TRANSCENDING THE COLD WAR

Transcending the Cold War

Summits, Statecraft, and the Dissolution of Bipolarity in Europe, 1970–1990

Edited by

KRISTINA SPOHR AND DAVID REYNOLDS

OXFORD
UNIVERSITY PRESS

OXFORD
UNIVERSITY PRESS

Great Clarendon Street, Oxford, OX2 6DP,
United Kingdom

Oxford University Press is a department of the University of Oxford.
It furthers the University's objective of excellence in research, scholarship,
and education by publishing worldwide. Oxford is a registered trade mark of
Oxford University Press in the UK and in certain other countries

Published in the United States of America by Oxford University Press
198 Madison Avenue, New York, NY 10016, United States of America

British Library Cataloguing in Publication Data

Data available

ISBN 978–0–19–872750–7

Jacket image: © REUTERS/Denis Paquin

There is a tide in the affairs of men
Which, taken at the flood, leads on to fortune;
Omitted, all the voyage of their life
Is bound in shallows and in miseries.
On such a full sea are we now afloat;
And we must take the current when it serves
Or lose our ventures.

Brutus, in *Julius Caesar*, act 4, scene 3

Let's say 'to hell with the past'.
We'll do it our way and get something done.

Ronald Reagan to Mikhail Gorbachev,
Geneva, 20 November 1985

Contents

List of Illustrations

List of Abbreviations

ABM	Anti-Ballistic Missile treaty
CBMs	confidence-building measures
CCP	Chinese Communist Party
CDU	Christian Democratic Union of Germany (*Christlich Demokratische Union Deutschlands*)
CPSU	Communist Party of the Soviet Union
CSCE	Conference on Security and Cooperation in Europe
CSU	Christian Social Union (*Christlich-Soziale Union*)
CTBT	Comprehensive Test Ban Treaty
DMZ	De-Militarized Zone
DRV	Democratic Republic of Vietnam
EC	European Community
EU	European Union
ERWs	enhanced radiation warheads
FBS	forward-based systems
FRC	Foreign Relations Committee, US Senate
FRG	Federal Republic of Germany
GDR	German Democratic Republic
GLCM	ground-launched cruise missiles
G7	Group of Seven
HVA	Main Directorate for Reconnaissance, GDR (*Hauptverwaltung Aufklärung*)
ICBMs	intercontinental ballistic missiles
INFs	intermediate-range nuclear forces
MAD	Mutual Assured Destruction
MBFR	mutual and balanced force reduction (talks)
MFN	Most Favoured Nation trade status
MIRVs	multiple independently targetable re-entry vehicles
NATO	North Atlantic Treaty Organization
NORAD	North American Aerospace Defense Command
NSC	National Security Council
NSDD	National Security Decision Directive
NVA	National People's Army of the GDR (*Nationale Volksarmee*)

PRC	People's Republic of China
SALT	Strategic Arms Limitation Talks
SDI	Strategic Defense Initiative
SED	Socialist Unity Party of Germany (*Sozialistische Einheitspartei Deutschlands*)
SLBMs	submarine-launched ballistic missiles
SPD	Social Democratic Party of Germany (*Sozialdemokratische Partei Deutschlands*)
SRINFs	shorter-range INFs
UN	United Nations

List of Contributors

James Cameron is a Stanton Research Fellow at Fundação Getulio Vargas in Brazil. His first book *The Secret Struggle: The Rise and Demise of America's First Missile Defense System, 1961–1972*, is under contract with Oxford University Press.

Jeffrey A. Engel is the founding Director of Southern Methodist University's Center for Presidential History in Dallas, Texas. Author or editor of nine books on American foreign policy, he is currently writing *When the World Seemed New: George H.W. Bush and the Surprisingly Peaceful End of the Cold War.*

Jonathan Hunt is Lecturer in Modern Global History at the University of Southampton. He is finishing his first book, provisionally entitled *Nuclear Containment: The Spread of Atomic Weapons and the Pax Americana.*

Michael Cotey Morgan is Assistant Professor of History at the University of North Carolina, Chapel Hill. He is the author of a forthcoming history of the Helsinki Final Act.

Gottfried Niedhart is Professor Emeritus at the University of Mannheim. His publications include *Entspannung in Europa: Die Bundesrepublik Deutschland und der Warschauer Pakt, 1966–1975* (2014).

Sergey Radchenko is Zi Jiang Distinguished Professor at East China Normal University in Shanghai, and Professor of International Politics at Cardiff University. His most recent book is *Unwanted Visionaries: The Soviet Failure in Asia at the End of the Cold War* (2014).

David Reynolds is Professor of International History at Cambridge University. His books include *Summits: Six Meetings that Shaped the Twentieth Century* (2007).

Daniel Sargent is Associate Professor of History at the University of California, Berkeley. He is the author of *A Superpower Transformed: The Remaking of American Foreign Policy in the 1970s* (2015).

Benedikt Schoenborn is a Senior Research Fellow at the Tampere Peace Research Institute, University of Tampere, Finland. His next book is entitled *Germany and European Peace: Through Reconciliation to Unification.*

Kristina Spohr is Associate Professor of International History at the London School of Economics. Her most recent book is *The Global Chancellor: Helmut Schmidt and the Reshaping of the International Order* (2016).

Chris Tudda is a Historian at the United States Department of State. His most recent book is *Cold War Summits: A History, from Potsdam to Malta* (2015).

Yafeng Xia is a Research Fellow at the Center for Cold War International History Studies, East China Normal University in Shanghai, and Professor of History at Long Island University, New York. His books include *Negotiating with the Enemy: U.S.–China Talks during the Cold War, 1949–1972* (2006).

Acknowledgements

This book reflects the long-standing interest of each of us in the challenges of summitry and statecraft during the Cold War and in the intricate interplay between structural forces and individual agency when explaining historical change. More particularly, it grew out of an international workshop held in Cambridge on 22–23 September 2014 and a witness seminar the following day at the Foreign and Commonwealth Office in London. These events were made possible by generous financial support from the following sources: a British Academy/Leverhulme research grant (RG73464); a conference fund grant from the Centre for Research in the Arts, Humanities, and Social Sciences (CRASSH) of Cambridge University; and a HEIF 5 grant from the London School of Economics. Our thanks to Simon Goldhill and Marie Lemaire of CRASSH; Ed Mayes and Mike Weaver of the Cambridge History Faculty; Susan O'Donnell, Kevin Keohane, and their staff at Christ's College, Cambridge; Marie Copperwaite of the LSE; and Patrick Salmon and his colleagues at the FCO. We are also grateful to Heonik Kwon and Harald Wydra for stimulating responses on the draft chapters, to Mathias Haeussler and Edoardo Andreoni for administrative support during and after the workshop, and to Odd Arne Westad and Mark Kramer for insightful comments on parts of the manuscript.

Robert Faber of Oxford University Press took a keen and constructive interest in the project from the beginning. Thanks also to others at OUP for helping to produce the book, especially assistant editor Cathryn Steele, copy-editor Fiona Tatham, and production manager Manikandan Chandrasekeran. Our deep gratitude, finally, to the contributors who probably got more than they bargained for when accepting our initial invitation to meet in the 'Original Cambridge', including our vigorous editing and the challenge of co-authoring chapters through hard summit bargaining.

ARKS, DJR, March 2016

Introduction

They were an unlikely pair and it was an almost inconceivable moment. American President George H.W. Bush and Mikhail Gorbachev, Secretary General of the Communist Party of the Soviet Union, sat together, relaxed and joking, in a joint press conference on 3 December 1989, at the end of their summit meeting in Malta (see Figure 0.1). 'We stand at the threshold of a brand-new era of U.S.–Soviet relations', Bush declared. 'And it is within our grasp to contribute, each in our own way, to overcoming the division of Europe and ending the military confrontation there.' Gorbachev concurred: 'We stated, both of us, that the world leaves one epoch of cold war and enters another epoch. This is just the beginning. We're just at the very beginning of our long road to a long-lasting peaceful period.' He added that 'the new era calls for a new approach. And thus, many things that were characteristic of the cold war should be abandoned' including 'force, the arms race, mistrust, psychological and ideological struggle ... All that should be things of the past'.

Fig. 0.1. A New Dawn: Bush and Gorbachev in Malta, 3 December 1989 (AP)

The Malta summit yielded no new treaties or agreements, not even a joint statement, but its message was clear. The world was moving out of the Cold War, which had defined international relations for more than four decades, and was on the verge of a new era of peace. This was a historic moment, and both men were acutely conscious of what Gorbachev called their 'special responsibility' as leaders of the superpowers for shaping the future. Bush expressed the hope and conviction that they could 'transform the East-West relationship to one of enduring cooperation'. He added, 'that's the future that I want to help in creating. And that's the future that Chairman Gorbachev and I began right here in Malta'. Both men also shared the view that, to quote Gorbachev, 'personal contacts are a very important element in the relations between leaders of state...I think our personal contacts help us implement our responsibilities and help us better interact in the interests of our two nations and in the interests of the entire world community'.[1]

Malta was a special meeting, effectively announcing the end of the Cold War, but it epitomized the larger attractions of personal summitry. Many politicians believe in themselves as historical actors. They like to take the initiative, they want to exploit and manage opportunities at potential turning points in world affairs. In short, they feel they have the ability to make history or at least, within the various constraints of time and place, to steer it in the right direction. In international affairs, a primary constraint is the attitude of other states because, in the case of extreme disagreements, their collisions can lead to war. The appeal of personal summits is to engage the leader of the other state in mutual interaction rather than violent confrontation. The summit, often held in a remote place or on neutral territory, serves as the arena in which leaders come face-to-face and on an equal footing aspiring to shape the future, freed—if only for the moment in this heady atmosphere—from old patterns, domestic politics, and bureaucratic red-tape. The belief in agency and the scope for interaction are essential ingredients of summitry. And productive interaction depends on dialogue. Some Cold War meetings between leaders proved disastrous: at Vienna in 1961 John Kennedy and Nikita Khrushchev talked at each other and past each other. Creative summitry requires a willingness to listen, a readiness to understand the other side's perspective, and the ability to explain one's own needs and interests persuasively—in short talking with, rather than against, the opposite number.

The 1970s and 1980s, the decades examined in this book, were a particularly intense and fruitful period for summitry. Initially these meetings sought to reduce the danger of war and advance détente—a diplomatic term signifying simply the relaxation of tension. By the mid-1980s, however, summit meetings took on a larger ambition, to defuse the Cold War itself, and by the end of the decade to move beyond the structure of bipolarity into a genuinely new era. It must be stressed that this profound shift in the international order was accomplished without war, unlike other moments of historical transition such as 1815, 1871, and 1945. Bush and Gorbachev certainly were both convinced action and interaction at the summit was of decisive importance in facilitating this remarkable process of peaceful change. But were they right?

Some may say that they were deluded, carried away by hubris, and that to take them seriously is to be swayed by outdated notions of Great Man history. There is indeed a large body of literature on the deeper structural changes that underlay the end of the Cold War. These include the mounting inefficiency of the Eastern bloc's planned economies, its technological backwardness as the world entered the IT age, the gradual loss of faith in Marxist-Leninist ideology, and the 'imperial overstretch' of the Soviet empire. All these long-term developments must surely be taken into account.[2] So, too, are interpretations that privilege history from below—generational change within the Soviet bloc, for instance, or the pressure of people power across Eastern Europe in the tumultuous year of 1989.[3] But all these factors take us only so far: they do not explain *when* and *how* the Cold War confrontation ended—why its dénouement occurred in 1989–90 and why this happened so peacefully. To explore those questions we must look more closely at statesmen, summitry, and statecraft. Structural and social change created the broad conditions within which leaders operated but how to respond to these was a matter of choice. Sometimes the response was cautious but at other moments leaders took greater risks—acting either from strategic calculation (the metaphor of chess) or out of a gambler's instinct (the throw of the dice). Whatever the impulse, decisive diplomatic moves could on occasion redefine the whole environment of international relations. Teasing out this interplay of political action and situational context lies at the heart of this book.[4]

Our chief protagonists were not acting entirely alone as diplomatic agents. Of course, each wanted to get personally acquainted with his counterpart, almost to unmask the other, and believed that more could be accomplished, more quickly, when face-to-face than through diplomatic correspondence or meetings between bureaucrats. In many ways they were right, as we shall see at crucial points in this book. But individual leaders, however remarkable, have the limitations of any human being. They cannot hope to grasp all the specialist issues at stake, they may have fundamental blindspots and misconceptions, and they will not be able to maintain alertness and acuity through long hours of conversation, usually contorted by translation and clouded by jet lag. In short, acting alone they cannot effect durable historical change. We shall see that advisers, ministers, and officials were often essential assistants— preparing the ground for productive summits, offering counsel during fraught negotiations, and implementing the agreements that had been reached. In this fundamental sense, summitry, though based on the agency of leaders, depends on teamwork. And also teamwork over time: summits often proved more effective when part of a process, rather than being one-offs. A planned sequence of meetings, or an intense flurry of summitry, helped to establish trust and enhance cooperation. In the process, creative networks were formed between governments and not just within them.

With this in mind we can discern a sharp contrast between the summits of the 1970s, which served as useful icebreakers but then failed to maintain momentum, and the meetings of the mid-1980s, when the cumulative weight of a series of summits helped break through the fundamental barriers of the Cold War. Admittedly, circumstances in the late 1980s were more propitious for radical change in the international order, but the chapters that follow argue that personal chemistry between leaders, their close partnerships with advisers, and the interactions between their entourages all played a vital role.[5]

In considering the prominence of summitry at the end of the Cold War, it is striking how little East-West summits figured in the first quarter-century after World War Two. The term itself was coined in 1950 when Winston Churchill called for a 'parley at the summit' with the Soviets to control the East-West arms race and avert a third world war. His word was quickly picked up in the international media and by 1955 the Geneva meeting between the leaders of America, Russia, Britain, and France was officially billed as a 'summit' by the US State Department.[6] But after Geneva there was little progress. The next 'Big Four' meeting, in 1960 in Paris, was aborted and the Kennedy-Khrushchev encounter in Vienna the following year was a dialogue of the deaf. The Soviet leader returned home believing that he could bully the green, young American president by placing nuclear missiles in Cuba—a gamble that took the world to the brink of nuclear war in 1962. Mutual shock about the Cuban Missile Crisis, however, pushed the superpowers into dialogue to restrain their spiralling nuclear arms race. To advance this process of negotiation and cut through the bureaucratic obstacles, summitry became the prime instrument of diplomacy, starting with the meeting between President Richard Nixon and General Secretary Leonid Brezhnev in Moscow 1972. Superpower summits in the 1970s and 1980s to advance nuclear arms control form one important strand of this book.

A second strand involves the German question. This was rooted in the aftermath of World War Two. Following the defeat of the Third Reich, Germany was divided among the four victor powers—America, Russia, Britain, and France—because they could not agree on the terms of a peace settlement. By 1949 two rival German states had come into existence: the Federal Republic of Germany (FRG) and the German Democratic Republic (GDR). The first was a client of the United States, the second a clone of the Soviet Union. This partition of Germany was part of a larger division of most of Europe into rival political blocs and military alliances—the North Atlantic Treaty Organization (NATO) and the Warsaw Pact—as the United States and the Soviet Union vied for control of the continent. In the late 1940s and 1950s this was a volatile face-off—on several occasions the two superpowers seemed close to war over Berlin—but the building of the Wall in 1961 effectively removed Berlin as a flashpoint. By the mid-1960s the division of both Germany and Europe seemed indisputable realities. Debate about whether to accept this as permanent or to seek to transcend division lay at the heart of subsequent Cold War diplomacy. In any attempt at transcendence, however, it was clear that one could not address the German question without grappling with the partition of Europe, and vice versa. Starting with the initial, bizarre encounter between the leaders of the two Germanies at Erfurt and Kassel in 1970, German summitry thus forms the second major dimension of this book.

Bipolarity was not, however, confined to Europe. America and Russia had global reach and also global pretensions: each was not just a 'country' but a 'cause'.[7] As well as being rivals for power and territory, they also embodied opposing ideologies—political pluralism versus a one-party state, liberal capitalism versus a command economy. This ideological confrontation was a core feature of East-West competition in Europe ever since 1945. But although Europe was the cockpit of the Cold War, over the next two decades superpower rivalry for place and position, for hearts and minds, spread across the so-called Third World. In the 1970s the Cold War became truly global.[8] By this time a third major player had also begun to emerge. The People's Republic of China (PRC), established in 1949 by the communist victory in the Chinese civil war, was originally a Soviet ally and a vehement foe of the Americans—fighting a full-scale war against them in Korea. During the 1960s, however, Mao Zedong repudiated the Soviet connection at every level, becoming a rival for territory and influence in Asia and a challenge to Moscow's monopolistic hold on the dogmas of Marxism-Leninism. In 1969 the two communist powers seemed on the verge of war. Meanwhile Beijing was extending feelers towards Washington. China had been able to reposition itself in this way between the two superpowers thanks to its size, population, and military might. This new international triangularity affected the dynamics of bilateral superpower interaction, especially in the summitry of the early 1970s and again in the late 1980s. Here we find a third strand in the chapters that follow.

* * * * *

What then were the international conditions that made summitry particularly attractive at the start of the 1970s? After the Cuban fiasco, Moscow built up its strategic nuclear arsenal to something approaching parity with the United States. Similarly China, now recovering strongly from the turmoil of the Cultural Revolution, was facing off against the Soviets. The Americans, meanwhile, were bogged down in Vietnam—their first serious check in the Cold War. The triangular configuration of global power was already apparent. In Europe, the Berlin Wall had imposed a new stability, both for Germany and the continent as a whole. All these developments stimulated international dialogue, and summitry should be seen as part of that process: an attempt by key leaders to promote novel forms of engagement in order to make international affairs safer and more predictable. This new era of détente provides the context for part one of our book, entitled 'Thawing the Cold War'.

Yet the leaders were not merely reacting to changes in the international situation. They also brought to bear their own 'mental maps' and emotional experiences. In the case of Germany, the subject of our first chapter, the essential catalyst was a change of government in Bonn in 1966, bringing about a 'Grand Coalition' of the Christian Democrats (CDU/CSU) and Social Democrats (SPD), through which the SPD leader Willy Brandt became foreign minister and then chancellor of an SPD-Free Democrat (FDP) coalition in 1969. As a former Mayor of West Berlin (1957–66), Brandt felt the pain of division as a gut issue, unlike previous chancellors such as Konrad Adenauer (a Rhinelander) and Ludwig Erhard (from Bavaria). Accepting the fait accompli of two states, Brandt nevertheless wanted to prevent total alienation between the peoples of East and West Germany and to keep open the possibility of eventual reunification. The conceptual framework for this policy had been elaborated by his adviser Egon Bahr during the 1960s, built around the slogan of 'change through rapprochement' (*Wandel durch Annäherung*) and the 'policy of small steps' (*Politik der kleinen Schritte*). The Brandt-Bahr partnership proved essential for Bonn's détente diplomacy, especially after Brandt had acceded to the chancellorship in October 1969. His 1970 meetings with East German leader Willi Stoph in Erfurt and Kassel were a first expression of this *neue Ostpolitik*—the story of the opening chapter of this book.

Our second summit, Beijing in 1972 (chapter 2), reflects similar personal impulses. Both President Richard Nixon and his National Security Adviser Henry Kissinger were convinced that the United States had to end its post-Korean War policy of treating 'Red China' as a pariah state. 'We simply cannot afford to leave China outside the family of nations', Nixon insisted in 1967. 'Communist China is a major fact of international life', declared Kissinger the following year; he visualized the world moving from a bipolar era to one of multipolarity.[9] This shared worldview prompted their opening to China in 1971–2; though tactical calculations about pressing the Soviets to the negotiating table also played a part. At the practical level, Kissinger acted as the secret go-between to set up the unprecedented meeting between the American and Chinese leaders in 1972. In some respects, his role paralleled that of Bahr for Brandt. On the Chinese side, there was a similar double act—Mao Zedong, founding father of the PRC, prided himself on being the 'philosopher', leaving his prime minister, Zhou Enlai, to handle all the practical details of diplomacy with Nixon and Kissinger in Beijing. Mao's motivation for a new relationship with the United States was both geopolitical and ideological: the mounting threat to China from the USSR and also his celebration of the PRC as the world's true revolutionary force, in antithesis to Washington's 'capitalist imperialism' and Moscow's 'socialist imperialism'.[10]

The Beijing summit of February 1972 was a global media event—the first time an American president had set foot in communist China and talked with its leaders. Three months later, in May, came an even bigger moment in the Cold War, when Nixon flew to Moscow for the first superpower summit in the Soviet capital—again prepared by Kissinger through secret visits and back-channel diplomacy (chapter 3). The Kremlin had been procrastinating about a meeting, seeking to maximize its advantages, but the Beijing summit aroused fears of a hostile Sino-American alliance and prompted a rapid change of mind. Nixon and Kissinger sought to regulate the spiralling arms race as well as to achieve stable multipolarity. For Brezhnev and his colleagues the intellectual and emotional impulses stemmed much more from the past. Like all the wartime generation, they were still haunted by the Nazi 'surprise attack' of 1941 and the titanic struggle that ensued for Soviet survival. What they wanted now was confirmation of the sphere of influence in Eastern Europe they had won by blood in 1945 and also American recognition of their status as an equal superpower, measured by strategic nuclear parity.

This triptych of German, Chinese, and Russian summits in 1970–2 was profoundly important as icebreakers in the Cold War. In each case there had previously been denial of the other side's existence: West Germany refused to acknowledge East Germany as an independent state; the United States had no diplomatic relations with the PRC and continued to recognize the rump Nationalist regime on Taiwan as rightful holder of China's seat on the UN Security Council. In the case of Soviet-American relations, formal diplomatic relations had existed since 1933 but the raft of agreements reached in Moscow in 1972 not only started to control the arms race but also extended relations between the two countries into many new areas including trade, technology, and culture. Each of these three summits entailed a journey of discovery, the beginnings of serious direct engagement with the alien Other.[11] These pioneering summits had impact precisely because they were not exercises in quiet, behind-the-scenes diplomacy, but were conducted in the glare of the international media and projected around the world. Brandt waving to the East German crowds from the window of his hotel in Erfurt, Nixon marching down the steps of Airforce One in Beijing with his hand outstretched to greet Zhou Enlai, or clinking champagne glasses with Brezhnev in the Kremlin—these images had an eloquence that no amount of words could convey. Although the Moscow meeting did yield some tangible agreements, the real significance of these three summits of the early 1970s lay in symbolism rather than substance. But the symbolism of discovering and beginning to humanize the Other helped to change the mood of international relations, aiding the process of détente.

Thawing the Cold War, however, did not imply that the era of confrontation was coming to an end—simply that the participants were less worried about imminent nuclear annihilation and therefore started to think about how to live with, and in, a world divided. Continued division in fact entailed continued competition—military, economic, and ideological—so the apparent stability was not as secure and predictable as it seemed. Part two of this book explores the uncertainties entailed in 'Living with the Cold War' during the rest of the 1970s and does so via different kinds of summits than those examined in part one. The Helsinki conference of July 1975 (chapter 4) involved no fewer than thirty-five countries, with America and Russia playing only a limited role; it was also the culmination of intricate lower-level diplomacy over the previous three years. Nevertheless, Helsinki built on the personal summitry of the early 1970s, in particular confirming the borders of 1945 and thus the position of the Soviet Union in Eastern Europe. Hence the elation in Moscow. But the Helsinki accords presaged change as well as stabilization: the Western states insisted on provisions that promoted human rights and freedom of movement. And in the years to come, these human features of the Helsinki Final Act would help to erode the Soviet bloc.

By the end of the 1970s, however, competition was again more evident than cooperation, generating renewed international instability. The triangularity espoused by Nixon and Kissinger had failed to provide a secure foundation for a multipolar world: Washington and Beijing did not establish full diplomatic relations until 1979 and by then China and Russia were engaged in a proxy war in Indochina. Nor had Soviet-American relations sustained the mood of détente created in Moscow in 1972. A second agreement on strategic arms limitation (the SALT II treaty) was delayed until 1979 and it failed to grapple with the issue of nuclear weapons stationed in Europe. All this generated uncertainty in Western Europe about the viability of détente at a time when the developed world was also wracked by the oil shock, economic recession, and rampant inflation. The summitry of 1978–9 (chapter 5) tried to address these problems, with the consolidation of the Group of 7 (G7) as an instrument of international economic governance and the Guadeloupe summit of January 1979—an attempt to re-establish the credibility of NATO's defence posture. These were different kinds of summits, meetings of allies rather than adversaries, characterized by far more informality than the set-piece summits examined in part one. While the G7 process became routine as fears about a fatal crisis of capitalism abated, the meeting at Guadeloupe remained unique but it led directly to NATO's 'dual track' decision of December 1979. This was taken just as the Soviets invaded Afghanistan. Together these events helped trigger what became known as a 'new Cold War' in which superpower dialogue was frozen out.

The ensuing arms race was a prime concern of a new series of superpower summits eventually initiated by Ronald Reagan and Mikhail Gorbachev in 1985, after a pause of some six years. Their encounters in Geneva (November 1985), Reykjavik (October 1986), Washington (December 1987), and Moscow (May–June 1988) are the subject of chapter 6. These four meetings were unprecedented in the history of Cold War summitry—yielding an agreement on nuclear arms reduction (the Intermediate-Range Nuclear Forces [INF] treaty of 1987), rather than simply arms limitation (as in the case of SALT I in 1972). Here, particularly, we see the cumulative power of summitry when conducted through a sequence of meetings between leaders who clicked as human beings and through several layers of sustained engagement amongst officials. The visions shared by the two men and the trust they established allowed the two superpowers to move beyond merely defusing the Cold War and towards what might be called the de-Othering of the adversary. Hence the title of part three of the book: 'Transcending the Cold War'.

Chapter 7 deals with the momentous year, 1989, and within it the place of three summits. Two of these took place in Beijing, between Deng Xiaoping and George H.W. Bush in February and between Deng and Gorbachev in June just before the Chinese leadership brutally cracked down on the pro-democracy demonstrators in Tiananmen Square. Bush entertained a long-standing belief in China's evolution into a future democratic partner and had conversely been sceptical about both Gorbachev himself and the Soviet Union's capacity to reform. But Tiananmen closed off the China option for the immediate future: the People's Republic would go its own way and the triangularity that had been a feature of the détente era would play no significant part in the diplomacy of the Cold War endgame in Europe. By contrast, when protests spread across the Soviet bloc during the second half of the year, Gorbachev did not use force to stop reform escalating into revolution—adhering to the Helsinki principles of 1975. Having paused to take stock of relations with Moscow in the first half of 1989, Bush in turn reoriented his foreign policy towards Europe and engaged seriously with Gorbachev in Malta in December. Their remarks, noted at the start of this introduction, demonstrate a shared eagerness to end the Cold War era, with its spiralling arms race and intense ideological struggle, and even to overcome the division of Europe itself.

That meant, above all, addressing the German question. The fall of the Berlin Wall in November put German unification at the top of the political agenda. Over the next few months, as East Germany began to disintegrate, Chancellor Kohl in Bonn moved decisively to absorb the former GDR terri-tories within the Federal Republic. But the prospect of a united Germany at the heart of Europe challenged the foundations of the postwar international order, around which the Cold War had been stabilized in the early 1970s. The question now was whether transcending the division of Germany would threaten the peace of Europe. Here summitry played a major role, as detailed in chapter 8. The American president, unlike his more sceptical British and French allies, had no fundamental objection to German unity but he insisted (and Kohl agreed) that unified Germany must remain anchored in a US-led NATO alliance. On this basis the German chancellor was able to negotiate freely with Gorbachev at meetings in Moscow and the Caucasus in

July 1990, where Kohl's chequebook diplomacy bought the withdrawal of Soviet forces from East German soil and secured Gorbachev's acceptance of unified Germany's NATO membership. In tandem, therefore, Bush and Kohl's summit diplomacy ensured both the emancipation of Germany as a united, sovereign state and also the persistence of America as a European power in the post-Cold War era. With the lifting of Germany's iron curtain, the East-West confrontation in Europe, rooted in the legacies of the Second World War, had been peacefully resolved. But the nature of the 'post postwar' order and especially the position of Russia within it would prove much more problematic.

NOTES

1. Remarks at Q&A session, 3 December 1989, 1.20pm on board 'Gorky', The American Presidency Project (henceforth APP) website, http://www.presidency. ucsb.edu/ws/index.php?pid=17900&st=&st1.
2. Federico Romero, 'Cold War Historiography at the Crossroads', *Cold War History* 14, no. 4 (2014), 685–703. For 'imperial overstretch' see Hannes Adomeit, *Imperial Overstretch: Germany in Soviet Policy from Stalin to Gorbachev* (Baden-Baden, 1998).For useful historiographically-based interpretations of the 1980s, see Jeremi Suri, 'Explaining the End of the Cold War: A New Historical Consensus', *Journal of Cold War Studies* 4, no. 4 (2002), 60–92, and Jane Zavisca, 'Explaining and Interpreting the End of Soviet Rule, *Kritika* 12, no. 4 (2011), 925–40.
3. Charles S. Maier, *Dissolution: The Crisis of Communism and the End of East Germany* (Princeton, NJ, 1997); Konrad H. Jarausch and Martin Sabrow, eds, *Weg in den Untergang: Der innere Zerfall der DDR* (Göttingen, 1999); Jacques Lévesque, *The Enigma of 1989: The USSR and the Liberation of Eastern Europe* (Berkeley, 1997); Stephen Kotkin with Jan T. Gross, *Uncivil Society: 1989 and the Implosion of the Communist Establishment* (New York, 2009); Constantine Pleshakov, *There Is No Freedom without Bread: 1989 and the Civil War that Brought Down Communism* (New York, 2009); Vladislav Zubok, *A Failed Empire: The Soviet Union in the Cold War from Stalin to Gorbachev* (Chapel Hill, 2009); Vladislav Zubok, 'With His Back Against the Wall: Gorbachev, Soviet Demise, and German Unification', *Cold War History* 14, no. 4 (2014), 619–45; Mary Elise Sarotte, *The Collapse: The Accidental Opening of the Berlin Wall* (New York, 2014).
4. On this theme of 'reciprocal interaction', see Maier, *Dissolution*, xiv–xv.
5. For the recent historiography of summitry, see David H. Dunn, ed., *Diplomacy at the Highest Level: The Evolution of International Summitry* (London, 1996); David Reynolds, *Summits: Six Meetings that Shaped the Twentieth Century* (London, 2007); Emmanuel Mourlon-Druol and Federico Romero, eds, *International Summitry and Global Governance: the Rise of the G7 and the European Council* (Abingdon, 2014); Günter Bischof, Stefan Karner, and Barbara Stelzl-Marx, eds, *The Vienna Summit and its Importance in International History* (New York, 2014); Chris Tudda, *Cold War Summits: A History, From Potsdam to Malta*

(London, 2015); Raymond Cohen, *Negotiating across Cultures: International Communication in an Independent World* (Washington, DC, 2nd edn, 1999); 115–27; G.R. Berridge, *Diplomacy and Theory* (Basingstoke, 2nd edn, 2002), 168–86; Jan Melissen, 'Pre-Summit Diplomacy: Britain, the United States and the Nassau Conference, December 1962', *Diplomacy & Statecraft* 7, no. 3 (1996), 652–87; J.G. Giauque, 'Bilateral Summit Diplomacy in Western European and Transatlantic Relations, 1956–63', *European History Quarterly* 31, no. 3 (2001), 427–45; David Reynolds, 'Summitry as Intercultural Communication', *International Affairs* 85, no. 1 (2009), 115–27; Alan S. Alexandroff and Donald Brean, 'Global Summitry: Its Meaning and Scope', *Global Summitry* 1, no. 1 (2015), 1–26.

6. Speech in Edinburgh, 14 February 1950, in Robert Rhodes James, ed., *Winston S. Churchill: His Complete Speeches* (New York, 1974), vol. 8, 7944. For background to Churchill's use of the term see Reynolds, *Summits,* 3, 409, and Jonathan Rose, *The Literary Churchill: Author, Reader, Actor* (New Haven, 2014), 404–5.

7. The terminology of Adam Roberts, adapting a phrase of Henry Kissinger's in 1984, in his essay 'An "Incredibly Swift Transition": Reflections on the End of the Cold War', in Melvyn P. Leffler and Odd Arne Westad, eds, *The Cambridge History of the Cold War,* 3 volumes (Cambridge, 2010), 534.

8. Odd Arne Westad, *The Global Cold War: Third World Interventions and the Making of Our Times* (Cambridge, 2005).

9. Jeremi Suri, *Henry Kissinger and the Making of the American Century* (Cambridge, MA, 2007), 181–3.

10. Chen Jian, *Mao's China and the Cold War* (Chapel Hill, NC, 2001), 239–44.

11. On the role of 'the Other' in international relations, building on the work of Edward Said, see for example Gertran Dijkink, *National Identity and Geopolitical Visions: Maps of Pride and Pain* (London, 1996); David Campbell, *Writing Security: United States Foreign Policy and the Politics of Identity* (Manchester, 1992); Ragnhild Fiebig-von Hase and Ursula Lehmkuhl, eds, *Enemy Images in American History* (Oxford, 1997); Linda Colley, 'Britishness and Otherness: An Argument', *Journal of British Studies* 31, no. 4 (1992), 309–29; and Andrew J. Rotter, 'Saidism without Said: Orientalism and U.S. Diplomatic History', *American Historical Review* 105, no. 4 (2000), 1205–17.

I

Thawing the Cold War

1

Erfurt and Kassel, 1970

Benedikt Schoenborn and Gottfried Niedhart

For twelve long minutes, the West German chancellor, Willy Brandt, looked down at the East German prime minister, Willi Stoph, and did not know what to say. It was 19 March 1970, late in the evening, at Erfurt station in East Germany. After a marathon thirteen-hour day of discussions Brandt, with his large delegation, had boarded the special train back to Bonn, and said farewell to Stoph. But the train did not move. Brandt stood at the carriage window, staring at Stoph who was freezing on the platform, one metre below. Angrily, Brandt turned to his staff and demanded immediate departure. But he was in the land of the command economy: the ministry of transport of the German Democratic Republic (GDR) had fixed the departure time for exactly 22.25. So Brandt had to stand at the train window, looking at Stoph with a forced smile amid the glare of the television cameras.

That snapshot summed up the day. During their official meetings the two leaders had delivered long monologues stating their opposite positions, rather than engaging in a meaningful dialogue. By the evening they had used up all their talking points and for a long awkward moment just looked at each other until the train finally started moving. Then Stoph politely wished Brandt a safe trip and added *'auf Wiedersehen'* (literally, see you again).[1] Their agreement to meet again two months later, in the West German city of Kassel, had been the only concrete result of the day. Nevertheless, the tremendous symbolism of the Erfurt summit of March 1970—the first-ever meeting of the leaders of the two Cold War German governments (see Figure 1.1)—presaged a thaw not only in German-German but in East-West relations as a whole. In fact it would prove a small, opening step on a long, slow journey towards overcoming the division of Europe.

The long deadlocked relations between Bonn and East Berlin would not start moving immediately after the two 1970 summits: official bilateral negotiations got going only by the end of the year, and then sluggishly. This was not surprising, given the divergent approaches of the two governments. The GDR

Fig. 1.1. Brandt and Stoph in front of Erfurt railway station, 19 March 1970 (Bundesbildstelle)

was determined not to move at all during the talks with Brandt. The very fact of a meeting with the 'class enemy' was difficult enough to reconcile with East German interests and ideology. Moreover, Moscow—determined to keep East Berlin under control—gave strict orders that no rapprochement was to result from the German-German summits. They were to be used merely to enhance the GDR's international recognition and public image.

While the Eastern side thus aimed at consolidating the division of Europe and the post-1945 territorial status quo, Brandt—like earlier governments of the Federal Republic of Germany (FRG)—hoped to transcend the Cold War confrontation in the long run. Bonn's goal was to bring about gradual changes in the East by creating channels in various ways to make little holes through the Iron Curtain. As will be shown, Brandt anticipated from the beginning that the immediate results of his meetings with Stoph would remain very limited and therefore aimed at starting regular contacts on lower levels. With the United States, Bonn's new sense of initiative towards the GDR created some underlying tension. Although the Nixon administration generally advocated détente, Brandt's eagerness to meet with Stoph raised fears that the subsequent momentum of German-German relations might get out of American control and endanger East-West stability.[2]

As we now know, of course, the Cold War order did not dissolve after Erfurt and Kassel. Rather, these summits were just the first in a long series of West German meetings with Eastern leaders, a process which decisively improved the political atmosphere in Europe and contributed to shift East-West confrontation towards negotiation and dialogue. The long-term effects of Brandt's Eastern policy proved significant, as illustrated by the retrospective view of veteran Soviet diplomat Valentin Falin: 'Without *Ostpolitik*, no Gorbachev'.[3] And, as later chapters will argue, without Gorbachev, the end of the Cold War in Europe would have been very different.

LONG-TERM GOALS: BRANDT REACHES OUT TO THE GDR

When Brandt was elected chancellor in October 1969 and in coalition with the small Liberal party set out to put his long planned *Ostpolitik* into practice, it appeared uncertain whether a summit with GDR leaders could be realized any time soon. Events seemed to evolve much faster on other fronts. Immediately after taking office, the Brandt government signed the nuclear non-proliferation treaty, thereby complying with a crucial Soviet demand previously unfulfilled by the former chancellor, Kurt-Georg Kiesinger. Negotiations with Moscow on the 'renunciation of force' started in December 1969. Simultaneously, Brandt arranged bilateral talks with Poland, which began in early February 1970. Bonn's recognition—*de facto* if not *de jure*—of the Oder-Neisse border between East Germany and Poland was another long-standing demand of the Eastern camp. Yet this would concede the loss of territory that had been German before 1945. Regarding the third contentious issue in Eastern affairs, diplomatic relations with the GDR, on 28 October 1969 Brandt publicly proposed negotiations and defined his position as follows:

> The federal government will continue the policy initiated in December 1966, and again offers the Council of Ministers of the GDR negotiations at government level without discrimination on either side, which should lead to contractually agreed cooperation. International recognition of the GDR by the Federal Republic is out of the question. Even if there exist two States in Germany, they are not foreign countries to each other; their relations with each other can only be of a special nature.[4]

By calling the GDR a state, Chancellor Brandt crossed a line previously respected by all his predecessors. The election of October 1969, which brought his Social Democratic Party (SPD) to full power after almost two decades in the political wilderness, was a decisive moment in West German history.[5] The previously dominant Christian-Democratic party (now in opposition) still argued that any state recognition of the GDR would perpetuate the division of Germany. Brandt's important choice of words about the two states not being foreign states—'*Auch wenn zwei Staaten in Deutschland existieren, sind sie doch füreinander nicht Ausland*'—followed closely on the policy recommendations by his adviser, Egon Bahr. In a detailed internal paper, Bahr argued that the GDR would most likely achieve its goal of international recognition anyway, and that Bonn should hasten to exploit the recognition element as leverage before time ran out. Bahr recommended aiming at a basic treaty (*Rahmenvertrag*) with the GDR which would offer equal status on the international level to the Eastern side, and at the same time consolidating the status and viability of Berlin under the Four-Power rights and institutionally interlock *(verklammern)* the two halves of Germany. Bahr's concept was designed to pursue the goal of German reunification in a changed international situation, and particularly to forestall any further 'drifting apart of the German people'.[6]

While Bahr's 1969 policy paper did not specify how he anticipated German reunification in the long term, his planning drafts of 1966 and 1968 had gone into some detail: the East German regime was to disappear eventually. With some variations on the steps proposed, Bahr had speculated in both these earlier drafts that East-West détente and the intensification of German-German contacts would lead to a situation in which foreign troops would withdraw from German territories. Deprived of any Soviet military presence and under pressure from the people of East Germany, Bahr expected that the puppet-like GDR government would ultimately collapse.[7] Brandt considered Bahr's scenario for moving towards reunification to be useful and important, but this was not the only planning concept he took into account when implementing his *Ostpolitik*. Indeed, as Brandt repeatedly emphasized, he attributed greater importance to ensuring peace than to establishing Germany's national unity.[8]

Brandt's means to create more peaceful relations with Eastern Europe has been defined as a 'policy of reconciliation'.[9] Two different aspects were included in this policy. First, the persistent efforts at reconciliation as a result of Germany's Nazi past, most famously symbolized by Brandt's gesture of kneeling at the Warsaw Ghetto memorial in December 1970. Second, reconciliation between Eastern and Western Europe by means of transcending the Cold War division in the long term. Brandt repeatedly insisted that he aimed at 'reconciliation' with the East, and thereby specifically included the GDR. While he used the term *Aussöhnung* for relations with Poland, he sometimes referred to the need for *Aussöhnung im Innern* (inner reconciliation) with regard to East Germans.[10]

The peace researcher John Paul Lederach has developed a conceptual framework outlining favourable elements and processes leading to 'sustainable reconciliation'.[11] While Lederach in his examples mostly discusses the period after the Cold War, we argue that some of his broader conclusions also shed useful light on the issues in this chapter. Indeed, to a large extent the general characteristics of the conflicts described by Lederach also apply to the FRG-GDR relationship in 1970: the conflicting groups 'live as neighbours and yet are locked into long-standing cycles of hostile interaction'; the conflicts are 'characterized by deep-rooted, intense animosity, fear, and severe stereotyping'; and the conflicting groups 'have direct experience of violent trauma'.[12]

Lederach proposes an interesting definition of what actually constitutes reconciliation. He describes it as a 'locus' creating time and space for encounter of the conflicting parties, a shared social space where antagonists engage in a process of building and eventually transforming relationships. As a first step in such a reconciliation process, the face-to-face expression of conflicting views (and possibly of accumulated anger or grievance) is of particular importance. Often after the lapse of some time, each side begins to take the antagonist's opinion seriously, and the confrontation then moves towards negotiation.[13] Seen in this light, Brandt's purpose in meeting with GDR leaders did not necessarily depend on concrete results emerging from the summits. From a reconciliation point of view, even a seemingly futile confrontation between FRG and GDR leaders might be a necessary initial face-to-face expression of antagonist views and thus a cathartic first step towards later normalization of German-German relations.

To be able to meet with Stoph in person, however, even if merely to express contradictory positions, Brandt first had to overcome considerable obstacles. On 17 December 1969 Bahr noted that, although the Soviet Union and others had responded 'objectively' to the various *Ostpolitik* initiatives of the new government in Bonn, the GDR had descended into 'nit-picking' and so far had not reacted in any constructive way.[14] The next day the Bonn official Dietrich Spangenberg, who had kept Bahr informed on internal developments in the GDR for more than two years, signalled a new development.[15]

OSTPOLITIK AS A CHALLENGE TO THE GDR

From the East German point of view the new government in Bonn meant some progress. Brandt's team seemed willing to go beyond the sterile practice of non-recognition and accept the GDR as a separate state. How to react to this development? This question divided the leadership of the country's ruling Socialist Unity Party (SED). The veteran Walter Ulbricht, still First Secretary of the party, wanted to be as active as Brandt and argued in favour of some kind of positive response. His designated successor, Erich Honecker, in principle shared Ulbricht's wish to have more stable relations with Bonn, not least in order to sustain the GDR's special economic relationship with the FRG. But, unlike Ulbricht, who tried to maintain a somewhat independent position within the Warsaw Pact, Honecker was much more willing to act in accordance with Soviet preferences. Therefore he kept his distance when Ulbricht summoned the Politburo of the Socialist Unity Party (SED) on 30 October 1969—only two days after Brandt's first policy statement as chancellor.

In Ulbricht's perception the political developments in the FRG signalled more than a simple change of government. Rather there was a societal shift, due to the 'progressive' segments within the West German society. 'Change has occurred in West Germany', he told the Politburo. That said, Ulbricht did not have any doubts about the offensive elements in Brandt's *Ostpolitik*: Brandt intends to 'penetrate us' and this could clearly have an 'effect' on the GDR. In order to avoid such a development, an Eastern counter-offensive was needed: 'If Brandt makes a new *Ostpolitik*, then we will make a new *Westpolitik*, one that truly deserves its name. We will make him sweat.' Ulbricht envisaged cooperation between the East and West German working classes, adding: 'The main force for a reunification of the nation is the working class.'[16]

Reunification on socialist terms, from the bottom up, was, of course, an absolutely unrealistic prospect. More relevant politically, it was anathema to Honecker and other members of the Politburo, among them Willi Stoph, head of government and Brandt's opposite number in the GDR.[17] In the ensuing controversy about the appropriate reaction towards Bonn's new *Ostpolitik*, Honecker gained the upper hand. Foreign Minister Otto Winzer was asked to prepare a paper demanding the full recognition of the GDR according to international law.[18] This was accomplished by 18 November 1969, including a draft for a German-German treaty.[19]

Winzer, in his capacity as foreign minister, was in charge of external relations and mainly concerned with the issue of support for the East German quest for full recognition of the GDR. With respect to internal security the Ministry for State Security was involved. There was no fear of an attack against the territory of the GDR. Rather it was Brandt's offensive via soft power that scared the Stasi—what became known as 'aggression on slippers'.[20] Shortly after the change of government in Bonn Markus Wolf, head of the *Hauptverwaltung Aufklärung* (*HVA*) and responsible for espionage in the West, produced a paper of over eighty pages for Erich Mielke, the formidable Minister for State Security, stressing the threat caused by *Ostpolitik* and exposing Brandt's policy as a purely tactical innovation. This was also the message for KGB chief Yuri Andropov whom Mielke and Wolf met in Moscow in mid November.[21] The Soviet Union ought to be aware of Brandt's true motives, they argued: 'new dangers and illusions' had to be considered. Dangers, because the 'socialist states', in particular the GDR, were going to be confronted with an 'intensification of the fight against socialism' by new means, among them trade relations. In other words, there would be increasing danger of what, in communist terminology, used to be labelled social democratization

(*Sozialdemokratismus*). Illusions also mattered, because, in Mielke's perspective, these dangers seemed to be underestimated in the socialist camp.[22] Responding, Andropov pointed out that one could not ignore some new elements in Brandt's policy. Although Brandt had 'thrown overboard' the line of his predecessor Kiesinger, one had to realize that the 'new tactic' was in the 'interest of *West* Germany, its monopolists and contrary to our interests'. Hence, the Warsaw Pact must form a 'united front'. Implicitly, Andropov warned the GDR of any steps without prior consultations with Moscow and he reminded Mielke of the advantageous position of the FRG, being 'bigger and richer' than the GDR.[23] What Andropov did not mention was that he himself was about to open a secret contact with the 'bigger and richer' Germany, leading to the establishment of a backchannel between the Kremlin and the chancellery in Bonn.[24]

Two weeks later the GDR leadership visited Moscow, first for bilateral consultations with the Soviet Union on 2 December and then for a Warsaw Pact summit on 3–4 December 1969. Beforehand Ulbricht informed the Soviets about his intention to send a 'confidential letter' to Brandt, announcing a draft treaty between both German states.[25] But Soviet party leader Leonid Brezhnev demanded he refrain from any steps of rapprochement with the FRG at a purely party level, in particular not liking the idea of a letter sent by the SED chief to the SPD leader. Contacts, he insisted, should be limited to the officials of the two states. First and foremost, however, Brezhnev complained about Article IV in the draft treaty, proposing that both German states would establish 'missions' with the function of embassies. Talk of 'missions', he warned, could be understood as a concession to the FRG. Brezhnev wanted to avoid this at all costs, not because he found this unreasonable but because the proposal emanated from Ulbricht. To maintain his position of dominance in the Soviet-GDR relationship, Brezhnev insisted on a maximal position demanding the de jure recognition of the GDR and the establishment of embassies in East Berlin and Bonn. Although he did not fail to add that it was unlikely that this maximal position could be achieved, 'one should proceed in this way'.[26] Brezhnev warned the East Germans not to relax the policy of strict delimitation: he wished to keep the opening to the West under Soviet control. This resulted in 'severe controversy' between Brezhnev and Ulbricht.[27]

GERMAN-GERMAN CONTACTS AND DISCONTENTS BEFORE THE SUMMIT

In accordance with Soviet instructions the GDR took several steps in response to Brandt's offer to enter into negotiations between the two German states.[28]

The first step was anything but negotiation. Ulbricht sent a draft treaty to the West German president Gustav Heinemann, demanding the full recognition of the GDR. Communication at the top level was somewhat archaic. The document was delivered in person on 18 December 1969 by Michael Kohl, state secretary in the office of the government, and Hans Voß, head of the West German department in the Ministry for Foreign Affairs. In Bonn they went to see Dietrich Spangenberg—former head of the *Senatskanzlei* in West Berlin, for a long time involved in informal contacts with East Berlin and now state secretary in the office of President Heinemann. Two days later Spangenberg travelled to East Berlin and delivered Heinemanns' answer: this stated that the FRG president had forwarded Ulbricht's letter to Chancellor Brandt.

The East German draft treaty was mainly a symbolic gesture. The SED leadership could be under no illusions that its wish for full recognition would ever be granted by any government in Bonn. This had already been made clear to East Berlin by Hermann von Berg, head of the Western department of Stoph's press office since 1962, and in this capacity in charge of informal contacts with Western officials and journalists, among them Spangenberg.[29] Two days prior to Brandt's first government statement a meeting with Bahr took place in Bonn at Bahr's request. He wanted to inform the GDR leadership in advance about the new government's policy towards the East in general and the GDR in particular. The aim was normalization in the mutual relationship on the basis of a *de facto* recognition of the GDR. Bahr insisted that any bilateral talks and negotiations had to achieve substantial progress for daily life (postal service, telephone contacts, and better opportunities for travel). As he put it, the 'man in the street' must feel some change.[30]

Stoph consulted Moscow and then invited the chancellor at short notice to meet him in what he called the 'capital of the GDR, Berlin'.[31] From now on the summit could be prepared. However, Stoph had to live with the inconsistency between the East German quest for de jure recognition and the more prag-matic Soviet attitude. In fact when Soviet foreign minister Andrei Gromyko came to East Berlin on 24 February 1970 and reported on the first round of his talks with Bahr he advised the SED Politburo that Bonn's recognition of the GDR's statehood would be tantamount to full international recognition. This, he added, would in any case occur on the part of the international commu-nity.[32] Between 2 and 12 March officials had to meet five times before they could agree the technical details of the summit, scheduled for 19 March.[33] On behalf of the GDR Gerhard Schüßler, deputy head of Stoph's office, was in charge of the talks. Bonn was represented by Ulrich Sahm from the chancel-lery. The main stumbling block was Brandt's intention to travel via West Berlin to the eastern part of the city, which was unacceptable to the GDR because West Berlin was regarded as an independent political entity where the FRG had no rights whatsoever. Eventually, both sides reached agreement on a new location for the summit: Erfurt in Thuringia.

By then only one week was left for detailed preparations. A press centre was set up for hundreds of journalists. To ensure that they gained positive impressions of the GDR, the city was hastily cleaned up, especially the area around the railway station. The conference venue was also renovated and the range of goods in the shops increased. Less visible were the Stasi's activities. On 13 March Mielke issued 'order No. 12/70', announcing various security measures and giving them the code name 'confrontation' (*Konfrontation*). The meaning of this strong language was crystal clear. From the Stasi's point of view the summit constituted a threat because it might trigger demonstrations in favour of Brandt. Any sign of agitation against the political order of the GDR had to be prevented. And the 'adversary' would do everything possible to reinforce the opportunity through infiltration and subversion.[34]

Two days prior to the summit the Politburo, together with Foreign Minister Winzer and various top officials of his ministry, gathered to decide the final version of Stoph's statement.[35] They approved the idea of a follow-up summit in the FRG. Brandt's wish to pay a visit to Buchenwald, the Nazi concentration camp near Weimar, was also discussed. Winzer would accompany the chancellor. Contrary to Brandt's wish and without informing him in advance, the Erfurt summit was organized like a state visit with national anthems and participation by the East German armed forces, the *Nationale Volksarmee* (NVA).[36]

BONN'S AGENDA FOR ERFURT

Meanwhile in Bonn, Brandt tried to put preparations for the first German-German summit into perspective and to keep expectations low. In public statements, he emphasized that he cared as much about *Westpolitik* as he did about *Ostpolitik* and that his bid to normalize relations with the East was mainly intended to catch up with the eastern policies of his Western partners, with whom he kept regular contact. Moreover, in early 1970 the fate and ultimate success of Bonn's new *Ostpolitik* and *Deutschlandpolitik* were rather uncertain. In mid-February, according to an American official with whom Brandt discussed the various initiatives of his envoys towards the Soviet bloc, the chancellor 'expressed real concern that all this frantic activity would arouse great hopes which would not be fulfilled', and was reported to be 'generally pessimistic about anything concrete coming out of all these activities'.[37]

Accordingly, in anticipation of the Erfurt meeting, Brandt was at pains to state that he did not expect any concrete results. He publicly attributed to the East German leadership 'a high level of stubbornness' and announced that the meeting aimed primarily at creating first contacts with a view to some kind of *modus vivendi* with the GDR to forestall 'the further alienation' of German from German.[38] He attached importance to the mere fact of a meeting taking place: 'After all, it must be possible for Germans and Germans to talk to each other again.'[39] At the same time, Brandt insisted that the social and political systems of East and West Germany were irreconcilable, and that there was no prospect of German reunification in the foreseeable future. At this moment, his objective was merely to keep the option of reunification open and to take some positive action with a view to 'overcoming the division of Europe' in the 1980s or possibly the 1990s.[40] Brandt hoped that Erfurt would be a beginning, and that a German-German dialogue would ensue: even if nothing came of it, he indicated that he deemed the meeting necessary.[41] On the one hand, this attitude corresponded with Brandt's objective of initiating a general process of reconciliation. On the other hand, for the credibility of his entire *Ostpolitik* it was vital to demonstrate readiness for talks with the GDR.

Brandt's staff, however, nurtured more ambitious goals for Erfurt. In their view the meeting should be used to create working groups on the various areas of tension, to initiate a dialogue on mutual respect and non-discrimination, and to improve communications and trade. Ultimately, they argued, Erfurt should lead to common institutions and to a legally binding normalization of relations between the GDR and the FRG 'for the time Germany remains divided'. In terms of practical planning, the exchange in Erfurt was to be substantial but not conclusive, in order to render a second meeting neces-sary.[42] Egon Bahr recommended pursuing the negotiations expeditiously, as the GDR might deliberately delay the talks in order to block Bonn's other initiatives to the East. Being in charge of negotiations with the Soviet leaders, Bahr also took advantage of his Moscow contacts to put pressure on East Berlin. On 12 March 1970 he sent a handwritten note to Brandt announcing that Moscow was 'forcing' Stoph to hold the Erfurt meeting.[43] In Bahr's estimation, in return for peace in the West from Bonn, the Soviets had 'moved in to unblock the talks' between East and West Germans.[44]

But as it turned out, Brandt's low expectations for the first German-German summit were justified. Hardly any real dialogue took place in Erfurt.

THE SUMMIT IN ERFURT: DUEL NOT DIALOGUE

On 19 March 1970, after crossing into the GDR, Brandt's special train stopped at Gerstungen, a small town close to the border in Thuringia. There, East German officials boarded the train, among them Michael Kohl and also Hermann von Berg who met Brandt for a brief moment. After that Berg informed Conrad Ahlers, Brandt's official government press spokesman, about some aspects of Stoph's opening statement.[45] At 9.30 the train arrived in Erfurt where Stoph welcomed Brandt on the platform and then walked with him across the square to the *Erfurter Hof*, a hotel just opposite the station. The authorities tried to prevent any contact between the public and the West German delegation but a huge crowd had gathered in the streets near the station since early morning and in the end, after Brandt had entered the hotel, the police and the Stasi could not stop the masses from flooding across the square shouting 'Willy Brandt to the window'. After some hesitation Brandt did appear at a hotel window for a moment, making a quietening gesture with his hands in an effort to calm the crowd. Turning back from the window, he saw that his staff had tears in their eyes. Shortly afterwards the GDR security authorities, seriously embarrassed, cleared the square and proceeded to organize hasty demonstrations in support of the East German regime. But the crowd moved to the city centre, where gatherings continued for the rest of the day.[46]

All this was widely reported by the international press, there in strength for the occasion, and the effect was palpable even for those not present. In Leipzig the historian Hartmut Zwahr, born in 1936 and SED party member since 1967, listened to the broadcast and became aware of the spontaneous gatherings. Although usually not an emotional person, he was deeply moved and had tears in his eyes when he heard the people in Erfurt declaring their 'belief in the unity of the nation'.[47]

At 10.00am the summit talks began in a conference room of the *Erfurter Hof* hotel. Stoph was accompanied by Foreign Minister Winzer because the GDR, in contrast to the FRG, regarded relations with the FRG as a matter of foreign policy rather than an inner-German domestic issue. Other senior members of the GDR delegation included the state secretaries Michael Kohl and Günther Kohrt as well as Gerhard Schüßler and Hans Voß. Leading figures in Brandt's delegation were Egon Franke, the Minister for Inner-German Relations; Wolfram Dorn, a member of the *Bundestag*; and Jürgen Weichert, an official of Franke's ministry—as well as Sahm, the meeting organizer, and Ahlers, the press spokesman. In addition to the morning and afternoon plenary sessions there were private conversations during and after lunch. In the evening, after Brandt's return from Buchenwald, Stoph and Brandt talked *à deux* for two hours. Speaking the same language, they needed no interpreter.[48]

Stoph began the morning by reading out a long statement for almost one hour. Brandt did not hear anything that was new. Stoph referred to the draft treaty and demanded the full recognition of the GDR. He described the current relationship between the two German states as 'completely abnormal' and asserted that the only solution was to establish 'diplomatic relations'. Otherwise a declaration on the renunciation of force would make no sense. According to Stoph, the 'division of the nation' stemmed from the FRG's membership of NATO: confronted with West German rearmament and the aggressive attitude towards the GDR, the 'securing of our border in 1961 was an act of humanity'. Stoph depicted the GDR as a 'modern socialist state': 'In our German Democratic Republic the working people, in free self-determination, organize the advanced socialist society.' That relations between both German states could be 'inner-German relations' because the 'unity of the nation', as postulated by Brandt, was pure fiction.

Responding, Brandt reiterated what he had already said elsewhere. He pleaded for a *modus vivendi* of both German states which belonged to different alliances and represented antithetical political and societal systems. The systemic conflict could not be solved. At the same time both sides agreed on the central principle that peace must be maintained. Consequently, one should concentrate on gradually improving the state of peaceful co-existence by better communication between both sides. Communication, in fact, was one of Brandt's key notions in his *Ostpolitik*. He believed that increased communication on the level of high politics as well as in the fields of trade relations and contacts between individuals would help to build bridges between East and West. Stoph, for his part, stressed the principle of non-interference in internal affairs.

In sum, Stoph wished to stabilize the political realities whereas Brandt, while respecting the territorial status quo for the time being, wanted ultimately to overcome it. Therefore he could not give an honest answer to Stoph's main question: 'What is your policy's strategic goal vis-à-vis the GDR?'[49] Brandt's long-term strategy aimed at the transformation of the GDR and the function of *Ostpolitik* was to start that process by inducing gradual change in the East.[50]

Unsurprisingly in the light of what transpired in the morning, the final *tête-à-tête* in the evening after Brandt's return from Buchenwald did not result in any rapprochement. There was agreement, however, that the summit per se had been useful. Controversial issues, such as the question of recognition and the status of West Berlin, were revisited. At the same time Stoph indicated East German interest in widening trade relations and in pragmatic regulations of questions like the postal service and road traffic. Brandt suggested communicating confidentially by special channels, similar to the West German-Soviet channel, and proposed von Berg as an envoy. Stoph did not express approval, but he did not reject the proposal.[51]

After Brandt's departure that night, Stoph gave a television interview to a tame journalist from the party. He asserted that the GDR had learned its lesson from history, contrary to the FRG, where the 'fatal forces of the past' did still exist. Asked how the people of Erfurt had reacted to this extraordinary day, Stoph, of course, could not admit that there had been a warm and enthusiastic welcome for Brandt. Instead he said he was grateful for the support of the population who wanted to strengthen their 'workers' and peasants' state' (*Arbeiter-und-Bauern-Staat*).[52] Behind closed doors the authorities were actually deeply concerned about the spontaneous demonstrations of support for the charismatic leader of the class enemy of the workers and peasants and they carried out urgent investigations as to why security planning had failed so badly. For the Stasi, Erfurt proved a rude shock.[53]

BONN'S JOURNEY, EAST BERLIN'S ROADBLOCK

In contrast to East Berlin, Bonn felt reassured by Erfurt and ready to continue on the long journey it had begun, even though little had been achieved during the official exchange at the summit. In his report to US President Richard Nixon, Brandt explained: 'From the practical standpoint the result is meagre, although I personally had not counted on anything more than a second meeting—in May and on the territory of the Federal Republic.' Brandt added that the East German side had insisted 'with penetrating resolve' on the formal question of diplomatic recognition. Nevertheless, he deemed it possible that some results on practical issues might emerge from future negotiations. Brandt also mentioned 'the many signs of solidarity' expressed in Erfurt by East German citizens, without overestimating the political significance of these gestures.[54]

On a personal level, what he called the 'pleasantly moderate' expressions of friendliness by East German people had made a profound impression on Brandt, as he admitted in a more private gathering two days after the summit. He described Erfurt as 'a strong human experience' and an encouragement for his efforts to cultivate contacts with the GDR. Brandt also made an interesting prediction. He said that the talks with the East German leadership were still an 'arduous business' and not many summit meetings might follow. Real progress might be achieved instead, less spectacularly, at lower levels.[55] As indicated in the preparatory documents for Erfurt, Brandt had always intended to use the German-German summits as ice-breakers: further progress would be made through less visible contacts. Overall, Brandt concluded that the Erfurt meeting had been useful to shed further light on the East German position and, as he so strikingly put it: 'to get a smell of each other'.[56]

Brandt's office noted that Stoph's arguments in Erfurt had been as expected. Now, Bonn needed to prepare a more concrete proposal for the next meeting in Kassel, in order to develop and firm up the contacts.[57] To this end a draft paper was elaborated in the following weeks (the so-called 'twenty points of Kassel'). While a third summit was deemed desirable in principle, special attention was paid to developing regular meetings on lower levels and to establishing 'permanent offices' in East Berlin and Bonn.[58] The FRG persisted in its policy of not recognizing the GDR according to international law, officially on the grounds that such a step was impossible as long as the Four Powers retained their rights over Germany as a whole. But this posture was, of course, a consequence of keeping unification as the ultimate objective.[59]

In the GDR preparations for Kassel were mainly focused on organizational aspects. A special commission headed by Honecker was in charge of everything. Regarding the summit itself, not much had to be done—Stoph was simply to stick to the position he had already taken in Erfurt—and when the Politburo met on 14 and 28 April it confirmed a stance formulated by Hermann Axen, namely that Kassel would end without any result. But, in order to facilitate some vague perspective for future contacts, Stoph was to propose an adjournment of discussions for the moment, to allow a pause for reflection (*Denkpause*).[60] Two weeks later, when this was suggested to the Soviet leadership, Brezhnev and Kosygin gladly agreed to a post-Kassel German-German '*Denkpause*'.[61]

THE SUMMIT IN KASSEL: TWENTY POINTS
BUT LITTLE DIALOGUE

At 8.00 on 21 May 1970, Willi Stoph's special train crossed the border from East to West Germany. He was accompanied by Foreign Minister Otto Winzer; State Secretaries Michael Kohl and Günter Kohrt; and a total of eighty-seven East German officials, information technicians, and journalists. In compliance with Stoph's exact wishes, Brandt's envoy Ulrich Sahm boarded the train a few minutes later and accompanied the visitors to Kassel railway station, where they were officially welcomed by Brandt and his summit team.[62]

The rest of the day did not run precisely according to the meticulously planned schedule. At the station, the East German visitors were booed by a group of protestors. The short car journey to the venue for the talks, the *Hotel Wilhelmshöhe*, went past more demonstrators, both right- and left-wing, whom the local police proved unable to keep at a distance. Brandt later wrote that 'our car was violently attacked' and that 'the smell of "Weimar" and its street battles hung in the air'.[63] The protest banners and slogans were directed against both Stoph and his host—for example, 'Brandt to the wall' (*Brandt an die Wand*). Security forces deemed the situation so dangerous that a scheduled wreath-laying ceremony honouring the victims of fascism was hastily cancelled. It eventually took place in the evening, when most protesters had left the city and the inhabitants of Kassel gave a warmer welcome to the guests from East Berlin and Bonn.[64]

The summit meeting took place between 10.00 and 19.30 with a pause from 11.30 to 16.30 and some shorter recesses—all used for less formal talks and several one-to-one meetings between Brandt and Stoph. Their personal notes and summaries have been published, as well as the statements and official minutes kept by both sides.[65] While the reports by Brandt and Stoph include some minor discrepancies regarding the one-to-one meetings—for example on the question of who first proposed a *Denkpause*—the minutes of the official talks between the two delegations are very similar. There is no doubt that the more relaxed atmosphere in the private conversations differed from the confrontational tone of the official meeting.[66]

The political tension between the two delegations was apparent from the outset, when Stoph interrupted Brandt's welcoming address to read a prepared statement in which he accused the FRG of systematically discriminating against the GDR and of permitting fascist and murderous agitation (*Mordhetze*) against its representatives. After this statement, Brandt could not even complete his next sentence before being interrupted again by Stoph, who vehemently protested about the tearing down of the GDR flag in front of the hotel. It turned out that three young men (sons of fugitives from the GDR), using false press cards, had managed to enter the premises and get hold of the flag before the police could intervene. Brandt, who had just been informed of the incident, offered his apologies. He emphasized that the purpose of the meeting was specifically to discuss the existing discrimination—on both sides—and to find ways to remedy the situation. In his turn he handed Stoph a lengthy note addressing the alleged 'judicial aggression' by the FRG against the East German regime.[67]

The key issue and prime stumbling block throughout the Kassel meeting was Stoph's insistence on Bonn's full and immediate de jure recognition of the GDR according to international law, whereas Brandt had no intention of making this move. The talks therefore soon reached deadlock. According to Stoph, unconditional respect for international law must necessarily be the first step towards resolving the 'cardinal problem of European peace'. He argued: 'Whoever refuses to accept international law as the basis for relations with another sovereign state obviously has intentions running counter to international law and the basic tenets of humanity.' Stoph demanded this 'guarantee for peace' before any further issue could be discussed and portrayed Brandt's evasive attitude as proof of Bonn's aggressive intentions towards the GDR.[68]

In an elaborate criticism of West Germany's *Ostpolitik* and *Deutschlandpolitik*, Stoph pointed out the innate contradiction between Brandt's public references to the 'unity of the nation' (*Einheit der Nation*) and the acknowledged impossibility of 'blending' (*vermischen*) the two different systems.[69] He then quoted the *Deutschlandvertrag* of 1955 as illustrating the real intentions of Bonn and the Western powers:

> Pending the peace settlement, the Three Powers and the Federal Republic will cooperate to achieve, by peaceful means, their common aim of a unified Germany enjoying a liberal-democratic constitution, like that of the Federal Republic, and integrated within the European Community.[70]

Stoph utterly rejected what he called 'destructive' ambitions against the socialist and peace-oriented GDR. In the same vein he dismissed Bonn's attempt to pursue the negotiations under an 'inner-German roof', which could only serve NATO's purpose of infiltrating the community of socialist states. Instead he reiterated that a dialogue had to take place between two independent and fully sovereign German states. In this context Stoph also rejected Brandt's reference to the Four Powers, and claimed that none of them had any rights over the GDR.[71]

In response, Brandt used part of his speaking time to counter Stoph's main accusations. Concerning the *Deutschlandvertrag*, Brandt argued that the paragraph quoted expressed the Western view in the context of the time, equivalent to objectives described in treaties between the GDR and the Soviet Union. The well-defined and higher-ranking goal of the *Deutschlandvertrag* was to prevent Germany from ever again endangering peace in Europe. Further, Brandt insisted that his position regarding international law was not unbending but stressed that 'first something needs to move in a positive direction' between the two German states.[72] Brandt also pointed out that East German trade greatly benefited from Bonn's official position, which stipulated that the two German states were 'not foreign countries' to each other.[73]

Brandt declared that, despite the fundamental differences of opinion and the regrettably 'polemic tone' of the discussion, his government would take Stoph's criticism seriously and investigate several of the points raised. The chancellor then endeavoured to shift attention towards topics of 'common interest' and 'points of contact'. In his opinion, these included not only the shared language and history, but also the common destiny of having been divided as a result of World War Two and especially their shared responsibility for preventing another war emanating from German territories. On the latest point, Brandt detected 'common beliefs'.[74]

To start regular talks and negotiations on topics of common concern, Brandt proposed his 'twenty points of Kassel'. This list combined principles (for example, non-discrimination, respect for sovereignty and human rights, commitment to peace); elements of a future agreement between the FRG and the GDR (such as the rights of the Four Powers); and domains of practical cooperation (for example, trade, passenger traffic, postal system and information, science, culture, and sports). Point nineteen stipulated the exchange of permanent representatives, and point twenty the membership of both German states in international organizations on the basis of a German-German treaty to be negotiated and signed.[75]

The meeting of the two delegations ended at 19.30 with Stoph's conclusion that Bonn was 'not yet ready' to establish relations with the GDR according to international law and thus needed a pause for reflection before discussions with the GDR government could be resumed. No communiqué was issued, no further summit agreed on.[76]

Fig. 1.2. Stoph says farewell to Brandt at Kassel station, 21 May 1970 (AP)

The notes of the more informal one-to-one meetings during the day never-theless show that both sides wanted further cooperation, notably at lower levels. For example, Stoph suggested that the ministries in charge of trade, traffic, and post should engage in negotiations to resolve issues in dispute and Brandt consented.[77] According to the West German record, Stoph privately expressed particular appreciation of German-German trade, admitting that this was at odds with his official position on the matter. Telephone and telex lines 'between our two houses' were considered useful by both sides. When Brandt proposed extending the contacts between Gerhard Schüßler and Ulrich Sahm to a higher political level, for instance by involving Michael Kohl and Horst Ehmke, Stoph remained noncommittal. Yet according to Brandt's notes, Stoph clearly had no desire to abort the existing contacts.[78]

Although the official meeting of the two delegations had ended with Stoph's harsh remarks on the 'hostile events' in the streets of Kassel, the East German leader concluded his private conversations with Brandt on a less confrontational note. The wreath-laying ceremony honouring the victims of fascism, said Stoph, had served to establish at least 'some common ground' (*Stück Gemeinsamkeit*).[79] He was referring to the fact that after 1933, both he and Brandt had been involved in resistance activities against the Nazi regime. The commonality thus established was bound up with the personalities of the two leaders, and would not have existed, for example, with Brandt's predecessor as chancellor, Kurt Georg Kiesinger.[80] After the ceremony, Stoph was accompanied back to the station, where he boarded the special train to return to the GDR (see Figure 1.2). This time the train left without delay.

ERFURT AND KASSEL: SMALL STEPS ON A LONG JOURNEY

The immediate results of the two meetings in Erfurt and Kassel were meagre, as Brandt himself conceded.[81] There had not even been agreement on a third summit to continue the contacts between the two Germanies. Rainer Barzel, the opposition leader in the *Bundestag*, claimed in late May 1970 that Bonn's new Eastern policy had reached a dead-end in Kassel. He argued that Brandt's rapprochement was not bringing about any of the desired changes in East Berlin or Moscow but rather a hardening of Eastern positions and an increase of Soviet influence in Europe.[82]

Yet from Brandt's perspective, the two summits could only be sensibly evaluated in the light of longer-term developments. When leaving for Erfurt, and again on his return to Bonn, Brandt had predicted that some time needed to elapse before 'a first stage' of improved relations with the GDR would begin to manifest itself.[83] After Kassel, he pledged to pursue détente towards East Berlin 'without illusions and with perseverance' and in close alignment with Bonn's relations to Moscow and Warsaw.[84] Brandt's ambition was to prepare the longer-term 'reconciliation' with the Eastern European states by moving gradually 'from confrontation to dialogue and to cooperation'.[85]

But if reconciliation was the goal, what mattered was not just the official exchanges at the summits. If we understand reconciliation as a social space for building a direct relationship between individuals, seemingly unimportant incidents at Erfurt and Kassel may also be seen as small contributions to an embryonic reconciliation process. These included the numerous East Germans waving at Brandt during his train journey to Erfurt; some citizens of Kassel smiling at Stoph after the summit; Schüßler and Sahm enjoying East German brandy after one of their many preparatory meetings; Ahlers trying to joke with GDR officials; Brandt sharing his sons' education plans with Kohl during lunch; and, not least, Stoph and Brandt earnestly contemplating each other's resistance against the Hitler regime during the wreath-laying ceremony in Kassel.[86]

Moreover, the reconciliation process needs to be studied not only at the top—between leaders like Brandt or Stoph—but also among actors on the middle level and at the grassroots. This parallels in some ways the distinction that has been made between *personal summits*, focusing on two leaders; *plenary summits*, complemented by the presence of specialist advisors; and *progressive summits* involving personal and plenary elements in series of meetings.[87] According to the study by Lederach referred to earlier, middle-range leaders in particular have significant potential to contribute to long-term reconciliation processes, notably by creating an infrastructure of sustained exchange and interdependence. Such actors usually have access to the top level and to networks behind the scenes, and often benefit from pre-existing relationships with their counterparts. Perhaps most important, middle-range leaders can meet in secret and therefore act more informally and flexibly. By contrast, as a result of their high public profile, top leaders often tend to be locked into maintaining a position of strength when meeting their opposite numbers, and—in keeping with this line of thought—are less prone to modify their attitude because their every move represents a high-stakes decision. In reconciliation processes, the key achievements of top leaders may be to set in motion a process of transition (for instance through a summit with the leader of the opposite side, as happened at Erfurt and Kassel) and later on to give public weight to results negotiated on lower levels. And at the grassroots, a mass of people may create pressure for change from below, which can ultimately lead to the end of a confrontation by exhausting the higher-level leaders.[88]

In light of these general observations, it seems noteworthy that Brandt was aware of the limits of his own capacities as West German chancellor and from the outset put great emphasis on institutionalizing contacts on middle-range levels. Much in line with the suggestion he made in Kassel, after a pause for reflection the German-German contacts officially resumed with a meeting of the State Secretaries Michael Kohl and Egon Bahr on 27 November 1970. Henceforth Bahr and Kohl met almost bi-weekly away from the cameras, preparing agreements on transit, traffic, and eventually the FRG-GDR Basic Treaty of 1972.[89] In parallel, different East and West German ministries established contacts—for example on matters of health, postal services, or cultural issues—and the important German-German trade cooperation expanded further. Crossing the border became easier, especially for families divided by the Berlin Wall. In terms of Bonn's initial objectives Erfurt and Kassel can therefore be judged a delayed success.

Given the crucial contribution of the people of East Germany and Eastern Europe to ending the Cold War by means of peaceful mass demonstrations in

1989, the grassroots level merits further mention. As Brandt and Bahr had hoped in 1970, at the end of the Cold War a feeling of togetherness (*Zusammengehörigkeit*) between ordinary folk in the two Germanies still endured. To what extent the summits in Erfurt and Kassel contributed to preserving this feeling cannot be determined. Yet it seems relevant to point out that the 1970 summits certainly created time and space for some grassroots encounters and for a Western leader to physically stand in front of Eastern people. Brandt's brief appearance at the hotel window in Erfurt making a pacifying sign to the East German crowd moved many of those present to tears. Even as far away as the United States, watching the scene on CBS television, some viewers were overwhelmed by emotion.[90] According to Brandt's own account, the mere fact of the summits taking place had awakened the otherwise 'hidden feeling of togetherness' in West Germany. He also received 'many moving letters from the GDR' in the aftermath of the meetings.[91]

While mostly undocumented, numerous brief moments of East-West encounter took place as a result of the vast media presence during both summits. About 400 journalists were present in Erfurt, forty-six of whom had accompanied Brandt on his special train. In Kassel reporters were admitted without restriction; from the GDR at least sixty journalists and six camera teams were present.[92] Yet the East German media were not eager to transmit Western statements. Whereas Stoph's Erfurt presentation was read out simultaneously on GDR television, the programme subsequently showed an old movie starring the comic actor Theo Lingen instead of relaying Brandt's statement. The party newspaper *Neues Deutschland* in its many reports about Erfurt and Kassel presented the GDR's policy of peace as the driving force behind the summits and also used strong Cold War language against the West. Bonn was described as 'imperialistic', Brandt as duplicitously dodging international law. Lacking a free and diversified press, the East Germans thus read about Erfurt and Kassel as class confrontations rather than attempts at détente and rapprochement. Still, in its back pages *Neues Deutschland* did reprint Brandt's official summit declarations. These issues were particularly popular with the East Germans and sold out quickly.[93]

The West German media reported at length on Erfurt and Kassel, being generally supportive of the summits as a first step towards changing the German-German confrontation. Before Erfurt, expectations of immediate results were generally low. When evaluating the two summits, and in the language used to describe the GDR, differences can be discerned according to political preferences. Conservative-oriented newspapers like *Die Welt* or *Bild* commented critically that Brandt conceded too much and gained too little. They referred to the 'DDR' only in quotation marks and still refused to accept East Berlin as a negotiating partner, depicting East Germany as a territory occupied by the Soviet Union. Due to its aggressive Cold War language, *Bild* journalists were not in fact admitted to Erfurt. Yet the majority of West

German newspapers tended to describe the summits, especially Erfurt, as a turning point and discerned small atmospheric changes that could gradually lead to a German-German rapprochement and East-West détente. For example, whereas before the summits Brandt had referred to the GDR leaders as stubborn, after Kassel the Western media detected in his description of Stoph as a 'calm and well informed man' a sign of evolution both in East Berlin and Bonn.[94]

Later comments by Brandt do not, however, suggest that he had created any particular personal bond with Stoph. At various anniversaries of the Erfurt and Kassel summits and in two volumes of memoirs Brandt expressed his own retrospective view. On the practical side, he emphasized several times that each of the 'twenty points of Kassel' was eventually accepted and implemented by the Basic Treaty of 1972.[95] On a personal level, he highlighted the 'overwhelming' sympathy he had felt at that hotel window in Erfurt, and stated that 19 March 1970 had perhaps been the most emotionally charged day of his whole life.[96]

For Willi Stoph, however, the summitry of 1970 seemed very different. Although officially embedded in a socialist community of brother states, he had to realize that his government was only a minor actor in the triangle between Bonn, Moscow, and East Berlin.[97] In Erfurt and Kassel he was forced to demand something that was not even the policy of the Soviet Union, namely recognition of the GDR according to international law. Highlighting the gap between East Germany and its superpower master, only one day after Kassel negotiations between Gromyko and Bahr in Moscow resulted in an accord which led to the Treaty of Moscow of August 1970. This committed each country to work towards normalizing relations and securing international peace without formal recognition. Right from the start of détente, Moscow controlled East Berlin in its relations with Bonn. Between November 1969 and the middle of May 1970 members of the SED leadership travelled to the Soviet capital four times in order to consult with the Soviets and keep in step.

To be sure, the FRG also had to maintain close contacts with its Western allies, in particular with the United States. But notwithstanding some uneasiness about the long-term consequences of 'a more independent German policy',[98] the Nixon White House never tried to put pressure on Bonn or even to block *Ostpolitik*. It understood that any attempt to slow down the pace of *Ostpolitik* would be futile. Rather than consulting with the Western superpower, let alone kowtowing, Bonn merely had to keep it well informed.[99] And Brandt was operating on fairly safe ground: his *Ostpolitik* turned out to be broadly compatible with Kissinger's policy of détente. As for the Warsaw Pact states, Brandt was aware that they did not support the maximalist goals pursued by Stoph in Erfurt and Kassel. For the Soviets the FRG had become its main economic and political partner in Western Europe and only in agreement with the FRG could Brezhnev hope to realize his favourite project, a Conference on European Security. The final arrangements for this were agreed when Brezhnev and Brandt met in the Crimea in September 1971, thereby starting a whole series of summits between Soviet and Western leaders which were pivotal to the era of détente.[100]

With regard specifically to bilateral German-German relations, although Brandt and Stoph showed respect for their mutually incompatible positions, their interaction was more like a duel than a dialogue: it did not generate trust between them. But what mattered above all was that the summits did take place, unlocking the German question for international diplomacy and paving the way for *de facto* recognition in the *Deutschlandvertrag* of 1972. For the moment this consolidated the two Germanies in their respective moulds, at a level of diminished tension and regularized contact. The next German-German summit in the FRG did not take place until 1987, when Chancellor Helmut Kohl received Honecker in Bonn.[101]

But the relations between each Germany and its respective superpower patron were ultimately decisive, as will become clear from later chapters of this book. Leonid Brezhnev made the essential point more tellingly than he knew when lecturing Erich Honecker in June 1970. He flatly stated that the Soviets considered that 'Erfurt and Kassel were of no avail' and that, instead of planning further summits, the GDR should concentrate on developing a clear socialist identity and solidarity within the community of socialist countries. He also warned that 'any rapprochement between the GDR and the FRG must be prevented', lest this erode the political stability and social strength of East Germany. Then Brezhnev added coldly: 'We have troops in the GDR. Erich, let us be clear and never forget: the GDR cannot exist without the power and the strength of the Soviet Union. Without us there will be no GDR.' In November 1989, what Brezhnev had said in July 1970 came true.[102]

NOTES

1. Claus Jacobi, 'Protokoll einer Reise durchs andere Deutschland', *Welt am Sonntag*, 22 March 1970; Jan Schönfelder and Rainer Erices, *Willy Brandt in Erfurt: Das erste deutsch-deutsche Gipfeltreffen 1970* (Berlin, 2010), 242–4.
2. Mary E. Sarotte, 'A Small Town in (East) Germany: The Erfurt Meeting of 1970 and the Dynamics of Cold War Détente', *Diplomatic History* 25, no. 1 (Winter 2001), 103.
3. Quoted in Timothy Garton Ash, *In Europe's Name: Germany and the Divided Continent* (New York, 1993), 119.
4. Regierungserklärung des Bundeskanzlers vor dem Deutschen Bundestag, 28 October 1969, in *Bulletin des Presse- und Informationsamtes der Bundesregierung* (henceforth *Bulletin*), 29 October 1969, 1122.
5. The SPD (and Brandt) had taken over in December 1966 some governmental responsibilities, as junior partner in the Grand Coalition with the CDU.

6. Hans-Peter Schwarz et al., eds, *Akten zur Auswärtigen Politik der Bundesrepublik Deutschland 1969, Band II: 1. Juli bis 31. Dezember 1969* (Munich, 2000), doc. 296, 1054–5.

7. Archiv der sozialen Demokratie, Bonn (henceforth AdsD), Depositum Bahr, Box 465, Manuskript *Was nun?*, 1966; Hans-Peter Schwarz et al., eds, *Akten zur Auswärtigen Politik der Bundesrepublik Deutschland 1969, Band I: 1. Januar bis 30. Juni 1968* (Munich, 1999), doc. 207, 812.

8. Sitzung des Bundeskabinetts, 7 June 1970, in Helga Grebing et al., eds, *Willy Brandt: Berliner Ausgabe, vol.* 6 (Berlin, 2005), 316; Benedikt Schoenborn, 'NATO Forever? Willy Brandt's Heretical Thoughts on an Alternative Future', in Jussi M. Hanhimäki et al., eds, *The Routledge Handbook of Transatlantic Security* (London, 2010), 76, 84.

9. For instance by Lily Gardner Feldman, *Germany's Foreign Policy of Reconciliation: From Enmity to Amity* (Lanham, 2012), 31–5, and in the Nobel Prize presentation speech by Aase Lionæs, 10 December 1971, http://www.nobelprize.org/.

10. AdsD, Willy-Brandt-Archiv (henceforth WBA), A3, Box 108, Brandt, 'Ringen um Aussöhnung im Innern', *Düsseldorfer Nachrichten*, 14 December 1960; WBA, A3, Box 207, Ansprache in Berlin, 29 April 1965; Brandt, 'Aussöhnung mit den Nachbarn im Osten', in *Bulletin*, 21 June 1968, 656; Brandt, 'Entspannung und Aussöhnung mit den Völkern Osteuropas', in *Bulletin*, 7 July 1970, 897.

11. John P. Lederach, *Building Peace: Sustainable Reconciliation in Divided Societies* (Washington, DC, 2010).

12. Lederach, *Building Peace*, 23.

13. Lederach, *Building Peace*, 34–5, 63–5.

14. AdsD, Dep. Bahr, 1/EBAA001026.

15. Since July 1969, Spangenberg had been the chief of the Office of the Federal President, Gustav Heinemann. For Spangenberg's reports to Bahr, see AdsD, Dep. Bahr, 1/EBAA000787.

16. Ulbricht during an extraordinary meeting of the Politburo in his country house in Dölln, 30 October 1969. *Dokumente zur Deutschlandpolitik, VI. Reihe, Band 1: 21. Oktober 1969 bis 31. Dezember 1970* (Munich, 2002) (henceforth *DzD VI/1*), doc. 10, 26–31.

17. Oliver Bange, 'The GDR in the Era of Détente: Conflicting Perceptions and Strategies', in Poul Villaume and Odd A. Westad, eds, *Perforating the Iron Curtain: European Détente, Transatlantic Relations, and the Cold War, 1965–1985* (Copenhagen, 2010), 66–7. See also Jochen Stelkens, 'Machtwechsel in Ost-Berlin: Der Sturz Walter Ulbrichts 1971', in *Vierteljahrshefte für Zeitgeschichte* 45, no. 4 (1997), 521–5; Marianne Howarth, 'Die Westpolitik der DDR zwischen internationaler Aufwertung und ideologischer Offensive (1966–1989)', in Ulrich Pfeil, ed., *Die DDR und der Westen: Transnationale Beziehungen 1949–1989* (Berlin, 2001), 85–6.

18. Monika Kaiser, *Machtwechsel von Ulbricht zu Honecker: Funktionsmechanismen der SED-Diktatur in Konfliktsituationen 1962 bis 1972* (Berlin, 1997), 331–2.

19. *DzD VI/1*, doc. 21, 61–4.

20. 'Aggression on slippers' (*Aggression auf Filzlatschen*) is attributed to Otto Winzer. There is no written evidence. But see the memoirs by Karl Seidel, head of the 'Department West Germany' in the East German Foreign Ministry from July

1970: Karl Seidel, *Berlin-Bonner Balance: 20 Jahre deutsch-deutsche Beziehungen. Erinnerungen und Erkenntnisse eines Beteiligten* (Berlin, 2002), 52.

21. Markus Wolf, *Spionagechef im geheimen Krieg: Erinnerungen* (Munich, 1997), 247.
22. Undated paper 'Disposition für Beratung', being a summary of Wolf's paper and serving as speaking notes for the meeting with Andropov. Der Bundesbeauftragte für die Unterlagen des Staatssicherheitsdienstes der ehemaligen DDR, Zentralarchiv, Berlin (hereafter BstU), MfS, SdM 1471. See also Siegfried Suckut, 'Probleme mit dem "großen Bruder": Der DDR-Staatssicherheitsdienst und die Deutschlandpolitik der KPdSU 1969/70', in *Vierteljahrshefte für Zeitgeschichte* 58, no. 3 (2010), 404–6.
23. A note on Andropov's assessment was taken after Mielke's return to Berlin, 17 November 1969. *DzD VI/1*, doc. 20, 58–61. See also Karl-Heinz Schmidt, *Dialog über Deutschland: Studien zur Deutschlandpolitik von KPdSU und SED (1960–1979)* (Baden-Baden, 1998), 211–15; Mary Elise Sarotte, *Dealing with the Devil. East Germany, Détente, and Ostpolitik, 1969–1973* (Chapel Hill, NC, 2001), 31.
24. Wjatscheslaw Keworkow, *Der geheime Kanal: Moskau, der KGB und die Bonner Ostpolitik* (Berlin, 1995), 26–32.
25. *DzD VI/1*, doc. 23, 67–70.
26. *DzD VI/1*, doc. 32, 93, doc. 33, 95–8.
27. See the account of two former East German Foreign Ministry officials Siegfried Bock and Karl Seidel, 'Die Außenbeziehungen der DDR in der Periode der Konsolidierung (1955–1972/73)', in Siegfried Bock, Ingrid Muth, and Hermann Schwiesau, eds, *DDR-Außenpolitik im Rückspiegel: Diplomaten im Gespräch* (Münster, 2004), 56.
28. For two detailed surveys, see Detlef Nakath, *Deutsch-deutsche Grundlagen: Zur Geschichte der politischen und wirtschaftlichen Beziehungen zwischen der DDR und der Bundesrepublik in den Jahren von 1969 bis 1982* (Schkeuditz, 2002); Schönfelder and Erices, *Willy Brandt in Erfurt.*
29. Hermann von Berg, *Vorbeugende Unterwerfung: Politik im realen Sozialismus* (Munich, 1988), 143ff.; Daniela Münkel, *Kampagnen, Spione, geheime Kanäle: Die Stasi und Willy Brandt* (Berlin, 2013), 36ff.
30. Memorandum of conversation by Bahr 26 October 1969, *DzD VI/1*, doc. 1, 3–4. For Berg's account, BStU, MfS, GH 25/87, vol. 8, 247–50.
31. Stoph to Brandt, 11 February 1970, *Dokumente zur Außenpolitik der Deutschen Demokratischen Republik 1970* (Berlin, 1972) (henceforth *DzA*), 770–2.
32. For a record of the meeting, see *DzD VI/1*, doc. 86, 298–324.
33. For a detailed account, see Schönfelder and Erices, *Willy Brandt in Erfurt,* 67–128.
34. BStU, MfS, SdM 1471, 81–92. Further on this aspect, see Oliver Bange, 'The Stasi Confronts Western Strategies for Transformation 1966–1975', in Jonathan Haslam and Karina Urbach, eds, *Secret Intelligence in the European States System 1918–1989* (Stanford, 2013), 170–208. See also Stefan Steck, *Neue Ostpolitik: Wahrnehmung und Deutung in der DDR und den USA (1961–1974)—Zur Symbolik eines politischen Begriffs* (Hamburg, 2012), 243–314.
35. Seidel, *Berlin-Bonner Balance,* 73–5.
36. Schönfelder and Erices, *Willy Brandt in Erfurt,* 136–7, 157–8. For the trip to Buchenwald, see Seidel, *Berlin-Bonner Balance,* 227–31.

37. Nixon Presidential Library, Yorba Linda, CA, Nixon Presidential Materials Staff, NSC, Country Files, Box 683, Telegram Rush (Bonn), 11 February 1970. The telegram refers to Brandt's conversation with 'an American official whom he knows well'.

38. Bericht zur Lage der Nation, 14 January 1970, in *Bulletin*, 15 January 1970, 51.

39. Vortrag des Bundeskanzlers in Kopenhagen, 13 February 1970, in *Bulletin*, 17 February 1970, 201.

40. Bericht zur Lage der Nation, 14 January 1970, in *Bulletin*, 15 January 1970, 52 ('Überwindung der europäischen Spaltung').

41. Erklärung des Bundeskanzlers im Deutschen Fernsehen, 18 March 1970, in *Bulletin,* 20 March 1970, 382.

42. AdsD, Dep. Bahr, Box 384/2, Aufz. Bahr, 19 February 1970 (quote); Bundesarchiv, Koblenz (henceforth BA), B136, Box 6689, Argumentation BK Erfurt, 16 March 1970; Hans-Peter Schwarz et al., eds, *Akten zur Auswärtigen Politik der Bundesrepublik Deutschland 1970, Band I: 1. Januar bis 30. April 1970* (Munich, 2001) (henceforth *AAPD 1970/I*), doc. 68, 292–4, Aufz. Ruete, 19 February 1970.

43. AdsD, Dep. Bahr, Box 429B, Bahr an Brandt, 12 March 1970.

44. Luncheon Conversation Kissinger-Bahr, 8 April 1970, *Foreign Relations of the United States 1969–76, vol. xl, Germany and Berlin, 1969–72* (henceforth *FRUS 1969–76, vol. xl*), https://history.state.gov/historicaldocuments/frus1969-76v40, doc. 206.

45. Berg, *Vorbeugende Unterwerfung,* 166. Note by Brandt, 21 March 1970, *DzD VI/1*, doc. 113, 441.

46. Schönfelder and Erices, *Willy Brandt in Erfurt,* 197–9, 202–8; Nakath, *Deutschdeutsche Grundlagen,* 70–3; Steffen Raßloff and Thomas Rothbart, 'Das erste deutsch-deutsche Gipfeltreffen 1970 in Erfurt', in Steffen Raßloff, ed., *'Willy Brandt ans Fenster!' Das Erfurter Gipfeltreffen 1970 und die Geschichte des 'Erfurter Hofes'* (Jena, 2007), 63–7; Sarotte, *Dealing with the Devil*, 46–8.

47. Hartmut Zwahr, *Die erfrorenen Flügel der Schwalbe—DDR und 'Prager Frühling': Tagebuch einer Krise 1968–1970* (Bonn, 2007), 336–8.

48. For the statements during the official sessions, see *DzD VI/1*, 398–437.

49. *DzD VI/1*, doc. 111, 421.

50. Gottfried Niedhart, '"The Transformation of the Other Side": Willy Brandt's Ostpolitik and the Liberal Peace Concept', in Frédéric Bozo, Marie-Pierre Rey, Bernd Rother, and N. Piers Ludlow, eds, *Visions of the End of the Cold War in Europe, 1945–1990* (New York, 2012), 149–62.

51. There are two records, one by Brandt and one by Stoph, see *DzD VI/1*, doc. 113, 438–42 and doc. 119A, 459–64.

52. *DzA*, 806–9.

53. Sarotte, *Dealing with the Devil*, 52–4.

54. *AAPD 1970/I*, doc. 126, 507–8, Brief Brandt an Nixon, 22 March 1970.

55. AdsD, WBA, A3, Box 340, Redemanuskript, Hörsaal der Kernforschungsanlage Jülich, 21 March 1970.

56. Vermerk Brandt über das Gespräch mit Stoph, 19 March 1970, *Berliner Ausgabe* VI, 281–8, at 287.

57. *AAPD 1970/I*, doc. 130, 515–17.

58. Hans-Peter Schwarz et al., eds, *Akten zur Auswärtigen Politik der Bundesrepublik Deutschland 1970, Band II: 1. Mai bis 31. August 1970* (Munich, 2001) (henceforth *AAPD 1970/II*), doc. 205, 770–1.

59. Luncheon Conversation Kissinger-Bahr, 8 April 1970, *FRUS 1969–76, vol. xl*, doc. 206.

60. Nakath, *Deutsch-deutsche Grundlagen*, 77–8. For the Politburo resolution of 28 April 1970, see *DzD VI/1*, doc. 134A, 506–9.

61. Honecker's notes on the talks in Moscow, 15 May 1970. *DzD VI/1*, doc. 139, 522.

62. BA, B136, Box 6688, Aufzeichnung Sahm, 6 May 1970; Programmablauf, 21 May 1970; Nakath, *Deutsch-deutsche Grundlagen*, 81.

63. Willy Brandt, *Erinnerungen* (Berlin, 1989), 228; Willy Brandt, *Begegnungen und Einsichten: Die Jahre 1960–1975* (Hamburg, 1976), 502.

64. *DzD VI/1*, doc. 144, 592–5, and doc. 146, 597–9; Arnulf Baring, *Machtwechsel: Die Ära Brandt-Scheel* (Stuttgart, 1982), 288–90. According to the *Frankfurter Allgemeine Zeitung* (23 May 1970), the protests were led by about 1,500 sympathizers of the DKP (Deutsche Kommunistische Partei), and about 250 sympathizers of the right-wing NPD (Nationaldemokratische Partei Deutschlands).

65. Many of the statements made in Kassel were published in the West German *Bulletin des Presse- und Informationsamtes der Bundesregierung*, on 22 and 23 May 1970, and a few others also appeared in the East German newspaper *Neues Deutschland* on the same days. The most complete publication of the minutes (East and West German versions) and personal notes is that in *DzD VI/1*, 529–603.

66. Vermerk Brandt, 21 May 1970, *Berliner Ausgabe* VI, 310 and 314; Brandt, *Erinnerungen*, 228–9. Likewise from the East German perspective: *DzD VI/1*, doc. 145, 595–601.

67. *DzD VI/1*, doc. 142, 529–47 for the West German minutes, and doc. 143, 548–92 for the East German minutes—here at 529–30 and 548–50. The East German record is significantly longer because it includes the written statements, read during the meeting, while the West German side recorded them separately.

68. *DzD VI/1*, doc. 143, 556–8.

69. *DzD VI/1*, doc. 143, 578.

70. *DzD VI/1*, doc. 143, 579. Stoph correctly quoted article 7.2 of the *Deutschlandvertrag* between the FRG, the United States, the United Kingdom and France, which entered into force on 5 May 1955.

71. *DzD VI/1*, doc. 143, 561–4. To prove the GDR's full sovereignty, Stoph referred to the treaty of 20 September 1955 between the GDR and the Soviet Union.

72. *DzD VI/1*, doc. 142, 541–3 (quote at 542).

73. *DzD VI/1*, doc. 142, 544 and doc. 143, 569. In line also with the West German tariff law of June 1961, the GDR indirectly participated in the Common Market. See also Brandt, *Begegnungen und Einsichten*, 504.

74. *DzD VI/1*, doc. 143, 568–76. Speech published also in *Bulletin*, 23 May 1970, 688–92.

75. Rede von Bundeskanzler Brandt in Kassel, 21 May 1970, *Bulletin*, 23 May 1970, 682–3. Likewise in *DzD VI/1*, doc. 143, 554–5.

76. *DzD VI/1*, doc. 143, 585–6.

77. *DzD VI/1*, doc. 146, 599, Notiz Kohl über Vieraugengespräch Stoph-Brandt, 21 May 1970.

78. Vermerk Brandt, 21 May 1970, *Berliner Ausgabe* VI, 311–12.

79. *DzD VI/1*, doc. 143, 591; Vermerk Brandt, 21 May 1970, *Berliner Ausgabe* VI, 314 (quote).

80. Kiesinger had joined the Nazi party in 1933 and rose to become deputy head of the Foreign Ministry's radio propaganda department during World War Two.

81. AdsD, WBA, A3, Box 364, Interview mit *Nordhessische Zeitung*, 21 July 1970.

82. Rede Barzels vor dem Bundestag, 27 May 1970, *Verhandlungen des Deutschen Bundestags*, 6. Wahlperiode, 2665–72. See also Herbert Lorenz, 'Wandlung durch Annäherung?', *Politisch-Soziale Korrespondenz*, 15 May 1970.

83. AdsD, WBA, A3, Box 339, Interview des Bundeskanzlers mit *Süddeutsche Zeitung*, 17 March 1970.

84. AdsD, Personalia, Willy Brandt, U/P, Box 1527, Pressekonferenz des Bundeskanzlers, 22 May 1970.

85. AdsD, WBA, A3, Box 364, Interview des Bundeskanzlers mit *Nordhessische Zeitung*, 21 July 1970.

86. Brandt, *Begegnungen und Einsichten*, 490 and 503. BA, N1474, Box 114, Tagebuch Sahm, 9 March 1970; *DzD VI/1*, doc. 148, 601 and doc. 147, 600; AdsD, Personalia, Brandt, BPA, Box 1834, *Lübecker Nachrichten*, 23 May 1970.

87. See David Reynolds, *Summits: Six Meetings that Shaped the Twentieth Century* (London, 2007), 7.

88. Lederach, *Building Peace*, 38–52.

89. Heinrich Potthoff, *Im Schatten der Mauer: Deutschlandpolitik 1961 bis 1990* (Berlin, 1999), 100–1.

90. AdsD, WBA, A8, Box 3, Brief Boelling (Washington) an Brandt, 28 March 1970.

91. Brandt, *Begegnungen und Einsichten*, 490 and 509.

92. BA, B136, Box 6688, Anreise der Delegationen, undated. Schönfelder and Erices, *Willy Brandt in Erfurt*, 192; Nakath, *Grundlagen*, 60.

93. Lisa Mundzeck, 'Der "Geist von Erfurt": Das Gipfeltreffen am 19. März 1970 in der deutschen Presse', in Steffen Raßloff, ed., *'Willy Brandt ans Fenster!': Das Erfurter Gipfeltreffen 1970* (Jena, 2007), 87–9 and 93–5; *Neues Deutschland*, 20–1 March and 22–3 May 1970. AdsD, WBA, A8, Box 2, Brief Bauer an Brandt, 27 May 1970.

94. David Binder, 'Brandt Asks Stoph to Unbend', *International Herald Tribune*, 23 May 1970 (quote); AdsD, Personalia, Brandt, BPA 1833–4, 1970 (newspaper collection); Mundzeck, 'Der Geist von Erfurt', 84–7 and 94–5.

95. See esp. AdsD, WBA, A3, Box 473, Manuskript, Rede in Kassel, 9 November 1972.

96. Brandt, *Begegnungen und Einsichten*, 500 (quote). For the second part of the sentence: Brandt, *Erinnerungen*, 226 (published in summer 1989).

97. Detlef Nakath, 'Das Dreieck Bonn – Ost-Berlin – Moskau: Zur sowjetischen Einflussnahme auf die Gestaltung der deutsch-deutschen Beziehungen (1969–1982)', in Pfeil, *Die DDR und der Westen*, 99–115.

98. Brandt during his first statement as chancellor in the Bundestag, 28 October 1969. *Verhandlungen des Deutschen Bundestags*, 6. Wahlperiode, 5. Sitzung, 31; 'Kissinger to Nixon on *Ostpolitik*, February 1970', in Jussi M. Hanhimäki and Odd Arne Westad, eds, *The Cold War: A History in Documents and Eyewitness Accounts* (Oxford, 2003), 338.

99. Judith Michel, *Willy Brandts Amerikabild und -politik 1933–1992* (Göttingen, 2010), 295–312.

100. Gottfried Niedhart, *Entspannung in Europa: Die Bundesrepublik Deutschland und der Warschauer Pakt 1966 bis 1975* (Munich, 2014).

101. The Soviet Union had prevented an earlier visit, against Honecker's wishes.

102. Brezhnev in conversation with Honecker, 28 July 1970. *DzD VI/1*, doc. 167, 669–71.

2

Beijing, 1972

Yafeng Xia and Chris Tudda

It seemed like fantasy. On 21 February 1972 President Richard Nixon stood up at a banquet in the Great Hall of the People in Beijing, to toast the leaders of communist China. In his speech, broadcast around the world by satellite and shown live on morning television in America, the president—formerly an inveterate anti-communist—waxed eloquent and emotional.

'What legacy shall we leave our children?' he asked. 'Are they destined to die for the hatreds which have plagued the old world, or are they destined to live because we had the vision to build a new world? There is no reason for us to be enemies. Neither of us seeks the territory of the other; neither of us seeks domination over the other; neither of us seeks to stretch out our hands and rule the world.' Nixon even quoted with approval the great ideologue of America's former enemy, against whom the United States had fought a bitter war in Korea only two decades before: 'Chairman Mao has written, "So many deeds cry out to be done, and always urgently. The world rolls on. Time passes. Ten thousand years are too long. Seize the day, seize the hour"'. Raising his glass, the American president declared: 'This is the hour, this is the day for our two peoples to rise to the heights of greatness which can build a new and a better world.'[1] Even Nixon's National Security Adviser Henry Kissinger, an unsentimental proponent of realpolitik who had endured innumerable diplomatic banquets, found himself 'deeply moved' by the occasion. As he commented later, 'when Richard Nixon could quote Mao Tse-tung to support American foreign policy on Washington's birthday, a diplomatic revolution had clearly taken place'[2] (see Figure 2.1).

After six days of intense negotiations between Nixon and the communist leaders and among the bureaucrats of the two countries, the president stood up again on 27 February at a banquet in Shanghai. 'We have been here a week', he declared. 'This is the week that changed the world.' Kissinger took the same view when reflecting on the summit a few years later: the leaders of China and America had come to the conclusion 'that they could conduct compatible

Fig. 2.1. Nixon and Zhou Enlai at a gymnastic show in Beijing, 23 February 1972 (AP)

foreign policies, revolutionizing world diplomacy. The bipolarity of the post-war period was over.'[3]

Were Nixon and Kissinger right? How far did summit diplomacy prove transformative?

FROM OPEN WARFARE TO QUIET CONVERSATIONS

It took the United States twenty years to reach a rapprochement with the People's Republic of China. The PRC had been created in 1949, after the communist victory in the country's long-running civil war which drove the Nationalist government to the island of Taiwan. The collapse of the Nationalist cause shocked the American public, which had idealized 'free China' as a democratic and valiant protégé. In the summer of 1949 American officials had tried to negotiate with the near-victorious leaders of the Chinese Communist Party (CCP), but the divergence over interests and ideology proved too great.[4] Now China had 'gone red', spreading the Cold War across East Asia, with the new regime in Beijing dependent on Moscow.

On 26 June 1950, the North Korean leader Kim Il-sung, with Soviet political and military support, invaded South Korea. Mao Zedong, the CCP Chairman, reluctantly gave his consent. But President Harry S. Truman reacted strongly to aid America's client in the South and he appealed to the United Nations

(UN) for international support. Since the Soviet Union was boycotting the UN because Taiwan, not the PRC, held China's Security Council seat, Truman was able to secure a Security Council Resolution that authorized the creation of an American-led UN force to repel the North Korean invasion. In September UN forces under General Douglas MacArthur landed at the port of Inchon, behind enemy lines, and trapped the North Korean army in the South. Over the next two months, the UN force advanced steadily deeper into North Korea, by November drawing close to the Chinese border. To pre-empt a feared American invasion, the Chinese army then invaded North Korea, pushing the American forces back below the 38th parallel into South Korea. After counterattacks by both sides, a military stalemate between the UN and Chinese forces ensued from July 1951 until an armistice was eventually signed in July 1953.[5]

The Korean War armistice negotiations opened the door for Chinese involvement in future international diplomacy. The PRC went on to participate in international gatherings, playing a major role at the Geneva conference on Indochina in 1954 and the Bandung summit of the 'non-aligned' states in 1955. The Korean armistice talks—America and the PRC's first face-to-face negotiations—also confirmed to US leaders the importance of direct contact with the Chinese. So both Washington and Beijing began to recognize the utility of talking to each other when trying to manage the confrontations of the Cold War in East Asia, even though they did not have formal diplomatic relations. To maintain communications they developed a special mechanism—the Sino-American 'ambassadorial talks'. Between 1955 and 1970 the Chinese and American ambassadors held 136 diplomatic conversations, first in Geneva and then in Warsaw. Despite a total impasse over the major issue of Taiwan, which caused two dangerous military crises in 1954–5 and 1958, the ambassadorial talks helped to deflect confrontations and provided a channel for transmitting information between the two antagonists during those difficult years.

In the mid-1950s, the Chinese leadership made a serious effort to improve relations with Washington. To show they were in earnest, they unilaterally released some detained Americans and offered to discuss less controversial issues such as the US economic embargo against China and the existing ban on cultural exchanges. In return, Beijing expected Washington to conduct serious, high-level discussions over the really significant issues: these included recognizing the legitimacy of the PRC, withdrawing American troops from Taiwan, and achieving an overall resolution of the Taiwan question.[6]

Despite the ambassadorial conversations, significant enmity continued to exist between the United States and the PRC. The alleged refusal by US Secretary of State John Foster Dulles to shake PRC Premier Zhou Enlai's hand at the 1954 Geneva Conference symbolized the gulf that existed between the two adversaries. Whatever the truth of the matter, this anecdote caused lasting damage—in the words of Mao's interpreter Ji Chaozhu becoming 'a legend in our foreign affairs, poisoning our relations with the United States for nearly two decades'.[7] More substantive for its geostrategic importance, in October 1964 China successfully tested an atomic bomb, and although US intelligence had anticipated the test, the reality sobered American policy-makers.[8] The planet's most populous country had now become the world's fifth nuclear power. Six months later, after US President Lyndon Johnson began bombing North Vietnam and significantly increased ground forces in South Vietnam, PRC Premier Zhou Enlai warned Washington via Pakistan that while 'China would not take the initiative to provoke a war with the United States', it would 'honor whatever international obligations it has undertaken' vis-à-vis Hanoi. Although both the Johnson administration and the PRC subsequently signalled that they did not want a repeat of the direct military confrontation that had occurred in Korea,[9] Mao made any Sino-American accommodation virtually impossible when he plunged China into the Great Proletarian Cultural Revolution in 1966. Radical Red Guards purged intellectuals and others considered to be 'capitalists'. Foreign governments were also a prime target. In January 1967, millions of Chinese students, responding to the quashing of a small Chinese student protest in Moscow, massed outside the Soviet embassy in Beijing, while in August Red Guards burned the office of the British Chargé d'Affaires. During 1968 the Chinese also repeatedly postponed further ambassadorial talks in Warsaw. Johnson administration officials predicted bleakly that unless and until 'the Maoists' lost power, the chances for improved Sino-American relations were remote.[10]

THE SINO-AMERICAN THAW

By mid-1969, however, the Chinese urgently needed to improve relations with Washington in order to break out of diplomatic isolation. They felt 'under siege' after the Soviet Union invaded Czechoslovakia in August 1968, declaring its right to intervene in any socialist country that deviated from the Moscow line. Mao interpreted the so-called 'Brezhnev doctrine' as an attack on his own legitimacy and his country's security. When two bloody conflicts between Chinese and Soviet border garrison forces broke out in March 1969 on Zhenbao Island in the Ussuri River (Damansky Island in Russian), followed by one in the northwestern border province of Xinjiang in August, China's situation dramatically worsened. The perception of an extremely grave military threat from the Soviet Union pushed Mao to decide to break through existing ideological constraints in order to improve relations with the United States.[11]

Meanwhile, Richard Nixon wanted to change American policy towards China. In 1967, before announcing his bid for the presidency, he wrote in the influential journal *Foreign Affairs* that the US must 'urgently come to grips with the reality of China'. The country, he said, could become a partner for stability if Washington could help pull it back 'into the world community'.[12] In his Inaugural Address in January 1969, Nixon said he wanted 'an open world' where 'no people, great or small, will live in angry isolation'. For his part, Mao, who had earlier read Nixon's *Foreign Affairs* article and recommended it to Zhou, ordered the CCP's official news organ, *Renmin Ribao* (*People's Daily*), to publish the president's Inaugural.[13]

During the fall of 1969 and the early winter of 1970, Nixon made several attempts to establish direct talks with China. The urgent need to reduce Beijing's support for Hanoi was an added incentive. To open channels the president and his national security adviser, Henry Kissinger, visited Pakistan and Romania and asked both Pakistani president Yahya Khan and Romanian president Nicolae Ceauşescu to serve as intermediaries.[14] The White House also tried discreetly to revive the Warsaw talks. In September 1969, Kissinger had instructed the American ambassador to Poland, Walter Stoessel, to inform his counterpart, should they meet, that Washington was ready for 'serious talks'. No such opportunity presented itself for several months. In the meantime Nixon announced in November that for 'budgetary reasons', he would remove the Seventh Fleet from the Taiwan Straits; its presence had been a major irritant in US-PRC relations since 1954. On 3 December, seizing his moment at a fashion show at Warsaw's Palace of Culture, Stoessel passed on his message through a senior interpreter from the Chinese embassy.[15]

Before Stoessel's overture, China regarded Nixon's probing about the Warsaw talks as only exploratory. But now Beijing responded quickly for it seemed convinced of the seriousness of the US offer. After receiving the Chinese embassy's report on the American ambassador's 'unusual behavior', Zhou immediately reported to Mao that 'the opportunity is coming; we now have a brick in our hands to knock at the door [of the Americans]'.[16] As a goodwill gesture, on 4 December 1969, with Mao's approval, Zhou ordered the release of two Americans who had been held in China since mid-February 1969, when their yacht had strayed into China's territorial water off Guangdong.[17]

On 20 January 1970, at what was the 135th ambassadorial meeting, Stoessel made another offer. The Nixon administration, he said, would consider sending an emissary to Beijing or receiving a Chinese representative in Washington for 'more thorough' talks. The Chinese viewed this change of attitude from the American side favourably since, as noted earlier, the Chinese had been seeking higher-level talks since 1955. The Chinese also allowed journalists to photograph the ambassadorial meeting for the first time since 1966.

Lei Yang, whom Zhou had personally chosen to represent China in Warsaw, repeated his government's 'principled position' that Taiwan was the crucial issue that prevented any improvement in the US-PRC relationship. He accused the United States of occupying the island and stated that the Chinese people would 'assuredly liberate Taiwan' and would 'not allow any country to occupy Chinese territory and to interfere in its internal affairs'. However Lei also said, 'We are willing to consider and discuss whatever ideas and suggestions the U.S. Government might put forward' in order to reduce tensions and fundamentally improve relations between China and the United States. 'These talks', he added, might 'either continue to be conducted at the ambassadorial level' or else be conducted 'at a higher level or through other channels acceptable to both sides'.[18]

Despite these overtures, the Warsaw channel had run its course. After American and South Vietnamese troops invaded Cambodia in early May, the Chinese cancelled a meeting for 20 May and the Warsaw talks never resumed.[19] The ambassadorial conversations had, however, served as a useful learning platform for the two antagonists. They provided American diplomats with keener insights into PRC's negotiating style and a greater knowledge of Beijing's positions on various issues. As the American record shows, preparations for the talks were also occasions for 'fresh thinking' about policies toward Beijing. Indeed there is reason to assert that these years left a rich set of policy options that could be drawn upon by future leaders in both China and the United States. Warsaw thus played an important part in mutual reconnaissance, which may have eased the task of subsequent negotiators, and it seems to have laid the foundation for Nixon's China policy.[20]

THE MAKING OF THE HIGH-LEVEL TALKS

After the collapse of the Warsaw channel, Nixon and Kissinger decided to covertly pursue China policy on their own, bypassing the State Department. They used Pakistani president Yahya Khan as a go-between. These early and indirect contacts between the White House and Beijing involved delicate exchanges on setting up an agenda for direct talks between the leaders of the two sides. In these exploratory communications, the Chinese focused on the withdrawal of US forces from Taiwan and the establishment of Sino-American diplomatic relations. The Americans sought a much broader, open-ended agenda that would include discussion of global and regional security issues.[21]

In October, Nixon told *Time* magazine: 'If there is anything I want to do before I die, it is to go to China.'[22] Suddenly his hopes seemed close to being fulfilled. On 8 December the Pakistani ambassador to the US, Agha Hilaly, gave the White House a secret message from Mao and Zhou Enlai: 'Taiwan and the Straits of Taiwan are an inalienable part of China which have now been occupied by foreign troops of [the] United States for the last fifteen years. Negotiations and talks have been going on with no results whatsoever. In order to discuss the subject of vacation of China's territory, called Taiwan, a special envoy from Pres. Nixon will be most welcome in Peking.' Nixon and

Kissinger immediately seized on this opportunity, replying that they would welcome high-level talks in Beijing, but they pressed their demands for a broad agenda. Haggling went on intermittently through the winter via Pakistan and also Romania.[23]

The major public breakthrough came in early April 1971, at an international table-tennis (Ping-Pong) tournament in Japan. Zhou artfully instructed the much better Chinese players to stress 'friendship first, competition second'.[24] With Zhou's evident encouragement, the members of Chinese and American teams met without difficulty in a friendly atmosphere and this was publicized in the world media. To prepare the ground at home for what would be nothing less than a veritable revolution in Sino-American relations, Mao decided to invite the American team to visit China after the tournament had finished.[25] On 7 April Zhou remarked that the visit would offer 'a very good opportunity to open the relations between China and the United States. In our handling of this matter, we must treat it as an important event, and understand that its significance is much larger in politics than in sports.'[26]

The American Ping-Pong team was given a grand public welcome to China and their activities were widely covered by the Chinese media.[27] The highlight of the visit was Zhou receiving the American and Chinese players in the Great Hall of the People on 14 April. Zhou's words would have been inconceivable even a year before: 'Your visit has opened a new chapter in the history of the relationship between Chinese and American peoples.' He predicted that 'this beginning again of our friendship will certainly meet with majority support of our peoples'.[28]

The White House was ecstatic. Kissinger privately credited Ping-Pong diplomacy and Nixon's China policy for creating a surge in 'goodwill' between the two countries. Because Nixon had 'played a hard, purposeful, controlled game' of diplomacy and not been 'too liberal' from the start, he claimed, the Chinese had been encouraged to make such a gesture. The president concurred, recalling that he had refused to recognize Beijing right off the bat because that would have given the game away without Chinese concessions. 'We're just going to take our own damn good time', Nixon said, and be 'quiet and enigmatic' about further moves. Kissinger claimed that it would have been easy to leak details to the public 'and make a big deal about it'. Instead they had accomplished more through secret diplomacy.[29]

Now Beijing moved quickly to make concrete plans for the high-level meetings with Washington that had been discussed for months. On 27 April, Hilaly handed Kissinger a handwritten message from Zhou. After apologizing for taking so long to follow up his message at the end of 1970, he requested 'direct discussions between high-level responsible persons of the two countries'. Zhou reaffirmed Beijing's desire to 'publicly receive an emissary in Beijing', be it Kissinger, Secretary of State William Rogers or 'even the President of the

U.S. himself for direct meeting and discussions', adding that Yahya Khan could arrange the meeting.[30]

Since the United States had been demonized as enemy No. 1 in China for over two decades, Mao and Zhou had to prepare the rank and file politically and psychologically for one of the biggest diplomatic transformations in the history of the PRC. At a meeting of the CCP Central Committee Politburo on 26 May, Zhou therefore carefully argued the case for talks. He contended that the power of the United States had declined in recent years. America's intervention in Vietnam had lost the support of American people, forcing Washington to establish contact with China in order to withdraw its troops completely from Indochina. These developments, Zhou asserted, provided China with 'an opportunity to improve Sino-American relations', which would be 'beneficial to the struggle against imperialist expansion and hegemonism, beneficial to maintaining peace in Asia as well as in the world, and beneficial to maintaining our country's security and pursuing the unification of the motherland in a peaceful way'.[31]

The Politburo meeting reached some measure of consensus, which was then summarized in a 'Politburo Report on the Sino-American Talks' drafted by Zhou. The main points were eight 'basic principles' that became China's new guidelines for relations with the United States. For their upcoming negotiations with America, the Chinese leaders agreed that they would not set preconditions for opening high-level meetings and recognized that they might not achieve all their goals. However, they knew the strategic difficulties Washington faced and saw these as opportunities to extract concessions. The Politburo reasoned that Nixon needed a successful negotiation to support his re-election campaign for November 1972.[32]

Meanwhile in America, the White House pondered the content of the historic message received on 27 April. The immediate issue was who would be sent as Nixon's emissary. Kissinger desperately wanted to go but the president knew that protocol usually demanded that Secretary of State Rogers, as the nation's chief foreign policy official, should meet with Zhou Enlai. Maybe, he told Kissinger, to show their seriousness, they should send Rogers. 'Kissinger rolled his eyes upward,' Nixon recalled in his memoirs. 'I knew that he would have opposed Rogers on personal grounds, but in this case he had good policy reasons. The secretary of state had too high a profile for these first talks' and there was no way a Rogers' visit to China could be kept secret. Kissinger and the president agreed that in some ways Ambassador David K. Bruce 'would be the ideal emissary' but they believed that his role as head of the American delegation negotiating in Paris with North Vietnam had soured him in Beijing's eyes. All the other possible candidates 'were insufficiently familiar with the nuances of Nixon's thinking'. Finally, the president said the words for which Kissinger had been yearning: 'Henry, I think you will have to do it.' Nixon then gave the thankless task of informing Rogers to his Chief of Staff H. R. 'Bob' Haldeman who spoke to Rogers about a week later.[33]

But it still took time to pin down the Chinese. On 10 May Kissinger gave Hilaly a message stating that the president was ready to visit China and that Kissinger would first undertake a 'strictly secret' preliminary visit. The Americans made clear that 'all subjects of mutual interest' should be on the table. It was not until 2 June that they received a reply, written after the crucial Politburo meeting, stating that both Mao and Zhou looked forward to the visits of Kissinger and Nixon and explicitly accepted 'each side would be free to raise the principal issue of concern to it'. Kissinger judged that 'this guaranteed a discussion of global issues that interested us most' including the war in Indochina and the Soviet threat. Moreover, Zhou had framed the Taiwan problem in a manner most susceptible to solution: the withdrawal of American forces. All in all, for Nixon and Kissinger, this seemed a historic moment. Kissinger claimed portentously that it was 'the most important communication that has come to an American President since World War II'. For his part, Nixon got out an unopened bottle of very old Courvoisier brandy and poured out two large snifters. 'Henry', he said solemnly, 'we are drinking a toast not to ourselves personally or to our success, or to our administration's policies which have made this message and made tonight possible. Let us drink to generations to come who may have a better chance to live in peace because of what we have done.'[34]

KISSINGER'S SECRET VISIT TO BEIJING

Since early 1971 Kissinger's staff had been preparing background material for a visit to Beijing.[35] They named the eventual briefing book 'Polo I' after Marco Polo, the fabled Venetian traveller to China in the thirteenth century—capturing the White House's sense of the China opening as an epic voyage of discovery.[36] In Beijing preparations were equally meticulous. The Chinese leadership established a special task force headed by Zhou and Marshal Ye Jianying, a senior Politburo member and vice chairman of the Central Military Commission, to handle all the technical and logistical matters.[37] According to Zhang Ying, a middle-rank official in the Information Department of the Foreign Ministry, extensive surveys on American history, politics, society, and especially US China policy since the founding of the PRC in 1949 were prepared. By June, all the Chinese officials assigned to work with the visiting Americans were moved into the state guesthouse, under strict instructions to keep Kissinger's visit secret even from their families. Zhou discussed almost every talking point with his senior associates and always sent the reports to Mao for his approval.[38]

Kissinger's cover for the visit was a trip to Pakistan, after which he would then secretly fly over the Himalayas. Initially, President Yahya Khan suggested that they tell the press that their American guest had decided to go off hunting for few days. But after Kissinger informed Hilaly that he had never even picked up a gun, let alone hunted, in his life, they decided to say that Kissinger had suffered a stomach ache (so-called 'Delhi belly') that required him to rest and recuperate in private. And so Foreign Minister Sultan Khan escorted a Kissinger's 'double'—the 'chubbiest' Secret Service agent in the American party—to a remote hill station while Kissinger and his staff flew off to China. Ironically, the double developed a real stomach ache, and the Foreign Minister had to scramble to find a doctor who had never seen or heard of Kissinger to treat the agent.[39]

The flight from Islamabad to Beijing took five hours. To smooth the journey Zhou had sent a group of four English-speaking Chinese foreign ministry officials to Pakistan to accompany Kissinger and his team. Despite the gap in protocol rank, Zhou, as China's premier, made a point of calling on Kissinger at the state guesthouse in Beijing, even though the national security adviser (equivalent of that of deputy cabinet secretary) was three levels down in the diplomatic hierarchy. Kissinger remembered this as 'a gesture of considerable courtesy', reflecting the 'extraordinary personal graciousness' that Zhou showed to the Americans throughout the visit, despite two decades of hostility, confrontation, and even war.[40]

During Kissinger's secret visit to Beijing in July 1971 and subsequent Sino-American talks, Zhou served as China's chief negotiator, in accordance with Mao's instructions.[41] Mao formulated China's grand strategy towards the Americans and had the final word on major policy decisions but Zhou was responsible for China's basic negotiation plan and was allowed the initiative for revising it during the talks, as and when necessary.[42]

Among the issues preoccupying the Chinese in July 1971, Zhou identified Taiwan as the top priority. The United States still recognized the Nationalist regime in Taipei as the official government of all of China and the rightful occupant of China's seat on the UN Security Council, whereas the PRC claimed those roles for itself. Knowing that Washington hoped to fudge the issue as part of its rapprochement with Beijing, Zhou wanted a firm commitment from the White House not to pursue a 'two China' policy or to categorize the sovereignty of Taiwan as 'an undetermined question'. Kissinger, by contrast, wanted to focus on Vietnam. He and Nixon believed that China could pressure the North Vietnamese to come to the bargaining table and negotiate an end to the war so the Americans could withdraw 'with our honor and self-respect'. Zhou, however, repeatedly refused to intervene in Hanoi's affairs and urged Kissinger to withdraw completely from Vietnam. That decision, he stressed, would best preserve American honour. Kissinger in turn said that the US would not abandon its South Vietnamese ally and would withdraw only after the North recognized South Vietnamese independence. This manoeuvring for position would continue in subsequent talks.[43]

The main priority in July 1971 was how to word the announcement of Nixon's trip to China. This did not come easily. According to Kissinger's staffer Winston Lord, the Americans wanted to 'make it look essentially that the Chinese wanted President Nixon to come to China. The Chinese essentially wanted to make it look as if Nixon wanted to come to China and that the Chinese were gracious enough to invite him.' Zhou wished it stated that Nixon was coming to China to settle the issue of Taiwan as the precondition for normalizing relations. Kissinger flatly refused, insisting that Nixon would not come as a supplicant and that he would be discussing a broad range of issues, not simply Taiwan or diplomatic normalization. Zhou reluctantly conceded that recognition was not an 'absolute' precondition for a summit, but insisted that the discussions should point in this direction.[44] The Chinese finally presented a draft that Kissinger found acceptable, which stated that, 'knowing of President Nixon's expressed desire to visit the People's Republic of China,' Premier Zhou 'has extended an invitation'. This formulation avoided the issue of who first proposed the summit.[45]

Timing had also been an issue. The Chinese preferred the presidential visit to take place in the summer of 1972, in the hope that Nixon would go first to Moscow. They worried that an American visit to China, coming out of the blue, might provoke the Russians, just three years after the grave border conflicts of 1969. Zhou said defensively that they were 'not afraid of anyone' but were 'not looking for unnecessary trouble'. But in the end he backed down and agreed to a date in the spring of 1972: this fitted the White House scenario of a largely symbolic visit to Beijing that would open the door for a substantive summit in Moscow. 'We're doing the China thing to screw the Russians and help us in Vietnam', Nixon told Kissinger. 'And maybe down the road to have some relations with China.'[46] It was also agreed that the Pakistani channel would now be terminated. Huang Zhen, the Chinese ambassador to France, and Nixon's hand-picked representative, General Vernon Walters, the military attaché at the US embassy in France, would now handle the secret discussions between the two nations.[47]

After his final discussion in Beijing, Kissinger cabled Nixon, describing his seventeen hours of conversations with Zhou as 'the most intense, important, and far reaching of my White House experience'. He also informed Nixon that Zhou had issued an invitation for a formal summit. Nixon responded with congratulations and said, equally grandiloquently, 'if we play the game up to the hilt from now on out, history will regard your effort as the most significant foreign policy achievement of this century'. He added, apparently without intended humour: 'When you return I intend to give you a day off in compensation for your superb service to the nation.'[48]

Kissinger's Second Visit

After Kissinger's secret visit, both governments prepared their people for the new policy. On 13 July Nixon spoke to the nation on television explaining that, in order to 'build a lasting peace in the world', he had sent his national security adviser to Beijing. He then read the agreed text of the summit invitation and said that he accepted it 'with pleasure', adding that the meeting was intended 'to seek the normalization of relations' between the two countries. He promised that this new policy would 'not be at the expense of our old friends'; nor, he said, was it 'directed at any other nation'—a disingenuous reference to the Soviet Union. 'We seek friendly relations with all nations. Any nation,' he continued, 'can be our friend without being any other nation's enemy.' He closed by saying that 'all nations' would benefit from Sino-US rapprochement.[49]

What became known as the 'Nixon shock' stunned America's Asian and European allies, who had been given as little as half an hour's notice of the announcement. While a minority of Americans complained, especially conservative Republicans, most of the country praised Nixon's initiative and looked forward to an improvement in Sino-US relations. Then, on 2 August, Rogers issued a carefully worded statement announcing that the United States would support the seating of the PRC in the United Nations General Assembly in the autumn but opposed 'any action to expel' Taiwan 'or otherwise deprive it of representation' at the UN. Knowing that both the PRC and Taiwan opposed the phrase 'two-Chinas', Rogers deliberately left it out of his statement. The US ambassador to the UN, George H.W. Bush, had canvassed members of the UN and concluded that Taiwan would be expelled at the next session—an outcome that America had sought to block for years. The administration therefore decided to make the best of the situation by using the 'dual representation' formula as a fig leaf to permit the PRC's inclusion while continuing to oppose Taiwan's expulsion. Again, although some conservative Republicans were upset, most Americans supported Rogers's plan.[50]

An unexpected political crisis in the CCP leadership in September 1971 made Kissinger's second visit, scheduled for October, easier to sell to Republican hardliners. Lin Biao, Mao's anointed successor, who had been known as Mao's 'closest comrade-in-arms' and 'best and most loyal student', allegedly opposed the opening to Washington and was plotting a coup to assassinate the Great Leader. On 13 September Lin, together with his wife, son, and a handful of supporters died in a mysterious plane crash in the Mongolian People's Republic.[51] The 'Lin Biao Incident' not only enhanced Zhou's political position but also damaged the myth of Mao's 'eternal correctness'. In order to cover up the domestic political crisis and reassert his declining authority Mao now sought a major foreign policy success.[52] Accordingly, Beijing notified Nixon through the Huang-Walters channel in Paris that the Lin Biao Incident would not change its preparations for Nixon's visit.

Kissinger's second visit to Beijing (codenamed 'Polo II') was intended to prepare the ground exhaustively for Nixon's summit. China, Kissinger warned Zhou Enlai, 'despite its long experience in handling outsiders, has never undergone anything like the phenomenon of a visit by an American President'. This would include Secret Service agents responsible for Nixon's safety, an entourage of administration staffers, reporters from print and broadcast media, and the like that would encompass 'several battalions'.[53] The main issue was the communiqué that would be issued after the summit which, like most such documents was not spontaneous but carefully scripted beforehand. Nixon had endorsed a draft by Kissinger that, in the latter's words, 'followed conventional style, highlighting fuzzy areas of agreement and obscuring differences with platitudinous generalizations', so that it 'implied more common ground than actually existed'. But when Kissinger handed this draft to Zhou on 22 October, the Chinese premier did not respond right away.[54] He took the draft to Mao, who was in high ideological mood, telling the premier, 'I have said many times that all under the Heaven is great chaos, so it is desirable to let each side speak out for itself.' If the American side wanted to talk about 'peace, security, and no pursuit of hegemony,' the chairman continued, the Chinese side should emphasize 'revolution, the liberation of the oppressed peoples and nations in the world, and no rights for big powers to bully and humiliate small countries'.[55] Zhou carefully explained to Mao that the Nixon administration faced a dilemma: as Kissinger had noted, the US could not withdraw from Taiwan before it had left Vietnam, nor would it end the war without preserving its honour.[56] But he responded to the Americans with a much more assertive document on 24 October, setting out very bluntly China's position on key issues leaving blank pages for America's counterblasts.

At first, Kissinger was surprised to receive China's response to his draft communiqué in this format. But after reading the document, full of what he called 'empty cannons', Kissinger began to see that 'the very novelty of the [Chinese] approach might resolve our perplexities'. He considered that 'the unorthodox format appeared to solve both sides' problem. Each could reaffirm its fundamental convictions, which would reassure domestic audiences and uneasy allies.'[57] Over the next twenty-four hours he and his staff toned down the most provocative parts of the Chinese text and developed some common points of agreement, seeking what Kissinger called 'a tone of firmness without belligerence'. Taiwan, as usual, proved particularly difficult. Zhou was especially sensitive to the possibility of Japanese expansion to Taiwan after eventual US withdrawal and kept trying to elicit an American commitment to prevent this from happening. Side-stepping all this, Kissinger came up with the following formula on Taiwan: 'The United States acknowledges that all Chinese on either side of the Taiwan Straits maintain that there is but one China. The United States Government does not challenge that position.' Reflecting on this later, Kissinger said that 'I do not think that anything I did or said impressed Chou [sic] as this ambiguous formula with which both sides were able to live for nearly a decade.'[58]

Meanwhile the United Nations was dealing with the Taiwan question. George Bush had introduced the Dual Representation Resolution in the UN General Assembly on 22 September.[59] During Kissinger's visit Zhou adroitly reminded him that Britain had decided in effect to abandon Taiwan— upgrading Sino-British relations to the ambassadorial level, recognizing Taiwan as simply 'a province of China', and indicating that it thus would vote for the resolution proposed by Albania to expel Taiwan from the UN. Kissinger left for home just as the UN voted by a seventy-six to thirty-five, with seventeen abstentions, for the Albanian resolution. None of the NATO allies voted with the United States.[60] And so America's dual representation formula failed, Taiwan was expelled from the UN, and in its place the PRC assumed China's seat in both the General Assembly and the Security Council.

Throughout the fall of 1971 Nixon kept talking about the significance of Sino-American rapprochement and his forthcoming summit in Beijing. A Nixon Tape of 10 November shows that he was almost obsessed about making his mark in history. From a public relations standpoint, he knew that the pictures of his meeting with Mao in Beijing would make the visit 'historic'. He predicted that the summit could affect not only 'the next generation' but 'the next century'. Nixon contended that 'no one sitting in this office' should miss such a chance to prevent a future confrontation with the PRC. For Nixon the summit was no electioneering gimmick but the culmination of a long-term geopolitical goal, which he had set out in his 1967 *Foreign Affairs* article about the future of Asia.[61]

THE SUMMIT

In the run-up to the summit, the Chinese government was very concerned to treat Nixon's party in a fashion that befitted China's sense of its place in the world. In Zhou's words, 'We are a sovereign nation. Nothing should be allowed to impinge upon our sovereignty.' He ordered that Nixon's reception 'must reflect the principles, styles, and strict disciplines of the proletarian class'.[62] During a meeting on 8 February 1972 attended by senior officials from Beijing, Shanghai, and Zhejiang, the cities and province which Nixon would visit, Zhou issued further guidelines: 'Neither cold nor warm; neither humble nor haughty; receiving him with politeness; and not imposing our opinions on him.'[63]

Nixon and Kissinger prepared for the summit by inviting the French author and politician André Malraux, a long-time acquaintance of Mao and Zhou, to the White House. Malraux dismissed China's involvement in Vietnam as an 'imposture' and said that Mao only cared about China and its survival. Nixon, he advised, should view Mao as a man who was nearing death and 'acting out the last act of his lifetime'. Kissinger also had words of advice for Nixon. He warned that 'when Zhou attacks, one has to be firm in substance but conciliatory in form. Because they never – They will always have superb manners.' Moreover, Kissinger explained, 'they don't expect us to agree with them. It's important, however, that we show we understand their point of view, not that we share it.' Lastly, he underlined the Chinese desire for concrete improvements in relations: 'cooperation in the abstract is of no interest to them. Peace in the abstract is of no interest to them'.[64]

Nixon's plane touched down in Beijing at 11.30 on the morning of 21 February 1972. Nixon and Haldeman had decided that no aides (especially Kissinger but also Secretary of State Rogers) should be seen by the television cameras. And so Nixon and his wife, Patricia, walked down the steps of the presidential plane alone. When he reached the bottom step, he made a point of extending his hand as he walked toward Zhou in order to correct the slight that Dulles had supposedly inflicted on him in 1954. Zhou, equally conscious of the importance of the handshake, stood there smiling, while trying not to seem too eager. 'When our hands met, one era ended and another began,' Nixon recorded in his memoirs. On their way to the state guesthouse, Zhou told Nixon, 'Your handshake came over the vastest ocean in the world – twenty-five years of no communication.'[65]

The Americans considered the welcoming ceremony formal and correct, but chilly.[66] There were about one hundred Chinese officials and social celebrities at the airport to meet the Americans. Two flags, one Chinese and one American, flew over the reception area, and the band played both national anthems. Nixon inspected a military honour guard, with contingents from each of the three People's Liberation Armies, but there were no other spectators or crowds, mainly since the two countries had not had formal diplomatic relations for so many years.[67]

Shortly after Nixon arrived at the state guesthouse, Zhou Enlai informed him that Mao was ready for a meeting.[68] The Chinese leader had been suffering from heart problems and a lung infection, which he had obstinately refused to let his doctors treat. Yet Mao, for whom Nixon's visit would confirm China's 'equal' position in the world of nations, eagerly wanted to meet the American president. On 1 February he therefore agreed to undergo physical therapy in order to walk and be in a condition to receive visitors.[69] For the meeting Mao put on a new suit and a new pair of shoes. His hair was freshly cut and his face cleanly shaved. He kept asking his aides for details of the exact arrival time and subsequent schedule. Awaiting the arrival of his guest, he was gripped by even greater nerves.[70]

When the American party departed for China from Andrews Air Force Base, they did not have an agreed time for the Nixon-Mao meeting. By not confirming the schedule for the president, Nixon aides believed, the Chinese wanted to keep the Americans off balance.[71] This was a typical practice of the Chinese emperor, indicating that the emperor (Mao) was the head of the Central Kingdom and that the Americans were coming to pay 'tribute'. The sense of status was equally evident when Nixon and Kissinger arrived at Mao's residence (Rogers had been deliberately excluded). According to Kissinger, 'Mao just stood there, surrounded by books, tall and powerfully built for a Chinese. He fixed the visitor with a smile both penetrating and slightly mocking, warning by his bearing that there was no point in seeking to deceive the specialist in the foibles and duplicity of man. I have met no one, with the possible exception of Charles de Gaulle, who so distilled raw, concentrated willpower.' This was even more impressive, Kissinger wrote, 'because it was so incongruous in relation to his physical condition'. For his part Nixon recalled that as soon as he entered Mao's book-lined study, his worries and anxieties vanished. '[W]hen he reached out his hand, and I reached out mine, and he held it for about one minute', hostilities between China and the United States that had begun more than twenty-five years earlier had symbolically dissolved.[72]

The meeting was more symbolism than substance, but behind the photographs and the banter Mao had a more serious purpose. After a few jokes about Kissinger's penchant for secret diplomacy, he told Nixon that he had voted for him in 1968. Nixon responded that Mao had 'voted for the lesser of two evils'. The Chinese leader objected: 'I like rightists... I am comparatively happy when these people on the right come into power.' Nixon responded that 'those on the right can do what those on the left talk about'. Mao agreed, noting that he had been opposed by 'a reactionary group' who failed and 'got on an airplane and fled abroad'. Nixon then asked if they could now address substantive issues. Mao refused to get into specifics, declaring that he would only 'discuss philosophical questions'.[73] But despite his continued banter he sent out some clear signals about policy.

Mao blamed his delays in responding to US easing of trade restrictions on his 'bureaucratic' insistence that the solution of major issues should precede the resolution of smaller issues like trade and reciprocal visits of private individuals. 'Later on', he conceded, 'I saw you were right, and we played table tennis.' He went on to label Taiwan a relatively minor internal Chinese dispute. Alluding to national security concerns, Mao made his point by omission: the likelihood of American or Chinese aggressive expansion, he opined, was 'relatively small... You want to withdraw some of your troops back on your soil; ours do not go abroad.' Obliquely, Mao was indicating that China feared the Soviet Union more than the United States. At the same time, in those few words ('ours do not go abroad'), he touched on key American preoccupations—the danger of Chinese intervention in the Vietnam War and possible challenges to vital US interests in Japan and South Korea. But what about the ideological struggle? With equal facility Mao now disposed of the ringing anti-American slogans that had been the hallmark of all his years in power. Laughing uproariously, he dismissed them as just the sound of 'a lot of empty cannons'. In only sixty-five minutes, Mao thus provided a set of signposts for both his American guests and also the Chinese bureaucracy.

Nixon allowed Mao to do much of the talking, but he nevertheless got his own points across. 'What brings us together', he reminded Mao, 'is a recognition of a new situation in the world and a recognition on our part that what is important is not a nation's internal political philosophy. What is important is its policy toward the rest of the world and toward us.'[74] With lines such as these Nixon and Kissinger conveyed what they wanted from the meeting, namely to leave China's 'fanatic' yet pragmatic leaders with an impression of American 'seriousness and reliability'. Nixon, perhaps taking Kissinger's advice, made statements that he hoped would encourage Mao and Zhou to view him as reliable, even though they had no reason to trust him: 'You will find I never say something I cannot do. And I will always do more than I can say.'[75]

Despite the restraint of the initial reception, the fact that Mao met Nixon within the first couple of hours of his arrival was truly significant. The following day, *Renmin Ribao* carried a photograph of Chairman Mao's meeting with President Nixon. This sent a clear signal to the world and to the Chinese people that Mao both personally approved of and recognized the historic importance of the event. 'It is all right to talk well', Mao told Nixon at the close of the meeting, 'and also all right if there are no agreements'.[76] For Nixon, the hour or so with Mao instantly put the whole China trip on a higher plane. It was, in fact, the highlight of his week.

Zhou, however, was Nixon's primary interlocutor during the Beijing summit. Throughout their closed door negotiations, he stuck to China's established principles, arguing on the basis of reason.[77] In this vein, Zhou once again refused to interfere in North Vietnamese affairs and Nixon finally realized that he would get no help from Beijing if he wanted to end the war. Nixon recalled, 'Zhou was tough and tenacious, but was flexible in working out our differences.'[78] The American president, meanwhile, endorsed Beijing's long-held contention that 'there is one China, and Taiwan is a part of China', promising that the United States would no longer issue statements about Taiwan's 'undetermined' status. He also said they would neither support Taiwanese independence nor back any Taiwanese attempt to take back Mainland China. Still, he reminded Zhou that the conservatives in the United States would not countenance an American troop withdrawal from Taiwan without guarantees from Beijing about not attempting a takeover of the island. He also repeated Kissinger's contention that a continued US military presence in East Asia would best prevent a revival of Japanese militarism.[79]

Kissinger and Vice Foreign Minister Qiao Guanhua, meanwhile, negotiated the final wording of the 'Shanghai Communiqué' issued at the end of the summit.[80] The Communiqué reiterated China's support for wars of national liberation and social revolution, while the United States affirmed its commitment to peace. Both conveyed their opposition to Soviet influence in Asia and the Pacific—euphemistically referred to as 'hegemony'. Not only did this confirm rhetorically the anti-Soviet underpinnings of the Beijing-Washington rapprochement but it also represented a rebuff to Moscow's earlier proposals for a Soviet-American partnership in the event that Beijing turned hostile to them both.[81] Although the Shanghai Communiqué did not mention the terms under which full normalization of diplomatic relations would take place, it became the basic instrument upon which an entirely new relationship was built. It embodied a *modus vivendi* for Chinese-American relations that fell short of full normalization but recognized that the two countries had common interests and that they needed to communicate as well as to work on gradually overcoming the remaining difficulties. The document served as the basic charter of the Sino-American relationship until the two countries finally normalized relations in 1979.

CONCLUSION

Nixon's China trip did accomplish its strategic and political goals. Through the vivid drama of summitry Nixon broke a twenty-two-year taboo in dealing with communist China. He and Mao engaged in a discussion that ended the isolation of the PRC from the West and America's isolation from China. Nixon had confided in Zhou that, when he was serving in the Eisenhower administration, his views had been no different from those of John Foster Dulles. 'But the world had changed since then', he said, 'and the relationship between the People's Republic and the United States must change too.'[82]

The Beijing summit made triangular diplomacy a reality and tipped the balance of power within it to the benefit of the United States. In the words of historian Jussi Hanhimäki, triangularity 'opened seemingly endless opportunities for achieving other goals, most specifically an end to the Vietnam War and an advantageous set of agreements with the Soviet Union'.[83] As Nixon hoped, his trip helped ensure future friction between the United States and the People's Republic would be decided at the negotiating table not on the battlefield.[84] Nixon and Kissinger also made particular efforts to build cordial personal relations with Mao and Zhou. Beforehand both men immersed themselves in Chinese culture and history, down to learning passages from Mao's poems and trying to eat with chopsticks. Bearing in mind the story of Dulles' historic snub, both showed obvious willingness to shake Zhou's hand. Aiming to dispel years of slights, hostility, and confrontation, they believed that personal amity and cultural symbolism were immensely important for America's sudden and dramatic rapprochement with China.

The historic Nixon-Mao handshake also stood as a great diplomatic victory for Beijing. A CCP Central Committee document hailed the summit for its success in utilizing the 'contradictions' of others (meaning the USSR), 'dividing up enemies, and enhancing ourselves,' and credited this success to Mao's 'brilliant decision' to invite the US president.[85] The Chinese leadership could now focus on the Soviet threat and avoid the possibility of fighting a two-front war. Furthermore, China gained US and world recognition of its legitimacy, of the validity of its national interests, and of its status as a major regional power with a rightful role in shaping international policies.

In sum, with these recalibrations in the diplomatic strategy of Beijing and Washington, the bipolar system of the early Cold War began to move into a new tripolar configuration. In the 1950s, China and the Soviet Union had formed an alliance and China was at the anti-US forefront in Asia. When the Sino-Soviet split took place in the 1960s, the Sino-Soviet alliance broke up. The direct outcome of this split was the division of the international communist movement and the weakening of the socialist bloc. Meanwhile, the Sino-Soviet antagonism and the new alignment between Beijing and Washington compelled Moscow to strengthen its armed forces along the Sino-Soviet border. Not only was this a heavy burden on Soviet national power, but it also threatened to divert the Kremlin from its struggle to confront the United States and control Eastern Europe. From now Beijing would adjust its foreign policy in an attempt to join forces with the United States to counter the Soviet Union. And Nixon's successors would operate in a new arena of triangularity that shifted the dynamics of international diplomacy. As will be discussed in chapter 7, this played an important part in the drama of 1989.

NOTES

1. Nixon, Toast at banquet in the Great Hall of the People, Beijing, 21 February 1972, The American Presidency Project (henceforth APP) website, http://www.presidency.ucsb.edu/ws/index.php?pid=3748&st=&st1=.
2. Henry Kissinger, *White House Years* (London, 1979), 1070.
3. Richard Nixon, Toast at banquet in the Shanghai Exhibition Hall, 27 February 1972, APP website, http://www.presidency.ucsb.edu/ws/index.php?pid=3755&st=&st1=; Kissinger, *White House Years*, 1096.
4. For details, see Yafeng Xia, *Negotiating with the Enemy: U.S.-China Talks during the Cold War, 1949–1972* (Bloomington, IN, 2006), 12–42.
5. See William Stueck, *The Korean War: An International History* (Princeton, NJ, 1997). For the Chinese perspective on the Korean War, see Zhihua Shen, *Mao, Stalin and the Korean War: Trilateral Communist Relations in the 1950s*, trans. Neil Silver (London, 2012).

6. For details, see Xia, *Negotiating with the Enemy,* chapters 3 and 4.

7. Ambassador Wang Bingnan claimed in his memoirs that the handshaking incident never happened. See Wang Bingnan, *Zhongmei Huitan Jiunian Huigu* (*Nine Years of Sino-American Talks in Retrospect*) (Beijing, 1985), 21–2. Xu Jingli, then Deputy Director of the Chinese Foreign Ministry Archives, claims that he has checked all the newly declassified Chinese diplomatic files, and concludes that this is a purely fabricated story. Xu Jingli, *Jiemi Zhongguo Waijiao Dangan* (*Declassifying Chinese Diplomatic Files*) (Beijing, 2005), 276–9. In his memoirs, Ji Chaozhu also recalled that the Geneva delegation heard that Dulles had instructed his entire entourage to avoid shaking hands with 'any of us "goddamned Chinese reds"'. Ji Chaozhu, *The Man on Mao's Right: From Harvard Yard to Tiananmen Square: My Life Inside China's Foreign Ministry* (New York, 2008), 126–7.

8. Memorandum for the Record, 15 September 1964, in *Foreign Relations of the United States, 1964–1968, vol. xxx, China* (henceforth *FRUS 1964–1968, vol. xxx*), https://history.state.gov/historicaldocuments/frus1964-68v30, docs 49 and 50.

9. James G. Hershberg and Chen Jian, 'Informing the Enemy: Sino-American "Signaling" and the Vietnam War, 1965', in Priscilla Roberts, ed., *Behind the Bamboo Curtain: China, Vietnam, and the World Beyond Asia* (Washington DC, 2006), 194–5.

10. Chi-Kwan Mark, 'Hostage Diplomacy: Britain, China, and the Politics of Negotiation, 1967–1969', *Diplomacy & Statecraft* 20, no. 3 (2009), 473–93; Paper Prepared by Alfred Jenkins, 9 October 1968, *FRUS 1964–1968, vol. xxx*, doc. 328.

11. For a discussion of the war scare in Beijing in 1969, see Yang Kuisong, 'The Sino-Soviet Border Clash of 1969: From Zhenbao Island to Sino-American Rapprochement', *Cold War History* 1, no. 1 (August 2000), 35–7; Xia, *Negotiating with the Enemy*, 138–9.

12. Richard M. Nixon, 'Asia after Vietnam', reprinted in *FRUS, vol. I, Foundations of Foreign Policy, 1969–1972,* https://history.state.gov/historicaldocuments/frus1969-76v01, doc. 3.

13. Chris Tudda, *A Cold War Turning Point: Nixon and Mao, 1969–1972* (Baton Rouge, 2012), 17.

14. See Steven Phillips, 'Nixon's China Initiative, 1969–1972', in International Conference of Editors of Diplomatic Documents, ed., *Documenting Diplomacy in the 21st Century* (Washington, DC, 2001), 135.

15. Xue Mouhong, ed., *Dangdai Zhongguo waijiao* (*Contemporary Chinese Diplomacy*) (Beijing, 1988), 219; Kissinger, *White House Years*, 188. See also US National Archives and Records Administration, College Park, Maryland (henceforth NARA), RG 59, Subject-Numeric files, 1967–1969, POL-US, Memorandum from Stoessel to Rogers, 3 December 1969.

16. See Jin Chongji et al., eds, *Zhou Enlai zhuan, 1949–1976* (*A Biography of Zhou Enlai, 1949–1976*) (Beijing, 1998) (henceforth *ZEZ*), vol. 2, 1087.

17. Li Ping et al., eds, *Zhou Enlai nianpu, 1949–1976* (*Chronology of Zhou Enlai, 1949–1976*) (Beijing, 1997) (henceforth *ZEN*), vol. 3, 336; *ZEZ*, vol. 2, 1088. See also Kissinger, *White House Years*, 188.

18. NARA, RG 59, Subject-Numeric files, POL CHICOM–US, Box 2187, Telegram 143 from the Embassy in Warsaw to the Department of State, 20 January 1970.

19. Kissinger, *White House Years*, 692.
20. Xia, *Negotiating with the Enemy,* 105, 133–4.
21. Xia, *Negotiating with the Enemy,* 146–52.
22. 'I Did Not Want the Hot Words of TV', *Time*, 5 October 1970.
23. Letter from Yahya Khan to Hilaly, 23 November 1970, in Fakir S. Aijazuddin, *From a Head, Through a Head, to a Head: The Secret Channel Between the US and China through Pakistan* (Oxford, 2000), 42–5; cf. Memorandum, Kissinger to Nixon, undated, in *FRUS 1969–1976, vol. xvii, China, 1969–1972,* (henceforth FRUS 1969–1976, *vol. xvii*), https://history.state.gov/historicaldocuments/frus1969-76v17, doc. 99. Kissinger, *White House Years*, 700–2.
24. Qian Jiang, *Xiaoqiu zhuandong daqiu: Pingpang waijiao muhou* (*Little Ball Moves Big Ball: Behind Ping-Pong Diplomacy*) (Beijing, 1997), 267–8.
25. For details, see Zhonggong zhongyang wenxian yanjiushi (CCP Central Committee Party Literature Research Office), ed., *Mao Zedong nianpu, 1949–1976* (*Chronology of Mao Zedong, 1949–1976*) (Beijing, 2013), vol. 6, 377; also Yafeng Xia, 'China's Elite Politics and Sino-American Rapprochement, January 1969—February 1972', *Journal of Cold War Studies* 8, no. 4 (Fall 2006), 13–17.
26. Qian, *Xiaoqiu zhuandong daqiu*, 236; Xu Dashen, ed., *Zhonghua renmin gongheguo shilu* (*A Factual Record of the People's Republic of China*) (Changchun, 1994), vol. 3, 698–9.
27. See Qian Jiang, *Pingpang waijiao shimo* (*Ping-Pong Diplomacy: The Beginning and the End*) (Beijing. 1987), 268–71.
28. Minutes, Zhou Enlai, Conversations with the American Table Tennis Delegation, 14 April 1971, in Zhonghua renmin gongheguo waijiaobu and zhonggongzhongyang wenxian yanjiushi (PRC's Ministry of Foreign Affairs and CCP Central Committee Party Literature Research Office), eds, *Zhou Enlai waijiao wenxuan* (*Selected Diplomatic Papers of Zhou Enlai*) (Beijing, 1990), 469–75; Kissinger, *White House Years,* 710.
29. Richard Nixon Presidential Library and Museum, Yorba Linda, California (henceforth RNPL), Conversation between Nixon and Kissinger, 14 April 1971, White House Tapes, Executive Office Building Conversation 28–16; and Diary Entry 17 April 1971, in *Haldeman Diaries CD Version* (New York, 1994), https://www.nixonlibrary.gov/virtuallibrary/documents/haldeman-diaries/haldeman-diaries.php.
30. Message from Zhou Enlai to President Nixon, 21 April 1971, *FRUS 1969–1976, vol. xvii*, https://history.state.gov/historicaldocuments/frus1969-76v17, doc. 118.
31. Yang Mingwei and Chen Yangyong, *Zhou Enlai waijiao fengyun* (*Diplomatic Winds and Clouds of Zhou Enlai*) (Beijing, 1995), 247–8.
32. See *ZEZ*, vol. 2, 1096; *ZEN*, vol. 3, 458–9. Mao approved Zhou's report on 29 May 1971. See Pang Xianzhi and Jin Chongji, eds, *Mao Zedong zhuan, 1949–1976* (*A Biography of Mao Zedong, 1949–1976*, hereafter *MZZ*) (Beijing, 2003), vol. 2, 1633.
33. Richard Nixon, *RN: The Memoirs of Richard Nixon* (New York, 1978), 549–50; Kissinger, *White House Years*, 716–18. RNPL, White House Tapes, Oval Office Conversation 518–13, Conversation between Nixon and Kissinger, 10.32am–11.11am, 12 June 1971.
34. Kissinger, *White House Years*, 727; Nixon, *RN*, 552.

35. John Holdridge, *Crossing the Divide: An Insider's Account of the Normalization of U.S.–China Relations* (Lanham, MD, 1997), 45.
36. Kissinger, *White House Years*, 734.
37. Gong Li, *Kuayue honggou: 1969–1979 nian ZhongMei guanxi de yanbian* (*Across the Chasm: The Evolution of China–U.S. Relations, 1969–1979*) (Zhengzhou, 1992), 108.
38. Zhang Ying, *Sui Zhang Wenjin chushi Meiguo: Dashi furen jishi* (*Serving in the United States with Zhang Wenjin: Account of an Ambassador's Wife*) (Beijing, 1996), 33–4; Zhang Ying, 'Random Recollection of Premier Zhou's Later Years', in Tian Zengpei and Wang Taiping, eds, *Lao waijiaoguan huiyi Zhou Enlai* (*Senior Diplomats' Remembrance of Zhou Enlai*) (Beijing, 1998), 375–6.
39. Sultan M. Khan, *Memories and Reflections of a Pakistani Diplomat* (London, 1997), 261–5.
40. Henry Kissinger, *On China* (New York, 2011), 238–9.
41. Li Danhui, 'Zhou Enlai in the Sino-American Rapprochement', *Lengzhan guojishi yanjiu (Cold War International History Studies)*, no. 6 (Summer 2008), 143.
42. Wei Shiyan, 'Inside Stories of Kissinger's Secret Visit to China', in Pei Jianzhang, chief ed., *Xin Zhongguo waijiao fengyun* (*Winds and Clouds in New China's Diplomacy*) (Beijing, 1991), vol. 2, 39–45; *ZEN*, vol. 3, 458–9, 467–8, 489, 491, 512.
43. RNPL, NSC Files, Files for the President, China Materials, Box 1032, POLO I Record, Memorandum of Conversation between Kissinger and Zhou Enlai, 9 July 1971.
44. 'Oral Interview with Winston Lord', *Frontline Diplomacy*, Library of Congress, and Memorandum of Conversation between Kissinger and Zhou Enlai, 9 July 1971, *FRUS 1969–1976, vol. xvii*, doc. 139.
45. Memorandum of Conversation between Kissinger and Chinese officials, 11 July 1971, *FRUS 1969–1976, vol. xvii*, doc. 142. See also Wei, 'Inside Stories of Kissinger's Secret Visit to China', 44–5; Kissinger, *White House Years*, 752–3.
46. White House Tape, 22 July 1971, *FRUS 1969–1976, vol. xvii*, doc. 142, note 2.
47. Gao Wenqian, *Wannian Zhou Enlai* (*Zhou Enlai's Later Years*) (Hong Kong, 2003), 439.
48. RNPL, NSC Files, Files for the President, China Materials, Box 1032, POLO I Record, Backchannel Message TOSIT 26 from Kissinger to General Haig, 11 July 1971, and Backchannel Message SITTO 88 from Haig to Kissinger, 11 July 1971; David Reynolds, *Summits: Six Meetings that Shaped the Twentieth Century* (London, 2007), 223.
49. 'Remarks to the Nation Announcing Acceptance of an Invitation To Visit the People's Republic of China', 15 July 1971, APP website, http://www.presidency. ucsb.edu/ws/index.php?pid=3079&st=&st1=.
50. 'Secretary Rogers Announces U.S. Policy on Chinese Representation in the U.N.', 2 August 1971, in Department of State, *Bulletin Vol. LXV, No. 1678*, 193–4. On the decision to omit 'two Chinas', as well as the administration's decision to 'oppose' rather than ignore an expulsion vote, see RNPL, Henry A. Kissinger Telephone Conversation Transcripts (Telcons), Chronological File, Box 10, Telephone Conversations between Kissinger and Rogers, 30 July 1971 and 2 August 1971.

51. Wang Nianyi, *Da dongluan de niandai (In the Years of Great Upheaval)* (Zhengzhou, 1988), 415–33. For an English narrative of the crisis, see Xia, 'China's Elite Politics and Sino-American Rapprochement', 3–28.

52. Gao, *Wannian Zhou Enlai*, 427–8, and Chen Jian, *Mao's China and The Cold War* (Chapel Hill, NC, 2001), 270.

53. RNPL, NSC Files, Box 1034, Files for the President, China Materials, Polo II, HAK China Trip, Transcripts of Meetings, Memorandum of Conversation between Kissinger and Zhou Enlai, 20 October 1971.

54. RNPL, NSC Files, Box 1034, Files for the President, China Materials, Polo II, HAK China Trip, Memorandum of Conversation between Kissinger and Chou En-lai, 4.15–8.28pm, 21 October 1971.

55. Wei Shiyan, 'Kissinger's Second Visit to China', in Pei Jianzhang, chief ed., *Xin Zhongguo waijiao fengyun (Winds and Clouds in New China's Diplomacy)* (Beijing, 1994), vol. 3, 67.

56. Gao, *Wannian Zhou Enlai*, 443. RNPL, NSC Files, Box 1034, Files for the President, China Materials, Polo II, HAK China Trip, Transcripts of Meetings, Memorandum of Conversation between Kissinger and Zhou Enlai, 9.50pm–11.40pm, 25 October 1971.

57. Kissinger, *White House Years*, 782, and Kissinger, *On China*, 269.

58. Kissinger, *White House Years,* 783; Memorandum of Conversation, 21 October 1971, 10:30am–1:45pm, *FRUS 1969–1976, vol. xvii*, doc. 162.

59. Gao, *Wannian Zhou Enlai*, 442, 441.

60. Kissinger, *White House Years,* 784.

61. RNPL, White House Tapes, Oval Office Conversation 616-10, Conversation between Nixon, Carl Curtis, and Clark MacGregor, 10 November 1971.

62. *ZEN*, vol. 3, 498.

63. *ZEN*, vol. 3, 511–12.

64. RNPL, White House Tapes, Oval Office Conversation 672-2, Conversation between Nixon and Kissinger, 15 February 1972.

65. Gao, *Wannian Zhou Enlai*, 396–7; Nixon, *RN*, 559–60; Wei, 'President Nixon's Trip to China', 85; Kissinger, *White House Years*, 1054–5.

66. Kissinger, *White House Years*, 1054; Holdridge, *Crossing the Divide*, 82.

67. Wei, 'President Nixon's Trip to China', 83–5.

68. Zhang Yufeng, 'A meeting with Nixon during Mao's illness', in Guo Simin and Tian Yu, eds, *Wo yanzhong de Mao Zedong (As I Saw Mao Zedong)* (Shijiazhuang, 1990), 267–9; Zhonghua remin gongheguo wajiaobu waijiaoshi bianjishi (Diplomatic History Research Office, PRC's Ministry of Foreign Affairs), 'This historical opening of Sino-American relations', *Dangde wenxian (Literature on the party)*, no. 3 (1991), 82.

69. For Mao's health during this period and its implications for the Nixon visit, see Li Zhisui, *The Private Life of Chairman Mao* (New York, 1994), 553–65. Kissinger mistakenly believed that Mao had suffered a series of strokes before the meetings. See Kissinger, *White House Years*, 1061.

70. He Di, 'The Most Respected Enemy: Mao Zedong's Perception of the United States', *China Quarterly* 137 (March 1994), 143.

71. 'Interview with Winston Lord on Nixon's Trip to China' cited in Nancy Tucker, ed., *China Confidential: American Diplomats and Sino-American Relations, 1945–1996* (New York, 2001), 270.

72. Kissinger, *White House Years*, 1057–9; Nixon, *RN*, 560.

73. *MZZ*, vol. 2, 1635–6; Wei, 'President Nixon's Trip to China', 86.

74. Transcript of Mao Zedong's Conversation with Nixon, 21 February 1972, cited in *MZZ*, vol. 2, 1638. For the American version, see Memorandum of Conversation between Nixon, Kissinger, Mao and Zhou, 21 February 1972, 2:50–3:55pm, *FRUS 1969–1976, vol. xvii*, doc. 194.

75. Nixon, *RN*, 563.

76. Memorandum of Conversation between Nixon, Kissinger, Mao, and Zhou, 21 February 1972, 2.50–3.55pm, *FRUS 1969–1976, vol. xvii*, doc. 194.

77. Gao, *Wannian Zhou Enlai*, 448.

78. Richard Nixon, *Leaders* (New York, 1982), 235.

79. Memorandum of Conversation between President Nixon and Zhou Enlai, 22 February 1972, 2.10–6.00pm, *FRUS 1969–1976, vol. xvii*, doc. 196.

80. For a detailed analysis of these arduous negotiations, see Tudda, *A Cold War Turning Point*, 192–7.

81. Raymond L. Garthoff, *Détente and Confrontation: American-Soviet Relations from Nixon to Reagan* (Washington, DC, rev. edn, 1994), 272.

82. Nixon, *RN*, 565.

83. Jussi M. Hanhimäki, *The Flawed Architect: Henry Kissinger and American Foreign Policy* (New York, 2004), 200.

84. RNPL, President's Handwriting Series, box 16, President's Office Files, White House Special File, Introductory Remarks (Re China), 17 February 1972.

85. CCP Central Committee, 'Notice on the Joint Sino-American Communiqué', 7 March 1972, cited in Gong, *Kuayue honggou*, 182.

3

Moscow, 1972

James Cameron

26 May 1972. In the vast expanse of St Vladimir Hall in the Kremlin Palace two men, flanked by diplomats and aides, bent over a huge table. Richard Nixon, the president of the United States, and Leonid Brezhnev, general secretary of the Communist Party of the Soviet Union, were signing agreements to limit the growth of the vast nuclear arsenal that each was aiming at the other, poised on hair-trigger alert (see Figure 3.1).

Their work completed, they stood up and exchanged the heavy leather-bound folders. Smiling with forced intimacy, the two leaders then sipped celebratory glasses of champagne. This ceremony, replete with symbolism, has been imitated on other occasions since 1972, from Jimmy Carter and Leonid Brezhnev's

Fig. 3.1. Nixon and Brezhnev signing the SALT I agreement in St Vladimir's Hall, Kremlin, 26 May 1972 (AP)

signature of the follow-on Strategic Arms Limitation Treaty (SALT II) in 1979, through to Barack Obama and Dmitry Medvedev's meeting in Prague to sign the New Strategic Arms Reduction Treaty (New START) in April 2010.

The list of accords signed in 1972 in Moscow was long. Over the course of one week of summit talks, ten were concluded, ranging from the sea to outer space. The capstone of the summit was the interim SALT agreement, limiting the number of strategic missile launchers, and the Anti-Ballistic Missile (ABM) Treaty, restricting each side's strategic defences. The two leaders also signed the Basic Principles of Relations, which set out a general framework under which their two governments pledged to deal with each other on the basis of 'peaceful coexistence', 'restraint', 'equality', and 'the renunciation of the use or threat of force'.[1]

These were momentous agreements, unprecedented in the previous history of the Cold War. To reach them Nixon and Brezhnev not only had to overcome their past hawkish instincts, but also a myriad of conflicting national interests that by the 1970s spanned the entire globe. The path to the summit was therefore long and tortuous, taking up almost all Nixon's first term as president. And only weeks before the Moscow meeting was supposed to take place, it was almost called off. Compared with what the summiteers hoped for, one would also have to say that the results of Moscow were modest. Nevertheless, the agreements signed in the Kremlin proved a significant benchmark for superpower relations over the subsequent two decades.

UNDERLYING MOTIVATIONS

Neither Nixon nor Brezhnev was a natural dove. In fact, Nixon had made his political name as an anti-communist crusader, rising to prominence in Congress on the back of his campaign to prove that Alger Hiss, a State Department official under suspicion of spying for the Soviet Union, had lied about his activities. Dwight D. Eisenhower selected Nixon as his running mate in the 1952 presidential election in order to reassure Republican conservatives. Nixon's 1959 trip to the Soviet Union as vice president had been contentious yet politically profitable after he got into an animated 'kitchen debate' with Nikita Khrushchev over the relative merits of American and Soviet consumerism.[2] In short, Nixon was a figure whose political trajectory had been fuelled by confrontation, not détente.

Time had not entirely mellowed Nixon's fundamental suspicion of communists in general and Russian communists in particular. Leaving most of the briefing papers for Moscow unmarked during his summit preparation, the president instead scribbled on the works of leading anti-communist intellectuals. Perusing Robert Conquest's congressional testimony on the nature and dynamics of the Soviet leadership, Nixon underlined the historian's assertion that the men in the Kremlin were 'morally and intellectually crippled' by Stalinism, due to the 'ruthless' way in which they had betrayed their fellow communists in the 1930s in order to secure 'their own promotion and survival'.[3] As for Daniel Bell's claim that the upheavals of Hungary and Poland in 1956 showed that even communists were capable of 'simple decency', Nixon considered this assertion really 'naïve—as far as Russia is concerned'.[4] The president's opinion of the Soviet general secretary as an individual was low: he dismissed the idea that he had 'great respect for Mr. Brezhnev' as 'bullshit'.[5]

Nor could anyone accuse Brezhnev of being a dyed-in-the-wool liberal. True to Conquest's analysis, he was a product of the Stalinist purges of the 1930s and the hugely destructive war fought by the Soviet Union against Nazi Germany between 1941 and 1945. Absent those factors, it is unlikely that Brezhnev—or indeed many of his colleagues—would have risen so far in the Soviet hierarchy. Part of the conservative cabal that had replaced the hard-charging Nikita Khrushchev, Brezhnev enjoyed significant support from military industry on which he lavished resources throughout his period in power. If Brezhnev was a believer in accommodation with the United States, he also held that such a settlement could only be achieved on the basis of Soviet military strength, equal in its fundamentals to that of its great rival.[6]

Nixon's broad understanding of Brezhnev's background appears to have been fairly accurate. Likewise, the Russians had a clear idea of the man with whom they were dealing in Washington. Anatoly Dobrynin, Soviet ambassador to the United States, warned his masters that Nixon's transition from anti-communist stalwart to champion of accommodation was more apparent than real. In his view, Nixon was 'petty and distrustful with a huge ego'. Moreover, Nixon continued to be motivated by his 'long-standing anti-communist ideology' and retained what Dobrynin called a 'heightened suspiciousness...regarding the Soviet Union's motives'.[7]

Neither side believed for a moment that the other might suddenly concede fundamental interests, thereby ending their competition. Instead, each inched towards pragmatic accommodation, animated by a distinctive vision that was born of domestic and international considerations. They saw a summit meeting as an opportunity to conserve the current balance of power in a way that would serve their broader foreign-policy aims.

On his side, Nixon envisaged summitry with Brezhnev as a way to arrest trends that had corroded the very basis of American post-war world leadership and consequently its strategy of globalized containment of the Soviet Union. Since the mid-1960s, the 'foundations' of containment had come under increasing pressure, as Moscow challenged Washington's nuclear superiority by engaging in a huge build-up of its intercontinental strategic striking power. At the same time, the Vietnam War accelerated the predictable deterioration of US economic hegemony as Western Europe recovered from World War Two, and America's NATO allies, notably West Germany, became increasingly assertive in their attempts to pursue foreign policies independent of the United States. America's entanglement in Southeast Asia also stirred up new opposition to containment at home, which manifested itself in mass youth protests against the country's involvement in the Vietnam War and a new congressional activism in foreign affairs that tried to limit Washington's foreign commitments and the preponderance of defence spending in the federal budget.[8]

Nixon's fundamental aim during his first term was to staunch this haemorrhage of power away from the United States. He sought to end the Vietnam War—or at least American involvement in it—in order to halt the broader domestic rebellion against containment. He also harboured ambitions to open relations with the People's Republic of China (PRC), thus facilitating American withdrawal from Southeast Asia and providing a counterweight to Soviet globalism. The idea of a summit with the Soviets fitted into this broader scheme. Through SALT he hoped to cap the Soviet offensive build-up; in return the United States would forgo its superiority in defensive systems. Through these new accords Nixon also aspired to grab the mantle of peace from his domestic critics, demonstrating how the United States could maintain global leadership while at the same time reducing some of its costs in blood and treasure that the American public was increasingly unwilling to bear. Through this complex of diplomatic initiatives, which would at once shore up the American position in the Cold War while limiting the possibilities for further growth in Soviet influence, Nixon hoped to continue the containment of Soviet expansion, but now through negotiation not confrontation.[9]

Brezhnev shared Nixon's desire to move to a period of negotiation, but for somewhat different reasons. His experience of Stalinism and the Great Patriotic War had made him staunchly conservative domestically but he also believed that war should be avoided at all costs. Brezhnev rejected the adventurism of his predecessor, Nikita Khrushchev, who, he thought, had brought the world to the brink of nuclear war with his reckless actions during the Cuban Missile Crisis in 1962. Instead of using nuclear weapons as a means to secure a dramatic realignment in global politics through audacious gambits, he 'wanted', according to historian Vladislav Zubok, 'to convert the growing power of the Soviet Union into the coin of international diplomacy and prestige'.[10] Brezhnev appears to have shared Nixon's overall sense that the 'correlation of forces' was shifting in favour of the Soviet Union. In fact, he sought to capitalize on this trend and gain something that had eluded both Stalin and Khrushchev—namely recognition by the United States of the Soviet Union's position as an equal superpower.

Such recognition was sought in two concrete forms, which together could provide the basis for a more ambitious long-term vision for the future of US-Soviet relations. The first was the acceptance of Soviet parity in intercontinental nuclear delivery vehicles. Throughout the strategic arms limitation negotiations, which ran from November 1969 right up to the summit, the Soviets stuck doggedly to this principle. They pushed consistently for a strong agreement on anti-ballistic missiles (ABMs), an area of Soviet weakness. At the same time, they constantly deflected American attempts to stop their build-up of offensive intercontinental ballistic missiles (ICBMs) until they felt they had a sufficient quantitative lead over the United States in the number of offensive missile launchers to compensate for their technological inferiority and for the positioning of American bomber aircraft in allied countries around the periphery of the Soviet Union. At the heart of this was the Soviet insistence that it be treated as a full peer of the United States. As Brezhnev's foreign-policy assistant, Andrei Aleksandrov-Agentov, argued, American 'acceptance of equality' between the two superpowers was 'the basis' of the Soviet under-standing of SALT's significance.[11]

The second element of equality would be acceptance by the United States of the inviolability of the post-World War Two borders in Central and Eastern Europe. Essential preconditions for this were recognition of Germany's eastern border, formalized in the Moscow Treaty of 1970, and the Four-Power agree-ment on rights and movement in Berlin (1971). Resolution of these issues, in which both America and Russia had a direct interest, opened the way for the Kremlin to ease tensions with the United States.[12] Brezhnev wanted to use the Moscow summit as a springboard for a pan-European security conference, which would apply the principle of the inviolability of borders and non-interference in internal affairs across the entire continent. In contrast with the Americans, who were primarily interested in SALT, for the Kremlin 'European security' held a 'special significance'.[13]

Taken together, Brezhnev hoped, SALT and European security could form the basis for a broader recognition by the United States of the Soviet Union's global role. While there were limited prospects for solving Third World conflicts in the near future—especially those between Israel and the Arabs, and India against Pakistan—Brezhnev wanted to ensure that the United States would now understand that it could no longer intervene in these regions unilaterally. Only consultation with the Soviet Union could prevent a clash between the two superpowers in such areas, and Brezhnev hoped that the USSR could use its new role as an indispensable mediator to shift the correlation of forces further in the Kremlin's favour.[14] Whereas Nixon hoped to continue containment by other means, Brezhnev's understanding of equality thus meant breaking out of the American straightjacket that the Soviet leadership felt had been imposed upon it since the end of the World War Two.[15]

Yet, like Nixon, Brezhnev also felt impelled towards accommodation because of what he saw as less favourable trends. The most important of these was the increasingly acrimonious split in the global communist movement between the Soviet Union and China. The Politburo was worried about a possible Sino-American rapprochement as early as December 1966, fearing encirclement on the basis of common 'anti-Soviet' disposition of the two states.[16] In 1969, Soviet and Chinese troops clashed over the disputed Zhenbao Island on the Ussuri river, in so-called 'skirmishes' that, as fellow analysts told then-CIA officer Robert Gates, left Chinese territory 'so pockmarked by Soviet artillery that it looked like a "moonscape".[17] Nixon, for his part, wished to use Soviet fears of an alliance between America and China to pressurize the USSR into concessions on a variety of issues, from arms control to Vietnam.

'What is détente?' Brezhnev asked in a 1977 speech—at a time when the much-derided process was already unravelling. 'Détente above all means overcoming the "Cold War" and transition to normal, equal relations among states'.[18] In these words lay the fundamental divergence between Soviet and American outlooks on the entire process of détente. Rather than seeing the diminished position of the United States in the late 1960s as 'normal', Nixon perceived it as an unnatural state of affairs with which he had to grapple in order to save the fundamentals of American influence in the world. He did so in the hope—which looked extremely optimistic in the late 1960s—that the United States would be able to, if not quite achieve 'eventual victory in the Cold War', then at least regain some of the vigour with which it had prosecuted the competition with the Soviet Union over the preceding twenty years.[19] For Brezhnev, the recent diminution of American power and the rise of the Soviet Union was exactly what he wished to preserve and extend through his negotiations with the United States. Given this fundamental disjuncture in aims, the demise of détente was woven into its very fabric.[20]

To be sure, the Moscow summit may not have happened at all if both sides had stuck to rigid understandings of their long-term goals. However, one party was under considerably more time pressure to compromise than the other. Nixon's desire to minimize the deleterious impact of the 1960s on the United States' international position was gradually superseded by baser political motives as the clock ticked down to the November 1972 presidential election. The Soviets, though keen to limit their enormous military budget and anxious about the growing challenge from China, were not constrained by any sort of electoral calendar. So the Politburo could sit doggedly on a position for months without any apparent political cost. During 1971 and 1972, we shall see that Nixon's need to satisfy the growing domestic demands for amelioration of the Cold War eroded Washington's hardline position to the extent that a summit became possible.

INITIAL APPROACHES

American domestic political pressures were especially evident in the summit's origins. Nixon had tried as early as June 1970 to get a quick SALT agreement that he could use, as he told Kissinger, to 'help our boys' in the congressional elections of that year.[21] After mediocre results in the November 1970 mid-terms, Nixon became increasingly set on a summit that he could present to the American public as a tangible result from the 'era of negotiation' that he had promised in 1968.[22] The blunt fact was that Nixon's and Kissinger's diplomatic strategy was not bearing fruit. Intensified bombing of North Vietnam and entreaties to the Soviets had failed to extract concessions at the Paris peace talks that could ease America's exit from Southeast Asia. Similarly, attempts to exploit the Sino-Soviet split by initiating dialogue with the PRC in a new policy of triangularity had not so far been successful.

According to Ambassador Dobrynin: 'On the eve of the New Year of 1971, there was growing irritation and impatience with Nixon in Moscow' and considerable scepticism that the president would make any significant concessions in order to move relations forward. With the Politburo constrained by its consensus style of decision-making, there was little chance of Moscow making the first move.[23]

This mutual wariness began to lift in early January 1971, when Kissinger came to Washington straight from a conference at Nixon's Western White House in San Clemente, California, to tell the Soviet ambassador that the Americans wanted to expedite negotiations on SALT, Berlin, and the Middle East.[24] SALT, the only one of these issues over which the Americans had full control, without need for negotiation with regional clients, became the natural focus for backchannel negotiations between Kissinger and Dobrynin as they sought to make progress. On 20 May 1971, the White House and the Kremlin announced a framework agreement for the conclusion of strategic arms talks. Conceding the primacy of the Kremlin's main objective, the limitation of defensive anti-ballistic missile systems, while pledging only to accept a less binding accord on capping the Soviet offensive build-up, the framework agreement really amounted to American movement towards the Soviet position. Moreover, it provided the essential foundation for a summit meeting that would be substantive for the United States. Nixon and Kissinger now began pushing for a firm Soviet commitment to hold a summit in late 1971.

For the Soviets, however, European security was as important as arms control. They refrained from inviting the Americans to Moscow until the Quadripartite Agreement on Berlin had been settled. Frustrated by Soviet procrastination, Kissinger made an overture to the People's Republic, travelling there in July 1971 to arrange a presidential visit to Beijing. The Soviets had clearly blundered by holding off on a summit and allowing the Chinese to get ahead of them. As Dobrynin later conceded in his memoirs, 'in [his] heart of hearts' he 'could only agree' with Kissinger's assertion that the PRC had stolen a march on the USSR by committing to a meeting first.[25]

However, Moscow recovered well from this initial upset, refusing to give way on substantive issues in return for a summit. This may have in part been

due to Brezhnev's limited room for manoeuvre within the collective leadership. However, Dobrynin also supported a policy of inertia for tactical reasons,
arguing that although Kissinger's journey to China was 'unquestionably of
major international significance', the Politburo should not panic. 'No less
ballyhoo preceded Kennedy's meeting with Khrushchev', Dobrynin noted
archly, 'and we all know how that turned out'. There continued to be 'profound objective differences' between the United States and the PRC that would
limit the extent of any rapprochement. For Nixon, Dobrynin estimated,
US-Soviet relations remained of 'paramount importance'. He advised that
the Kremlin should sit tight and wait for further American moves.[26]

This policy paid off: the Americans began to intensify their efforts to
'prove', in Dobrynin's phrase, that Soviet-American relations would not suffer
as a result of Kissinger's visit to Beijing.[27] On 5 August, on Foreign Minister
Andrei Gromyko's suggestion, Nixon for the first time sent a letter directly to
Brezhnev, rather than Alexei Kosygin who as head of the Soviet government
was the figure technically in charge of state-to-state (as opposed to party-to-
party) relations. Although the letter did not mention the possibility of a
summit, Kissinger told Dobrynin that the president hoped he would 'still
receive a response in this connection'.[28]

On 10 August, in answer to Kissinger's entreaties, the Kremlin issued a
formal invitation to Nixon, which the president accepted a week later. The
rapidity of the American response is surprising at first glance, because it
neutralized a potential card in Nixon and Kissinger's game of triangular
diplomacy with the USSR and China. The Beijing meeting being in hand,
the US could have extracted concessions from the Soviets on SALT in
exchange for a Moscow summit and the restoration of diplomatic parity
between the communist world's two most important rivals. With the Soviets
pocketing the American acceptance, however, the US was back to business as
usual at SALT, bargaining over the number of ABM sites each side should be
allowed, with little progress on offensive limitations. It is therefore hard to
agree with Kissinger's contention that news of the Beijing summit gained
the United States immediate traction on major issues with the Soviet Union.[29]
As Dobrynin rightly surmised, for Nixon the attraction of having two major
meetings in the capitals of the United States' erstwhile enemies in an election
year overrode any nickel and dime haggling over the details of SALT.

TO THE SUMMIT

Befitting the domestic political importance of the summit, the American side
planned for Moscow to be a multimedia extravaganza. Without any precedent
for a presidential visit to the Soviet Union, Nixon's staff raided the itineraries

and communiqués of other Western leaders for ideas, including West Germany's Willy Brandt, Harold Wilson of Great Britain, Charles de Gaulle of France, and Pierre Trudeau of Canada. They also looked at Dwight D. Eisenhower's aborted 1960 summit and even Nixon's vice-presidential kitchen debate visit in 1959.[30] In the end Washington agreed on a nine-day visit, with regional stops in Leningrad and Kiev. The public symbolism of each moment was choreographed to the last detail, in some cases almost absurdly. Nixon's PR team decided that David Eisenhower, the late president's grandson and Nixon's son-in-law, should say goodbye to the president at Andrews Air Force Base in order to underline the fact that Nixon was 'doing something that [President] Eisenhower was unable to do'—a point that was likely lost on most members of the American public.[31]

The White House's obsession with the media caused problems in the Kremlin. With less than two months to go, the American television networks complained that Moscow was being even more obstructive than the Chinese had been.[32] Desiring the widest possible coverage of the summit, the Americans presented the Soviets with an accreditation list of 250 journalists. The Soviets claimed that it would be extremely difficult to issue so many visas on time.[33] However, it is more likely that they were worried that, with time to kill in Moscow, journalists might peek behind the façade that was hastily being thrown up and see the realities of Soviet life. The Kremlin wanted to put on the best possible face and undertook extensive urban renovations in preparation for the summit. The US ambassador, Jacob Beam, reported on the work undertaken in Leningrad. Nevsky Prospekt, the city's central street, 'was completely repaved', he noted. 'The road from the city to the airport was widened by one lane', with workers drafted in to tend the flora and fauna that the president would pass in his motorcade. The Kirov ballet company was told to keep its most accomplished dancers on standby, just in case the president decided he would like to see a performance.[34] All this reflected a deep insecurity about the media scrutiny to which the Soviet Union would be subjected during Nixon's nine-day visit. The public works involved were enormous. One only has to imagine the possibility of Nixon ordering the resurfacing of Times Square and the widening of Grand Central Parkway to speed Brezhnev's progress from Kennedy Airport into midtown-Manhattan. In the end, compromises were reached on media issues. The Soviets eventually let in 111 correspondents, plus 71 broadcast support staff.[35]

On the American side there was anxiety of a different sort, but it also touched on Soviet pride. Some within the White House were worried about the physical safety of the president when flying in the Soviet aircraft that the Kremlin offered to ferry Nixon around the USSR. Brent Scowcroft, then on the staff of the National Security Council (NSC), presented a list of 'hair-raising' incidents, including Soviet pilots using road maps to navigate over the United States.[36] Nixon was unconcerned. 'I don't really give a damn,' he told

Kissinger, 'I've ridden in their planes many times before'.[37] His staff relented. Nixon did travel around the USSR in Soviet planes—though not without the odd mishap, to acute Soviet embarrassment. According to Dobrynin, at one point Soviet Premier Alexei Kosgyin was reduced to 'swearing at' a hapless Soviet pilot after one of the summit planes suffered a technical malfunction.[38]

VIETNAM INTERVENES

Just as the issues appeared to be lining up for the final approach to the summit, Vietnam almost destroyed everything. On 30 March the North Vietnamese army launched a huge offensive across the De-Militarized Zone (DMZ). The 'Easter Offensive', as it became known, crushed South Vietnamese forces. Only a few days after the initial assault, the American embassy in Saigon estimated that the South's military position was 'on the verge of collapse'.[39]

Both superpowers immediately realized the danger that the North Vietnamese attack posed to the summit and tried to reduce its impact. On the American side, Nixon was initially intent on doing everything possible to smash the offensive, regardless of the chance that Moscow would cancel the summit. Kissinger sought to limit the fallout in his meeting with Dobrynin on 3 April, relaying Nixon's 'hope that the military response he is forced to undertake... will not negatively impact Soviet-US relations in other fields,' and that the initial attacks would be limited in deference to Soviet sensitivities.[40]

In Moscow, similarly, the Ministry of Foreign Affairs had no desire to see the summit fall through. As the bombing escalated, Dobrynin proposed to the Kremlin that the Soviets could broker talks between the United States and the Democratic Republic of Vietnam (DRV) during Nixon's trip to Moscow. The White House, however, revived an earlier Soviet proposal that Kissinger travel to Moscow to talk through the outstanding problems with the Soviet leadership.[41] Dobrynin held out little hope that these discussions would lead to substantive progress on Vietnam. Instead, he advised the Kremlin leadership to conduct themselves with Kissinger on the basis that Nixon was still willing to come to Moscow, concentrating on areas of potential progress— presumably in order to keep the summit on track.[42]

That is not how Nixon saw the situation, however. When Kissinger flew to Moscow, accompanied by Dobrynin, he had explicit instructions from the president to make Soviet pressure on the DRV the prerequisite for substantive negotiations about the summit.[43] Kissinger made token demands along these lines but in ways that showed his desire not to jeopardize the summit. At his first meeting with Brezhnev, for instance, Kissinger outlined the American position very directly: the Americans simply wanted to effect 'an honourable withdrawal' of the last US troops and would then allow what he called 'the political process' to take its course. If this were not clear enough, Kissinger underlined that the United States was 'prepared to let the real balance of forces in Vietnam determine the future of Vietnam'.[44] He did, however, threaten American reprisals that could endanger the summit if the North Vietnamese did not desist from their offensive. Brezhnev, for his part, passed on a proposal from Hanoi for talks, blaming the offensive on a Chinese attempt to derail the summit, whereupon Kissinger responded that he would demand the withdrawal of DRV units to the north of the DMZ. With this shadow boxing out of the way—and despite Nixon's repeated orders to get back to Vietnam—Kissinger and the Soviets turned to matters that could be directly solved at the summit.[45]

For the Soviets, the most pressing issue was securing Kissinger's agreement on their draft of the 'Basic Principles of Relations'. The Soviets had asked about the possibility of a statement of principles in January and the Americans had responded with a draft in mid-March. But the paper Brezhnev handed Kissinger at the conclusion of their first meeting was heavily revised. In particular, the Soviets had elevated the vague American pledge that countries in the world could 'co-exist peacefully' into a statement affirming 'peaceful coexist-ence' as the central guiding principle of US-Soviet relations.[46] As every Soviet-ologist knew, this formulation signified the continuation of class struggle by the Soviet Union without the threat of annihilation in a superpower war. Kissinger, however, was not worried about the Soviet revisions. Without checking with Washington, he concurred with the Basic Principles agreement 'in principle and basic outline', delegating his Soviet affairs assistant, Helmut Sonnenfeldt to hammer out the details with Georgii Kornienko, head of the US department at the Soviet Ministry of Foreign Affairs. According to Kornienko, even Sonnenfeldt was not that interested in the details, hurrying to redraft the agreement so that he could leave and find out what Kissinger was telling Gromyko on the Middle East. The Soviet document was accepted with minor changes.[47]

The State Department was not told of the Basic Principles of Relations, which was probably just as well. A few weeks later, Foggy Bottom told the NSC explicitly that at the summit the United States 'should avoid ... any reference to "peaceful coexistence"'.[48] How significant the American concession of peaceful coexistence proved to be is hard to say. The short answer is that, while it mattered little diplomatically in 1972, and certainly helped Brezhnev make the case domestically for the summit, the Basic Principles became one of the sticks that later American opponents of détente would use to beat the Nixon and Ford administrations for their 'appeasement' of the Kremlin.

Kissinger's trip to Moscow kept the summit on the road. But despite progress on a number of other issues, Vietnam remained intractable. After a 'brutal' meeting in Paris between Kissinger and the DRV negotiator Le Duc Tho, and with the military situation in the South becoming more parlous by the day, Nixon temporized over his next move. His central anxieties were twofold. First, how to respond militarily to the near-collapse of the South Vietnamese in the face of Hanoi's onslaught. Second, assuming the Soviets would retaliate in some way to American action and recalling Khrushchev's cancellation of Eisenhower's 1960 trip to Moscow, whether to pre-empt such a 'humiliating' move by taking the initiative himself to call off his summit with Brezhnev.[49]

Both Kissinger and Nixon were in favour of American air strikes. If Nixon went 'to Moscow without having done anything', Kissinger advised on 3 May, the president would lose 'all credibility', not only in Vietnam, but in the Middle East and South Asia. 'Henry, that argument has sold me a thousand per cent,' Nixon responded. However, unlike Kissinger, who by early May favoured cancelling the summit in order to punish the Russians for not restraining their client, Nixon began to demur on whether it was wise to call off the meeting.[50] It appears to have been the White House chief of staff, H.R. 'Bob' Haldeman, who suggested that Washington should 'go ahead and bomb and see what happens'.[51] The idea stuck. Nixon delivered an address on 8 May announcing the mining of North Vietnamese ports and the interdiction of ships heading towards the DRV, emphasizing that these measures were 'not directed against any other nation'.[52] Kissinger passed a copy of the president's speech to Dobrynin, together with a letter to Brezhnev explaining American motivations and urging that the two sides must 'not slide back toward the dark shadows of a previous age'. The White House was calling the Kremlin's bluff. Now all it could do was wait.[53]

Those in Moscow who identified themselves as sponsors of détente were, on balance, in favour of going ahead. This camp included Brezhnev, Gromyko, and the Ministry of Foreign Affairs. Despite his personal experience of American bombing on a visit to Hanoi in February 1965 and earlier scepticism, Prime Minister Alexei Kosygin also concluded that the summit should be held. However, the détente group was counter-balanced by a strong coterie of opponents of a summit, including Minister of Defence Marshal Andrei Grechko, President Nikolai Podgorny, and Ukrainian First Secretary Petro Shelest.[54]

Although the content of the Politburo debate is still secret, the manner in which it was presented to the wider Communist Party gives some idea of the way in which the Soviet leadership justified its decision to go ahead with the summit. In order to garner the widest possible support, the Politburo convened a plenum of the Central Committee for 19 May. In a speech that must have lasted well over two hours, Brezhnev piled on example after example to show the advantages the USSR had obtained from détente. The most significant issue on which the Soviet Union had made progress, he argued, was European security. With the ratification of the Moscow Treaty by the West German Bundestag, Brezhnev emphasized, the Soviet Union had secured 'the gains of the Second World War' for which the USSR 'had struggled' for more than twenty-five years. 'The core of the whole agreement,' Brezhnev noted, was 'the inviolability of borders'.[55]

Turning to the subject of the summit, Brezhnev outlined the Politburo's achievements in negotiations with the United States. An agreement to ban nationwide ABM systems, Brezhnev argued, would prevent the United States from building protection of its homeland that could embolden American foreign policy in the direction of greater 'aggression and adventurism'. The agreement on offensive weapons would leave the Soviets ahead in inter-continental ballistic missiles and submarine-launched ballistic missiles (SLBMs) and free to pursue qualitative improvements. These two agreements, along with others, such as those on technical cooperation and health, meant that the accords to be signed in Moscow would be far more significant than those reached during Nixon's visit to Beijing. At the same time, the United States had pressured West Germany to ratify the Moscow Treaty. These successes, Brezhnev asserted, had come from the fact that 'the correlation of forces between us and the U.S... is more favourable to us than at any time in the past'.[56] Now was the time, the Soviet leader implied, to lock in these gains by getting Nixon to sign on the dotted line at the summit.

Turning finally to Vietnam, Brezhnev heaped scorn on the American bombing campaign. Having done so, however, he went on to criticize the North Vietnamese for overemphasizing the 'military means of struggle' and not paying enough attention to the 'political means'. Mirroring American arguments, Brezhnev implied that the DRV was acting against its own self-interest, slowing down the withdrawal of American troops by launching the offensive. Using information the Soviets had picked up on Nixon's meetings in Beijing, Brezhnev claimed that the US strikes could have been encouraged by the Chinese, in whose interest it was to derail improvements in the Soviet Union's relations with both capitalist and communist countries.[57]

The question Brezhnev posed implicitly, therefore, was simple: was the Soviet Union willing to throw all of these gains away, and forgo the chances of yet more, for the sake of the narrow self-interest of one member of the socialist camp, who was probably acting as an unwitting instrument of the Chinese? Withdrawing Nixon's invitation would only serve the PRC's interests, leading, as Brezhnev prognosticated, to 'an American-Chinese rapprochement on an explicitly anti-Soviet basis'. Brezhnev answered his own question: 'By deciding to hold the meeting, we proceeded firstly in the interests of the Soviet people [and] the Soviet state.'[58] With the full support of the Central Committee, bolstered by Marshal Grechko's endorsement of the merits of SALT, the summit was on.[59]

THE SUMMIT

On 22 May, after a stopover in Austria, Nixon landed at Vnukovo Airport outside Moscow. Podgorny and Kosygin were there to meet him. Full honours for a visiting dignitary were observed and the route to the Kremlin was bedecked with American and Soviet flags. The main streets, however, were eerily quiet: the crowds that usually lined the pavements had been pulled by the Soviets as a form of symbolic punishment for the continuing American action in Indochina.[60]

After Nixon's arrival at the Kremlin, Andrei Alexandrov-Agentov, Brezhnev's assistant, invited the president for an unscheduled 'eye-to-eye' meeting with the general secretary in his office, a ten-minute walk away. After an initial pro forma chiding on Vietnam, Brezhnev did his best to reach out to Nixon. According to the general secretary's interpreter, Viktor Sukhodrev, who was the only other person present apart from the leaders, the two men attempted to bond over jokes at the expense of bureaucrats on both sides—words which, he noted dryly, 'in one way or another most leaders like to utter'. The meeting overran and the two leaders' advisers were kept waiting—again an occurrence that would become something of a tradition for American and Soviet leaders.[61]

Despite the image of relaxed bonhomie that he tried to project at their first meeting, Brezhnev was nervous. Later in the visit, he turned to Sukhodrev. 'Vitia, you have participated in these kinds of meetings many times. How do you think my first talk with Nixon went? How do you think he took my revelation [*otkrovenie*]?' The bilingual Sukhodrev, struggling not to burst out laughing at the general secretary's poor Russian, reassured his boss that Nixon had been favourably impressed by Brezhnev's frankness [*otkrovennost'*]. The meeting, he declared, had been a 'worthy beginning to the American president's visit to our country'.[62]

This initial moment of personal rapport was atypical of a summit that mainly comprised formal sit-downs between Soviet and American principals and failed either to establish a personal connection between the protagonists or to resolve any substantive disagreements in areas beyond those already marked up for resolution at the summit. There were many reasons for this stilted formalism. Kissinger ascribes much of the difficulty in engaging the Kremlin leadership on concrete matters to the Soviets' intense nerves and their idiosyncratic negotiating style. None of the troika—Brezhnev, Kosygin, and Podgorny—could commit to anything that had not been agreed beforehand with the others, meaning that their room for manoeuvre during the summit meetings was generally very limited. The visitors also quickly discovered, as Kissinger later put it acidly, that the advance agenda was 'largely theoretical', with the Americans occasionally 'kept waiting for hours while the Soviet leaders caucused, attended Politburo sessions, or simply disappeared'. The Soviets unilaterally changed the topics of meetings at the last minute, leaving Nixon and his entourage with barely enough time to assemble the appropriate specialists, let alone come up with anything to say beyond their standard talking points.[63]

Yet such explanations for the lack of fluidity during the summit place more blame than is justified on Soviet habits. Nixon was hardly the easiest person to get on with at the best of times and his ponderous style was very different to Brezhnev's. Nixon set his preferred tone at the first plenary, delivering lengthy statements on the status of US-Soviet relations, and noting that the two sides were 'meeting here not because of sentiment, but because [the principals were] pragmatic men'. Brezhnev, by contrast, made far shorter contributions that were lighter on substance and interspersed with a few jokes in an attempt to break the ice.[64] Progress towards better personal understanding was not forthcoming over the next few days. At their concluding one-on-one, the general secretary's opening gambit was to tell Nixon a Russian 'anecdote about the sex life of older men'. The prudish Nixon responded by noting how much he appreciated getting to know the general secretary but then immediately switched topics to the final communiqué.[65]

Relations between the sides—both leaders and staff—remained distinctly transactional, therefore, with prearranged accords signed and difficult geopolitical questions left mostly on the sidelines. The two superpowers inked deals establishing joint committees to coordinate cooperation in a range of areas, including science and technology, health, and the environment.[66] They announced a space agreement that included a joint Apollo-Soyuz mission in 1975, during which the two craft would dock in orbit.[67] And, closer to earth, there was an accord on incidents at sea that aimed to prevent a clash between the US and Soviet navies through the observation of a set of rules when operating in close proximity; it even included a prohibition on certain types of simulated attacks that one could launch against the other.[68] Civilian traffic between the superpowers was made considerably easier through a maritime agreement, which guaranteed access for non-military ships to more than forty ports in each country.[69]

Preoccupied with security issues, Nixon paid little attention to these agreements on what he considered minor questions. But they did help to flesh out a programme that was otherwise dominated by the nuclear arms accords, thereby giving greater credence to the idea that the Moscow summit represented the beginning of a new era across the full range of US-Soviet relations. The Soviets, by contrast, placed real emphasis on the establishment of a joint American-Soviet economic commission that could open the way to lucrative technology transfer deals in areas such as American natural gas extraction equipment.[70] In a meeting with Nixon on 25 May, Kosygin pressed for a commitment to prioritize the granting of Most Favoured Nation (MFN) trade status to the Soviet Union. Perhaps wishing to retain some leverage to ensure future Soviet good behaviour, Nixon promised expeditious action on Export-Import Bank credits, but underlined that the power to grant MFN rested with Congress.[71] Ultimately, Nixon's emphasis was proved correct. Although an MFN agreement was signed in October 1972, the 1974 Jackson-Vanik Amendment dashed Soviet hopes by prohibiting MFN status for any country that did not allow free emigration.

Totally intractable geopolitical issues were dealt with in a variety of ways depending on the sensitivity of the question. On the evening of 24 May, for instance, Nixon, Kissinger, and a few aides were suddenly whisked off to a dacha outside Moscow to endure a three-hour diatribe from Brezhnev, Podgorny, and Kosygin on Vietnam. Brezhnev now declared that the American desire for a summit, whilst 'continuing the cruel conflict in Vietnam... [was] quite incompatible', while Kosygin condemned Nixon for behaving 'even more cruelly... than Johnson'.[72] After the meeting was over, it was back to jokey bonhomie lubricated with large amounts of cognac. Such a display, Kissinger surmised, was designed to provide a transcript that the Soviets could then present to their North Vietnamese allies to reassure them that the Kremlin had used the summit as an opportunity to press Hanoi's interests.[73] The Politburo may also have seen the incident as a useful tool in selling détente to the Party leadership. At a subsequent Central Committee meeting, Gromyko certainly made great play of how 'burned' Nixon had felt as a result of the meeting, and implied, tendentiously, that the pain thereby inflicted had speeded up conclusion of the Paris Peace Accords.[74]

Other areas of recurring superpower confrontation were given perfunctory discussion, probably so that both sides could tell their regional allies that they had gone over the issues while reassuring them that no deals had been concluded above their heads. For instance, Nixon and Brezhnev did not touch on the Middle East until the afternoon of 26 May, and then only lightly, because neither side wanted to derail the most important process now in train: the final concluding moves of the eighteen-month SALT negotiations.[75]

Addressing the nuclear arms race—a defining element of the superpower Cold War rivalry—SALT was the main event of the summit. With this in mind, Nixon and Kissinger wanted to conclude the accords in Moscow and to do so alone, without the perennially abused American SALT delegation, marooned in Helsinki where the detailed arms control talks had been held. This led to a situation that could be broadly characterized as organized chaos. The final negotiating sessions on SALT were conducted, as Kissinger admitted, 'sporadically between [the] president's meetings with [the] Soviet leadership'.[76] This was particularly galling for Gerard Smith, leader of the American SALT delegation, given that he could quite easily have hopped on a plane to help nail down the final details. In his memoirs Kissinger claims that the idea of moving Smith to Moscow was simply never discussed.[77] In fact, Kissinger told Smith explicitly to 'stay in place' until the agreement had been 'wrapped up'.[78] Even if Smith had been present, this would not have solved all the problems, however, because Kissinger also had to run each position by a sceptical secretary of defense, Melvin Laird, as well as the joint chiefs of staff—all of whom were back in Washington.

Nixon and Kissinger were determined not to share the limelight for the signing of SALT. In consequence they kept at arm's length senior military and arms control specialists who could have helped make the agreements water-tight, or at least more credible to hawks back home. Given the seeming irrelevance of many of the details at stake, such as whether to include obsolete Soviet Golf-class submarines (which had 'surface-to-fire' missiles with a range of less than 700 miles), the modern reader can sympathize with Kissinger's dismissal of much of the arms control arcana.[79] Nevertheless, by going it alone and neglecting specialist advice, Nixon and Kissinger left themselves vulnerable when opponents of strategic arms control later tried to unpick the agreements.

With SALT signed at a ceremony late on the evening of 26 May, Nixon flew to Leningrad the next day for a sightseeing tour, which included the Piskaryev Cemetery where hundreds of thousands from the Siege of Leningrad in 1941–4 were buried. He was deeply moved by the diary of Tanya, a twelve-year-old girl, who calmly recorded the deaths of each of her family before the final sad entry: 'Only Tanya is left'. The guide, choking with emotion, added: 'Tanya died too'.[80] Returning to Moscow, he addressed the Soviet people on television the following evening. The speech was carefully crafted to steer away from anything remotely controversial, with Nixon personally crossing out references to the fact that the United States and the Russian Empire had both fought against Germany in World War One—probably for fear of suggesting that he had a positive view of the tsarist period.[81] In his speech, however, Nixon highlighted the human element of détente in a way that was often lacking in his private discussions, mentioning the story of Tanya. He also told Soviet listeners that American people were 'idealists. We believe deeply in our system of government. We cherish our liberty'. Yet at the same time, Nixon emphasized that Americans, however much they liked their own system, had 'no desire to impose it on anyone else'.[82] Despite some reference to the importance of common humanity, therefore, Nixon's conservative understanding of the aims and limits of détente shone through. The speech went over well. Brezhnev expressed his wish that the two sides would refrain from 'propa-ganda' in the future, just as they had during the summit. Nixon agreed: 'Let's keep the rhetoric cool'.[83]

On 29 May, Nixon signed the summit communiqué and the Basic Prin-ciples of Relations, which Kissinger and Gromyko had finalized while he was in Leningrad. He also met the Soviet leaders for one last time. Then he took to the air again, stopping over in Kiev before flying on to Teheran to meet with the Shah of Iran. On 1 June, in another marathon travel day, Nixon dropped in on Warsaw to meet with the Polish government, before returning home to address a joint session of Congress live on television that evening.

IMPACT AND RESULTS

As soon as Nixon had left Moscow, the administration spin machine moved into top gear. Burying his earlier disquiet about the results of SALT, Laird instructed his Pentagon staff to contact almost every major figure in US nuclear domestic politics, including all surviving former secretaries of defense, as well as a selection of high-profile nuclear scientists and strategists.[84] Administration spokesmen fanned out across the United States, speaking to the regional press and selling Moscow on all the major television talk shows.[85] Extra effort was put into winning over cold warriors who had the potential to derail congressional assent to the SALT accords, such as senators Henry Jackson and Barry Goldwater, as well as California Governor Ronald Reagan.[86] Kissinger was naturally at the forefront of these efforts, describing the SALT agreements to congressional leaders expansively as 'without precedent in the nuclear age; indeed, in all relevant modern history'.[87]

Yet, looking beyond the hyperbole of the moment, the substance of the SALT accords is less impressive than it seemed. The Anti-Ballistic Missile (ABM) Treaty banned systems that both sides had secretly concluded were incapable of providing a significant defence against a nuclear first strike from the other side. The SALT I Interim Agreement, covering offensive weapons, capped the number of ICBMs and SLBMs at fantastically high levels. It was only binding for five years, did not limit strategic bombers aircraft, and did nothing to inhibit the development of the newest and more deadly offensive warhead technology—multiple independently-targetable re-entry vehicles (MIRVs)—which increased up to twelvefold the number of targets that could be hit by a single missile. SALT underlined the fact that, despite the warm words expressed in Moscow, fundamental elements of the superpower competition remained unchanged.[88]

In the aftermath of the summit, both sides were caught in a double bind. Nixon hoped, as he told Brezhnev, that SALT was 'the hors d'oeuvre. Next comes the main course'.[89] Moscow was supposed to be the beginning of greater achievements through further summitry. Yet at the same time, both sides had to insure themselves against the possibility that détente could unravel. This endowed the selling of the summit with a curiously schizophrenic quality. While making statements regarding the prospects for further cooperation, Kissinger also claimed to travelling journalists that, regardless of the Basic Principles Agreement, it was 'perfectly possible that six months from now' the two superpowers would be 'again in a period of extreme hostility'.[90] The Soviets, for their part, were not as confident about the soundness of the Basic Principles as Brezhnev's enthusiastic advocacy of the agreement at the summit implied.[91] 'We understand,' he had told the Central Committee a few days beforehand, 'that neither this, nor any other document can change the reactionary-aggressive nature of American imperialism on its own'. He described the Basic Principles only as a 'solid basis for the long-term development of relations with the United States', useful as an 'additional means of containment' of US power that helped to strengthen 'the peace-loving forces within the American people'.[92] The importance of the Basic Principles in Soviet eyes should therefore be seen in this light—more a way to reinforce pre-existing internal and external constraints on Nixon than as an expression of sincere belief in the agreement's intrinsic power. Certainly neither side saw the Basic Principles Agreement as a magic bullet that would suddenly transform the dynamics of the superpower rivalry.

Faced with the impossible task of predicting which areas of Soviet-American relations would see a major improvement, whilst at the same time cautioning that a fundamental transformation was not in prospect, both sides inevitably made commitments they could not fulfil. During his speech before the Central Committee, Brezhnev had argued that the Moscow summit could advance the USSR's Middle East policy and help stave off American pressure on Salvador Allende of Chile.[93] Only a summit, he implied, could consolidate the Soviet position in the Third World. Yet in July 1972, President Anwar Sadat threw 20,000 Soviet advisers out of Egypt, part of a growing Egyptian-Soviet estrangement that was deepened by the Yom Kippur War of October 1973. And in September 1973 Allende was overthrown by a right-wing military coup, supported by the United States and its regional ally, Brazil.[94]

In contrast to Brezhnev, Nixon had to sell the summit afterwards, not before. In his address to Congress on 1 June, Nixon also overstated some of his gains. While cautioning that what Moscow did would not lead to 'instant peace', Nixon nevertheless proclaimed the 'beginning of the end of that era that began in 1945'.[95] As the November election approached, Nixon leant more towards the latter sentiment than the former. He talked increasingly about a 'generation of peace' between the United States and the Soviet Union—a phrase that he had considered 'too euphoric' for his congressional address.[96] Nixon was assuming a continuation and intensification of Soviet-American summitry but the sequence of annual meetings in America in 1973 and Russia in 1974 petered out after his political demise. Even without Watergate, however, it is difficult to see how Nixon's promise of a generation of peace would have been fulfilled given America's humiliating exit from Vietnam, the USSR's continued nuclear build-up, and further Soviet gains in Africa—all of which Brezhnev considered natural consequences of the shift in the correlation of forces that he hoped the Moscow summit would solidify.

Herein lay a fundamental divergence regarding what the Moscow summit and détente in general were supposed to achieve. 'As our motherland becomes more powerful, as we develop our economy more successfully and deal with our internal issues,' Brezhnev predicted, 'the greater the authority of the Soviet

Union in the international arena, the louder will ring the voices of Soviet diplomats and the more attentively they will listen in the rest of the world'.[97] Yet as the Soviet Union gathered confidence, moving towards greater activism beyond its traditional Eurasian area of operation, it would face increasing pushback from the United States. The shift in the correlation of forces would prove far more temporary than Brezhnev predicted.

The Moscow summit, therefore, neither triggered a permanent shift in the correlation of forces towards the Soviet Union nor did it lead to a generation of peace. Its main agreements stuck to the old diplomatic themes of borders and armaments. By freezing both, it was explicitly conservative. Yet, unlike Nixon's other major 1972 meeting in Beijing, Moscow was a substantive summit, with deals concluded on a whole range of issues. In achieving this Soviet and American leaders gained for the first time a sense that, to borrow Margaret Thatcher's famous phrase from the 1980s, they could 'do business together'.[98] To be sure, the Brezhnev-Nixon relationship was never going to blossom into the kind of partnership enjoyed by Reagan and Gorbachev—not least because both men lacked the strain of rebellion against the verities of post-1945 international relations that characterized their successors. Their main aim was to strengthen trends that would control the arms race and to create a framework for further dialogue. Personal relations may have been staid, even forced, often manipulative and transactional, but they showed that the Cold War was not an uncontrollable, promethean force. Human agency mattered. Agreements could be reached to defuse the potential for conflict. In short, the Cold War could be stabilized in ways that served the vital interests of its two main antagonists. To a generation that had lived through the Cuban crisis, this seemed a ray of hope for the future.

NOTES

1. Text of the 'Basic Principles of Relations Between the United States of America and the Union of Soviet Socialist Republics', 29 May 1972, The American Presidency Project (APP) website, http://www.presidency.ucsb.edu/ws/?pid=3438.
2. Robert Dallek, *Nixon and Kissinger: Partners in Power* (New York, 2007), 16–26.
3. Richard Nixon Presidential Library, Yorba Linda, CA (hereafter RNPL), NSC Files, President's Trip Files, Box 476, Hearings before the Subcommittee on National Security and International Operations of the Committee on Government Operations United States Senate Ninety-First Congress, First Session, Part 1 with Robert Conquest, 15 December 1969.
4. RNPL, NSC Files, President's Trip Files, Box 476, Annotated extracts from Daniel Bell, *The End of Ideology: The Exhaustion of Political Ideas in the Fifties* (Glencoe, IL, 1960).

5. 'Conversation between Richard Nixon and Henry Kissinger, 19 April 1972', in Douglas Brinkley and Luke A. Nichter, eds, *The Nixon Tapes: 1971–1972* (Boston, 2014), 499.
6. Vladislav M. Zubok, *A Failed Empire: The Soviet Union in the Cold War from Stalin to Gorbachev* (Chapel Hill, NC, 2007), 194–7, 200–2; Steven J. Zaloga, *The Kremlin's Nuclear Sword: The Rise and Fall of Russia's Strategic Nuclear Forces, 1945–2000* (London, 2002), 101–3, 118.
7. Anatoly Dobrynin, 'Memorandum of Telephone Conversation (USSR)', 11 May 1971, in David C. Geyer and Douglas E. Selvage, eds, *Soviet-American Relations: The Détente Years, 1969–1972* (Washington, DC, 2007), 351.
8. Mario Del Pero, *The Eccentric Realist: Henry Kissinger and the Shaping of American Foreign Policy* (Ithaca, NY, 2009), 29–42. For the connection between youth protest and détente, see Jeremi Suri, *Power and Protest: Global Revolution and the Rise of Détente* (Cambridge, MA, 2003). On Congress, see Robert D. Johnson, *Congress and the Cold War* (New York, 2006), 144–241.
9. Raymond L. Garthoff, *Détente and Confrontation: American-Soviet Relations from Nixon to Reagan* (Washington, DC, rev. edn, 1994), 33–7.
10. Zubok, *A Failed Empire*, 201 and at 214.
11. A.M. Aleksandrov-Agentov, *Ot Kollontai do Gorbacheva* (Moscow, 1994), 226–7.
12. Zubok, *A Failed Empire*, 210–13.
13. Leonid Brezhnev, 'O mezhdunarodnoi deiatel'nosti TsK KPSS posle XXIU s"ezda partii', 22 November 1971, fond 2, opis' 3, delo 251, 57, in *Plenumy Tsentral'nogo Komiteta Kommunisticheskoi partii Sovetskogo Soiuza, 1941–1990: iz fondov Rossiiskogo gosudarstvennogo arkhiva noveishei istorii* (Woodbury, CT, 2001) (henceforth *Plenumy TsK KPSS, RGANI*).
14. Leonid Brezhnev, 'O mezhdunarodnom polozhenii', 19 May 1972, fond 2, opis' 3, delo 270, 6–20, in *Plenumy TsK KPSS, RGANI*.
15. Garthoff, *Détente and Confrontation*, 40–73.
16. Leonid Brezhnev, 'Vneshniaia politika Sovetskogo Soiuza i borba KPSS za splochennost' mirovogo kommunisticheskogo dvizheniia', 12 December 1966, fond 2, opis' 3, delo 45, 111, in *Plenumy TsK KPSS, RGANI*.
17. Robert M. Gates, *From the Shadows: The Ultimate Insider's Story of Five Presidents and How They Won the Cold War* (New York, 1996), 36.
18. Garthoff, *Détente and Confrontation*, 40.
19. Andrew Preston and Fredrik Logevall, 'Introduction: The Adventurous Journey of Nixon in the World', in Andrew Preston and Fredrik Logevall, eds, *Nixon in the World: American Foreign Relations, 1969–1977* (New York, 2008), 10.
20. Garthoff, *Détente and Confrontation*, 1126–9.
21. Richard Nixon-Henry Kissinger Telcon, 11 June 1970, KA03097, in William Burr, ed., *The Kissinger Telephone Conversations: A Verbatim Record of U.S. Diplomacy, 1969–1977*, Digital National Security Archive, http://nsarchive.gwu.edu/NSAEBB/NSAEBB193/press.htm. Nixon wanted to replicate the public relations boost of President Lyndon Johnson's brief summit with Soviet Premier Alexei Kosygin in Glassboro, New Jersey, in 1967.
22. Richard Nixon, Address Accepting the Presidential Nomination at the Republican National Convention in Miami Beach, Florida, 8 August 1968, APP website, http://www.presidency.ucsb.edu/ws/?pid=25968.

23. Anatoly Dobrynin, *In Confidence: Moscow's Ambassador to America's Six Cold War Presidents (1962–1986)* (New York, 1995), 209.
24. Dobrynin, *In Confidence*, 210–11.
25. Dobrynin, *In Confidence*, 226, 233.
26. 'Telegram from Ambassador Dobrynin to the Soviet Foreign Ministry', 17 July 1971, in Geyer and Selvage, eds, *Détente Years*, 401–4.
27. 'Telegram from Ambassador Dobrynin to the Soviet Foreign Ministry', 17 July 1971, in Geyer and Selvage, eds, *Détente Years*, 403.
28. 'Memorandum of Conversation (USSR)', 5 August 1971, in Geyer and Selvage, eds, *Détente Years*, 425.
29. Henry Kissinger, *White House Years* (Boston, MA, 1979), 837–8.
30. RNPL, NSC Files, President's Trip Files, Box 474, Theodore Eliot, Jr to Kissinger: President's USSR Visit—Itineraries of Other Major Western Leaders who Have Visited the USSR, 25 March 1972; and Helmut Sonnenfeldt to Henry Kissinger: USSR Visit—President Eisenhower's Planned Visit in 1960, 21 March 1972; and Eliot, Jr to Kissinger, 'President's USSR Visit: Itineraries of President Nixon on Previous USSR Trips, 23 March 1972; RNPL, NSC Files, President's Trip Files, Box 475, Recent Summit Communiques, undated.
31. RNPL, White House Special Files Staff Member and Office Files (hereafter SMOF), H.R. Haldeman, Box 108, Dwight L. Chapin to Haldeman: David Eisenhower, 4 May 1972.
32. RNPL, White House Special Files SMOF, John Scali, Box 6, John Scali to Haldeman: TV Coverage of the President's Visit to Russia, 23 March 1972.
33. RNPL, NSC Files, President's Trip Files, Box 474, Dwight Chapin to Kissinger and Ronald Ziegler, Russia, 4 May 1972.
34. RNPL, NSC Files, President's Trip Files, Box 475, Jacob Beam: Leningrad Reactions to the President's Visit, 2 June 1972.
35. RNPL, White House Special Files SMOF, Ronald Ziegler, Box 37, Total Press List, undated.
36. RNPL, NSC Files, President's Trip Files, Box 474, Scowcroft to Kissinger and Haldeman: Presidential Travel Aboard Soviet Aircraft, 11 April 1972.
37. Conversation between Richard Nixon, Henry Kissinger and Bob Haldeman, 1 May 1972, Brinkley and Nichter, *Nixon Tapes*, 519.
38. Dobrynin, *In Confidence*, 255.
39. Jussi Hanhimäki, *The Flawed Architect: Henry Kissinger and American Foreign Policy* (New York, 2004), 203.
40. 'Memorandum of Conversation (USSR)', 3 April 1972, in Geyer and Selvage, eds, *Détente Years*, 639.
41. 'Telegram from Ambassador Dobrynin to the Soviet Foreign Ministry', 10 April 1972, in Geyer and Selvage, eds, *Détente Years*, 654–5; 'Memorandum of Conversation (USSR)', 12 April 1972, in Geyer and Selvage, eds, *Détente Years*, 657–8.
42. 'Telegram from Ambassador Dobrynin to the Soviet Foreign Ministry', 19 April 1972, in Geyer and Selvage, eds, *Détente Years*, 675–9.
43. 'Memorandum from President Nixon to Presidential Assistant Kissinger', 20 April 1972, in Geyer and Selvage, eds, *Détente Years*, 679–80.

44. 'Memorandum of Conversation (U.S.)', 21 April 1972, in Geyer and Selvage, eds, *Détente Years*, 687.

45. 'Memorandum of Conversation (U.S.)', 21 April 1972, in Geyer and Selvage, eds, *Détente Years*, 695; Hanhimäki, *The Flawed Architect*, 207–8; David Reynolds, *Summits: Six Meetings that Shaped the Twentieth Century* (New York, 2007), 233–4.

46. Kissinger, *White House Years*, 1131–2; 'Memorandum of Conversation (U.S.)', 21 April 1972, in Geyer and Selvage, eds, *Détente Years*, 696–7. RNPL, NSC Files, Henry A. Kissinger Office Files, Box 21, Joint Communique, HAK handed to D 3/17; RNPL, NSC Files, Country Files, Box 72, Osnovy vzaimootnosheniï mezhdu Soiuzom Sovetskikh Sotsialisticheskikh Respublik i Soedinennymi Shtatami Ameriki; and 'Basic Principles of Relations Between the Union of Soviet Socialist Republics and the United States of America'—Handwritten US changes on Soviet draft, 22 April 1972.

47. 'Memorandum of Conversation (U.S.)', 22 April 1972, in Geyer and Selvage, eds, *Détente Years*, 710; Georgii Kornienko, *Kholodnaia voina: svidetel'stvo eë uchastnika* (Moscow, 1995), 144–5.

48. RNPL, NSC Files, President's Trip Files, Box 475, William Rogers to Nixon: Moscow Visit—Communiqué, 19 May 1972.

49. Kissinger, *White House Years*, 1169, 1176.

50. Conversation between Nixon and Kissinger, 3 May 1972, *Foreign Relations of the United States, 1969–1976, vol. xiv, Soviet Union, October 1971–May 1972* (henceforth *FRUS 1969–76, vol. xiv*), https://history.state.gov/historicaldocuments/frus1969-76v14, doc. 187.

51. Editorial Note, *FRUS 1969–76, vol. xiv,* doc. 188.

52. Richard Nixon, Address to the Nation on the Situation in Southeast Asia, 8 May 1972, APP website, http://www.presidency.ucsb.edu/ws/?pid=3404.

53. 'Memorandum of Conversation (U.S.)', 8 May 1972, in Geyer and Selvage, eds, *Détente Years*, 800; 'Letter From President Nixon to General Secretary Brezhnev', 8 May 1972, in Geyer and Selvage, eds, *Détente Years*, 803–4.

54. Dobrynin, *In Confidence*, 248; Zubok, *A Failed Empire*, 218–20.

55. Brezhnev, 'O mezhdunarodnom polozhenii', 19 May 1972, fond 2, opis' 3, delo 270, 23, 36–7, in *Plenumy TsK KPSS, RGANI*.

56. Brezhnev, 'O mezhdunarodnom polozhenii', 19 May 1972, fond 2, opis' 3, delo 270, 43–4, 50–7, in *Plenumy TsK KPSS, RGANI*.

57. Brezhnev, 'O mezhdunarodnom polozhenii', 19 May 1972, fond 2, opis' 3, delo 270, 57–64, in *Plenumy TsK KPSS, RGANI*.

58. Brezhnev, 'O mezhdunarodnom polozhenii', 19 May 1972, fond 2, opis' 3, delo 270, 67, in *Plenumy TsK KPSS, RGANI*.

59. Andrei Grechko, 'Obsuzhdenie doklada "O mezhdunarodnom polozhenii"', 19 May 1972, fond 2, opis' 3, delo 270, 129–30, and 146, in *Plenumy TsK KPSS, RGANI*.

60. Viktor M. Sukhodrev, *Iazyk moi—drug moi: Ot Khrushcheva do Gorbacheva* (Moscow, 1999), 265–6.

61. Sukhodrev, *Iazyk moi*, 266–70.

62. Sukhodrev, *Iazyk moi*, 275–6.

63. Kissinger, *White House Years*, 1210–11.
64. 'Memorandum of Conversation (U.S.)', 11am–1pm, 23 May 1972, in Geyer and Selvage, eds, *Détente Years*, 842–7.
65. 'Memorandum of Conversation (U.S.)', 10.20am–12.20pm, 29 May 1972, in Geyer and Selvage, eds, *Détente Years*, 991.
66. Reynolds, *Summits*, 251–2.
67. RNPL, NSC Files, President's Trip Files, Box 478, Space Cooperation, undated.
68. RNPL, NSC Files, President's Trip Files, Box 478, Incidents at Sea, undated.
69. RNPL, NSC Files, President's Trip Files, Box 478, Maritime Agreement, undated.
70. RNPL, NSC Files, President's Trip Files, Box 475, Peter G. Peterson to Nixon: Economic Announcements at the Moscow Summit, 19 May 1972.
71. 'Memorandum of Conversation (U.S.)', 2.10–3.50pm, 25 May 1972, Geyer and Selvage, eds, *Détente Years*, 924.
72. Memcon, Brezhnev-Nixon et al., Meeting held at Brezhnev's dacha, 24 May 1972, *FRUS 1969–76, vol. xiv*, doc. 271.
73. Kissinger, *White House Years*, 1227–8.
74. Andrei Gromyko, 'Obsuzhdenie doklada "O mezhdunarodnoi deiatel'nosti TsK KPSS po osushchestvleniiu reshenii XXIU s"ezda partii', 27 April 1973, fond 2, opis' 3, delo 299, 49–50, *Plenumy TsK KPSS, RGANI*.
75. Kissinger, *White House Years*, 1246.
76. RNPL, NSC Files, President's Trip Files, Box 480, Kissinger to Gerard Smith, 25 May 1972.
77. Gerard Smith, *Doubletalk: The Story of SALT* (Lanham, MD, 1985), 408–10; Kissinger, *White House Years*, 1230.
78. RNPL, NSC Files, President's Trip Files, Box 480, Kissinger to Gerard Smith, 24 May 1972.
79. RNPL, NSC Files, President's Trip Files, Box 480, Kissinger to Gerard Smith, 25 May 1972.
80. Richard Nixon, *RN: The Memoirs of Richard Nixon* (London, 1978), 616–17.
81. RNPL, White House Special Files SMOF, President's Personal File, Box 76, Moscow TV Address 4th Draft, 25 May 1972.
82. Richard Nixon, Radio and Television Address to the People of the Soviet Union, 28 May 1972, APP website, http://www.presidency.ucsb.edu/ws/?pid=3437.
83. 'Memorandum of Conversation (U.S.)', 29 May 1972, in Geyer and Selvage eds, *Détente Years*, 993.
84. RNPL, White House Special Files SMOF, Charles Colson, Box 80, Louis Thompson, Jr: Notification of SALT Agreement, 1 June 1972; Ben Plymale to Julian Levine: Briefing of Scientific Community on SALT, 26 May 1972; and Colson to Haldeman: Soviet Union Summit Follow Up, 31 May 1972.
85. RNPL, White House Special Files SMOF, Charles Colson, Box 80, Charles Colson to Alvin Snyder, 31 May 1972.
86. RNPL, White House Special Files SMOF, Charles Colson, Box 80, Plan of Action for Ratification of the SALT Agreements, undated; and Colson to Alexander Haig, 23 May 1972.
87. RNPL, White House Special Files SMOF, Charles Colson, Box 80, Congressional Briefing by Kissinger, 15 June 1972.

88. Garthoff, *Détente and Confrontation*, 189.
89. 'Memorandum of Conversation (U.S.)', 7.20–9.55pm, 23 May 1972, in Geyer and Selvage, eds, *Détente Years*, 860.
90. RNPL, NSC Files, President's Trip Files, Box 475, Press Conference of Kissinger, Press Center—Dniepro Hotel, Kiev, 29 May 1972.
91. 'Memorandum of Conversation (U.S.)', 22 May 1972, in Geyer and Selvage, eds, *Détente Years*, 833.
92. Brezhnev, 'O mezhdunarodnom polozhenii', 19 May 1972, fond 2, opis' 3, delo 270, 49, in *Plenumy TsK KPSS, RGANI*.
93. Brezhnev, 'O mezhdunarodnom polozhenii', 19 May 1972, fond 2, opis' 3, delo 270, 67, in *Plenumy TsK KPSS, RGANI*.
94. Svetlana Savranskaya and William Taubman, 'Soviet Foreign Policy, 1962–1975', in Melvyn P. Leffler and Odd A. Westad, eds, *The Cambridge History of the Cold War, volume II: Crises and Détente* (Cambridge, 2010), 153; Tanya Harmer, 'Brazil's Cold War in the Southern Cone: 1970–1975', *Cold War History* 12, no. 4 (2012), 659–81.
95. Richard Nixon, 'Address to a Joint Session of the Congress on Return From Austria, the Soviet Union, Iran, and Poland', 1 June 1972, APP website, http://www.presidency.ucsb.edu/ws/?pid=3450.
96. Kissinger, *White House Years*, 1255. RNPL, White House Special Files SMOF, President's Personal File, Box 76, Summit Report to the Congress and the Nation, Fifth Draft', 31 May 1972.
97. Brezhnev, 'O mezhdunarodnom polozhenii', 19 May 1972, fond 2, opis' 3, delo 270, 74, in *Plenumy TsK KPSS, RGANI*.
98. Margaret Thatcher TV Interview for BBC, 17 December 1984, Margaret Thatcher Foundation website, http://www.margaretthatcher.org/document/105592.

II

Living with the Cold War

4

Helsinki, 1975

Michael Cotey Morgan and Daniel Sargent

On the morning of 30 July 1975, President Gerald Ford greeted General Secretary Leonid Brezhnev at the US ambassador's residence in Helsinki (see Figure 4.1). Photographers snapped pictures as the two leaders exchanged congratulations. Just days earlier Apollo and Soyuz spacecraft had docked in orbit and American astronauts had shaken hands with Soviet cosmonauts. 'They go up', Brezhnev exclaimed, and 'they meet somewhere in the limitless vastness of space'. However 'fantastic' this space summit had been, Brezhnev and Ford's terrestrial meeting carried greater consequences for the Cold War—and spawned far greater controversy.[1]

Fig. 4.1. Ford and Brezhnev at US embassy, Helsinki, 30 July 1975 (AP)

The two leaders had come to the Finnish capital to celebrate, with thirty-three other statesmen, the successful conclusion of the Conference on Security and Cooperation in Europe (CSCE) and to sign the Helsinki Final Act, a 22,000-word agreement. The Act was the culmination of nearly three years of bureaucratic negotiations among diplomats from the Soviet Union, the United States, Canada, and almost every European country. They dealt with a staggering array of subjects—state sovereignty and military security, trade and technology, the movement of people, and the exchange of information—that tied together the many strands of détente. The CSCE process had developed in three stages: first, multilateral preparatory talks in the suburbs of Helsinki (1972–3), then full-scale CSCE negotiations in Geneva (1973–5), and finally a summit of the leaders back in Helsinki from 30 July to 1 August 1975—three days of speeches and dinners, climaxing in a solemn signing ceremony.

In content and ambition, the Helsinki summit resembled the great peace conferences of the past; in size it even eclipsed Vienna in 1815 and Paris in 1919. But unlike them, Helsinki did not follow a cataclysmic military conflict: this was an attempt in what remained a *cold* war to establish some rules of engagement for the two sides. What also mattered about Helsinki were the informal meetings between leaders that took place on its margins. The Ford-Brezhnev encounter was replicated by numerous quiet conversations between East and West Europeans and among the leaders of each bloc. These, too, would be part of Helsinki's legacy.

For Brezhnev, the Final Act opened a new era in international politics. 'This is a victory of reason', he told the assembly of statesmen in Finlandia Hall. 'This is the prize of people who cherish peace and security.'[2] The Soviet press joined the celebration: 'Let us remember this day', declared *Pravda*. 'It will enter history as the most important landmark on the road to durable peace in Europe.'[3] American reactions were not so euphoric. The Final Act itself, Ford argued, mattered less than 'practical and concrete results': without Soviet follow-through, the CSCE would become 'the latest chapter in a long and sorry volume of unfulfilled declarations'. The American press, for its part, was downright hostile. The Final Act, according to the *New York Times,* gave 'political and psychological endorsement to Soviet hegemony over Eastern Europe',[4] while the *Wall Street Journal* damned its recognition of Europe's postwar frontiers as 'a formal version of Yalta, without Yalta's redeeming features'.[5] Columnist William Safire stated bluntly: 'we were had'.[6] The *New York Times* went so far as to say that the CSCE 'should not have happened'.[7] This torrent of criticism echoed the views, and indicated the influence, of exiled Soviet writer Aleksandr Solzhenitsyn, who had denounced the CSCE as 'an amicable agreement of diplomatic shovels' that would 'bury and pack down still-breathing bodies in a common grave'.[8]

In the years after Helsinki, however, a new consensus about the Final Act would emerge in the United States and the West at large. Politicians and pundits began to hail the summit as a turning-point in the Cold War, not as the strategic setback and moral sellout that critics of the Final Act perceived in 1975.[9] This reversal reveals the divergences between the consequences of the Final Act and expectations at the time. The Soviet leaders who initiated the CSCE achieved less than they sought, but did not understand the meagreness of their achievements until after the summit. Their American counterparts, by contrast, had at first disparaged the CSCE as a distraction and allowed their Western European allies, who were more hopeful for the process, to take the lead, which the US government backed late in the day, pressing the Soviets for concessions. Ultimately, the combination of the USSR's impatience for an agreement and the Western allies' obduracy on the terms broke the diplomatic impasse into which the CSCE negotiations had fallen. This resulted in a deal that reflected Western values more than Eastern imperatives.

ORIGINS

The CSCE was, in origin, the USSR's idea, though the Soviets persuaded neutral Finland to act in May 1969 as its official promoter.[10] To understand the Kremlin's thinking, it is is necessary to move beyond the arms race and the the strategic parity that underpinned SALT I to consider the larger context of East-West relations during the 1960s. The idea of the CSCE emerged from the multiple crises that befell the Soviet bloc in the 1960s, which cumulatively threatened to sap Moscow's power and erode the bloc's political, economic, and social systems. Within the Warsaw Pact, the USSR struggled to contain the centrifugal pressures that exploded in Czechoslovakia in 1968. The suppression of the Prague Spring strained the bloc's cohesion and demonstrated that the Kremlin's influence in Eastern Europe rested upon the threat of force. Communist ideology had lost any mass appeal it might once have claimed.[11] Outside Europe, the picture looked similarly grim. The Sino-Soviet alliance collapsed acrimoniously during the 1960s, degenerating into border clashes that imperilled Soviet security.[12] To make matters worse, the socialist economy was sputtering. Nikita Khrushchev searched in vain for a solution, eventually losing the support of his Politburo colleagues, who overthrew him in 1964. His successors Alexei Kosygin and Leonid Brezhnev fared little better.[13] In sum, Soviet claims to legitimacy at home and across Eastern Europe had worn thin. By the late 1960s, after years of relative stability in Europe, the old arguments that Western imperialism, fascism, and revanchism posed a mortal danger to the peoples of Eastern Europe lacked any credibility. Moscow could no longer rely on these outworn bugbears to justify heavy military spending and tight social controls. Tired of shortages and stagnant living standards, citizens began to question the Party's long-standing promises that communism would eventually yield material plenty. A small but growing dissident movement began to challenge the party-state; many more East Europeans subsided into cynicism and apathy.

Amid crisis, the Kremlin sought new options. The challenge was to redress the East bloc's problems without violating the Soviet system's core tenets. To this end, Brezhnev aimed to shore up the USSR's international influence, revive its economy, and rebuild its legitimacy. These interlocking components defined his strategy for East-West détente. The Soviet Union sought to defuse long-standing tensions over the division of Germany and the status of Berlin and gain international acceptance of the territorial and political changes that had followed World War Two. Formal Western recognition of the Soviet bloc's right to exist would salve Eastern European leaders' long-standing anxieties about their status in international society and confirm that the socialist regimes were there to stay. Stable frontiers in Europe, in turn, would allow Moscow to shift its attention to the Sino-Soviet border. Normalized relations with the Western Europeans and the Americans would also open new markets to Soviet exports and give the USSR access to financial capital, consumer goods, and the latest technology. At the same time arms control agreements should make it possible for the Kremlin to redirect military spending to more productive economic use, boosting standards of living and bringing mass prosperity within reach. With the implementation of all these steps, Brezhnev hoped to rejuvenate the Soviet bloc and present himself as the architect of a new era of peace and stability, confirming his personal grip on power.

Moscow's new strategy coincided with a parallel crisis of the Western alliance. During the 1960s, NATO also lost cohesion and legitimacy. After the Cuban Missile Crisis, the Cold War had stabilized and fears of war with the Warsaw Pact declined. If these trends continued, Western political leaders feared, voters might conclude that NATO served no purpose or, worse, stood in the way of peace.[14] Further, some Western European leaders chafed at American leadership. In 1966, French president Charles de Gaulle shocked Washington by withdrawing from NATO's military command.[15] These existential challenges prompted NATO to articulate a new *raison d'être* in the Harmel Report of 1967. Military defence should remain a core task, the report concluded, but NATO should also seek to foster East-West détente. This all-weather approach would guarantee the Alliance's relevance whether relations with the Soviet bloc improved or soured anew.[16] By working for peace instead of just preparing for war, NATO could make a fresh appeal for its citizens' support and prove that it had not outlived its usefulness.

The proponents of East-West détente sought new relations with the East, but priorities, and their strategic implications, varied across the West. From 1969 President Richard Nixon sought to expand American leverage by circumventing the constraints on American power. Working with National Security Adviser Henry Kissinger, Nixon aimed to curtail military expenditures while forging more constructive relationships with Moscow and Beijing. By gaining some respite from Cold War pressures, Nixon believed that the United States could secure the breathing room it needed to recover from Vietnam without ceding global primacy to the Soviet Union.[17] His static détente strategy aimed to de-escalate the East-West struggle in order to stabilize the Cold War order. It resembled Brezhnev's own strategy more closely than it did the priorities of Washington's West European allies.

Leading Western European statesmen pursued more dynamic strategies of détente, focused less on stabilizing the Cold War than on overcoming it. In 1969, as noted in chapter 1, the new West German chancellor Willy Brandt made *Ostpolitik* his foreign policy priority. By normalizing relations with the East, Brandt sought to mitigate the Cold War's human costs for the Germans, for instance by making it easier to reunite families that had been divided by the Berlin Wall. He hoped that closer contacts at every level of state and society would encourage more profound changes over the long run, culminating ultimately in Germany's peaceful unification.[18]

French President Georges Pompidou crafted a similar strategy and harboured similar hopes. As de Gaulle's loyal heir, Pompidou sought political and economic cooperation between France and the Soviet bloc for stability and French freedom of action, but he also hoped that the dynamics of 'interpenetration' would transform the Cold War. 'The more contacts we have with the East', Pompidou told Nixon in 1970, 'the more liberty will become contagious.'[19] In the competition of ideas and values, both Brandt and Pompidou reasoned, liberal democracy and capitalism would eventually triumph, bringing the Cold War to a peaceful conclusion by remaking the Soviet bloc in the West's image.

As these competing strategies took shape in the West, the Finns made their proposal to host preparatory talks for a pan-European security conference. Out of this, Soviet leaders wanted to achieve *de jure* recognition of Europe's postwar frontiers and, by implication, the legitimacy of the continent's communist regimes. In effect the CSCE would be the peace conference that never happened after 1945.[20] Despite their general enthusiasm for détente, American and West European leaders greeted this proposal with scepticism, seeing in it an attempt to sap NATO's resolve by sowing discord among the allies. A conference would give Moscow a bullhorn to denounce the West for the postwar division of Europe and proclaim that peace was within reach if only NATO would cooperate. Western citizens might be gulled, draining support for military spending and undermining NATO's fragile legitimacy.[21] On the other hand, rejecting the conference proposal also carried risks. If NATO rebuffed the East's overture, the West's citizens might conclude that the alliance was not serious about peace.[22] So danger lay in both directions. Some of the smaller NATO members nonetheless embraced the proposal, hoping that a pan-European conference would give the diplomatic minnows a rare opportunity to bargain with the whales.

After weighing the risks at length in 1970–1, Western leaders concluded that the CSCE proposal offered them considerable leverage. If the Soviets wanted a conference, they would have to pay for it and it was therefore up to NATO to name the price. The Allies declared, first, that they would participate in a security conference only once Bonn's negotiations with Moscow, East Berlin, and Warsaw had been concluded and the four occupying powers had hammered out an agreement on the status of Berlin. This stipulation strengthened the negotiating position of the Federal Republic (FRG) and ensured that unresolved arguments about Germany would not cause a pan-European exercise to collapse in recriminations.[23] Second, NATO pressed the Soviets to agree to conventional disarmament talks, known as the mutual and balanced force reduction talks (MBFR)—an idea that had been debated by the two blocs since 1966. Western experts doubted that the two sides could agree on troop cuts but, even if the talks went nowhere, MBFR would be useful to demonstrate the Alliance's peaceful intentions to domestic audiences. This was particularly important in the United States, where political forces led by Democratic Senate Majority Leader Mike Mansfield, were calling for a unilateral 50 per cent reduction of US forces in Europe. Mansfield's proposal garnered substantial support, prompting Nixon to embrace MBFR, so that he could claim to be progressing towards Mansfield's goal on terms that would secure a parallel reduction in Soviet arms. On the other side, MBFR held few attractions for Soviet leaders, because the Warsaw Pact had long relied on conventional superiority as the foundation of its security. Still, once the United States had connected it to the security conference proposal, Moscow could not reject MBFR outright.[24]

Most significantly, the Western Allies demanded a broader agenda for the security conference. The Warsaw Pact wanted this to discuss only a few basic principles—respect for frontiers and the renunciation of force—as well the promotion of economic, scientific, and technological cooperation. These ideas catered to Brezhnev's static détente concept but did little for the West. NATO therefore crafted its own list of priorities, including human rights, the freer movement of people, and the exchange of ideas and information.[25] This enlarged agenda challenged the foundations of the Soviet system, which relied on absolute state authority and tight controls on individual freedoms. NATO's agenda therefore embodied a transformative conception of détente, at odds with Brezhnev's more conservative interest in confirming the status quo.

PREPARATORY TALKS

On 22 November 1972, diplomats from across Europe and North America descended on the Helsinki University of Technology's student union (Dipoli), the unlikely venue for the CSCE's multilateral preparatory talks. The timing was not accidental. Earlier that year, the West German Bundestag's ratification of the Eastern Treaties and the conclusion of a four-power treaty on the status of Berlin had satisfied NATO's two preconditions. At the Nixon administration's insistence, the preparatory talks had also been delayed until after the presidential election at the beginning of that month, when the president was returned for a second term.

Once the talks got underway, the Kremlin wanted to conclude them as fast as possible, eager to convene a final summit of political leaders that would anoint Brezhnev as Europe's peacemaker. The Western allies refused to be rushed. They had no intention of leaving the negotiating table until they had achieved their own goals. The interplay between Soviet haste and Western patience coloured the negotiations from beginning to end, affecting every subject that the CSCE discussed over the next two-and-a-half years. These were divided into three loose 'baskets'. Basket I contained a set of principles guiding relations between the participant states; Basket II dealt with economic and technological cooperation, and related issues; and Basket III was devoted to cooperation over humanitarian issues, including freer movement and freedom of information.

From the outset, the Soviets focused their attention on Basket I, in particular the issue of Europe's postwar borders. They were delighted with the success of Brandt's *Ostpolitik* and wished to push it several steps further. Now that the FRG had recognized *de facto* the territorial status quo, Soviet leaders wanted all the NATO allies to do the same in a legally-binding treaty. 'The chief political result of the all-European conference', Brezhnev explained, 'must be to entrench in international law on a multilateral basis... the inviolability of the present frontiers of the European states.'[26] His goals were partly idealistic and partly pragmatic. Affirming postwar borders would vindicate the war's sacrifices by protecting 'the territorial and political realities that emerged in Europe' after 1945.[27] Yet by stabilizing peace in Europe, the CSCE would also sanctify communism's hold over Eastern Europe, offering international affirmation of the Soviet bloc's rightful existence.

Some Western leaders were appalled by Moscow's proposals. To be sure, none of the NATO allies had immediate ambitions to alter the map of the continent. 'No one is challenging the existing frontiers,' Kissinger told Soviet Ambassador Anatoly Dobrynin.[28] But accepting frontiers *de facto* was profoundly different from legally recognizing their immutability. The very idea was anathema to West Germany, whose Basic Law enshrined the goal of German reunification within its constitutional fabric. Indeed, Willy Brandt argued when he signed the Moscow Treaty that the border between the two German states could in time be erased. The other Western Allies followed Bonn's lead, resolving that the CSCE should not become a full peace conference or result in a formal peace treaty. Hammering out a legally binding treaty would drastically complicate the CSCE process because of the need to ensure the compatibility of any treaty with other international legal instruments, while calling the CSCE a peace conference would implicitly accept the continent's frontiers as permanent. Instead, NATO would sign a declaration that the frontiers were only 'inviolable' not 'immutable'. Borders were not sacred or eternal: they could be redrawn but only through international agreement.

The irreconcilability of Eastern and Western goals forced the preparatory talks into calculated ambiguity. After months of argument in Helsinki, the participants completed the agenda for the fully-fledged CSCE negotiations, which eventually opened in Geneva in September 1973. The English-language version of the list of 'principles' governing relations between states included the '*inviolability* of frontiers', just as the NATO allies wanted. The equally-authoritative Russian and German versions used words drawn from the Warsaw Pact's own proposals—*nerushimost'* and *Unverletzlichkeit*. All these words allowed a variety of connotations, including sanctity and immutability, depending on your negotiating position. East and West Germans, for example, disagreed about how to interpret *Unverletzlichkeit*: each regarded the term as an affirmation of its own position.[29] CSCE negotiators argued furiously about these shades of meaning, not least because the FRG and its West European allies demanded an explicit declaration that the principle of 'inviolability' would not preclude borders being changed peacefully—notably in the case of Germany.[30]

The impasse dragged on for months. Early in 1974 Brezhnev raised the issue directly with Henry Kissinger, recently confirmed as US secretary of state. In Kissinger's view, the United States had little at stake but, to soothe the Soviets, he agreed to press the stubborn Western Europeans to back down. His intervention had little effect. Eventually, Brezhnev's impatience for a summit overcame his resistance and the Soviet delegation in Geneva accepted a clause that borders could be changed peacefully, on condition that this must not appear as an integral part of the principle on inviolability.[31] Here was a major concession but the West Germans—for whom this was a matter of national importance—still haggled with the Soviets for much of 1974 about the precise wording of this clause.[32]

The Soviets regarded the declaration on frontiers as the centrepiece of the CSCE, while the Western Allies wanted to concentrate on the human dimension of détente in ways that would target the foundations of Soviet power. First, they wanted the CSCE to repudiate the 'Brezhnev doctrine'. Proclaimed in 1968 to justify the crushing of the Prague Spring, the doctrine authorized the USSR to use force to preserve socialism in Eastern Europe. This made a mockery of state sovereignty. If the CSCE declared that the principles of sovereignty and non-interference applied everywhere, regardless of a state's social system or its membership in an alliance, the Soviets might have a harder time keeping their satellites in line.[33] Second, the Western Allies wanted to establish human rights as a fundamental 'principle' in Basket I.[34] Doing so implied that respect for human rights was not merely a domestic matter but a concern of statecraft, even an issue of international peace. Human rights and sovereignty nonetheless stood in mutual tension: the first mandated attention to—if not intervention in—another state's domestic affairs; the latter insisted that domestic politics were the business of no-one but the government in question.

Soviet diplomats attacked the Western proposals from every direction. Non-intervention, they said, implied respect for 'the political, economic, and social foundations' of other states, including the special rules that its system of government entailed.[35] Foreign Minister Andrei Gromyko put the matter bluntly: there was a 'visible boundary between the two social worlds,' which the CSCE must not violate.[36] In a similar vein Soviet diplomats argued that the international system rested on the bedrock of sovereignty, giving each state 'supreme authority' over its internal affairs. Human rights therefore had no place on the list of principles. Besides, the Soviet and other communist constitutions already guaranteed their citizens' rights: a new agreement would be superfluous.[37] Much like the Western demands, Moscow's response contradicted itself. It repudiated outside interference in its internal affairs but reserved the right to dictate the domestic policies of its own Allies. After much haggling, human rights were eventually added to the 'list of principles', in exchange for including the inviolability of frontiers. However, Soviet diplomats continued to insist that sovereignty trumped human rights. Each state, they argued, must retain the authority to decide for itself how to put human rights into practice and so the CSCE should restrict itself to a vague declaration. Going into detail would only pull the negotiations into what Soviet negotiators called the muck of 'ideological quarrels'.[38] The Western Allies remained unmoved. By June 1974 the talks were deadlocked on this issue.

Economic questions (Basket II) should have been less contentious because, in theory, all participants stood to gain from expanded cooperation. Moreover, the USSR had already negotiated a series of bilateral agreements over the transfer of goods and technology across the Cold War divide. The Lada car factory in Tolyatti on the Volga, built with Italian know-how in 1966 and named for the Italian communist leader Palmiro Togliatti, exemplified the economic benefits of détente. The Soviets wanted the CSCE to formalize and expand economic relations. At the top of Brezhnev's list was 'equality of rights' in international trade,' which entailed the USA granting 'most-favored nation' (MFN) status for the USSR and an end to Western rules that discriminated against imports from the communist bloc.[39] If they could sell their products in the West, the Soviets and their allies could earn hard currency to purchase the technology and consumer goods that figured prominently in their plans for economic rejuvenation.

The Western Allies were willing to consider the Soviet proposals but again wanted something in return. Generally they felt that the benefits of East-West trade outweighed the risk of giving the communist regimes material succour. And they calculated that exposing the Soviets and their allies to Western products and mores could coax them to liberalize and open up their societies. The West Germans called this idea *Wandel durch Handel* (change through trade), but even Bonn was cautious.[40] For the Soviets to gain MFN status by itself was of no value to America and Western Europe. The Soviets and their allies lacked the hard currency needed to buy Western imports and their own poor-quality manufactures found few buyers in the West. Western officials therefore decided that if the Soviets wanted MFN status, they would have to make concessions of a different sort. Under the proposed terms of 'reciprocity' East bloc governments should relax their controls on foreign trade, publish previously classified economic statistics, provide better working conditions for foreign businessmen, and generally make it easier for Western corporations to do business in the East.[41] Whereas the Soviets wanted grandiose principles from the CSCE process, the Western Allies preferred modest but practical measures.

But the MFN issue was entangled with the issue of Congressional approval and the consequent politicking in Washington. Senior Democratic Senator Henry 'Scoop' Jackson argued that the United States should not confer MFN status on any country that impeded the emigration of its citizens. He attacked the trade agreement that Nixon and Brezhnev had signed in October 1972, wherein Nixon had promised MFN status to the USSR. Nixon denounced Jackson for meddling in foreign policy but Jackson had most of Congress on his side. Making the conferral of MFN status on 'non-market' countries conditional upon those countries permitting their citizens to emigrate freely, the Jackson-Vanik amendment to the Trade Bill—named for Jackson and his Democratic co-sponsor Congressman Charles Vanik—passed Congress in December 1974. It made the MFN question a dead letter in Geneva.[42] Predictably, the frustrated Soviets rejected Western demands for reciprocity. Even without Jackson's troublemaking, however, it is unlikely that Brezhnev would have contemplated the far-reaching economic reforms that reciprocity entailed. The purpose of the CSCE, in his view, was to strengthen the communist economic model, not to dismantle it. Although trade should have been the most tractable subject at the CSCE, here, too, work ground to a halt in early 1975.

The most violent arguments in Geneva erupted over the West's proposals on societal openness and military transparency, which targeted the mechanisms of communist control. The first issue was freedom of information and freer movement of people (Basket III). NATO countries sought to promote wider access to Western books and newspapers, an end to the jamming of radio broadcasts, and the elimination of barriers to travel and emigration. In the best-case scenario, if the communists cooperated, these steps would loosen the regimes' grip on their societies. In the worst case, if they refused to cooperate, the debate would focus international attention on the regimes' mistreatment of their citizens. The propaganda generated could help Western officials who worried that their own citizens perceived no moral distinctions across the Iron Curtain. In a fight over freer movement, the West could reclaim the moral high ground.[43]

The West's second major openness proposal (in Basket I) was for greater transparency in the military sphere. With MBFR the subject of separate talks, Western governments decided to work on 'confidence-building measures' (CBMs) at the CSCE. They proposed the exchange of military observers and the advance notification of troop movements and manoeuvres in order to reduce the risk of war through stronger relationships and ultimately mutual understanding and trust.[44] President Dwight Eisenhower's abortive Open Skies proposal of 1955 had rested on similar logic.[45] The West thought that, even if the CBM idea foundered, it would still benefit because the initiative would have reminded their citizens that Cold War security threats persisted and that NATO's military deterrent remained essential. The Soviets were apprehensive about both proposals. In their view, freer movement was a blatant Western device for ideological subversion. Without controls and censorship, Soviet leaders feared, educated workers would flee westward and counter-revolutionary ideas would spread, undermining social and economic stability.[46] The West's proposals on CBMs, in Soviet eyes, also went too far. All military questions, the Soviets argued, should be relegated to the MBFR talks.[47]

Overall, Baskets I and III proved the most troublesome in Geneva. The Western Allies even fell out among themselves, arguing about how hard to push the Soviet bloc. French officials warned that NATO's steep demands might prompt the Soviets to abandon the CSCE, ruining a golden opportunity for the West. At the other end of the spectrum, Dutch officials wanted NATO to present its most ambitious demands up front, and give ground only in exchange for Soviet concessions. For their part, the Americans did not regard the CSCE process as a vital national interest and stayed aloof from many of the debates, especially in Basket III. 'Take CSCE. We never believed in it', Kissinger said in February 1973. 'We want to get it over with. Otherwise people will think something really important is going on.'[48] Amid these arguments, Soviet diplomats tried to subjugate all issues to the primacy of state sovereignty, agreeing to discuss freer movement in Basket III but only so long as the discussion presumed 'full respect' for principles established in Basket I. In the Soviet view, the sovereignty proviso (placed first on the list of principles) would forestall all undesirable consequences.[49] In addition, Soviet diplomats proposed a preamble to Basket III that would subordinate the substantive provisions on freer movement to the prerogatives of sovereignty and the norm of non-interference in domestic affairs.

As they fought a diplomatic war of attrition, Western negotiators concluded that patience and unity offered the best hope of success. Moscow's desire for a successful conference, they reasoned, would eventually oblige Brezhnev and his colleagues to back down. The CBM negotiations similarly mired the negotiators in squabbles over parameters: how many troops would have to be involved in an exercise to require notification; how many days' advance notice would be required; and, crucially, to how much of the USSR's territory the rules should apply. The ferocity of Soviet resistance led some Western participants to doubt whether a deal could ever be reached. In the winter of 1974–5, the Geneva negotiations were stalemated across all three baskets. The prospects for an agreement looked bleak.

NEGOTIATIONS

Ironically, it was the deterioration of superpower relations that helped break through all these logjams and pave the way to the Helsinki summit. Understanding the CSCE endgame thus requires situating the pan-European dialogue within a broader panorama of Cold War politics. The weakening of America's position vis-à-vis the Soviets in 1974–5 helped push the Ford administration into stronger support of the CSCE process, in particular backing its European allies over a tough line on Basket III.

Soviet-American détente had been in decline since the Nixon-Brezhnev summits of 1972 and 1973. The president's resignation in August 1974 in the Watergate scandal removed one of détente's chief architects from the scene. His successor Gerald Ford was a caretaker president, which left Secretary of State Henry Kissinger as the main defender of détente's accomplishments.[50] Critics of the Soviet Union seized on Nixon's disgrace as their opportunity, none more so than Scoop Jackson, who railed against détente's amorality. Echoing Soviet dissidents like Andrei Sakharov and Aleksandr Solzhenitsyn, Jackson called détente an accommodation with totalitarianism and urged instead the promotion of human rights in the Soviet bloc.[51] As the 1970s progressed, the clamour against détente mounted. The midterm elections of November 1974 expanded the Democratic majority in Congress, which inclined towards idealism in foreign policy not hard-nosed pragmatism. 'Détente', wrote Zbigniew Brzezinski, a leading Democratic foreign-policy intellectual, 'is a conservative balance of power arrangement, devoid of any moral content'.[52]

Critics also indicted détente's pusillanimity. Arms control, especially the SALT I Interim Agreement of 1972, consigned the United States to parity with the Soviet Union, if not inferiority, critics argued. This concern animated a nascent neoconservative movement that Eugene Rostow's Coalition for a Democratic Majority exemplified. 'In terms of real defense capability', the Coalition proclaimed, 'the United States is . . . pursuing a policy of unilateral disarmament'.[53] This was hyperbole, but the technical compromises upon which military détente had been built lent credibility to the allegation. SALT I after all permitted the Soviet Union more intercontinental and submarine-launched ballistic missiles than the United States (2,347 against 1,710), although this was offset by wide margins of US superiority in other areas, such as heavy bombers (USA 450, USSR 155). Still, détente's ranks of critics would not tolerate any permanent arms control treaty that did not achieve numerical parity (the 1972 deal was a temporary arrangement). Kissinger's reluctant decision to seek clear numerical symmetry as part of SALT II at the Vladivostok summit in December 1974 (with missiles and heavy bombers limited to a total of 2,400 on each side) was a sign of the disfavour into which détente had fallen in America and the domestic political constraints on policy. Détente could only continue if the US administration was seen to be acting tough with the Kremlin.[54]

Meanwhile, the Cold War was hotting up across the Third World. In the Middle East the October 1973 war was contained but, as a result, Egypt shifted towards the American camp. Kissinger's general efforts in its aftermath to exclude Soviet influence from the Middle East frustrated Moscow, which bolstered its ties with Syria, Iraq, and Libya. Moscow also capitalized on opportunities afforded in southern Africa by the collapse of the Portuguese Empire, supporting Cuban troops engaged in a 'war of national liberation' in Angola.[55] Still, in March 1975, Kissinger felt that Angola was 'an aberration'. 'On the whole', he said, Moscow had 'stuck by détente'.[56] But this position was much harder to sustain after the debacle that spring in Indochina. Between March and August 1975 communist forces overran first Vietnam, then Laos, and finally Cambodia—bringing to a humiliating end a quarter century of American efforts to contain the red tide in Southeast Asia. The fall of Saigon enraged critics of détente in the United States.[57] Kissinger fumed that the domestic political context was becoming increasingly unfavourable to the easing of East-West tensions, and chafed at Moscow's support for Hanoi. 'We need to challenge the Soviet Union', Kissinger advised Ford in April. 'Détente is not consistent with what they have been doing in Southeast Asia.'[58] Kissinger himself took a hard public line in a speech in St Louis on 12 May. Developments in Vietnam and elsewhere represented 'a heavy mortgage on détente', Kissinger declared, as he espoused the black-and-white ideological binaries that high-ranking American officials had largely abandoned in the years of détente: 'We are not neutral in the struggle between freedom and tyranny.'[59] More substantively, Kissinger insisted that détente, in and of itself, was not Washington's foremost objective. Rather, the Ford administration considered 'our allies and friends our first priority'.[60] This line from his St Louis speech was pregnant with implications for CSCE. He and Ford wanted to avoid a rift in Soviet-American relations but they needed to show their toughness on Western concerns in tandem with their European allies.

During the winter of 1974–5 the Soviets had hoped to cut through the impasse in Geneva by getting the United States to impose upon the West Europeans a Final Act congruent with Moscow's expectations. Among the allies, Great Britain still ranked among the most obdurate, especially over Basket III. When Prime Minister Harold Wilson and Foreign Secretary James Callaghan visited Moscow in February 1975, Gromyko had tried 'to browbeat' them[61]—a tactic that, to the British, smacked of desperation. 'The Russians', British diplomats inferred, were 'in more of a hurry to complete the CSCE than they generally liked to admit'.[62] To prevail in areas of substantive disagreement, British diplomats now reasoned, the West should remain patient and united because Moscow's evident desperation for rapid resolution of the CSCE process would lead it to make concessions that would serve Western interests. These negotiating tactics placed a particular burden on Washington, which would have to take the lead in any tough NATO line. Days after Wilson and Callaghan left Moscow, Henry Kissinger arrived. Predictably, Gromyko enjoined Kissinger to bring the Geneva talks to a prompt conclusion. Could the United States not impose its 'authoritative word', Gromyko asked, and compel its allies to take 'a more realistic approach' to the CSCE? The secretary of state promised that Washington would seek to 'speed up the work of the European Security Conference', but he warned that adverse political currents at home were inhibiting the Ford administration from taking a 'too visibly active' role.[63]

Working behind closed doors, however, Kissinger was able to act as broker, especially to resolve the prolonged dispute between West Germany and the USSR over the language about peaceful change of borders. Moscow had already conceded that the Final Act would not describe borders as 'immutable' but there remained the issue of when and how borders might be changed. In Moscow, Kissinger and Gromyko confected a sentence that (almost) resolved the issue. 'Frontiers', it read, 'can be changed in accordance with international law, by peaceful means, and through agreement'.[64] After eventually adding, at Bonn's insistence, a comma after the word 'changed', Kissinger and Gromyko's text prefigured the resolution of the impasse over borders on terms agreeable to West Germany. At stake was not grammar but the range of circumstances under which Europe's post-1945 borders could be redrawn and Germany reunified. Thanks to European firmness and Kissinger's late démarche the Final Act would therefore incorporate a flexible formula on borders, rather than the absolute consecration of the territorial status quo that Moscow had sought when the CSCE started.

The end of the process was now coming into sight. During February and March 1975 Harold Wilson and President Valéry Giscard d'Estaing of France both suggested that a concluding heads-of-state summit could convene as soon as July 1975.[65] President Ford concurred in a letter to Brezhnev that noted the coincidence with the thirtieth anniversary of the end of World War

Two.[66] As a summer summit loomed, the critics circled. William Safire was among the sharpest. 'In case you haven't heard,' Safire wrote in April, 'World War II will soon be coming to its official end. The Russians won.'[67] Similarly Ronald Reagan, former California governor and prospective presidential candidate, called for the abandonment of the CSCE 'unless the Western nations are allowed uninhibited access...to the Eastern European nations'.[68] Against Reagan, Ford insisted that abandoning the CSCE would be counterproductive. 'If we didn't participate', the president asserted, 'it would appear that we were sulking and going back to the Cold War'.[69] Instead, as also urged by US negotiators in Geneva, he intended to use Soviet eagerness for a summer summit to extract final concessions that might appease his domestic critics and satisfy the Europeans.[70]

The success of this tactic would depend, in part, on talks between Henry Kissinger and Andrei Gromyko in Vienna in mid-May. Facilitating American efforts, the British delegation in Geneva had already formulated a 'global' solution to the various disputes over human rights and free movement and rallied the NATO countries behind it.[71] The encounter in Vienna was more caustic than usual. Gromyko lambasted the West's insistence on affirming freedom of information and for the press in the Final Act. 'That's a new one in international practice', he complained. Gromyko clearly understood the transformative implications of Basket III: 'We'd never accept broadcasting that undermined our system.' What had changed since earlier meetings was Kissinger's position. Unlike previous encounters, when he had ridiculed West European attachments to human rights and transnational contacts, the secretary of state now rebuffed Soviet complaints and blamed their negotiators for the lack of 'substantial progress' at Geneva. He warned bluntly that he was 'not optimistic' about the prospects of convening a summit in the summer of 1975. Moscow's attempt to drive a wedge between Washington and its European allies had clearly failed.

The Soviet Union responded to the British global proposal with a demand for broad and substantive revisions—a counterproposal that Kissinger dismissed as 'worthless and foolish'.[72] Henceforth, the NATO countries closed ranks, refusing to countenance further revisions. Kissinger now openly espoused the virtues of a 'hard-line position'.[73] 'No more concessions to the Soviet Union,' he told Ford: 'If they want a conference, let them concede'. Meeting with British, French, and German foreign ministers, Kissinger encouraged his allies to stand their ground.[74] Within a matter of weeks, the Soviets backed down with concessions that satisfied Western leaders but offered no cause for jubilation. The British global proposal had, after all, represented NATO's bottom line, not its maximal agenda. Meeting in Brussels, Kissinger and Callaghan concurred that Basket III's accomplishments were ultimately meagre and 'unenforceable'.[75]

Now CBMs remained the sole outstanding source of disagreement: should the CSCE's signatories notify each other in advance of military manoeuvres? The Soviet Union demanded more flexible parameters; the West, and Bonn in particular, favoured more onerous requirements, especially concerning the size of the zone, measured in distance from the border, for which notification would be required. Again Moscow appealed to Washington as broker; again the Americans would not play ball.[76] In late June the USSR finally accepted a Swedish compromise. This required countries to notify each other of military manoeuvres involving more than 25,000 troops taking place within 250 kilometres of international borders and within twenty-one days of the start of the exercises.[77] From NATO's vantage point, the compromise was acceptable, not optimal. Still, Moscow's desire to convene a summit in July 1975 had at least catalysed agreement on terms that the NATO countries including West Germany, could tolerate. With the dispute resolved, the long CSCE dialogue slouched towards Helsinki.

Meeting again in mid-July, Kissinger agreed with Gromyko that 'practically all questions have been agreed upon'.[78] By now Moscow had abandoned its long-standing demand for the inclusion of language on the universal expansion of MFN status, which was totally incompatible with the Jackson-Vanik amendment. At the last minute an unforeseen and bizarre obstacle nonetheless emerged when tiny Malta demanded a reframing of the proposed Mediterranean Declaration. The country's prime minister, Dom Mintoff, wanted the CSCE to enter into dialogue with *all* countries bordering the Mediterranean and to seek the reduction of armed forces in the region. The Maltese bid for influence united Gromyko and Kissinger in disdain for 'Mintoff the Terrible'—even joking about assassination—but this did not resolve the real dilemma that Mintoff posed.[79] While Gromyko favoured ignoring his demands and convening the Helsinki summit without him, Kissinger worried that excluding Malta would violate 'the consensus rule prevailing in the conference', alienate other small countries, and throw the CSCE process into new deadlock. To avoid this danger, the NATO countries agreed to accept Malta's proposal and the Soviets acquiesced.[80] With this deal, the Geneva negotiations ended, and the CSCE proceeded to Stage III: the summit that would approve the Final Act and establish a new European security order.

SIGNING

When the thirty-five heads of state and government convened in Helsinki at the end of July, little more had to be decided (see Figure 4.2). After Stage I in Helsinki had prepared for the talks, Stage II in Geneva had defined the substance of the Final Act. All that remained was for the assembled leaders

Fig. 4.2. Helsinki summit, Finlandia Hall, 1 August 1975 (AP)

to affix their signatures to the accords. But, rather than being a binding treaty, the Helsinki Final Act had the status of a political declaration. Indeed, upon completion, the Finnish government transmitted the document to the United Nations with the stipulation that 'neither the final act nor any of the documents referred to in it are treaties or international agreements'.[81] This ranked among the most important of the details negotiated during Stage II, especially for the Ford administration, which for domestic reasons could not risk the Final Act being misinterpreted as a binding treaty. Most of this highly choreographed summit was devoted to speeches, with each leader allowed twenty minutes, and concluded with a signing ceremony, at which the heads of state and government sat on the stage in French alphabetical order. This meant that the two Germanies were placed next to each other. In essence, Helsinki would be pro forma event, a rite of consecration upon the diplomats' work. The only opportunities for improvisation at this pre-fabricated gathering would be offstage, in the informal talks conducted on the margins of the summit and in the language used by the leaders in their addresses in Finlandia Hall. These would have a significance of their own.

For both Brezhnev and Ford the Final Act and the Helsinki summit served complex and rather different purposes. Even if the USSR had conceded substantive ground during the preparatory talks, especially on Basket III, Brezhnev had achieved in Basket I a long-sought objective—*de facto* recognition of the 1945 frontiers—that had eluded his predecessors. Crucially, Brezhnev would be able to open the Twenty-Fifth Congress of the Communist Party of the Soviet Union in February 1976 with a landmark diplomatic accomplishment to his credit. American Sovietologists hoped that this achievement would cement Brezhnev's authority and his policy of détente against such rivals as KGB chief Yuri Andropov.[82] For the Ford administration, in contrast, the signature of the Final Act promised only to weaken the president's position at home. Ford went to Helsinki despite strong domestic pressure to abstain because he believed that détente depended on it. He and Kissinger considered the Final Act to be a fair compromise that achieved 'modest' gains for the West, rather than the sellout blasted by the sceptics. They struggled to convey their message to the public but, ultimately for Ford and Kissinger, marketing Helsinki itself was a lower priority than sustaining the momentum of détente, which Ford attempted to do in two bilateral meetings with Brezhnev.

The two superpower leaders met twice on the summit's sidelines. These encounters offered opportunities to reflect upon the past, present, and future of Soviet-American relations.[83] For his part, Ford stressed both his commitment to East-West dialogue and the relaxation of tension, while emphasizing the force of the adverse headwinds at home. 'We have those on the right as well as on the left', Ford declared, who 'would like to undermine what we have tried to implement'. He added: 'I came here despite the criticism in the United States, because I believe in detente.' Brezhnev expressed his appreciation of the president's efforts. 'We in the Soviet leadership are supporters of your election', he said, and 'will do everything we can to make that happen'. Progress on strategic arms control was nonetheless elusive in Helsinki: mutual goodwill aside, the delegations remained deadlocked over technical issues. Ford held out the prospect of a summit at Camp David, the presidential retreat, in the fall of 1975 but the impasse on arms control made this seem a remote prospect. In bilateral superpower relations, Helsinki would prove a plateau, not a way-station on the path to higher ground. After Helsinki, Ford and Brezhnev would never meet again.

More significant at Helsinki were the talks that Ford held with his British, French, and West German counterparts. Meeting at the British ambassador's residence, the West's leading statesmen reflected on the Final Act, which they judged a success. But then they debated their common predicament of 'economic and social disorder and rising unemployment' following the 1973-4 oil shocks.[84] The 'self-evident inability' of governments 'to do anything in the face of this crisis', warned French president Valéry Giscard d'Estaing, was 'a serious weakness for the West', upon which the USSR would 'play'. West German Chancellor Helmut Schmidt circulated a 'private memorandum' arguing for concerted international action to address 'economic problems' that were, he asserted, 'a greater threat to the West than the Soviet Union'.[85] Schmidt urged Ford: 'Your strong leadership is needed'. The president then endorsed the proposals of Giscard and Schmidt for an economic summit of the leading capitalist countries.[86] And so at Helsinki the leaders of the West started to pursue collaborative solutions to their shared dilemmas. Helsinki precipitated the Rambouillet Summit of November 1975, in which Japan and Italy also participated, and the subsequent annual economic summits of the so-called Group of Seven (G7).

In a larger sense Helsinki did prove a pivot of world politics, although not in the way that Brezhnev had intended. Whereas summits between adversaries—Erfurt/Kassel, Beijing, and Moscow—had defined world politics in the early 1970s, summits between allies—especially the G7 meetings and Guadeloupe 'Big Four' (chapter 5)—would characterize the second half of the decade, as détente soured, capitalism faltered, and the industrialized countries collaborated to manage the uncertainties that accompanied economic globalization.[87]

The real action took place in these private bilaterals, but the public speeches in Finlandia Hall highlighted the different meanings attached by various actors to the Final Act. Stage II had decreed that the order of the speeches would be chosen by lot, and so Harold Wilson opened the proceedings. Proclaiming 'freedom and peace' to be 'indivisible', the British prime minister defended Basket III, elaborating the dynamic détente concept the West European countries had championed at the CSCE.[88] 'Détente', he declared, 'means little if it is not reflected in the daily lives of our peoples'. Later on Brezhnev naturally took a contrasting view. International peace, he insisted, depended upon governments abiding by 'the correct and just principles of relations among States'. None should try to dictate to another 'the manner in which they ought to manage their internal affairs'.[89] Thus, for all the strenuous diplomacy of the past three years, the fundamental rationale of the CSCE remained ambiguous. The Final Act remained, in a certain sense, an empty document, whose substantive meaning would have to be defined by future actions and choices on the international stage.

Ford's remarks manifested not only the paradoxes inherent within the Final Act but also the tensions that had from the outset bedevilled US policy towards the CSCE. The initial draft of the president's speech, prepared by the State Department, was cautious, even deferential when it came to Soviet bugbears like freedom of movement and human rights. Unwilling to acquiesce in a Soviet concept of détente and concerned about 'how his words would sound at home', Ford decided to take a tougher rhetorical stand. He asked his counsellor and speechwriter Robert Hartmann to devise an alternative to the State Department's 'diplomatic gobbledygook'.[90] Hartman did so, with considerable presidential input. The revised address paid obeisance to 'non-intervention, sovereign equality...territorial integrity, [and] inviolability of borders', but Ford enveloped these commitments within a transformative vision of détente. 'It is important', he declared, focusing on Brezhnev, 'that you recognize the deep devotion of the American people and their Government to human rights and fundamental freedoms'.[91] The audience in Finlandia Hall gave Ford a standing ovation. The president would nonetheless struggle to convey a transformative vision of Helsinki to American voters.

*　*　*　*　*

Reflecting on Helsinki summit at the end of the twentieth century, Kissinger rounded on its critics. 'The peoples of Eastern Europe', he concluded, were 'demonstrably better off' as a result because the accords cracked the Soviet bloc open to the West's liberalizing influence.[92] The Final Act, Kissinger asserted with hindsight, had emboldened critics within the Warsaw Pact countries. When, for instance, a group of Czechoslovak dissidents constituted themselves as Charter 77 two years after Helsinki, they called upon their government to honour the commitments it had made when signing the Universal Declaration of Human Rights and the Helsinki Final Act. This was more or less what the champions of progressive détente had envisaged although Kissinger, an advocate of stable spheres of influence, had not himself embraced such a conception of the Final Act until late in the process. Only under pressure from domestic critics, West European allies, his own representatives in Geneva, and, ultimately, the president whom he served, did Kissinger come around in the last months of the CSCE saga to accept the transformative conception of the Final Act. Helsinki, in the end, did much to advance West Europe's more dynamic approach to détente that was distinct in crucial respects from the narrow, transactional relationship that the superpowers had established in their détente of the early 1970s.

In the context of the Cold War, Helsinki was *sui generis*. This was a much vaster undertaking than any other summit, whose enormous scope at times almost became its undoing—as was the case when Dom Mintoff, who represented fewer people than the mayor of Helsinki, nearly derailed the negotiations at the eleventh hour. Also unlike other summits, the diplomacy that culminated in Finlandia Hall had evolved across multiple sites, involved hundreds of diplomats from thirty-five countries, and dragged on for two-and-a-half years. Its formalism was at odds with the creativity of past bilateral summits, but the informal and private encounters in the wings of Helsinki—especially the quadripartite conversation at the British ambassador's residence—offered a pattern that Giscard, Ford, Schmidt, and Wilson would try to replicate at Rambouillet a few months later in November.

Viewed within the thawing of East-West relations in the 1970s, the Helsinki Summit emerged in part from the Soviet-American détente that Nixon and Brezhnev had pioneered. This found its fullest expression in the arms control agreements signed in Moscow in 1972. Superpower détente unfolded amid a Sino-American rapprochement that had the effect of triangulating the Cold War's core rivalries and pushing the Kremlin to consolidate its East European sphere of influence.[93] Meanwhile, West European leaders sought an alternative, dynamic détente that aimed not only to stabilize the Cold War but eventually to transcend it. Contact diplomacy at the European level, notably but not exclusively Brandt's *Ostpolitik*, was intended to pierce and erode the Iron Curtain at a human level. So one might say that superpower détente framed the CSCE process but the West European countries steered its course, inserting language affirming human rights and universal freedoms as basic commitments for European international politics. Brezhnev signed the Final Act because he presumed, wrongly, that these concessions in Basket III were inconsequential compared with what he had got in Basket I and because he was determined, for domestic political reasons, to complete the CSCE before the end of 1975. Ford signed the Final Act because he believed it was necessary to sustain the momentum of détente and because he hoped, erroneously, that American voters would, in the end, appreciate Helsinki's transformative potential. Both men would be proven wrong. Far from affirming the Brezhnev doctrine, Helsinki helped over the next fifteen years to weaken the USSR's grip on Eastern Europe. Voters in the United States nonetheless concluded that 'we lost in Helsinki', in the words of Jimmy Carter, Ford's successful opponent in the 1976 presidential election. But in time the leaders of the West, including Gerald Ford, who gambled at Helsinki on human freedom and hoped to overcome Cold War divisions, would win some vindication through the revolutions of 1989.

NOTES

1. Memorandum of Brezhnev-Ford Conversation, 30 July 1975, *Foreign Relations of the United States, 1969–1976, vol. E-15, Documents on Western Europe, 1973–1976* (henceforth *FRUS, 1969–1976, vol. E-15*), https://history.state.gov/historicaldocuments/frus 1969-76ve15p2, doc. 329.
2. L. Brezhnev, 'Speech at the Helsinki Conference on Security and Cooperation in Europe', in Leonid Brezhnev, *Peace, Détente, and Soviet-American Relations: A Collection of Public Statements* (New York, 1979), 98.
3. Yu. Zhukov and Yu. Kuznetsov, 'Pobeda Razuma', *Pravda*, 2 August 1975, 7.
4. 'Ford vs. Solzhenitsyn II', *New York Times*, 24 July 1975, 23.
5. 'Jerry, Don't Go', *Wall Street Journal*, 23 July 1975, 14.
6. 'Super Yalta', *New York Times*, 28 July 1975, 21.
7. 'European Security . . .', *New York Times*, 21 July 1975, 14.
8. 'Solzhenitsyn Warns Congress of Pacts', *Los Angeles Times*, 16 July 1975, B11.
9. See, for example, George W. Bush, 'Statement on the 30th Anniversary of the Helsinki Final Act', 1 August 2005, http://georgewbush-whitehouse.archives.gov/news/releases/2005/08/20050801-3.html; Henry Kissinger, *Years of Renewal* (New York, 1999), 635–63; Daniel Thomas, *The Helsinki Effect: International Norms, Human Rights, and the Demise of Communism* (Princeton, NJ, 2001); Sarah B. Snyder, *Human Rights Activism and the End of the Cold War: A Transnational History of the Helsinki Network* (New York, 2011).
10. Thomas Fischer, '"A Mustard Seed Grew into a Bushy Tree": The Finnish CSCE initiative of 5 May 1969', *Cold War History* 9 no. 2 (2009), 177–201; Thomas Fischer, *Neutral Power in the CSCE: The N+N States and the Making of the Helsinki Accords 1975* (Baden-Baden, 2009).

11. Matthew J. Ouimet, *The Rise and Fall of the Brezhnev Doctrine in Soviet Foreign Policy* (Chapel Hill, NC, 2003).
12. Lorenz M. Lüthi, *The Sino-Soviet Split: Cold War in the Communist World* (Princeton, NJ, 2008), 340–4.
13. Alec Nove, *An Economic History of the USSR, 1917–1991* (New York, 3rd edn, 1992), 378–93.
14. Frédéric Bozo, 'Détente versus Alliance: France, the United States and the Politics of the Harmel Report (1964–1968)', *Contemporary European History* 7, no. 3 (1998), 343–60.
15. Georges-Henri Soutou, 'La décision française de quitter le commandement intégré de l'OTAN (1966)', in Hans-Joachim Harder, ed., *Von Truman bis Harmel: Die Bundesrepublik Deutschland im Spannungsfeld von NATO und europäischer Integration* (Munich, 2000), 185–208.
16. Andreas Wenger, 'Crisis and Opportunity: NATO's Transformation and the Multilateralization of Détente, 1966–1968', *Journal of Cold War Studies* 6, no. 1 (2004), 22–74.
17. Daniel J. Sargent, *A Superpower Transformed: The Remaking of American Foreign Relations in the 1970s* (New York, 2014), esp. 59–67.
18. Timothy Garton Ash, *In Europe's Name: Germany and the Divided Continent* (New York, 1993), 65ff.
19. Archives du Ministère des Affaires Étrangères, Paris (henceforth AMAE), Secrétariat général—Entretiens et Messages—vol. 40, Pompidou-Nixon Memcon, 24 February 1970.
20. Politburo Memorandum from Andrei Gromyko, 27 August 1969. Rossiiskii Gosudarstvennyi Arkhiv Noveishei Istorii, Moscow, F. 3, Op. 72, D. 287, Direktivy dlya dvustoronnikh konsul'tatsii so stranami-uchastnitsami Varshavskogo dogovora i dlya soveshchaniya ministrov inostrannykh del etikh stran po voprosam, svyazannym s sozyvom Obshcheevropeiskogo soveshchaniya.
21. National Archives and Record Administration, College Park, Maryland (henceforth NARA), RG 59, Executive Secretariat Conference Files, 1966–1972, Box 488, Memorandum from Rogers to Nixon, Your Participation in the NATO Ministerial Meeting (10–11 April 1969), 7 April 1969; AMAE, Secrétariat général—Entretiens et Messages—vol. 37, Rogers-Debré Memcon, 9 April 1969; Nixon Presidential Materials Project, College Park, Maryland (henceforth NPMP), NSC Files, Box 709, Memorandum from Kissinger to Nixon, Soviet Initiative for a European Security Conference, 4 April 1969.
22. NARA, RG 59, Subject Numeric Files, 1970–73, Box 1703, Current West European Attitudes toward a European Security Conference, 3 April 1969; and, Telegram from Oslo to the State Department, 8 January 1970.
23. AMAE, Affaires Étrangères—Fonds EU—Organismes Internationaux et Grandes Questions Internationales—Sécurité, 1966–70, 2032, Memorandum, Problèmes posés par l'éventuelle convocation d'une Conférence sur la Sécurité Européenne, 20 November 1969.
24. Memorandum from Kissinger to Nixon, Brezhnev on Mutual Troop Reductions in Europe, 15 May 1971, *FRUS 1969–1976, vol. xxxix, European Security* (henceforth *FRUS 1969–76, vol. xxxix*), https://history.state.gov/historicaldocuments/

frus1969-76v39, doc. 49; and Henry Kissinger, *White House Years* (Boston, 1979), 1124–64.

25. NARA, RG 59, Executive Secretariat Conference Files, 1966–1972, Box 488, Briefing paper by J.G. MacCracken, European Security Conference, 3 April 1969; AMAE, Affaires Étrangères—Fonds EU—Organismes Internationaux et Grandes Questions Internationales—Sécurité, 1966–70, 2036, Telegram from Quai d'Orsay to Moscow, 4 July 1969; Archives Nationales, Paris, 5 AG 2/1010, Pompidou-Brandt Memcon, 30 January 1970.

26. Stenogramm des Freundschaftstreffens führender Vertreter der kommunistischen und Arbeiterparteien der sozialistischen Länder, 31 July 1972, Parallel History Project on Cooperative Security (henceforth PHP).

27. Stenogramm des Freundschaftstreffens führender Vertreter der kommunistischen und Arbeiterparteien der sozialistischen Länder, 31 July 1972, PHP.

28. 'Memorandum from Kissinger to Nixon, Conversation with Soviet Ambassador Dobrynin', 22 December 1969, in David C. Geyer and Douglas E. Selvage, eds, *Soviet-American Relations: The Détente Years, 1969–1972* (Washington, DC, 2007).

29. Politisches Archiv des Auswärtigen Amts, Berlin (henceforth PAAA), Bestand MfAA, C 374/78, MfAA Memorandum, Argumentationshinweise zu den beiliegenden Schluβempfehlungen der Konsultation über die Vorbereitung der Sicherheitskonferenz in Helsinki, n.d. [June 1973]; The National Archives, Kew, London (henceforth TNA), FCO 41/1303, Telegram from Elliott, UK Embassy in Helsinki, to Douglas-Home, FCO, CSCE/MPT: Meeting of Political Directors on 24 and 25 May: Principles, 23 May 1973.

30. PAAA, B28 111547, Auswärtiges Amt Memorandum, Sprechzettel für die Sitzung des KSZE-Unterausschusses am 17./18.7.73 in Kopenhagen, 10 July 1973; TNA, FCO 41/1304, Minute from Burns, WOD, to Gordon, TRD, CSCE Principles, 20 August 1973.

31. NPMP, HAK Office Files, Box 76, Kissinger-Brezhnev Memcon, 25 March 1974.

32. TNA, FCO 33/2365, Elliott, UK Mission in Geneva, to James, FCO, CSCE: German and Berlin Problems, 18 July 1974.

33. NPMP, NSC Files, Box 709, Memorandum from Kissinger to Nixon, Soviet Initiative for a European Security Conference, 4 April 1969; PAAA, B28 109306, Memorandum from von Groll, Konferenz über die Sicherheit und Zusammenarbeit in Europa: Politische Aspekte der Sicherheit, 7 January 1971.

34. NARA, RG 59, Central Foreign Policy Files, 1970–3, Box 2264, US Delegation to NATO to the State Department, East-Est [sic] Negotiations Study: Principles Governing Relations between States, 4 November, 1971. See also PAAA, B28 109306, Memorandum from the West German Delegation to NATO, Eventual CSCE agenda item on the improvement of interstate relations by adopting a conference document on principles governing relations between states, 10 August 1972.

35. TNA, FCO 41/1307, Minute by UK Mission in Geneva, Note for the Record: Sub-Committee 1 (Principles), 22 November 1973.

36. Speech by Andrei Gromyko, in Igor I. Kavass, Jacqueline Paquin Granier, and Mary Frances Dominick, eds, *Human Rights, European Politics, and the Helsinki*

Accord: The Documentary Evolution of the Conference on Security and Co-operation in Europe, 1973–1975, Vol. I (Buffalo, NY, 1981), 47.

37. TNA, FCO 28/2168, Memorandum from Fall to Solesby, CSCE: Human Rights, 19 October 1973; TNA, FCO 41/1306, Letter from Bishop, UK Mission in Geneva, to Burns, FCO, CSCE: Sub-Committee I: Principles, 12 October 1973. Stiftung Archiv der Parteien und Massenorganisationen der DDR im Bundesarchiv, Berlin (henceforth SAPMO), DY 30/J IV 2/2/1501, GDR Politburo Memorandum, Bericht über die 2. Phase der Konferenz für Sicherheit und Zusammenarbeit in Europa (Stand: 5. April 1974) und Direktive für das weitere Auftreten der Delegation der DDR, 23 April 1974.

38. TNA, FCO 41/1307, Minute by UK Mission in Geneva, Note for the Record: Sub-Committee I (Principles), 26 November 1973.

39. Rede des Leiters der sowjetischen Delegation auf der Tagung des Politischen Beratenden Ausschusses, Genossen L.I. Breschnew, in Prag, 25 January 1972, PHP.

40. AMAE, CSCE 1969–1975, Box 27, Pour le Ministre de la part de JP Brunet, 17 October 1972; and Garton Ash, *In Europe's Name*, 249.

41. TNA, FCO 41/1060, Project de rapport du Groupe Ad Hoc au Comité Politique (IIème partie), 24 October 1972.

42. TNA, FCO 30/2484, Minute from Key to Cloake, CSCE: Commercial Exchanges Sub-Committee: MFN, 4 April 1974. Noam Kochavi, 'Insights Abandoned, Flexibility Lost: Kissinger, Soviet Jewish Emigration, and the Demise of Détente', *Diplomatic History* 29, no. 3 (June 2005), 503–30; Kissinger, *Years of Renewal*, 305–6.

43. TNA, FCO 28/2458, Memorandum from Tickell to Wiggin and Goulding, CSCE: Basket III, 15 March 1974.

44. G. Bennett and K. Hamilton, eds, *Documents on British Policy Overseas: The Conference on Security and Co-operation in Europe, 1972–1975, series III, vol. 2* (London, 1997) (hereafter *DBPO III, vol. 2*), doc. 9.

45. On the rationale for Eisenhower's Open Skies proposal, see James J. Marquardt, 'Transparency and Security Competition: Open Skies and America's Cold War Statecraft, 1948–1960', *Journal of Cold War Studies* 9, no. 1 (Winter 2007), 55–87.

46. Comrade Todor Zhivkov's Speech at the Meeting of the Warsaw Treaty's Political Consultative Committee in Prague, 25 January 1972, PHP. See also MfAA Memorandum: About Some Current Questions Concerning the Multilateral Preparations for the European Security Conference, 18 October 1972, http://digitalarchive.wilsoncenter.org/document/110100.

47. NPMP, HAK Office Files, Box 70, Anatoly Dobrynin Memorandum, Talking Points with Dr Kissinger (all-European conference), n.d. [16 January 1973]; *DBPO III, vol. 2*, doc. 21.

48. TNA, FCO 41/1284, Telegram from Douglas-Home, FCO, to UK Embassy in Helsinki, Meeting of Political Directors on 14 May: CSCE: Baskets I, II, and III, 16 May 1973; AMAE, Affaires Étrangères—Organismes Internationaux et Grandes Questions Internationales—Sécurité, 1971–1976, 2926, Telegram from the French Embassy in the Hague to the Quai d'Orsay, Attitude néerlandaise à l'égard de la CSCE, 5 July 1973. Memorandum of Kissinger-Thorn Conversation, 21 February 1973, *FRUS 1969–76, vol. xxxix*, doc. 129. For more on US views, see Sargent, *A Superpower Transformed*, 215–17.

49. TNA, FCO 28/2172, Telegram from Elliott, Helsinki, to FCO, CSCE/MPT: Basket III, 29 March 1973; PAAA, B28 111543, Auswärtiges Amt Memorandum, MV-KSZE, Korb III, (menschliche Kontakte, Kulturaustausch, Informationsfluß): Einleitung des Mandats, 25 April 1973; 'Final Recommendations of the Helsinki Consultations, 8 June 1973', in Great Britain: Foreign and Commonwealth Office, ed., *Selected Documents Relating to Problems of Security and Cooperation in Europe, 1954–77* (London, 1977), 149–51.

50. Kissinger stresses Watergate's disruptive consequences for foreign policy in his book, *Years of Upheaval* (Boston, 1982), 1030–1.

51. On human rights in the 1970s, see, inter alia, Barbara Keys, *Reclaiming American Virtue: The Human Rights Revolution of the 1970s* (Cambridge, MA, 2014). Insider accounts emphasize preoccupation with the Soviet Union, as do Jeri Laber, *The Courage of Strangers: Coming of Age with the Human Rights Movement* (New York, 2005) and Aryeh Neier, *The International Human Rights Movement: A History* (Princeton, NJ, 2012).

52. Jimmy Carter Presidential Library, Atlanta, Georgia (henceforth JCL), Zbigniew Brzezinski Materials, Trilateral Commission File, Box 1, Zbigniew Brzezinski to Sidney Hertzberg, 7 November 1973.

53. JCL, Campaign Files (1976), Issues Office (Eizenstat), Foreign Policy, Box 16, Coalition for a Democratic Majority, Task Force on Foreign Policy, Statement No. 2, For an Adequate Defense. On the Coalition, see Justin Vaïsse, *Neoconservatism: The Biography of a Movement* (Cambridge, MA, 2010).

54. For a table on 'aggregate strategic force limits' based on US Senate hearings, see Zbigniew Brzezinski, *Power and Principle: Memoirs of the National Security Adviser 1977–81* (London, 1983), 163; Kissinger, *Years of Upheaval*, 1173.

55. On Soviet reactions to US policy in the Middle East, see Raymond L. Garthoff, *Détente and Confrontation: American-Soviet relations from Nixon to Reagan* (Washington, DC, 1985), 442–57; and Vladislav Zubok, *A Failed Empire: The Soviet Union in the Cold War from Stalin to Gorbachev* (Chapel Hill, NC, 2007), 240–1. On Soviet policy in Angola, see Odd Arne Westad, *The Global Cold War: Third World Interventions and the Making of Our Times* (Cambridge, 2005), 218–41, and Piero Gleijeses, *Visions of Freedom: Havana, Washington, Pretoria, and the Struggle for Southern Africa, 1976–1991* (Chapel Hill, NC, 2013), 25–31.

56. Gerald Ford Presidential Library, Ann Arbor, Michigan (henceforth GFPL), National Security Adviser Files, Box 18, Memorandum of Conversation between Ford, Kissinger, Rumsfeld, Scowcroft, and Cheney, 8 March 1975.

57. Memorandum from Sonnenfeldt to Kissinger, 16 April 1975, *FRUS 1969–1976, vol. xvi, Soviet Union, August 1974–December 1976* (henceforth *FRUS 1969–76, vol. xvi*), https://history.state.gov/historicaldocuments/frus1969-76v16, doc. 142.

58. Minutes of NSC Meeting, 9 April 1975, *FRUS 1969–1976, vol. x, Vietnam, January 1973–July 1975*, https://history.state.gov/historicaldocuments/frus1969-76v10, doc. 212.

59. Henry Kissinger, 'The Challenge of Peace', 12 May 1975, in *Department of State Bulletin* 72, no. 705 (1975), 705–12.

60. Ibid.

61. *DBPO III, vol. 2,* doc. 112.

62. *DBPO III, vol. 2*, doc. 113.
63. Memcon, Gromyko-Kissinger, 16 February 1975 and Memcon, Gromyko-Kissinger et al., 17 February 1975, FRUS *1969–76, vol. xxxix*, docs 270 and 271.
64. Memorandum from the Counselor of the Department of State (Sonnenfeldt) to Secretary of State Kissinger, 28 September 1974, *FRUS 1969–76, vol. xxxix*, doc. 252.
65. Levin, 'Backslaps in Moscow'; 'Soviet Union and France Make Détente Pledge', *The Times*, 25 March 1975, 9.
66. Letter from President Ford to Soviet General Secretary Brezhnev, 1 March 1975, *FRUS 1969–76, vol. xxxix*, doc. 276.
67. William Safire, 'Ending World War II', *New York Times*, 14 April 1975, 31.
68. Ronald Reagan, 'West Should Bolster Defense', *Los Angeles Times*, 25 May 1975, C3.
69. Editorial Note, *FRUS 1969–76, vol. xxxix*, doc. 281.
70. Memorandum from Denis Clift of the National Security Council Staff to Secretary of State Kissinger, 16 May 1975, *FRUS 1969–76, vol. xxxix*, doc. 282.
71. Minutes of Secretary of State Kissinger's Staff Meeting, 16 May 1975, *FRUS 1969–76, vol. xxxix*, doc. 283; and *DBPO III, vol. 2*, docs 119–22.
72. Memcon, Schmidt-Kissinger et al., 21 May 1975, *FRUS 1969–76, vol. xxxix*, doc. 289.
73. Memcon, Ford-Kissinger-Scowcroft, 26 May 1975, *FRUS 1969–76, vol. xvi*, doc. 153.
74. Memcon, Quadripartite Breakfast on Berlin, 28 May 1975, *FRUS 1969–76, vol. xxxix*, doc. 293.
75. Editorial Note, *FRUS 1969–76, vol. xxxix*, doc. 295.
76. For the bilateral back-and-forth, see Oral Message from Brezhnev to Ford, undated, Telcon: Kissinger-Dobrynin, 17 June, 1975, and Note from Ford to Brezhnev, undated, *FRUS 1969–76, vol. xxxix*, docs. 303, 307–8.
77. *DBPO III, vol. 2*, no. 127.
78. Memcon, Luns and NATO Perm. Representatives at the White House, 19 June 1975, *FRUS 1969–76, vol. xxxix*, doc. 310.
79. Minutes of Secretary of State Kissinger's Staff Meeting, 7 July 1975 and Editorial Note, *FRUS 1969–76, vol. xxxix*, docs 311 and 315.
80. Editorial Note and Telegram from the Mission in Geneva to the Department of State, 21 July, 1975, *FRUS 1969–76, vol. xxxix*, docs. 317–8. See also section in the Helsinki Final Act 'Questions relating to Security and Co-operation in the Mediterranean', http://www.osce.org/mc/39501?download=true.
81. Telegram from the Mission in Geneva to the Department of State, 21 July 1975, *FRUS 1969–76, vol. xxxix*, doc. 318.
82. For Andropov's critique, see *FRUS 1969–1976, vol. xxxix*, doc. 304; and Anatoly Dobrynin, *In Confidence: Moscow's Ambassador to Six Cold War Presidents (1962–1986)* (New York, 1995).
83. GFPL, National Security Adviser Files, Kissinger Memcons and Reports, USSR Memcons and Reports, Box 1, Brezhnev Memcons, Helsinki, 1975.
84. Sommet monétaire, Extract from French record of Quadripartite Lunch, 31 July 1975, Margaret Thatcher Foundation website, http://www.margaretthatcher.org/document/110973.

85. Private Memorandum on International Concertation of Economic Action by Schmidt, undated, *FRUS 1969–1976, vol. xxxi, Foreign Economic Policy, 1973–1976* (henceforth *FRUS 1969–76, vol. xxxi*), https://history.state.gov/historicaldocuments/frus1969-76v31, doc. 95.

86. Memcon, Schmidt-Ford et al., 27 July 1975, *FRUS 1969–76, vol. xxxi,* doc. 94.

87. Sargent, *A Superpower Transformed*, esp. 165–260. On summits, see, inter alia, George de Menil and Anthony M. Solomon, *Economic Summitry* (New York, 1983); Robert D. Putnam and Nicholas Bayne, *Hanging Together: The Seven-Power Summits* (London, 1984); and Michael C. Webb, *The Political Economy of Policy Coordination: International Adjustment since 1945* (Ithaca, NY, 1995).

88. Wilson speech, 30 July 1975, http://www.cvce.eu/obj/discours_de_harold_wilson_helsinki_30_juillet_1975-fr-49805ee6-3bda-4149-bf17-b7be2241af79.html.

89. Brezhnev speech, 31 July 1975, http://www.cvce.eu/obj/discours_de_leonid_brejnev_helsinki_31_juillet_1975-fr-3567f2ca-a5f7-464d-9336-763edc090f0d.html.

90. Robert T. Hartmann, *Palace Politics: An Inside Account of the Ford Years* (New York, 1980), 342–5.

91. Gerald Ford, Address in Helsinki, 1 August 1975, The American Presidency Project website, http://www.presidency.ucsb.edu/ws/index.php?pid=5137&st=&st1=.

92. Kissinger, *Years of Renewal*, 652.

93. Chinese diplomats opposed the CSCE from beginning to end.

5

Bonn, Guadeloupe, and Vienna, 1978–9

Kristina Spohr and David Reynolds

It looked like a fun occasion. Four middle-aged men, sitting around the table in a beach hut in the Caribbean, as if waiting for their first round of drinks (see Figure 5.1). But the so-called 'sunshine summit' was actually serious business, bringing together the 'Big Four' of the Western world. Valéry Giscard d'Estaing and Jimmy Carter, the presidents of France and the United States, together with Prime Minister James Callaghan of Britain and West German Chancellor Helmut Schmidt met on the Caribbean island of Guadeloupe in the New Year of 1979 to review Alliance relations in the context of a deteriorating international situation. Détente was in decline, superpower arms-control discussions had become bogged down, and the Soviets were expanding their influence in Africa and Asia, as well as building up their conventional and nuclear forces in Europe.

The years 1978–9 marked a transitional phase in the evolution of Cold War summitry. Superpower summits did continue, albeit sporadically because of Soviet-American discord: Vienna in July 1979 was in fact the long-awaited successor to Moscow in May 1972, concluding the Strategic Arms Limitation Treaty (SALT II). But alongside East-West meetings, new West-West summitry was emerging—addressing economic problems through the Group of Seven (G7) process, notably the Bonn meeting of July 1978, and grappling with strategic issues, in the case of the Guadeloupe Four in January 1979. These gatherings among Western leaders were deliberately informal—to facilitate a franker and more spontaneous dialogue than was possible in set-piece summits such as the three meetings discussed in the first part of this book. And they were intended to shore up the West in an increasingly turbulent world—amid global economic crisis, worsening superpower relations, and the uncertainties engendered by the rise of China. They also represented an attempt by the leading powers of Western Europe to exert greater influence on American policy and thereby on superpower relations, especially over issues of European security.

Fig. 5.1. Summitry on the Beach: Schmidt, Carter, Callaghan, and Giscard at Guadeloupe, 5 January 1990 (Jimmy Carter Library)

In 1978–9 international relations were also on the cusp, between the waning of détente and the onset of a 'New Cold War'. Helsinki 1975 had marked the apogee of hopes for a fundamental change in the nature of relations across the 'Iron Curtain', the aspiration of living together on the same continent according to mutually agreed principles. As the decade progressed, however, the West's high hopes of further rapprochement with the East evaporated. Summitry at the end of the 1970s was about living with the Cold War in a different sense: the West was trying to cope with the challenges of an increasingly tense and unpredictable world.

G7 SUMMITRY AND GLOBAL ECONOMIC GOVERNANCE

The roots of the G7 go back at least to 27 July 1975, just before the Helsinki summit, when Schmidt met the then American president, Gerald Ford, in Bonn. They discussed the recent public statement by Giscard about the urgent need for an 'international economic summit' among the leaders of the main Western industrial countries to address the global economic crisis— double-digit inflation, stagnant growth, and politically dangerous levels of unemployment, not seen in the West since the Great Depression of the 1930s. Schmidt stressed his agreement with the French president, adding: 'Giscard says what I have been saying since a year ago'. Indeed at the NATO Council in June 1974 the chancellor had emphasized that the 'very, very grave dangers' of the world economy were as vital for the security of the Western Alliance as more familiar issues of East-West arms talks. To Ford, Schmidt underlined the broader repercussions of the worldwide recession: 'The West is undergoing the greatest political crisis since World War Two. The functioning of the democratic industrial nations is at stake.' If this were a political or military crisis, Schmidt went on, 'the leaders would get together and act. Since it is economic, we leave it to our finance ministers.' But, he warned, 'if we leave it this way for five years, there will be a political disaster'.[1]

The Ford-Schmidt discussion on 27 July set the stage for their meeting with Giscard and Harold Wilson of Britain on the margins of the Helsinki Conference a few days later (chapter 4). The four of them agreed to hold an economic summit that autumn and to include Prime Minister Takeo Miki of Japan. Giscard and Schmidt did not want a formal, highly public affair because that tended to stifle free and frank discussion and raise public expectations of dramatic results. Their model was derived from the so-called 'Library Group'—informal and private gatherings of finance ministers from these five countries in which they had participated in 1973–4.

The first of the economic summits took place near Paris on 15–17 November 1975, at the *Château de Rambouillet*—a former royal castle that had become the summer residence for French presidents. The setting evoked what Callaghan, then Britain's foreign secretary, rather archly called 'the country house atmosphere that Giscard had intended and in which he felt so much at home'.[2] The summit (which included Italy at the insistence of Giscard as host) was intended to show the world that Western leaders were getting to grips with the economic crisis. In itself, Rambouillet did not accomplish much by way of concrete decisions and policies but it helped establish a road map for the future. The conference declaration ended: 'We intend to intensify our cooperation on all these problems in the framework of existing institutions as well as in all the relevant organizations.'[3] Some commentators were sceptical—the London *Spectator* scoffed that Rambouillet was 'more hot air than hot news'—but *Die Zeit* saw at least 'a weak ray of hope for the world economy'. The German paper picked up on Ford's statement about 'a new spirit—a spirit of cooperation and confidence stemming from a deeper understanding of our common destiny and our joint conviction that free peoples can master their future'.[4]

Ford and Miki were particularly keen to turn economic summitry into a process, supported by bureaucratic machinery. Schmidt and Giscard, on the other hand, wanted to keep future discussions small and personal, with the emphasis on reaching real decisions. Over the next three years the G7, as it was known after the inclusion of Canada (1976), became institutionalized as an annual event—increasingly bureaucratized while also making policy. Faced with a highly volatile global financial system after the collapse of the Bretton Woods order of fixed exchange rates, the G7 leaders felt it essential for politicians to assume a greater role in the governance of international financial relations— what one scholar has called a regime of 'surveillance'.[5] Determined to avoid protectionist answers to the unprecedented combination of recession and inflation ('stagflation'), the G7 saw one of its main tasks as being the coordination of national policies. The international economic managers of the future would no longer be the IMF or the World Bank but an elite coterie of Western statesmen.

Driving the whole process was a growing recognition of the world's economic 'interdependence'. This was particularly evident before and during the Bonn G7 summit of July 1978. In a clash of priorities in 1977–8 Schmidt had kept up his mantra about the need to control inflation whereas Carter, the new American president, backed by Japan and Britain, favoured a coordinated Keynesian policy. By the summer of 1978, with German growth stalling, Schmidt was reluctantly moving towards a stimulus package if the Americans took robust action to control their own inflation, strengthen the dollar, and reduce oil imports. But the devil was in the details and these had to be decided in Bonn. When Schmidt welcomed his visitors at the opening session, he alluded to the city's equivalent of Rome's seven hills—the *Siebengebirge* on the other side of the Rhine. 'We are seven delegations', he declared in a phrase widely reported in the press, 'and we must avoid having each one climb his own summit, but stay together and climb the peak which confronts us all'.[6]

The meeting in Bonn ended with the declaration of 'a comprehensive strategy' to 'create more jobs and fight inflation, strengthen international trading, reduce payments imbalances, and achieve greater stability in exchange markets'. The G7 leaders stressed that they were 'dealing with long-term problems, which will only yield to sustained efforts. This strategy is a coherent whole, whose parts are interdependent. To this strategy, each of our countries can contribute; from it, each can benefit.' Although the main deal was between America, Germany, and Japan, all seven countries made specific commitments: to borrow Schmidt's phrase, they deliberately roped themselves together at the summit to reach their common goal of global economic recovery. In the words of American journalist Flora Lewis, 'the acceptance that no single country or group of countries could be expected to bear the brunt of an overall effort was the source of the intense satisfaction among leaders'. Or, as Schmidt put it pithily a few years later: 'the world economy is our fate. It can only be directed through collaboration.'[7]

Despite its achievements, however, Bonn revealed some of the flaws of institutionalized summitry (see Figure 5.2). The G7 was already being transformed from Giscard and Schmidt's idea of a small, intimate gathering to what one journalist called 'a full-fledged media event' with some 2,500 reporters in attendance[8]—five times the number who had covered Rambouillet.

Fig. 5.2. G7 Summit, Bonn, 17 July 1978 (Bundesbildstelle)

Later G7 summits would follow this trend, becoming highly public, intensely bureaucratic, and pre-packaged by so-called 'sherpas'. But none of this should detract what had been accomplished by those very first meetings. Looking back on the trajectory of the G7 between 1975 and 1978, Schmidt was sure that 'if there hadn't been these four summits in the last four years, the world economy would most likely have tumbled into an equally deep depression to that of 1930s'.[9] Similarly Callaghan, by this time Britain's prime minister, was convinced that 'economic summits of the kind that took place at Bonn foster a sense of political and economic direction in handling the world's problems'. More than that—they generated a sense of trust among the key leaders. Callaghan, like Schmidt, had no doubt that 'each summit meeting had reinforced our confidence in one another, despite the fact that we could obviously not expect to wipe all the world's problems off the face of the earth in two days'. The process of collaboration was as important as concrete results.[10]

GUADELOUPE: THE WESTERN 'BIG FOUR'

Meanwhile, détente was on the wane and progress on arms control seemed increasingly problematic. Traditional Cold War problems were back with a vengeance. The Guadeloupe summit of 5–6 January 1979 was intended to get a grip on this deepening security crisis. The initiative came from Schmidt, who pushed the idea when talking with Carter's national security adviser, Zbigniew Brzezinski, on 3 October 1978. The German chancellor said he felt 'uneasy' that there was no forum in which the four Western leaders most directly engaged in the political-strategic problems of NATO could meet for free and frank discussion. So far they had held such conversations fleetingly on the margins of other large and formal gatherings, such as NATO Council meetings or the 1975 Helsinki Conference on Security Cooperation in Europe. Schmidt had in mind the same model as the 'Library Group', which had also been the chrysalis of the G7. By the summer of 1978 Carter was receptive to the idea, as was Callaghan, so Schmidt felt encouraged to sound out Giscard. The latter agreed to act as host—hence the choice of the French island of Guadeloupe as the conveniently secluded venue.[11]

The patronage of France was important for all the participants. Carter did not want to be seen as sponsor of the summit, for fear of 'resentments from other governments at such an exclusive meeting' and of possible retaliation by Moscow in the ongoing SALT II negotiations. Callaghan was happy to include France because this would give Britain support for its own interests as a European nuclear power. Schmidt was pleased for Giscard to take public responsibility for a proposal that had emanated from the Federal Republic of Germany—given the taboo about the FRG as a nuclear power in its own right. The summit was particularly significant for Giscard because President Charles de Gaulle had pulled France out of the NATO command structure in 1966 and the country had thereafter stood aloof from all multilateral discussions about nuclear weapons and its own *force de frappe*. By 1979, however, France was concerned about the growing nuclear imbalance in Europe and its exclusion from the high-level talks by then underway within NATO on the issue. French diplomats were also unsettled by the way the FRG now appeared ready to 'mark its interest in a field in which it had always avoided any engagement', maybe even trying to 'define European nuclear defence' without owning such weaponry.[12]

Carter, Giscard, Schmidt, and Callaghan therefore all saw compelling reasons to meet as a quartet with special interests and responsibilities. But the format of their meeting was equally important. Guadeloupe fitted Carter's desire for 'some very small and isolated island where the protagonists could be effectively insulated from the press'. He did not 'underestimate the difficulties which press attention would create'.[13] Most of the planning was handled by each leader's inner circle, excluding most of the wider bureaucracy, and no foreign ministers were invited to attend. The aim was to survey world problems as a quartet, with only one key adviser from each country and a minimum of publicity. All the leaders wanted the talks to be held in a friendly and relaxed atmosphere, without any pressure to produce a formal communiqué or declaration. As a British journalist noted on 8 December, the day after the summit was announced: 'The Guadeloupe hideaway is designed to restore the informality of Rambouillet.' That was indeed what transpired, with the leaders spending forty-eight hours together at a luxury hotel, living in beach bunga-lows accompanied by their wives. 'We gossiped on the grass outside our huts', Callaghan later recalled, 'ate together informally, and even when our formal discussions took place they were held in an open, round thatched hut. For recreation Carter jogged, Giscard played tennis and I sailed a small dinghy. We all spoke English. There were no position papers, no fixed agenda...and only one reception.'[14]

After a *tour d'horizon* of global problems (China, Africa, and the Middle East) in the first session, the leaders devoted most of their time to the central issue of nuclear security in Europe. The core of their discussions was the so-called 'grey area' problem of Soviet intermediate-range nuclear forces (INFs), not addressed in any current arms control negotiations. The Kremlin had managed to keep these missiles out of the SALT II forum, which dealt with weapons of 'intercontinental' range (over 5,500 kilometres). Nor were INFs under discussion in the talks about mutual and balanced force reductions (MBFR): these were concerned with the conventional balance between NATO and the Warsaw Pact.

From 1976 the Soviets had started deploying SS-20 missiles—a new gener-ation of more mobile and accurate INFs, each with three independently targetable warheads—at a time when NATO had no modern INFs at all. The SS-20s were directed on North-West Europe with Germany as the front-line. Hence Schmidt's special concern. He spoke out on the matter at a lecture in London in October 1977, noting that because SALT had the effect of neutralizing superpower *strategic* nuclear capabilities, 'in Europe this magni-fies the significance of the disparities between East and West in nuclear tactical and conventional weapons'. He demanded a balance at *all* levels—what he called the 'full range of deterrence'. Such a balance could be achieved either through arms build-up or arms reduction. Schmidt made clear his strong preference for the latter.[15]

INF modernization was already under discussion among NATO bureaucrats—in the High-Level Group—but no decision could be taken by the Alliance without agreement among the heads of government. The issue was particularly sensitive for two reasons. Firstly, anti-nuclear feeling was on the rise among the Western publics and their leaders did not wish to be stigmatized as war-mongers for adding a new spiral to the nuclear arms race. Most NATO politicians therefore preferred to procrastinate. Secondly, Western Europe's leaders lost confidence in Carter during the neutron-bomb fiasco of 1977–8. The American president had dithered over the introduction of enhanced radiation warheads (ERWs), a battlefield nuclear weapon—initially pressing his allies for deployments and then suddenly abandoning the whole project in the spring of 1978. Schmidt felt particularly humiliated, having gone out on a limb for Carter despite vocal opposition from his Social Democrat rank-and-file. And the Soviets gained a major propaganda victory, with NATO left publicly in disarray about its strategic posture. These various concerns prompted the three Western European leaders, especially Schmidt, to seek a proper face-to-face discussion with Carter about the grey area—to avoid another shambles like the neutron bomb and show real political leadership for the rest of NATO.

Discussion about these issues at Guadeloupe was blunt and at times heated. Schmidt's tendency to lecture particularly wound up Carter, with whom personal relations had been strained ever since Schmidt openly supported Ford during the 1976 election campaign. Giscard recalled that Schmidt took 'visible pleasure in going into all the details' of SALT II, and 'expressing critical judgments' on the way these negotiations were being handled, which in turn 'visibly irritated' Carter.[16] Nevertheless the long debate, running to several hours over two sessions, allowed the leaders to get deep anxieties off their chest and on to the table in a way that would have been impossible through correspondence or even formal summits. And real progress was made. In the first session Carter spent some time updating his colleagues on the protracted SALT II negotiations with Moscow. Despite continuing differences on several issues, the president was confident that the treaty could be signed at the next superpower summit, which at this point he hoped would take place in February. Fearing difficulties over the treaty's ratification by the Senate he sought its endorsement by Britain, France, and West Germany to help persuade opinion back home. Although Schmidt and Callaghan had serious misgivings about American handling of SALT II, all three allies—both in private and in public afterwards—gave Carter the backing he wanted. For the president, this alone made Guadeloupe worthwhile.

In addition, Guadeloupe forced Carter to face up to the grey-area problem for the first time—an important development and one that was highly gratifying for Schmidt. By the end of the meeting, after tangled discussions, the president said that at his upcoming summit he would warn Brezhnev that he intended to modernize American forward-based systems (FBS) in Europe, in other words introducing Pershing II and ground-launched cruise missiles (GLCM) to counter the Soviet SS-20s. But, following Schmidt's desire for arms reduction, Carter also said he would bring all these INFs—existing Soviet missiles and future American ones—to the negotiating table. He was not specific about whether this would be done in SALT III, once the existing superpower treaty had been concluded, or in a separate arena. But Schmidt now felt confident that the tangled issues of SS-20s and Cruise were going to be addressed at the forthcoming superpower summit.[17]

After their meeting, the four leaders held an upbeat but anodyne press conference, which gave little away apart from European support for SALT II—but Callaghan told the press: 'The forty-eight hours we spent together has been worth forty thousand Foreign Office telegrams.'[18] Behind the scenes real progress had been made. NATO's 'Big Four' were moving towards a clear policy of INF modernization. But equally they wanted to explore the idea of arms reduction in future superpower talks. Here was the genesis of NATO's eventual dual-track decision. The challenge was now how to tie together the two tracks—in content and in timing. Furthermore, the Big Four had to persuade the other eleven NATO members, suspicious of any *directoire*, to follow their lead. These two challenges would absorb much of the Alliance's energies for the rest of 1979. But in the meantime, Carter had to deliver on his promises about SALT II—and that would prove no easy task.

VIENNA: SALT THAT HAD LOST ITS SAVOUR

Despite all the fanfare, the Interim Strategic Arms Limitation agreement of 1972, SALT I, was of restricted scope and duration. It simply set a cap on ballistic missile launchers for each side and was to run for only five years. The SALT II negotiations were intended to produce a longer-term agreement, covering the whole gamut of strategic systems including aircraft. Another challenge was that the negotiators had to wrestle with major changes in weapons technology—especially because missiles were now being developed with several warheads: the so-called MIRVs (multiple, independently-targetable re-entry vehicles). A fundamental problem was the issue of verification. SALT I had no mechanism for on-site inspection: both sides relied on electronic means of surveillance, whose adequacy was increasingly questioned on Capitol Hill.

Negotiating SALT II was therefore always going to be difficult. Leonid Brezhnev and Gerald Ford had made a start at their Vladivostok summit of November 1974. They agreed on a general framework of ten years' duration that set aggregate limits of 2,400 missile launchers and heavy bombers for each side, of which 1,320 could be MIRVed. And so they hoped to sign the treaty the following spring. But major disagreements arose about whether Soviet Backfire bombers and American Cruise missiles should be counted as strategic systems. Negotiations were then almost derailed by the change of administration in Washington. When Carter became president in January 1977 he sought a more radical agreement than the Vladivostok formula, involving 'deep cuts' to a ceiling of 1,800 on both sides. This partly reflected his own idealism but also a desire to differentiate himself from the Ford-Kissinger arms control policy that was now under attack from right and left. In his words, he wanted 'proposals that would push the *limitation* talks into *reduction* talks'. Under Carter, American diplomacy also placed a novel emphasis on human rights. The president, to quote Brzezinski, 'resolved to make a break with the recent past, to bring the conduct of foreign affairs into line with the nation's political values and ideals, and to revitalize an American image which had been tarnished by the Vietnam experience'.[19]

When Carter set out this assertive new agenda in his very first meeting with Soviet ambassador Anatoly Dobrynin, less than two weeks after his inauguration, he was firmly advised not to 'test Moscow'.[20] Ignoring this clear warning, the president set out his aspirations for arms control and human rights in a long letter to Brezhnev on 14 February 1977. The general secretary replied in highly undiplomatic language, stating 'bluntly' that, whereas the Soviets wanted to build on the 'balanced and realistic approach' taken at Vladivostok, Carter's new arms reduction agenda was 'unconstructive' and contained 'deliberately unacceptable proposals'. Brezhnev was equally direct about Carter's human rights policy and his agitation on behalf of leading Soviet dissidents such as Andrei Sakharov and Alexander Ginzburg, vowing that the Kremlin would 'resolutely respond' to 'interference in our internal affairs, whatever pseudo-humanitarian slogans are used to present it'. Although shaken by Brezhnev's letter, Carter still sent Secretary of State Cyrus Vance to Moscow at the end of March with a radical arms reduction package that Dobrynin warned beforehand would have no chance of being accepted. The fact that Carter also unveiled his proposals publicly before the United Nations added to Kremlin suspicion that he was, in Dobrynin's words, 'merely trying to achieve a propaganda victory'. The Soviet Union's equally public rejection of Vance's mission, without anything offered in return, rounded off a disastrous couple of months in Soviet-American relations that seriously delayed SALT II and from which the Carter presidency never fully recovered.[21]

Carter's persistence on both arms reduction and human rights reflected his underlying Christian idealism but also the diplomatic naiveté and political inflexibility of a complete Washington outsider whose only executive experience was as a one-term governor of Georgia. In most areas of foreign policy he preferred a bold, 'comprehensive' approach rather than building more modestly and incrementally on past agreements. Yet the administration's problems were structural as well, rooted in the tension between Vance and Brzezinski, which ensured that the White House did not speak with a single voice. Vance's priority was to sustain détente and complete SALT II on the basis of the Vladivostok guidelines, whereas Brzezinski—an acerbic Polish-American— was much more hawkish towards Moscow. When the president had appointed them, his line—according to aide Hamilton Jordan—was that 'Zbig would be the thinker, Cy would be the doer, and Jimmy Carter would be the decider'. But Carter was a details man, prone to see several sides of an issue, who ultimately found it very hard to make up his mind. He also signally failed to stop the feuding among his advisers and, in particular, to curb Brzezinski's increasing tendency to encroach on Vance's turf and make public statements about policy. In fact, the president relied heavily on Brzezinski's incisive advice (often bluntly presented) and felt much closer to him personally than to Vance, seeing Brzezinski as a fellow outsider whereas the more buttoned-up secretary of state seemed to epitomize the East Coast Establishment.[22]

Intertwined with their divergent approaches towards Moscow, Vance and Brzezinski also held different views of Beijing. Under the leadership of Deng Xiaoping the People's Republic of China (PRC) had embarked on a momentous programme of economic reform and had also emerged as a weighty, if imponderable, factor in international diplomacy. The United States was now moving towards full recognition of the PRC. Whereas the Republicans had procrastinated since Nixon's pioneering visit in 1972 on whether to abandon American commitments to Taiwan, a Democrat president found it politically easier to take such a momentous step. In May 1978 Carter sent Brzezinski to Beijing with the message that 'the United States has made up its mind on normalization'. For Vance this would simply signify an acknowledgement of China's status as a global power. But Brzezinski saw China in the context of triangular politics—as a useful instrument in America's dealings with Moscow—and wanted to exploit the Kremlin's anxiety about its Asian neighbour and rival. His mission to Beijing was undertaken after a full-scale battle with Vance. He had, in his own words, become 'preoccupied with Moscow's misuse of détente to improve the Soviet geopolitical and strategic position' in the Middle East and the Horn of Africa, and believed that 'a strategic response was necessary'—in other words by 'playing the China card'. Brzezinski did not conceal these feelings from the media. During his visit to China, according to *Time* magazine, he raced his hosts along a section of the Great Wall joking: 'Last one to the top fights the Russians in Ethiopia.'[23]

Brzezinski's reference to Moscow's misuse of 'détente' highlights a basic conceptual difference between the two superpowers. For the United States 'détente' signified the beginnings of a more stable and peaceful world in which the Soviet Union and its satellites might then gradually open up and adopt American political values. The Kremlin, by contrast, saw détente more narrowly as a bilateral relationship and viewed superpower nuclear parity enshrined in SALT I as a sign that the era of American hegemony was on the wane. It therefore had no qualms about strengthening the USSR's sub-strategic armaments, for example by introducing SS-20s and building up their conventional forces. Détente and peaceful co-existence with the West would serve to 'make the world safe for historical change' on Marxist-Leninist lines. The Kremlin was particularly alert in the 1970s to the crisis of capitalism amid the OPEC revolution and 'stagflation' and to the final collapse of Western imperialism in Africa. Soviet military aid to Cuban guerrillas in Angola, for example, was intended to accelerate a trend of history that seemed to be moving inexorably in their favour. As Brezhnev told Warsaw Pact allies in November 1978, 'the strengthening of the positions of socialism in the world in recent years is an incontrovertible fact'.[24]

The emergence of China and the shifting dynamics of the global Cold War were factors that complicated the discussions on SALT II. So did Carter's insistence on human rights—to which the Kremlin became increasingly allergic. Although SALT talks had resumed in Geneva in May 1977, the atmosphere was now very suspicious and the technical issues (such as MIRVs, mobile launchers, and verification) proved hard to resolve. Essentially the two sides went back to the Vladivostok outline as a base, but the Americans tried to insert some elements of the comprehensive package that Carter had thrust at them in the spring. In other circumstances, top-level intervention by political leaders might have cut through some of the bureaucratic logjams—as would be the case in the Reagan-Gorbachev summitry of 1985–6—and during the summer of 1977 Carter did press for an early meeting with Brezhnev in the hope of improving relations and expediting a SALT II deal. But the Politburo was determined not to hold a summit until the SALT treaty was ready for signature. Although such linkage was a familiar Soviet tactic, for instance in 1971–2 before SALT I, another consideration now played a part in Moscow's thinking. Brezhnev's health was in rapid decline: addicted to cigarettes, alcohol, and prescription drugs, he had suffered several strokes and heart attacks. It was clear to his colleagues that, although the Soviet leader might be able to preside over a signing ceremony, he was incapable of conducting a summit that entailed real debate and bargaining.[25]

Carter's own diplomatic priorities also zig-zagged around. By the end of 1978, with his domestic popularity slipping and the re-election campaign looming, he desperately needed a foreign-policy success. Normalizing relations with China became his top goal, yet he failed fully to appreciate the effect this would have on relations with the Soviets or on the increasingly delicate Vance-Brzezinski dynamic within his administration.

The United States and the People's Republic initiated formal diplomatic relations on New Year's Day 1979, prompting a warning from Brezhnev against any Western arms sales to China. In what Carter described as an 'almost paranoid' tone, the Soviet leader stated that 'the question here is of arming a country with the biggest ground forces, a country whose leaders proclaim for all to hear the inevitability of a new world war and are driving in practice at unleashing such a war'. Soviet fears about what normalization portended would affect their handling of SALT—encouraging tougher bargaining on the details.[26]

The issue became even more fraught in the New Year. The Soviet Union and Vietnam had signed a 'friendship treaty' to support the latter in its deepening border conflict with Pol Pot's genocidal regime in Cambodia. In response, the Chinese—Cambodia's main ally—played the 'America card' against Moscow. When Deng Xiaoping made a state visit to America—the first by any PRC leader—at the end of January 1979, the Chinese did their best to represent normalization as the beginnings of a Sino-American axis.

This exacerbated Soviet suspicions and also encouraged them to drag out negotiations, to ensure that a SALT summit would not occur in the shadow of Deng's visit. While in Washington, the Chinese leader told Carter privately that his forces were planning a 'punitive strike' into Vietnam to administer 'an appropriate limited lesson'. The president warned Deng that such action would be 'a serious mistake' and could easily 'escalate into regional conflict'; nevertheless, when the Chinese incursion began on 17 February, the Soviets suspected American complicity.[27]

Brezhnev told Carter that the attack was 'a direct manifestation' of Beijing's 'expansionistic, hegemonistic aspirations'. He noted that it was 'undertaken soon after Deng Xiaoping's visit to the USA' during which he had uttered 'direct threats' to Vietnam. 'Is this', asked Brezhnev darkly, just 'a simple coincidence?' Carter immediately called in Dobrynin to assure him that 'we have no secret agreements with China' and (more disingenuously) that 'we have had no private information on Vietnam'. He added: 'tell President Brezhnev that I want to meet with him so that we can prove that we are as friendly with the Soviet Union as with China'. The ambassador left the White House musing that this was the first time Carter had failed to mention human rights: he sensed that the president was 'beginning to show a real interest in a shift in our relationship' towards reduced confrontation. Even though the Chinese pulled back from Vietnam after three weeks, American fears of a possible Sino-Soviet conflict seem to have energized Carter's determination to secure an arms control treaty as soon as possible.[28]

While Brzezinski used China normalization to advance his own policy agenda, Vance pushed through the final stages of the arms control agreement. The endorsement of SALT that Carter had gained from his Western European allies at Guadeloupe in January strengthened his hand. In the first half of 1979 Vance and Dobrynin met almost every week—some two dozen discussions overall—in an effort to resolve the remaining problems. The White House had become increasingly worried about whether a SALT II treaty would be ratified by the Senate, so US negotiators went over the small print obsessively, prompting Soviet accusations of nit-picking.[29]

A crunch issue was verification, especially 'telemetry encryption'—electronic signals from missile tests, some of which the Soviets encoded. These signals were essential to monitor the Kremlin's compliance with arms control agreements, and therefore encryption had developed into a big issue on Capitol Hill (especially after the United States lost two crucial detection stations in Iran, following the fall of the Shah and the establishment of an Islamic theocracy). Carter made the point dramatically in a letter to Brezhnev on 7 March: 'I must tell you in all candor that the terms and future observance of our agreement concerning telemetry encryption is an issue that goes to the heart of the prospects for SALT II ratification, the verification and viability of the SALT II treaty, and the future stability of the strategic relationship between us.' In reply

Brezhnev said he was 'surprised' Carter had raised the issue, because it had been 'considered already closed by mutual agreement of the sides', and he accused the United States of introducing 'many far-fetched things that are not related to the agreement'. It took until the end of March to find a mutually acceptable form of words, namely that encryption was permissible except where it impeded verification of 'compliance with the provisions of the agreement'—a formulation that still offered considerable scope for interpretation on both sides.[30]

At long last, on 11 May 1979, Vance was able to announce agreement on the draft of a SALT II treaty and to state that Carter and Brezhnev would sign it in the middle of June. Brezhnev was too feeble to travel to America; Carter in turn said he could not travel to Moscow because Congressional hawks would accuse him of yet more concessions to the Soviets, further imperilling ratification. So they settled on Vienna—a neutral capital, close to Moscow, and the venue for the Kennedy-Khrushchev summit of 1961. That ill-judged and stormy encounter was on the mind of Brzezinski when preparing briefing memos for the president. He reminded Carter that the summit would take place at a time of 'unusual uncertainty and difficulty' because of the growth of Soviet power, their interventions in the Third World, and the 'trauma of a succession crisis' in Moscow. The Kremlin's message to Washington, in a nutshell, was 'no surprises' at the summit; their approach was 'one of extreme caution'. In this vein Brzezinski advised Carter to concentrate on a small range of issues: consummating SALT II and initiating SALT III, giving impetus to further Soviet-American arms control measures, and warning the Kremlin that its actions were trespassing on 'our vital interests' in various Cold War hot-spots.[31]

Carter reacted angrily to these memos. At several points he scrawled 'too timid' and demanded: 'let us list what we want & work for it'. The president noted in his diary that he was 'really peeved' with the 'timidity' of Brzezinski's memo. 'Every presumption was that we would fail, with analyses of how we would cover up failure. I told him to set maximum goals and work toward them.' Carter added sarcastically: 'I wasn't just interested in going to Vienna to the opera.'[32] Here was another example of Carter's idealistic preference for comprehensive proposals with sweeping implications for Soviet-American relations at a time when even Brzezinski, instinctively hawkish and bold in his approach, favoured a low-key summit to tie up SALT II and put down markers for the future. On 12 June, just before they departed for Vienna, Brzezinski told the president that this was going to be 'a sober, working summit—one which is not designed to generate excessive expectations' and advised that 'in talking to Brezhnev he ought to focus on two simple themes—arms cuts and regional restraint. Trying to do more than that is going to be counterproductive.'[33]

Carter, energetic and optimistic as ever, threw himself into things as soon as he arrived in the Austrian capital—jogging a few miles on the first morning before a final planning meeting with Vance. This was all a big contrast with Brezhnev, who was sluggish, hard of hearing, and erratic in attention. Most of the time he read from prepared statements and, even then, often needed prompts. Clearly he could not handle the cut-and-thrust of debate. This accorded with Dobrynin's advice to Brzezinski beforehand: 'Carter knows so much more on all of these issues than Brezhnev' so that 'Brezhnev will be on the defensive and embarrassed if Carter presses him'. Avoiding any embarrassment of the old man was also the advice from Averell Harriman, former US ambassador to Moscow, who told Carter that 'Brezhnev's firm commitment was to keep war away from the Soviet Union'. He said that the Soviet leader 'considered the Vienna summit as one of the great events of his life: they have done everything to avoid failure'. For Brezhnev and his colleagues—having secured recognition at Helsinki for their postwar geopolitical position in Europe—Vienna 1979, building on Moscow 1972 and SALT I, was an essential part of securing American recognition of the Soviet Union as an equal superpower.[34]

The first meeting on 15 June was simply a staged exchange of statements by Carter and Brezhnev in front of their Austrian hosts in the Hofburg Imperial Palace. The two leaders got down to serious business on the 16th especially in their pre-dinner meeting to approve the draft SALT II treaty. Brezhnev observed that, despite its limitations, 'the Treaty, in its present form, met the interests of both states and was consistent with the principle of equality and equal security'; Carter said it was 'the result of ten years of effort, involving skill and patience', and extravagantly praised Brezhnev's role. Both men agreed that SALT II was 'part of a continuing process which ultimately would lead to much greater control of the destructiveness of nuclear weapons'. They then confirmed the agreed form of words on telemetry encryption and verification and also tied up the issue of the Soviet Backfire bomber. This was one of the few moments of the summit where Vance and Dobrynin's script allowed Brezhnev a cameo moment as a negotiator, proposing—apparently spontaneously—that the USSR would not produce more than thirty Backfires a year, to which Carter would respond. In the event both leaders flubbed their lines but the eventual outcome essentially followed the script.[35]

Apart from concluding SALT II, the summit was also supposed to look ahead to SALT III. Here the handling was even sloppier. At their pre-dinner meeting on 16 June Brezhnev raised the question of medium-range missiles in Europe. He said that the 'grey-area' issue, as the West called it, was actually a rather 'foggy' concept because Soviet SS-20s could not reach the United States whereas American nuclear weaponry in Europe could hit the USSR. So, he added, it was 'very difficult to determine' which of these systems were 'grey' and which were 'black'—a point that Carter did not pick up. Towards the end of the meeting the president suggested that they discuss American and Soviet INFs the following morning, but in fact there was no discussion of Soviet INFs in the form of the SS-20 in Vienna.[36] At the same time Carter had made a crucial concession within the SALT II treaty, which included an additional protocol prohibiting for three years (until 31 December 1981) the deployment of modernized American INFs, namely Cruise missiles. Cruise was a system that Carter had treated principally as a tradable bargaining chip against Soviet ICBMs to get SALT II but which Schmidt always regarded as a direct counter to the Soviet SS-20s. It is clear that Carter was pre-occupied with the strategic dimension of nuclear issues, which especially concerned the United States. By comparison, Euromissiles were pushed to margins of the talks. This flatly contradicted the assurance Carter had given to Schmidt, Giscard, and Callaghan at Guadeloupe that he would address the SS-20 problem during his summit with Brezhnev.

The last morning in Vienna, 18 June, was devoted to signing the SALT II treaty with full ceremony in the Hofburg. The language was appropriately flowery and optimistic. Brezhnev, reading as usual from his prompt cards, expressed the hope that the treaty would generate 'a more favorable climate for solving other problems of Soviet-American relations'. Carter called SALT II 'a historic contribution to world peace' and announced that both leaders had agreed to visit each other's country. They also expressed the hope that summitry would become frequent, even routine, 'for the purpose of understanding each other better', without 'having to wait for a crisis or some other momentous event'. At the end the two of them shook hands and, Carter added, 'to my surprise we found ourselves embracing each other in the Soviet fashion. There is no doubt there were strong feelings of cooperation between us at this moment' (see Figure 5.3).[37]

SALT II was an advance on SALT I. It set equal aggregate limits—2,400 strategic nuclear delivery vehicles (missiles and aircraft) for each side, with equal limits on total numbers of MIRVs and on the number of warheads per missile or aircraft. It also established more rigorous procedures for electronic verification. Despite the upbeat mood at the end of the summit, however, two major problems immediately loomed large. First, there was no guarantee that the SALT II treaty would be ratified by the US Senate. This had worried the Carter administration all through the negotiations and also deeply unsettled the Soviets as to the predictability of American policy. Secondly, there was the European dimension of superpower arms control. The question of the Eurostrategic balance, especially the Soviet arsenal of SS-20s, which had preoccupied the NATO allies at Guadeloupe had not been addressed to their satisfaction at Vienna. These two issues would form the focus of international relations for the rest of 1979.

Fig. 5.3. A Sweet Embrace, and SALT II: Carter and Brezhnev in Vienna, 18 June 1979 (AP)

INTO THE 'NEW COLD WAR'

Carter had always been extremely anxious about obtaining ratification of the SALT II treaty, which under the US Constitution would require a two-thirds majority of the Senate. The midterm elections of 1978 left the Democrats with a majority of fifty-eight to forty-one in the upper house: this meant that the president would need some Republican support, at minimum eight votes. Yet it had been clear to him for months that the Republicans, having failed in 1978 to block his immensely controversial treaty giving up American control of the Panama Canal, were going to make a fundamental political issue out of SALT II. And his own party was no means united behind him. A long-standing opponent of détente was Democrat Senator Henry 'Scoop' Jackson of Washington, who compared Carter's trip to Vienna in 1979 with Neville Chamberlain going to Munich in 1938. Carter's aide, Hamilton Jordan told Dobrynin that the president was so stung by this analogy that he refused to use an umbrella when arriving in Vienna, despite the pouring rain.[38]

Another key figure among the Democrats was Senator Frank Church of Idaho who, as chairman of the Foreign Relations Committee (FRC), would be responsible for shepherding the treaty through all-important hearings. Church was well-disposed to SALT in principle but, feeling vulnerable in a re-election year to attacks on him as a 'dove', he decided to play up reports about a 'Soviet brigade' in Cuba and started a firestorm in the media with his statement to the press on 4 September: 'There is no likelihood whatever that the Senate would ratify the SALT II Treaty as long as Russian combat troops remain stationed in Cuba.' Church suspended FRC hearings on the treaty until Carter offered satisfactory explanations. The president was furious, noting in his diary that the Soviet troop presence in Cuba 'is obviously not a threat to our country, not a violation of any Soviet commitment—but politically it's devastating to SALT'. He fumed that Church had been 'absolutely irresponsible'. Critics of the treaty seized on the issue. If American intelligence could not even detect a brigade of commies in Cuba, they asked, how could it verify Soviet compliance with a complex arms control treaty.[39]

The Senator was not entirely to blame: the whole story had been mangled by misinformation across Washington—for which Vance, Brzezinski, and the CIA were largely to blame—and Carter's subsequent attempts to reassure the nation only served to draw further attention to the issue. The furore also played into the abiding division between his advisers. Vance talked tough in public but, behind the scenes, he tried to dampen the flames and confine the problem to Cuba itself. On the other side, Brzezinski, supported by Defense Secretary Harold Brown, wanted to highlight the global implications—stressing 'Cuban activism worldwide on behalf of Soviet interests' and urging Carter to warn Moscow that he would move closer to Beijing if Soviets failed to cooperate. So angry did Brzezinski become with Carter's handling of the issue that, for the only time in his tenure as national security adviser, he came close to resigning.[40]

It was not until 1 October, after a month of political frenzy, that Carter made clear to the American public that in fact the brigade was neither combat-ready nor even new: it had been stationed in Cuba since 1962 with the full knowledge of President John F. Kennedy and subsequent administrations. Only then did Church resume the Senate hearings on the SALT II treaty.[41] All in all the whole business was a remarkable botch by the Democratic establishment. 'Politically,' Vance acknowledged later, 'the administration had been seriously hurt by the episode'. In Brzezinski's view, 'the Cuban crisis shook public confidence in the Administration' and 'heightened public hostility toward the Soviet Union. It also deprived us of momentum in the SALT ratification process. Approximately one month of time was lost.'[42]

After the Cuban debacle, Carter tried to regain the initiative on SALT by intensive lobbying of key senators. But he was knocked back onto the defensive again by another totally unforeseen event: the Iranian hostage crisis. On 4 November Islamic militants seized fifty-two members of the US embassy in Teheran. The release of these American citizens became, for the embattled Carter, the litmus test of his whole presidency. In effect he became the greatest hostage of the crisis, diverting his time and emotional energy away from arms control.

Five days later Church's FRC voted nine to six in favour of SALT II, with two Democrats among the opposition. The FRC report stated that the treaty 'would make a positive contribution to American security and foreign policy interests, provided that the United States also vigorously undertakes necessary measures to maintain deterrence and essential equivalence' and 'improve theater nuclear and conventional capabilities'. The latter point was a reminder of the European dimensions of détente that had been neglected by Carter in Vienna. On the other hand, the Senate Armed Services Committee, of which 'Scoop' Jackson was a prominent member, voted on 4 December overwhelmingly against the treaty, with ten against, none in favour, and seven abstentions. Its report, largely the work of Jackson and his hawkish aide Richard Perle, damned the treaty as favouring the Soviets, lacking adequate verification protocols, and therefore 'not in the national security interest'. Although the Armed Services Committee had no jurisdiction over foreign treaties, its high-profile onslaught was a damaging blow for the president. Senate majority leader Robert Byrd remained hopeful of a final, positive vote on the floor of the Senate before Christmas, but the eventual outcome clearly hung in the balance.[43]

The administration's erratic behaviour regarding SALT also had international implications. Across the Atlantic European allies found Washington's dithering deeply disconcerting. After all, the treaty was not only essential to stabilize the superpower relationship, but also to expedite progress on nuclear arms control in Europe. German Defence Minister Hans Apel told the American press that NATO would be in 'real crisis' if the Senate failed to ratify SALT II.[44] This made it seem all the more important that the Alliance should adopt a strong and united front on the problem of Euromissiles.

To be sure, Carter, Schmidt, Giscard, and Callaghan had outlined a two-track approach to this issue at Guadeloupe in January. The details, however, took the rest of 1979 to nail down. The Americans and British, particularly keen to modernize NATO's INF arsenal, focused on the specifics of track one. The Germans, desperate not to lose sight of arms control and SALT III, pressed for a special Alliance working group to explore various limitation or reduction options under a second track. By the spring of 1979 the two tracks were being bonded together in an intricate package: NATO's collective decision for an evolutionary modernization of INFs—involving from the outset a commitment both to produce and deploy—would be combined with a *simultaneous* offer to the Soviets to negotiate limits on both new American and Soviet INF systems. The inbuilt automaticity within and between the two tracks was intended to prevent the sole selection or prioritization of either. This *uno actu* concept (as the Germans named it) represented a clear difference from the sequential approach touted at Guadeloupe which entailed first pursuing modernization before embarking on any negotiations with the Soviets.[45]

The real problem during the summer of 1979 was to find NATO countries that would commit to deploy modernized INF systems, specifically Pershing II and Cruise missiles. The British were willing from the start, but some countries opted out, and others were strategically irrelevant; the Schmidt government insisted that there must be at least one non-nuclear deployment partner to complement Britain. By July the Carter administration had drawn up a draft deployment programme covering allied countries—West Germany, Britain, Italy, Belgium, and the Netherlands.[46] The Belgian and Dutch governments, faced with strong anti-nuclear movements, remained doubtful about domestic support and in the end postponed any decision on deployment. In September, however, Italy's new coalition government offered a firm commitment, thereby giving Schmidt the continental partner he wanted.

The German chancellor was, however, not satisfied about the way the negotiation track was developing. Since Cruise was already under discussion as strategic weaponry, the second track could not be disentangled from the SALT process. Schmidt welcomed the signing of the SALT II treaty. But he remained unhappy at the asymmetry of the agreement because the Soviet SS-20s were not included while the treaty contained the detested protocol prohibiting for three years the deployment of long-range ground- and submarine-launched cruise missiles. This weakened the strength of track one. Worse still, Schmidt discovered that Carter, in his references to SALT III at Vienna, had not even discussed the SS-20s at the summit with Brezhnev, despite his pledge at Guadeloupe to do so.[47] And this was all the more irritating because in Washington on 6 June, less than two weeks before the summit, the chancellor had been assured by the president that he would pursue 'mutual limitation of Eurostrategic weapons' in the American agenda for SALT III which would be explored at Vienna.[48] Once again, it seemed, Jimmy Carter could not be relied upon. And then, when meeting Soviet Foreign Minister Andrei Gromyko a week later, Schmidt realized that the Kremlin was also utterly unwilling to discuss its SS-20s.[49] It was obvious that the Soviets saw future arms-control initiatives and negotiations primarily as a tactical device to forestall NATO nuclear modernization. For Schmidt this was a sobering moment.

The chancellor was now determined to move the Alliance as a whole to a clear decision. In doing so, unlike his Belgian and Dutch counterparts, he was willing to fly in the face of strong pacifist opposition within his own party and the population at large. And, despite continued rumblings, in early December his fellow Social Democrats endorsed the dual-track policy at their party conference. On the 12th, at a Special Meeting of NATO defence and foreign ministers in Brussels, all the Allies acquiesced in the dual track through a carefully worded communiqué.[50]

The Ministers have decided to pursue these two parallel and complementary approaches in order to avert an arms race in Europe by the Soviet TNF [theatre nuclear forces] build-up, yet preserve the viability of NATO's strategy of deterrence and defence and thus maintain the security of its member States.

a. A modernization decision, including a commitment to deployments, is necessary to meet NATO's deterrence and defence needs, to provide a credible response to unilateral Soviet TNF deployments, and to provide the foundation for the pursuit of serious negotiations on TNF.

b. Success of arms control in constraining the Soviet build-up can enhance Alliance security, modify the scale of NATO's TNF requirements, and promote stability and détente in Europe in consonance with NATO's basic policy of deterrence, defence and détente...[51]

In this way the Americans and British had secured NATO's commitment to INF modernization and deployment. At the same time the continental Europeans—led by West Germany—had gained the inbuilt commitment to negotiate, with a view to possible nuclear arms reduction. After protracted arguments within the Alliance, NATO had managed to hang together. This was a significant diplomatic achievement.

*   *   *   *   *

Yet any arms control negotiations on INF depended on the willingness of Washington to make proposals (problematic given the Senate deadlock on SALT II) and equally on the willingness of Moscow to talk. Within days of the NATO meeting in Brussels, however, the Soviet communist party newspaper, *Pravda*, declared that the dual-track decision had completely 'destroyed the basis for talks on medium-range weapons' in Europe. And then on Christmas Day thousands of Soviet troops were airlifted into Afghanistan to safeguard Moscow's crumbling position there. As soon as he heard the news, Carter exclaimed: 'There goes SALT II.'[52]

On 3 January 1980 the president sent Majority Leader Byrd a letter asking him not to bring the treaty to the floor of the Senate for a vote but to leave it on the calendar for future action. 'Because of American disgust with the Soviet invasion', Carter explained in his memoirs, 'the treaty would have been defeated overwhelmingly' but 'to withdraw it from the Senate might have made it almost impossible to resubmit in the future or for most of its terms to continue to be observed. This action was the best I could do at the time to keep it alive.'[53]

The next day the president delivered a televised address to the American people, calling the invasion 'a serious threat to peace' and insisting that it was not possible to 'continue to do business as usual with the Soviet Union'. He went on to announce that he had recalled the US ambassador from Moscow and had imposed economic sanctions, especially on grain exports and technology transfers. The president's determination to punish the Kremlin for invading Afghanistan was rooted in his reading of appeasement in the 1930s.

'History teaches, perhaps, very few lessons', he declared. 'But surely one such lesson learned by the world at great cost is that aggression, unopposed, becomes a contagious disease.'[54] Within days the president also called on the US Olympic Committee not to participate in the upcoming Moscow Olympics—a hugely important prestige project for the Kremlin. Elaborating on his geopolitical reasoning, Carter declared that the invasion 'endangers neighboring independent countries and access to a major part of the world's oil supplies. It therefore threatens our own national security, as well as the security of the region and the entire world.'[55]

In such an atmosphere, the prospects for any meaningful American-Soviet negotiations had completely evaporated. Although Carter did send a US delegation to Geneva in the autumn of 1980 to open the negotiation track on INFs, the discussions rumbled on inconclusively and were then suspended after Carter lost the November election. And because SALT II remained in limbo, there was also no chance of moving into SALT III or indeed any superpower talks about strategic nuclear weapons. The new Reagan administration, furthermore, had doubts about the dual-track decision and, generally, about the chances of any productive arms control talks with the Kremlin.

Carter later stated that 'our failure to ratify the SALT II treaty and to secure even more far-reaching agreements on nuclear arms control was the most profound disappointment of my Presidency'. Soviet ambassador Anatoly Dobrynin blamed Carter himself. 'One of the main reasons for his failure was the incompatibility between his ideas, some of which were very good, and his ability to put them into practice. He lacked flexibility. Seeking to achieve the best, he would underestimate tangible assets ... As he pursued the wonderful bird of his dream—a drastic reduction in nuclear weapons—he let go of the bird in his hand, the ratification of the SALT II treaty.' Dobrynin's verdict is perhaps too personalized a judgement. But, by rejecting a quick SALT II treaty based on the Ford-Brezhnev deal at Vladivostok in 1974 and pressing instead for 'deep cuts', Carter managed to derail the whole process. Negotiating a new and broader agreement then took more than two years and Brezhnev refused to hold a summit with Carter until a draft treaty was ready to sign. By the time the two leaders did meet the whole climate for arms control had changed. Brezhnev's health was in terminal decline and the Soviets had been unsettled by America's normalization with China. For its part Washington was disturbed by intensified Soviet activism in the Third World and suspicion of détente was now rife among the American public and politicians. The treaty was finally signed in Vienna in July 1979 but it had come too late. In the words of Raymond Garthoff, SALT II was therefore 'a case in which the operation was a success, but the patient unfortunately died'.[56]

This was all a far cry from the optimism of the *annus mirabilis* of 1972, when Nixon journeyed to Beijing and to Moscow. Then summit diplomacy seemed to be transforming the dynamics of the Cold War and offering hope for a more peaceful and cooperative future. But the Helsinki conference—intended to be a stepping-stone to making the Cold War more liveable, particularly in the heart of Europe—turned out to be the pinnacle of détente. As the decade neared its end superpower relations turned chillier and their competition became increasingly global in scope. Europe was caught precariously in the middle. The 1970s had proved a particularly fraught decade for America's West European allies, as the post-war boom collapsed into a crisis of capitalism and the tentative efforts to pierce the Iron Curtain fizzled out in renewed strategic insecurity. Living with the Cold War had become a matter of muddling through. In this climate summitry proved primarily a device to hold the West together.

By 1980 Western governments had closed ranks. But superpower détente was dead; indeed the United States and the Soviet Union were entering what became known as a 'new Cold War'. Their leaders were no longer talking. Summitry froze.

NOTES

1. Bonn meeting of 27 July 1975, quoted variously from the German and American record in Horst Möller et al., eds, *Akten zur Auswärtigen Politik der Bundesrepublik Deutschland 1975, Band I: 1. Juli bis 31. Dezember 1975* (Munich, 2006) [henceforth *AAPD 1975/II*], doc. 222, 1035–6, and *Foreign Relations of the United States, 1969–1976, vol. xxxi, Foreign Economic Policy, 1973–1976,* (henceforth *FRUS 1969–76, vol. xxxi),* https://history.state.gov/historicaldocuments/frus1969-76v31, doc. 94.

2. James Callaghan, *Time and Chance* (London, 1987), 479–80.

3. 'The Rambouillet Declaration', 17 November 1975, Margaret Thatcher Foundation website, http://www.margaretthatcher.org/document/110957.

4. Robert Mauthner, 'Rambouillet: Did the Summit Work?', *The Spectator,* 22 November 1975, 8; Klaus-Peter Schmid, 'Wir fanden einen neuen Geist', *Die Zeit,* 21 November 1975, 2; Ford, Remarks to the Press, 17 November 1975, The American Presidency Project (henceforth APP) website, http://www.presidency. ucsb.edu/ws/index.php?pid=5383&st=&st1.

5. Harold James, *International Monetary Cooperation since Bretton Woods* (Oxford, 1996), ch. 10, esp. 263.

6. Schmidt in Flora Lewis, 'President of "the Club"', *New York Times,* 17 July 1978, at A1. See generally Joan E. Spero and Jeffrey A. Hart, *The Politics of International Economic Relations* (London, 5th edn, 1997), 35–6.

7. Bonn Economic Summit Declaration Issued at the Conclusion of the Conference, 17 July 1978, APP website, http://www.presidency.ucsb.edu/ws/index.php?pid= 31093&st=&st1. Flora Lewis, '7 Industrial Nations Pledge to Spur Jobs, Curb Inflation; U.S. Ready to Cut Oil Imports', *New York Times,* 18 July 1978, A1; 'Die Weltwirtschaft ist unser Schicksal', *Die Zeit,* 25 February 1983, http://pdf.zeit.de/ 1983/09/Die-Weltwirtschaft-ist-unser-Schicksal.pdf.

8. Terence Smith, 'Reporter's Notebook: Neither All Work Nor All Play at the Economic Conference', *New York Times*, 17 July 1978, A3.

9. 'Das Wichtigste: Den Absturz vermeiden', *Die Zeit*, 21 July 1978, http://pdf.zeit.de/1978/30/das-wichtigste-den-absturz-vermeiden.pdf.

10. James Callaghan, *Time and Chance* (London, 1987), 485–6, 497. On the evolution of the G7, see more generally Robert D. Putnam and Nicholas Bayne, *Hanging Together: Cooperation and Conflict in the Seven-Power Summits* (London, 2nd edn, 1987), and Emmanuel Mourlon-Druol and Federico Romero, eds, *International Summitry and Global Governance: The Rise of the G7 and the European Council, 1974–1991* (London, 2014), chs 2 and 3.

11. Zbigniew Brzezinski, *Power and Principle: Memoirs of the National Security Adviser, 1977–1981* (London, 1983), 294–5; Horst Möller et al., eds, *Akten zur Auswärtigen Politik der Bundesrepublik Deutschland 1978, Band II: 1. Juli bis 31. Dezember 1978* (Munich, 2009) (henceforth *AAPD 1978/II*), doc. 293, 1457 and 1462, n. 47. For fuller discussion see Kristina Spohr, 'Helmut Schmidt and the Shaping of Western Security in the late 1970s: The Guadeloupe Summit of 1979', *International History Review* 37, no. 1 (2015), 167–92.

12. Ilaria Parisi, 'From the Sidelines to the Heart of the European Nuclear Question: France at the Guadeloupe summit of January 1979', unpublished paper—presented at the Conference 'Cold War Summitry: Transcending the Division of Europe, 1970–90', 22–23 September 2014, 8–9, notes 44–5.

13. The National Archives, Kew, London, (henceforth TNA), PREM 16/1984, DEFENCE—'Grey Area' Medium Range Nuclear Weapon Systems: Arms Control and Deployment 4.10.1978–4.4.1979, Peter Jay to FCO, tel. 4261, 26 October 1978.

14. Jonathan Kandell, 'Carter to meet three Western European leaders', *New York Times*, 8 December 1978, A10; Jonathan Steele, 'An island summit for four', *The Guardian*, 8 December 1978, 1; Callaghan, *Time and Chance*, 544.

15. Helmut Schmidt, 'The 1977 Alastair Buchan Memorial Lecture', *Survival* 20, no. 1 (Jan–Feb 1978), 4.

16. Valéry Giscard d'Estaing, *Le pouvoir et la vie: vol. 2—L'affrontement* (Paris, 1991), 375.

17. TNA, PREM 16/1984, Extract from Four-Power Discussions in Guadeloupe 5/6 January 1979: Third Session, 1. In deference to strong pressure from Giscard and Callaghan, however, Carter promised not to include their national deterrents in any bargaining with Brezhnev.

18. Ian Aitken, 'Salt to sugar', *Guardian*, 8 January 1979, 11.

19. Raymond L. Garthoff, *Détente and Confrontation: American-Soviet Relations from Nixon to Reagan* (Washington, DC, 1985), 442–6; Jimmy Carter, *Keeping Faith: Memoirs of a President* (New York, 1982), 216; Brzezinski, *Power and Principle*, 124. Cf. Betty Glad, *An Outsider in the White House: Jimmy Carter, his Advisors, and the Making of American Foreign Policy* (Ithaca, NY, 2009), 47–51.

20. Anatoly Dobrynin, *In Confidence to America's Six Cold War Presidents, 1962–1986* (New York, 1995), 384–6, 394; Carter-Dobrynin conversation, 1 February 1977, *Foreign Relations of the United States 1977–80, vol. vi, Soviet Union* (henceforth *FRUS 1977–80, vol. vi*), https://history.state.gov/historicaldocuments/frus1977-80v06, doc. 3.

21. Carter to Brezhnev, 14 February 1977, and Brezhnev to Carter, 25 February 1977, *FRUS 1977–80, vol. vi*, docs 7 and 12; Dobrynin, *In Confidence*, 392.
22. Hamilton Jordan, *Crisis: The Last Year of the Carter Presidency* (London, 1982), 47; Cyrus Vance, *Hard Choices: Critical Years in America's Foreign Policy* (New York, 1983), 31, 35–6. See generally Glad, *An Outsider in the White House*, 29–40.
23. Brzezinski, *Power and Principle*, 196; Garthoff, *Détente and Confrontation*, 703. For fuller discussion, see Glad, *An Outsider in the White House*, 119–41.
24. Garthoff, *Détente and Confrontation*, 49; Dobrynin, *In Confidence*, 407–8; Brezhnev, speech of 22 November 1978, in Vojtech Mastny and Malcolm Byrne, eds, *A Cardboard Castle? An Inside History of the Warsaw Pact, 1955–1991* (Budapest, 2005), 418.
25. Dobrynin, *In Confidence*, 397–8; see also Chris Tudda, *Cold War Summits: A History, from Potsdam to Malta* (London, 2015), 133–4.
26. Garthoff, *Détente and Confrontation*, 709; Vance, *Hard Choices*, 110–12; Carter diary, 31 December 1978, quoted in Carter, *Keeping Faith*, 201; Brezhnev to Carter, 27 December 1978, *FRUS 1977–80, vol. vi*, doc. 168.
27. Vance, *Hard Choices*, 112–13; Memcon, Deng-Carter, 29 January 1979, Carter presentation to Deng, 30 January 1979, *FRUS 1977–80, vol. xiii, China,* (henceforth *FRUS 1977–80, vol. xiii*) https://history.state.gov/historicaldocuments/frus1977-80v13, doc. 206.
28. Dobrynin, *In Confidence*, 418–19; Brezhnev to Carter, 18 February 1979, and Memcon, Carter-Dobrynin, 27 February 1979, *FRUS 1977–80, vol. vi*, docs 173 and 176.
29. Dobrynin, *In Confidence,* 420; James Reston, 'Mr. Vance: the year ahead', *New York Times*, 10 January 1979, A23.
30. Carter to Brezhnev, 7 March 1979, Brezhnev to Carter, 11 March 1979, and Carter to Brezhnev, 27 March 1979, *FRUS 1977–80, vol. vi*, docs 180, 181, 184.
31. Memos, Brzezinski to Carter, 24 and 29 May 1979, *FRUS 1977–80, vol. vi*, docs 196–7.
32. Ibid.; Jimmy Carter, *White House Diary* (New York, 2010), 25 May 1979, 321–2.
33. Brzezinski, *Power and Principle,* 341.
34. Brzezinski, *Power and Principle,* 340; Carter, *White House Diary,* 6 June 1979, 324.
35. Memcon, Carter-Brezhnev meeting, 5.35pm, 16 June 1979, *FRUS 1969–1976, vol. xxxiii, SALT II, 1972–1980,* (henceforth *FRUS 1969–76, vol. xxxiii*), https://history.state.gov/historicaldocuments/frus1969-76v33, doc 239; cf. Vance, *Keeping Faith,* 134–5; Brzezinski, *Power and Principle,* 341.
36. Memcon, Carter-Brezhnev meeting, 5.35pm, 16 June 1979, *FRUS 1969–76, vol. xxxiii,* doc. 239.
37. Memcon, Carter-Brezhnev meeting, 18 June 1979, 11.50am, *FRUS 1969–76, vol. xxxiii,* doc. 240; Carter, *Keeping Faith,* 261.
38. Carter, *Keeping Faith*, 224; Dobrynin, *In Confidence*, 422; cf. Glad, *An Outsider in the White House*, 111.
39. George C. Wilson, 'Church: No Treaty If Brigade Remains', *Washington Post*, 6 September 1979, A1-2; Carter diary, 5 September 1979, quoted in Carter, *Keeping Faith*, 263. See more generally Gloria Duffy, 'Crisis Mangling and the Cuban

Brigade', *International Security* 8, no. 1 (Summer 1983), 67–87; David Newsom, *The Soviet Brigade in Cuba: A Study in Political Diplomacy* (Bloomington, IN, 1987).

40. Brzezinski, *Power and Principle*, 346–52.
41. Frank Church later told his son that his handling of the Cuban brigade story was the biggest mistake of his life. And it did not even pay off politically: in November 1980 Church lost the Senate seat he had held since 1956. See Glad, *An Outsider in the White House*, 195–6.
42. Vance, *Hard Choices*, 364; Brzezinski, *Power and Principle*, 352.
43. Tudda, *Cold War Summits*, 151; Vance, *Hard Choices*, 366–7
44. 'German Fears "Real Crisis" If Arms Pact Not Ratified', *Los Angeles Times*, 3 October 1979, A2.
45. Horst Möller et al., eds, *Akten zur Auswärtigen Politik der Bundesrepublik Deutschland, Band I: 1. Januar bis 30. Juni 1979* (Munich, 2010) (henceforth *AAPD 1979/I*), doc. 114, 507–9; Politisches Archiv des Auswärtigen Amts, Berlin (henceforth PAAA), B150 1979, Abt. 2 to Bundesminister, Betr.: Kabinettssitzung am 2. Mai 1979, 30 April 1979.
46. *AAPD 1979/I,* docs 142 + 144.
47. Horst Möller et al., eds, *Akten zur Auswärtigen Politik der Bundesrepublik Deutschland, Band II: 1. Juli bis 31. Dezember 1979* (Munich, 2010) (henceforth *AAPD 1979/II*), doc. 211, 1028–33. See also PAAA, B150 1979, Fernschreiben Nr. 2335, Washington to Bonn AA, 22 June 1979. For the SALT II treaty and protocol, see BA 136/17749, Betr.: SALT II—hier: Inhalt des Vertrages und der Begleiturkunden, 19 June 1978.
48. *AAPD 1979/II*, doc. 211, 1028–33. See also PAAA, B150 1979, FSNr. 2335, Washington to Bonn AA, 22 June 1979. Jimmy Carter Library, Atlanta, Georgia, Zbigniew Brzezinski collection, Box 36, subject file, serial XS (5–9/79), Memcon, Carter-Schmidt talk, 6 June 1979.
49. *AAPD 1979/I*, docs 188 and 193, 905–18 and 937; cf. PAAA, B150 1979, Bundes-kanzleramt to Wallau, Ministerbüro AA, Vermerk über das Gespräch des BK mit PM Nordli am 12.7.1979, 13 July 1979.
50. TNA, 28/3697, NATO TNF Modernisation (1979—part D), Telegrams (nos 329 and 330) by Sir Clive Rose (Head of UK delegation to NATO) to FCO on 'Joint Ministerial Meeting: TNF Modernisation and Arms Control', 12 December 1979.
51. See Special Meeting of Foreign and Defence Ministers in Brussels, Chairman: Mr J. Luns, http://www.nato.int/docu/comm/49-95/c791212a.htm.
52. Strobe Talbott, *Deadly Gambits: The Reagan Administration and the Stalemate in Arms Control* (New York, 1985), 40; Glad, *An Outsider in the White House*, 197.
53. Carter, *Keeping Faith*, 475.
54. Jimmy Carter, Address to the Nation on the Soviet Invasion of Afghanistan, 4 January 1980, APP website, http://www.presidency.ucsb.edu/ws/index.php?pid=32911&st=&st1.
55. Letter to President of the US Olympic Committee, 20 January 1980, APP website, http://www.presidency.ucsb.edu/ws/index.php?pid=33059&st=&st1=.
56. Carter, *Keeping Faith*, 265; Dobrynin, *In Confidence*, 375; Garthoff, *Détente and Confrontation*, 822.

III

Transcending the Cold War

6

Geneva, Reykjavik, Washington, and Moscow, 1985–8

Jonathan Hunt and David Reynolds

The sight of the leaders of the United States and the Soviet Union strolling amicably together past St Basil's Cathedral captivated onlookers in Red Square on 31 May 1988 (see Figure 6.1). Even more striking was what the two leaders actually said. Five years earlier, President Ronald Reagan had likened the USSR to an 'evil empire', which exported communist revolution even as it crushed dissent within the Soviet bloc. Yet on that spring day in 1988 he sang a new tune. When asked by one American reporter whether he still believed that his hosts were 'the evil empire', he recanted: 'I was talking about another time, another era.' Standing beside him, Mikhail Gorbachev felt vindicated; via backchannels in March he had urged Reagan to make precisely such a statement. The president's words signalled an acknowledgement that a new Soviet Union was emerging thanks to Gorbachev's reforms. The Soviet leader uttered a single word in reply: 'Right.'[1]

That moment in Red Square was the high-water mark of an amazing odyssey for each leader. Reagan had entered the Oval Office in January 1981 as a tough-talking anti-communist. He left eight years later having presided over a revolution in world affairs as East-West relations evolved from the resurgent antagonism of the 'New Cold War' after the Soviets' 1979 invasion of Afghanistan to peaceful engagement by the end of his second term in January 1989. In Moscow, Gorbachev became general secretary of the Communist Party of the Soviet Union (CPSU) in March 1985 as a cautious domestic reformer. When his political career ended in December 1991, the Cold War was history. So were his party and his country.

Gorbachev's domestic reforms required a major revision of Soviet foreign policy in order to end an arms race whose costs were bankrupting vital sectors of the national economy. Reagan seized on Soviet anxieties, not only for narrow American advantage, but also because of his utopian vision of a nuclear-free

Fig. 6.1. Reagan and Gorbachev in Red Square, 31 May 1988 (Ronald Reagan Library)

world. Capitalizing on a rare moment of convergence in international politics, often in defiance of their more hawkish advisers, the two leaders transformed superpower relations through face-to-face diplomacy in a remarkable series of four summits between 1985 and 1988.[2] Their parleys in Geneva, Reykjavik, Washington, and Moscow started by establishing personal trust and culminated in a treaty abolishing intermediate-range nuclear forces (INF)—the first time that the United States and the Soviet Union had agreed to eliminate an entire category of nuclear weapons. Even though the backlash against the treaty among the military in both capitals retarded progress on a superpower strategic arms reduction treaty (START), the INF treaty signed in Washington in 1987 significantly defused tensions in the European theatre at a crucial juncture in the Cold War. The contribution of summitry to these achievements is the theme of this chapter.

SHUFFLING TOWARDS A SUMMIT

In the 1980 presidential campaign, Reagan contrasted his assertiveness about America's might and right against Jimmy Carter's alleged feebleness in response to the Iranian hostage crisis and the Soviet invasion of Afghanistan. But Reagan's attitude to diplomacy was more nuanced once in office.[3] This was evident in National Security Decision Directive (NSDD) 75 in January 1983, which delineated three guiding principles for US policy towards the USSR: first, 'to contain and over time reverse Soviet expansionism'; second, to promote 'the process of change in the Soviet Union'; and third, 'to engage the Soviet Union in negotiations to attempt to reach agreements'.[4] Reagan's long-standing antipathy toward communism and his brusque dismissal of Nixon and Kissinger's policies of détente inspired fierce rhetorical claims, such as his declaration that 'the march of freedom and democracy' would 'leave Marxism-Leninism on the ash-heap of history, as it has left other tyrannies'.[5] His conviction that 'military strength is a prerequisite to peace' was used to justify the massively increased defence budgets of his early years. Nonetheless, Reagan wanted to encourage any signs of greater pluralism in the Soviet system: hence his support for dissidents demanding human rights or religious freedom. The president believed that a combination of geopolitical muscle and diplomatic flexibility might persuade the Soviets to renounce their 'religious bent for global hegemony'. He warned that stark ultimatums would 'make it impossible for them to give in'; his preference was to 'sit around a table and tell the Russians quietly'.[6] Even though any summit was clearly a long way off, Reagan's private letters to Soviet leaders were intended to establish some kind of personal rapport.[7] George Shultz, secretary of state from 1982 to 1989, supported the president, believing that a two-pronged strategy of fortifying national strength while conducting limited and firm dialogue could yield 'a more stable', if still 'competitive', Soviet-American relationship.[8]

Reagan's intellectual complexities were most evident in his approach to nuclear weapons. It is ironic that the president who advocated 'peace through strength' and authorized one of the biggest arms build-ups of the Cold War did not, at heart, believe in the nuclear option. He was convinced that the Pentagon's deterrence doctrine of Mutual Assured Destruction (MAD) was literally mad because the human cost of a major US-Soviet nuclear war would be annihilation. Many of Reagan's advisers believed that he could never have brought himself to authorize the use of nuclear weapons. Since his days in Hollywood, Reagan held what has been described as a 'visionary, even utopian' belief in nuclear abolitionism. His gut instinct was confirmed by a visit in the summer of 1979 to the North American Aerospace Defense Command (NORAD) in Colorado Springs—nerve centre for tracking a potential nuclear attack—which was carved into the Rocky Mountains and encased in steel and concrete. In response to Reagan's questioning, however, the commanding general admitted that one Soviet SS-18 missile 'would blow us away' and that the best NORAD could do for any American city was to give its people ten to fifteen minutes notice of their extermination. Reagan was appalled. 'We have spent all that money and have all that equipment', he told an aide, 'and there is nothing we can do to prevent a nuclear missile from hitting us'.[9]

Yet Reagan also felt that the nuclear arms race would serve as an ideological litmus test, proving the superiority of capitalism over communism in providing both guns and butter. He accordingly pursued contradictory aims as president, hoping to eliminate nuclear weapons entirely, while using massive military spending to apply pressure on the Soviets. His ends were peaceful but the means he used were often confrontational. And he failed to rein in the internecine feuding amongst his advisers—Reagan had no less than six national security advisers during his eight years in office—which only added to the confused and discordant messages emanating from Washington.

The practice of 'quiet diplomacy' was therefore a minor theme of Reagan's first term. Superpower relations remained fundamentally adversarial, with tensions exacerbated by Soviet human rights violations and geo-ideological competition in Central America. The president's public statements added fuel to the fire. On 8 March 1983 he branded the Soviet Union an 'evil empire' at an evangelical conference in Florida. Two weeks later, on 23 March, he unveiled his Strategic Defense Initiative (SDI)—a programme to build a shield of space-based defences and neutralize ballistic missiles with the intent of eventually rendering nuclear weapons 'impotent and obsolete'. But what Reagan offered as the prelude to a nuclear-free world was seen by the Soviets as a new and alarming high-tech twist to the arms spiral. This was also the view of many critics in the West, who dubbed the initiative 'Star Wars'. The president's rhetoric infuriated Moscow. Veteran foreign minister Andrei

Gromyko denounced his 'organized crusade' against the Soviet Union and said that any tally of evil in the two systems would show that 'the height of the curve for the U.S.A. would be hundreds of times higher than ours'.[10]

Relations sank to a new low that autumn. In September Soviet MiGs mistakenly shot down a South Korean civilian passenger jet that had strayed into Soviet airspace, killing 270 people. Reagan damned the attack as a 'crime against humanity...an act of barbarism, born of a society which wantonly disregards individual rights and the value of human life and seeks constantly to expand and dominate other nations'. In November Moscow over-reacted to a NATO exercise 'Able Archer'. The KGB alerted the Kremlin that this might be the build-up to a Western surprise attack on the USSR and the Soviets readied their nuclear forces to pre-empt a NATO strike. CIA Deputy Director Robert Gates later admitted a general failure in Washington 'to grasp the true extent of [Soviet] anxiety'.[11]

Diplomacy had also broken down over arms control. SALT II remained unratified and the second track of NATO's 1979 Brussels decision (namely negotiations over INF) had completely stalled. To be sure, in November 1981 Reagan had proposed a zero-zero solution to the INF conundrum, offering to cancel NATO's future Cruise and Pershing deployments if the Soviets would dismantle their existing SS-20s and other INFs. On Reagan's part this was a genuine expression of his anti-nuclear creed but the Pentagon saw it merely as a public relations gesture. And the Kremlin—as the American hawks always expected—naturally rejected the 'zero option' as one-sided. After the Soviets walked out of arms control talks in 1983 the Americans went ahead with the implementation of track one, to strengthen and modernize NATO's INF posture by deploying Cruise and Pershing II missiles in Germany, Italy, and the United Kingdom. These new NATO deployments began in 1984, despite intense public opposition from peace groups and the European left. Not only had arms control proved ineffectual, but the nuclear confrontation in Europe seemed to be escalating to new and more dangerous levels.

The Soviet panic about Able Archer shocked Reagan, who was incredulous that the Russians might believe that America wanted to attack them, and this prompted one of his most conciliatory speeches to date in January 1984, when he imagined an American couple and a Russian couple sitting down together and discovering their shared humanity—a mutual love of family, home, and above all peace. He also continued his effort to engage with his Soviet counterparts through personal letters. But there was no stability of leadership in the Kremlin. Leonid Brezhnev passed away in November 1982; Yuri Andropov died in February 1984, and his successor, Konstantin Chernenko, followed just over a year later in March 1985. 'How am I supposed to get anyplace with the Russians', Reagan asked his wife Nancy, 'if they keep dying on me?'[12] Fortunately for the president, a fourth Soviet leader who was actually interested in dialogue stuck around long enough for them to meet.

GENEVA: A SPARK OF MUTUAL TRUST

Mikhail Gorbachev acceded to power on 11 March 1985. Born in 1931, he was a generation younger than his predecessors, as well as most of the Politburo, and also twenty years junior to Reagan. Gorbachev was the first Soviet leader not to have served in the Great Patriotic War. In place of the national trauma of Hitler's 'surprise attack' in 1941, the formative political influence on him was Khrushchev's 'secret speech' of 1956 revealing the grim excesses of Stalinism. The travels to the West that Gorbachev undertook in the 1970s and 1980s were another significant experience, opening his eyes to the limitations of the Soviet system and the need for 'new thinking'. He prized empirical knowledge above party dogma and turned for guidance to critics of Soviet foreign policy like the well-travelled Aleksander Yakovlev and intellectuals from the International Department of the Central Committee such as Anatoly Chernyaev, who became his principal foreign-policy adviser in February 1986. Gorbachev was the first university-educated general secretary, with a degree in law; his wife Raisa lectured in sociology. Although Gorbachev remained rooted in Marxist-Leninism, he believed that the existing Soviet system had failed to deliver the goods, both literally and metaphorically. He was especially impressed by Scandinavian models of social democracy and sought to emulate their ideas and practices without, however, fully rejecting collectivist philosophy. Like Reagan, he was therefore a man of paradox—a product of his own society who was nonetheless ready to think heretically.[13]

Taking advantage of Chernenko's funeral, Reagan sent Vice-President George H. W. Bush with a letter inviting the new Soviet leader to meet him in Washington at the 'earliest convenient opportunity'.[14] Although in his reply Gorbachev evaded the question of venue, he expressed complete agreement that a summit was desirable, albeit in the form of 'a meeting to search for mutual understanding on the basis of equality' rather than necessarily concluding 'some major documents'. Gorbachev began to consolidate his control over Soviet foreign policy. A crucial step at the end of June was the replacement of the veteran hardliner Gromyko (known to the Americans as 'Grim Grom') with Eduard Shevardnadze, the Communist Party leader in Georgia whose lack of foreign policy experience and reliance on Gorbachev's patronage made him a reliable lieutenant. He was also far more open than his predecessor. 'I like it when a person does business with a smile and gets the point of a witty remark', Shevardnadze observed, in a clear dig at Gromyko. 'We achieve little with dour solemnity and immobile facial muscles.'[15]

For now, however, the new leader's priority was domestic reform. At his nomination, a Politburo member declared that change was imperative: 'we cannot postpone questions of economic development—they will not wait'.[16] Yet the Soviet Union had fallen behind economically not just because of an outmoded industrial base but also because 20 or 30 per cent of gross domestic product was being diverted to military ends.[17] Hence Gorbachev's desire to reduce Cold War tensions.

The balance of power in Washington was also tilting in favour of dialogue. All through Reagan's first term hawks in the Pentagon and National Security Council (NSC) had encouraged a policy of confrontation. But after the president's re-election in November 1984 he felt politically freer to pursue his inclinations for quiet diplomacy. The White House believed that the United States was now in a stronger bargaining position thanks to Alliance solidarity, the successful Cruise and Pershing deployments, and Soviet alarm at SDI.[18] At the same time Shultz was gradually gaining the upper hand in his battle to wrest control of Soviet-American relations into the hands of the State Department. An economist by training and an experienced business leader, Shultz knew how to combine toughness with negotiation—both with the Soviets and in the bear-pit of Washington politics. 'Strength and realism can deter war', he told senators in 1983, 'but only direct dialogue and negotiation can open the path to lasting peace'. He also favoured making incremental progress in Soviet-American relations wherever possible—rejecting the Nixon-Kissinger tactic of strict 'linkage' between issues whereby progress in one area was contingent on progress in the others. In January 1985, even before Gorbachev gained power, Shultz persuaded the Soviets to resume arms control negotiations in Geneva, which they had so abruptly abandoned four-teen months earlier. His determined pursuit of diplomatic opportunities and his growing rapport with Shevardnadze established a vital back-channel between Washington and Moscow.

Reagan and Gorbachev's readiness to meet built on this new thaw in Soviet-American relations. In contrast with the Brezhnev-Gromyko era, Gorbachev saw summitry as a vital opportunity for mutual reconnaissance between two leaders rather than a carefully-scripted moment of political theatre to consummate a long diplomatic negotiation. Reagan shared his faith in the value of personal contact at the top. But this was a high-risk business. The White House was particularly concerned to dampen public expectations that the summit would produce a dramatic breakthrough.[19] Because the Soviet leader remained unwilling to go to Washington—that would seem too much like being America's poodle—they eventually settled on Geneva, in neutral Switzerland, as a mutually acceptable venue reflecting their equality as superpowers.

The two sides approached the summit with different goals in mind. The Kremlin tried to resist American efforts to get human rights and regional conflicts on the agenda but Reagan kept pursuing these issues, speaking to the UN in October about 'a broader vision of world leadership' that went 'beyond arms control' to truly reflect 'Western ideals'.[20] Moscow wanted to keep the focus of the summit on the arms race, with Gorbachev waging a 'star peace' campaign to depict SDI as the lone obstacle to nuclear arms control. A new and dynamic radicalism was now transforming Soviet foreign policy.

Chernyaev had outlined some of its key elements as early as 1982: withdrawal from Afghanistan, non-intervention in Eastern Europe, removal of European SS-20s, military cuts, and more open borders.[21] Summitry was deemed critical to the success of this diplomatic grand design. Yakovlev counselled Gorbachev that Reagan wanted to be remembered as a 'great peace-maker President' and encouraged him to 'get a personal impression' of Reagan in Geneva. As a test, Gorbachev proposed a 50 per cent cut in both sides' nuclear arsenals if the United States would abandon Star Wars. Such a concession was inconceivable in Washington but the Reagan administration was not of one mind on how to exploit SDI. Defense Secretary Caspar Weinberger and CIA Director William Casey—both viscerally suspicious of the USSR—insisted that weapons programmes, especially SDI, were non-negotiable, whereas Shultz wanted to keep them up his sleeve as possible 'bargaining chips'.[22] Characteristically Reagan was reluctant to arbitrate the 'many irreconcilable differences', leaving US policy in this vital area inchoate.[23]

Both leaders approached the summit in a mood of uncertainty, struggling to decipher each other's mixed signals. Gorbachev had admonished Reagan back in March that 'trust is an especially sensitive thing', which would 'not be enhanced, for example, if one were to talk as if in two languages: one for private contacts and the other, as they say, for the audience'. Here was a clear reference to the grating dissonance of the two Reagans—the would-be diplomatist and the strident ideologue.[24] The American failure to come up with a draft communiqué in advance of the summit, due to the bureaucratic infighting over SDI, aroused particular suspicion in Moscow; it seemed to suggest that the United States was not serious about the meeting. In Washington, those prepping the president for the summit highlighted similar contradictions in their adversary. Veteran diplomat Jack Matlock, now a senior adviser in the NSC, diagnosed a split Soviet personality that would 'lie and cheat' or 'stonewall a negotiation', but could also be 'candid to a fault—grovelling in his nation's inadequacies'. (Reagan called Matlock's essay 'one of the best things I have read on the Soviet Russian psychology'.)[25] For his part Shultz depicted Gorbachev as a 'curious blend of new and old', ready for reform but 'not about to squander the legacy of Soviet power'.[26] Lessons from previous Cold War encounters were not deemed encouraging: Kenneth Adelman, director of the Arms Control and Disarmament Agency, judged summits a 'risky business at best' that had 'clearly not helped moderate Soviet behavior'.[27] On the eve of the summit, neither side entertained high expectations, though Shultz had at least managed to secure a more united American delegation by keeping the ever-obstructive Weinberger off the plane.[28]

The long-awaited encounter took place in Geneva from 19 to 21 November 1985, in the full glare of the world's media. (Almost all the city's 12,000 hotel rooms had been booked for months and the Americans took over the entire 500-room Intercontinental for staffers and the White House press corps.[29])

Reagan hosted the first day's meetings in a private villa on Lake Geneva; on the second day the leaders moved downtown to the Soviet embassy. The summit combined plenary meetings—featuring long and often formulaic statements, especially by the president—with informal one-on-one encounters that were mediated only by interpreters. The public face of each leader was on display in the plenaries, as Reagan and Gorbachev indulged in ideological sloganeering and dug in on entrenched positions—human rights for Reagan, SDI for Gorbachev. Debate on the latter issue became particularly intense on the second day, with the Soviet leader insisting that SDI could allow the Americans to mount a first strike on the USSR and Reagan reiterating his mantra that SDI would be a 'shield' not a 'spear'. 'Do you take us for idiots?' Gorbachev exploded at one point. Ironically the novelty of using simultaneous translation in the plenaries, which speeded up business and more naturally connected words to body language, also allowed the exchanges to become more heated with Gorbachev frequently cutting in before Reagan's translator had finished.[30]

Ultimately the plenaries mattered less than the personal tête-à-têtes, all of which overran their allotted time because the two men were surprised to find that they clicked. Chatting on day one before a roaring fire in a pool house overlooking Lake Geneva (see Figure 6.2), Gorbachev began to grasp 'on a human level' Reagan's utopian hopes for SDI, while also getting across his own passionate fear of 'starting an arms race in a new sphere'. By the time they left the pool house they had agreed—to the delight of Shultz—on further summits

Fig. 6.2. Reagan-Gorbachev fireside chat at Fleur d'Eau, Geneva, 19 November 1985 (Ronald Reagan Library)

in Washington and Moscow.[31] As they parted on the first evening, the two men 'locked hands and eyes with real affection'; according to Reagan's official biographer: 'I have rarely seen such mutuality.' Gorbachev remembered what he called a 'spark of electric mutual trust which ignited between us, like a voltaic arc between two electric poles'. The president also responded on a human level. 'You could almost get to like the guy', he admitted that evening to his Chief of Staff Don Regan.[32] At the end of the summit the two leaders issued a joint statement that 'nuclear war cannot be won and must never be fought'—Reagan's formulation, which Gorbachev had embraced.[33] None of this overrode each man's fierce ideological commitment, or their frequent mutual frustration—Gorbachev being particularly prone to fume about the 'banalities' that Reagan often uttered. Yet that spark of mutual trust was never truly extinguished.

REYKJAVIK: THINKING THE UNTHINKABLE

By the criteria that the Americans had set beforehand—'to establish personal contact and, if possible, to develop an agenda for negotiations'—Geneva proved a success.[34] White House officials wanted to schedule the second summit expeditiously on the assumption that 'momentum' was now with them.[35] Gorbachev was more ambivalent. He praised 'the spirit of Geneva' but complained that Reagan had been facile and intransigent.[36] To increase the pressure on the White House, on 15 January 1986 he publicized a three-stage plan to eliminate nuclear weapons by the new millennium. The superpowers would sign a Comprehensive Test Ban Treaty, halve their strategic arsenals, and drastically reduce INF forces. Britain, France, and China would then join them in multilateral talks to shrink nuclear forces worldwide. The process would culminate with the international community formalizing the abolition of nuclear weapons in a treaty.[37] Reagan admitted that the speech was, 'at the very least', one 'hell of a propaganda move', but he disliked being upstaged and resented Gorbachev giving him only one day's advance notice.[38] The president stopped handwriting his letters to Gorbachev to get across 'without saying so, that the use of proposals for propaganda is not helpful'.[39]

Gorbachev's *démarche* shrewdly exploited a deepening defence debate within NATO, exacerbated by SDI. Multilateralists in Washington such as Reagan's arms control fixer Paul Nitze wanted to maintain a balance of terror based on credible deterrents for both sides.[40] Unilateralists such as NSC staffer Robert Linhard believed that stability would be achieved by making SDI 'as effective as possible as soon as possible'.[41] Western European allies, most vocally British Prime Minister Margaret Thatcher, sided with Nitze, dismissing anti-ballistic missile (ABM) systems as too speculative to rely upon and, if ever implemented, likely to decouple American security from that of Western Europe.

The debate also had a very public dimension. As early as April 1982 an NSC report pinpointed mushrooming anti-nuclear sentiment in Europe and America as 'the most important national security opportunity and challenge of this Administration'.[42] Both SDI and START were therefore deliberately framed as steps towards nuclear disarmament. But this did not quell the growing movement for a nuclear 'freeze' which, by 1986, was attracting significant support from mainstream religious organizations in the United States. To counter Gorbachev's peace campaign the NSC recommended an American declaration renouncing first use of nuclear weapons, on the grounds that this was 'near and dear to the hearts of disarmamenters and Catholic Bishops'.[43] But Reagan's attitude to anti-nuclear feeling was more sympathetic. Shultz told one British official that even though many US 'arms control experts' belittled abolition, the president shared the 'growing unease' about nuclear weapons and was seeking a 'stable pattern within which to reduce them'.[44] At a National Security Planning Group meeting in February, Reagan rebuffed Weinberger and other hawks when they dismissed Gorbachev's disarmament plan as a 'publicity stunt', ordering a response that 'we share their overall goals' and 'now want to work out the details'.[45]

Early planning for Gorbachev's American summit envisaged a grand tour of the United States from Washington to Los Angeles.[46] But that was before the Chernobyl disaster changed the terms of debate. The disastrous meltdown at the Ukrainian nuclear power plant on 26 April 1986 was the worst civilian nuclear accident of the Cold War era, releasing over four hundred times more radioactive material than the bomb dropped on Hiroshima in 1945, with fallout spreading across much of Eastern and Central Europe from the Baltic to the Mediterranean. Equally damaging for the Kremlin was the fact that the first significant information about the scale of the disaster came from Sweden and was not officially acknowledged in Moscow for several days. The impact of the disaster on Gorbachev and like-minded colleagues was immense. 'Just a puff and we can all feel what nuclear war would be like', he told the Politburo. He asked them to imagine what a real nuclear war 'would mean for Europe with its concentration of population'.[47]

Chernobyl injected new passion into Gorbachev's quest to abolish nuclear weapons. It also underlined the importance of his policy of *glasnost*—variously translated as openness, transparency, or even freedom of information—to appease critics of the Chernobyl cover-up at home and abroad. Yet he was also increasingly alarmed at the hawkish rhetoric from the president and his advisers, intended in part to resist Congressional attempts to rein in defence expenditures by fanning the flames of domestic anti-communism. The Soviet leader feared, in short, that the spirit of Geneva was evaporating fast and the

consequences of inaction for the USSR would be grave. 'If we do not compromise now on some questions, even very important ones', Gorbachev
warned his foreign policy advisers, 'we will be pulled into an arms race beyond
our power, and we will lose this race, for we are presently at the limit of our
capabilities'. His plan, outlined by Chernyaev, was still for mutual 50 per cent
cuts in all types of nuclear weapons, giving priority to the removal of all Soviet-
American INFs from Europe. The Pershing IIs, he asserted, were like 'a gun
pressed to our temple'. On a larger plane, Gorbachev made clear that 'my
ultimate goal is the liquidation of nuclear weapons'.[48]

These concerns lay behind the letter that the Soviet leader sent to Reagan on
15 September 1986. He proposed 'a quick one-on-one meeting' in Iceland or
London, perhaps for just a single day, in order to generate 'instructions to our
respective agencies on two or three very specific questions, which you and
I could sign during my visit to the United States'. The questions Gorbachev
identified were: (i) extending the duration of the ABM treaty of 1972 and
strengthening its content, especially by restricting R&D on space weapons
to 'laboratories'; (ii) accepting the Soviet INF proposals for the 'complete
elimination' of Soviet and American medium-range missiles in Europe; and
(iii) agreeing to a complete moratorium on nuclear testing. There had been 'no
movement on these issues' since Geneva, Gorbachev argued, and everything
would 'continue to mark time' unless the two of them provided 'a major
impetus' from the very top 'to demonstrate political will'.[49]

Historian James Graham Wilson has observed that Gorbachev's letter
offered Reagan more Soviet concessions 'than in the entirety of his presidency
up to that time'. But Washington does not seem to have appreciated just how
serious and radical Gorbachev was. Discounting his concrete proposals, the
NSC complained of the Soviet leader's 'coyness' about his real intentions and
advised the president to 'smoke him out in your discussions'. Shultz saw the
offer of a meeting as evidence that Reagan's policy of negotiation from
strength was paying off. Their aim, he said, should be 'to produce substantive
progress (but no agreements per se) at Reykjavik that will enhance the chances
for a successful summit in the U.S.' He wanted the agenda to highlight two
issues: arms control, especially START, and human rights. The Americans
clearly approached Reykjavik as a preparatory meeting for the real 'summit' in
the United States. No one foresaw the drama that would ensue in Iceland.[50]

Reagan and Gorbachev met at Höfði, a government guesthouse just outside the windswept Icelandic capital, on 11 October. The venue was suitably
secluded yet cramped: for one presidential briefing, American staffers had
to use a tiny upstairs bathroom, with three senior aides standing in the tub.
When Reagan walked in he said, 'I'll take the throne' and sat on top of the
toilet.[51] Unlike Geneva, Reykjavik was intended as a strictly business affair,
mainly one-on-one. But it went beyond the single day originally envisaged
because the four plenary meetings and related discussions among advisers

gained a momentum of their own focusing, under the stimulus of Gorbachev's radical package, largely on arms control—contrary to the wider American agenda. At the first session the Soviet leader proposed a mutual 50 per cent cut in strategic nuclear forces, the 'complete elimination' of Soviet and American INFs in Europe, and total adherence to the ABM treaty of 1972 for at least another ten years, followed by a period of three to five years in which the two superpowers would negotiate about how to proceed. During this interval, R&D into space weapons would not be conducted 'outside of laboratories'.[52] Without this last provision, as Gorbachev's briefing papers noted, 'it would be impossible for the Soviet Union to reduce its strategic nuclear forces because that would objectively help the United States to achieve a decisive military advantage over us'. The Soviets did not expect to strangle SDI completely but wanted to prevent the Americans from using their head start in space weaponry to extract concessions from the USSR in nuclear arms talks. 'If the United States does not test these weapons over the next 10 years, that will allow us to decrease our lag behind them in creating the space-based echelon of ABM defense.' Seeing SDI in this overall context of linked diplomatic bargaining Gorbachev was therefore adamant that the 'package' had to be accepted as a whole: his offer of radical arms cuts was conditional on Reagan accepting a brake on SDI.[53]

Nitze, whose government service stretched back to World War Two, called the Soviet proposal 'the best we have received in 25 years'.[54] But to Gorbachev's chagrin, Reagan did not respond enthusiastically in the first session. Sticking to his prompt cards, he reiterated his commitment to the principle of SDI and emphasized that any INF deal must take account of such weapons in Asia as well. The president also highlighted the issue of verification, trotting out a Russian proverb he had recently learned, '*doveryai no proveryai*'—'trust, but verify'—which would become his mantra.[55] After a lunch break that afforded the Americans time to assess Gorbachev's proposals, the two men got down to details. Reagan said that they would accept a mutual zero in Europe on INFs if an acceptable deal was also reached on INFs in Asia. Gorbachev was receptive. On what the Soviet leader called 'space weapons' Reagan kept insisting that SDI was a peaceful technology that the United States was ready to share. This inflamed the nerve Reagan had touched in Geneva. 'Excuse me, Mr President', Gorbachev finally exploded: 'You are not willing to share with us oil-well equipment, digitally guided machine tools, or even milking machines. Sharing SDI would provoke a second American revolution! Let's be realistic and pragmatic.'[56] Despite this outburst, the leaders set up two groups of staffers to work through specific problems. One group dealt with arms control, the other with a range of diplomatic issues including human rights, regional conflicts, and improved contacts and communication. While the latter group finished its work by midnight, the arms controllers—headed by Nitze and his Soviet counterpart, Marshal Sergei Akhromeyev—laboured until four in the morning, as the Americans tried to pick apart what the Soviets kept insisting was a single package. Although the two sides moved closer to the idea of a 50 per cent cut in strategic forces, the Soviets still linked this to agreement on controlling the testing of SDI. 'We brought closer our positions on strategic weapons quite well', a weary Akhromeyev summed up, 'but completely disagreed on the ABM. This makes strategic weapons reductions impossible...Regretfully our work today did not lead to big results.'[57]

The next morning, at the start of a session that ran from 10.00am until 1.35pm, Gorbachev complained that the Americans seemed resistant to his offers. The United States 'did not appear to feel obliged to take Soviet concerns into account, while the Soviets had met American concerns'. On INFs, they agreed on a zero option for Europe and 100 missiles each in Asia. But on SDI the two leaders dug in, with Reagan quoting Marx and Lenin and Gorbachev fuming about the president's 'evil empire' rhetoric. In desperation, Shevardnadze asked if they could at least reach an agreement about the duration of the ABM treaty but Gorbachev cut that off: 'I made a specific package proposal, and I would ask you to treat it as such.' Reagan inquired whether all the progress they had made should be thrown away because of this Soviet insistence on linkage.[58]

After a cursory survey of the other working group's suggestions, they agreed to pause for thought and re-convene in mid-afternoon. The discussions resumed at 3.25, only for the Americans to take an hour-long break at 4.30 as they tried to come up with a form of words that would satisfy Gorbachev's concerns about confining the testing of SDI to 'laboratories'. Shultz, Nitze, and Adelman wanted to meet him halfway, but National Security Adviser John Poindexter and Assistant Secretary of Defense Richard Perle would not budge.[59] Eventually the American group settled on the ten-year timeframe for respecting the ABM treaty but refused to limit SDI R&D to laboratories; at the end of the ten years 'either side could deploy [space-based] defenses if it so chose'.[60] They also switched what would be eliminated during years five to ten from 'strategic offensive arms' to 'offensive ballistic missiles'—probably to retain US advantages in cruise missiles and long-range bombers.

When the leaders reconvened at 5.30, there ensued an increasingly frazzled discussion between men who were now teetering between exhilaration and exhaustion. From the minutes it is unclear whether they were talking about eliminating strategic weapons, ballistic missiles, or nuclear weapons as a whole. But ultimately neither leader would budge on what both agreed was 'one word'—'laboratories'. Gorbachev insisted it was 'unacceptable' for him to offer 'deep reductions in nuclear weapons' while allowing the Americans to 'conduct all sorts of research that would go against the ABM Treaty, and put weapons in space': he would be denounced at home as a 'dummy' (*durak*). The president responded in kind, as 'one political leader to another'. If he did what Gorbachev asked, he would lay himself open to the extreme anti-Soviet right who were already 'kicking his brains out'. In the cold prose of the American minutes:

> The President said that he could not give in.
> Gorbachev asked if that was the last word.
> The President said yes.[61]

Reykjavik's denouement obscured its momentousness.[62] When cameras recorded the two leaders' haggard faces and tense body language as they left Höfði, a tragic requiem became the media's dominant theme. Privately, however, the participants, despite outbursts of anger, were hopeful. It was significant that Gorbachev chose not to heed instructions from the Politburo to 'make everything public' if Reagan refused to react positively. 'In no sense would I call Reykjavik a failure', Gorbachev told his team on the flight home. 'It is a step in a complicated and difficult dialogue. I am even more of an optimist after Reykjavik.'[63] Reagan expressed similar sentiments. In a national address he portrayed himself as standing firm on human rights and SDI while proposing 'the most sweeping and generous arms control proposal in history'. Although the Soviets had not accepted the American offer, he said 'we are closer than ever before to agreements that could lead to a safer world without nuclear weapons'. This was no mere rhetoric. Matlock concluded that 'the extent of agreement on key points was unprecedented'; according to Chernyaev, the meeting proved to Gorbachev that he and Reagan could 'do real business' together after all.[64]

At Reykjavik, the two leaders changed the whole tenor of the arms control debate. By sharing their dream of a nuclear-free world, they had dared to think the unthinkable.

WASHINGTON: DOING THE UNPRECEDENTED

Once again, however, coming down from the summit proved an anti-climax— and an occasion for second thoughts. Gorbachev increasingly believed that Reagan 'was not free in making his decisions', opining that he and Shultz 'have their hands and feet tied by the military-industrial complex'.[65] The Soviet leader was also acutely conscious of the growing budget crisis in the USSR. So although remaining obdurate about his 'package' approach to arms control negotiations, he now shifted ground on restricting SDI R&D to the 'laboratory'. On 30 October, undeterred by dyspeptic comments from Gromyko, the Politburo agreed that it would accept testing anywhere except in space. There was a catch however. They would not disclose this new position to the Americans until the White House made clear its definition of 'laboratory'.[66]

In Washington, too, the autumn of 1986 was a time for second thoughts—or more accurately a counterattack by hawkish critics of the president appalled at how far he had (nearly) gone. Neither quiet diplomacy nor top-level summitry had forged a consensus within the administration or in Congress. Even the exact nature of what had transpired in Iceland was a matter of dispute. Reagan had been imprecise and inconsistent in his subsequent remarks to the nation, noting that ballistic missiles and SDI had been the main issues at stake before lamenting that 'all that work toward eliminating nuclear weapons' might 'go down the drain'.[67] To Thatcher, he recalled a proposal that would have halved all nuclear weapons and then eliminated ballistic missiles. The *Washington Post* quoted sources on Capitol Hill who recalled him praising nuclear abolition in front of members of the Congress.[68] Seeking a clearer line while also trying to rein in his boss, Poindexter urged the president to 'step back from any discussion of eliminating all nuclear weapons' and instead to focus on 'offensive ballistic missiles'. He warned that removing nuclear weapons from Europe would undermine Atlantic relations because NATO allies feared a costly transition to conventional defences and he remarked on how they were exhibiting 'new (and ironic) appreciation for SDI' after it had scuttled a disarmament deal in Iceland.[69] Thatcher, in particular, was aghast at Reagan's anti-nuclear rhetoric. 'How could he do it?' she exclaimed. 'What is he doing?' Descending on the president at Camp David on 14 November with a draft in her handbag, she secured a joint statement affirming their commitment to NATO's policy of nuclear deterrence.[70]

The Pentagon also did its best to turn back the clock on Reykjavik. Tipped off by a Soviet official that there was clear 'give' in Moscow on SDI, Shultz wanted to 'get away' from the word 'laboratory' and allow arms control negotiators in Geneva to discuss 'exactly what activities are permitted and what activities are prohibited under the ABM Treaty'.[71] But Weinberger was unyielding. He took his reservations straight to Reagan—trivializing Soviet concessions, lambasting attempts to revise defence policy 'through the back door', and categorically rejecting any 'limitations' on SDI.[72] He and the Pentagon eventually prevailed. Shultz was instructed not to make the ABM Treaty 'more restrictive' than in 1972 and in consequence Shevardnadze never revealed that laboratories were no longer the Politburo's red line.[73]

In Gorbachev's eyes, Reagan seemed to be disavowing Reykjavik. The White House declared that it would stop abiding by the SALT II treaty. Gorbachev protested 'not only that they are not doing anything in the spirit of Reykjavik, but they are removing all breaks from the arms race'. Financial considerations weighed heavily on him. Even a limited 'asymmetric' response to SDI would cost his government $30–40 billion, when Moscow was already pouring $4 billion per year into Afghanistan. Meanwhile he was under attack from the military who, he told the Politburo, were 'hissing among themselves' about the way he was supposedly 'disarming the country'.[74]

In an effort to impose a concerted policy in Washington, the NSC took firm control of preparations for presidential directive NSDD 250—even demanding that the draft be returned in a couple of hours to forestall stonewalling or fundamental criticisms.[75] Entitled 'Post-Reykjavik Policy', NSSD 250 turned the anti-nuclear radicalism of Reykjavik into a more specific evolutionary plan for eventually eliminating ballistic missiles. Yet even this was controversial within the Beltway. The Joint Chiefs of Staff promptly responded that abolishing ballistic missiles would entail a massive compensatory increase in spending on conventional forces.[76]

NSDD 250 was issued on 3 November 1986, only to be immediately overtaken by events. That same day news broke about a secret administration operation to sell arms to Iran and then use the proceeds to finance anti-communist Contra guerrillas in Nicaragua—both prongs of which violated Congressional legislation. By 25 November Poindexter had resigned in response to accusations that he had shredded presidential documents; the scandal spread to finger Weinberger and even the president himself. Reagan felt obliged to set up a special commission and, although not directly implicated in its findings, he formally apologized to the nation in a televised address in March 1987. The Iran-Contra affair—for a time spoken of as a second Watergate—tarnished Reagan's hitherto 'Teflon' reputation and sapped the president's own morale.

Even more damaging for his presidency were the mid-term Congressional elections held on 4 November 1986. The Democrats tightened their grip on the House of Representatives to a majority of eighty seats while also regaining control of the Senate with a ten-seat margin of fifty-five to forty-five. Now that his opponents were in full control of Capitol Hill, Reagan feared that the days of generous funding for SDI were over. In desperation Weinberger vainly urged the president to approve immediate testing outside the laboratory and called for phased deployment as early as 1993. Despite all Weinberger's bluster, however, Reagan's was now a 'weakened presidency'.[77]

The implications of Iran-Contra and the Congressional elections were not lost on the Soviets. In a long memo on 25 February 1987 Yakovlev urged Gorbachev to exploit the diplomatic opportunity—in particular by 'untying' the arms control 'package' that the USSR had placed on the table at Reykjavik. The ideas in the package still worked, both as policy and as propaganda, Yakovlev contended, but 'the "package" in its present form only ties our hands' because the Reagan administration could represent it as 'our final position' and thereby continue the deadlock on arms control. The following day Gorbachev and the Politburo agreed to 'untie the package', planning a dramatic speech by the Soviet leader in mid-March to win over world opinion and kick-start negotiations. 'As difficult as it is to conduct business with the United States,' Gorbachev lamented, 'we are doomed to it. We have no choice.' He cautioned his colleagues that 'we should not build our policy on illusions.

We should not count on capitalism suffering an economic crisis', as Marxism-Leninism predicted, adding that 'competition will continue in any case . . . Our main problem is to remove the confrontation. That is the central issue of our foreign policy.'[78]

The danger of American backtracking and the imperatives of Soviet reforms made limited arms control agreements more appealing. Gorbachev's domestic agenda was now moving into high gear. Sensitive to the drumbeat of American pressure on human rights, in December 1986 he had released the celebrated dissident Andrei Sakharov from house arrest. Gorbachev knew full well that Sakharov would now criticize the Soviet government relentlessly but his decision was a hugely symbolic signal to the West, addressing one of Reagan's major critiques of the 'evil empire'. Shevardnadze set up a human rights bureau in the Foreign Ministry and began to ease restrictions on the emigration of Soviet Jews. In January 1987 Gorbachev told the party plenum that the 'further democratization of Soviet society' was the most urgent task facing the CPSU. He also enlarged the concept of *perestroika* beyond its previous connotation of 'economic restructuring' to become the signature for his whole ethos of leadership. His book *Perestroika: New Thinking for Our Country and the World*, published in America on 3 November 1987, proved a global bestseller. It helped to disseminate his concepts of 'reasonable sufficiency' in weaponry, rather than an ever-accelerating arms race, and of a 'common European home' instead of a nuclear face-off across the iron curtain. In all these respects Gorbachev was strengthening his position for radical arms control agreements, especially on theatre nuclear forces in Europe.[79]

Facing a Soviet leadership that was increasingly coherent and bold, Reagan's administration remained divided and cautious. The key figure in brokering an eventual deal was George Shultz. In an effort to pick up the momentum after Reykjavik, he held direct talks with Gorbachev and the Soviet leadership on 13–14 April 1987. Shultz's trip aroused a storm of protest on Capitol Hill, already up in arms about sensationalized reports of Soviet spies infiltrating the US embassy in Moscow. Before the secretary of state set off, Weinberger—playing his customary role as spoiler—had inveigled the president into signing instructions (immediately leaked to the press) that, in Shultz's words, were almost intended to ensure that 'I came back from Moscow without any progress toward an agreement'.[80]

In Moscow he found Gorbachev at his most intemperate: 'I have an impression listening to you', he told Shultz, 'that you are walking around hot porridge and cannot make a decision to do anything'. Eventually their talks did make headway, in three areas. Gorbachev agreed to a 'global zero' for intermediate-range nuclear forces, roughly 1,000 to 5,500 kilometres in range, thus covering Soviet and American arsenals in both Europe and Asia. Shultz wanted to include shorter-range INFs (SRINFs), from 500 to 1,000 kilometres in range, a category in which the USSR had some 160 missiles operationally deployed and the United States none at all. Gorbachev responded by proposing to abolish all SRINFs in Europe—an offer that greatly benefited the United States—but, because of his tight brief, Shultz was left in the embarrassing position of having to argue for the right to reach equality by building new American SRINFs. An incredulous Gorbachev exclaimed: 'But we want to eliminate these missiles', to which Shultz replied lamely: 'We want to have the right to have an equal level'. Gorbachev also proved surprisingly radical on verification—an issue that had bedevilled the negotiation of SALT II in 1978–9. In the spirit of *glasnost*, he sketched out a comprehensive regime of on-site inspections that went further than the Americans themselves were willing to go. In the light of his new 'reasonable sufficiency' thinking, with national security no longer seen as a zero-sum game, the precise size of the Soviet nuclear arsenal—so sensitive for his predecessors, haunted by 1941—was no longer of decisive importance.[81]

Traditional Cold War axioms of military superiority were, however, still very much ascendant in Washington. Shultz returned from Moscow with the outlines of an INF deal, to which the president was receptive because of his need for a foreign-policy success to redeem the Iran-Contra debacle. But Shultz still had to battle with administration hawks and opponents on Capitol Hill and to convince the president's alter ego that the Soviets were serious. Privately Reagan assured his old friend William Buckley, a noted anti-communist ideologue, in May: 'I have not changed my belief that we are dealing with an "evil empire".' And he kept up the propaganda war with a rousing speech in front of the Berlin Wall at the Brandenburg Gate on 12 June. Challenging the Soviet leader to show that *perestroika* and *glasnost* were more than 'token gestures', the president called for one 'unmistakable' sign of his commitment to 'freedom and peace': 'Mr Gorbachev, tear down this wall!' He had made this demand many times before but repeated it in this headline-catching venue to show he was not a politically crippled president and to prove his continued toughness in dealing with Moscow.[82]

Shultz also had to secure the agreement of America's NATO allies for the 'double-zero' deal on INFs and SRINFs in Europe. Even though the British and French nuclear deterrents had always been excluded from bargaining, Thatcher deplored what she saw as an erosion of nuclear deterrence and it took until 12 June for NATO to approve. There followed a protracted wrangle about the SRINFs in West Germany—Pershing 1As—which Washington and Bonn regarded as 'German missiles' even though the United States owned and controlled their nuclear warheads. Chancellor Helmut Kohl eventually agreed in late August to eliminate the Pershing IAs as part of the overall settlement with the Soviets. Weinberger's Pentagon—obstructive to the end—had tried to get round this with the ploy of converting Pershing II missiles into short-range Pershing IBs and turning them over to the Germans, but Kohl refused.[83]

Gorbachev was eager for a summit in America to sign the INF Treaty but he, too, had to square his conservative critics. Here luck played into his hands. On 28 May a single-engine plane had landed in the middle of Red Square and taxied to a stop in front of St Basil's Cathedral. The pilot was an eccentric West German teenager, Mathias Rust, who had improbably managed to evade all Soviet air defences along the way. This hugely embarrassing incident gave Gorbachev a pretext to 'retire' some 150 senior officers, from Defence Minister Marshal Sergei Sokolov downward—thereby removing (peacefully) a higher percentage of the Soviet military elite than in Stalin's notorious purge of 1937. In their place Gorbachev promoted officers who were more loyal and open-minded.[84] On 9 July he secured Politburo approval for a double-zero on INFs and SRINFs in Europe and Asia, asserting confidently that this would 'make a strong impression in China, Japan, and the whole of Asia...We will get a huge political victory.' The new policy was announced two weeks later.[85]

Gorbachev also moved to staunch the 'bleeding wound' in Afghanistan—warning the Politburo that without decisive action the war might go on 'for another 20-30 years'. He therefore engineered a transfer of leadership in Kabul from communist strongman Babrak Karmal to Mohammed Najibullah, a moderate politician who, at Gorbachev's behest, embraced a policy of national reconciliation aimed at constructing a coalition government.[86] When Shevardnadze visited Washington in mid-September, he told Shultz in confidence: 'We will leave Afghanistan. It may be in five months or a year, but it is not a question of it happening in the remote future. I say with all responsibility that a political decision has been made.' Shultz was acutely conscious that this was a 'dramatic moment' because the Kremlin's intervention in Afghanistan at Christmas 1979 had sparked the 'New Cold War' and had also proved a massive drain on national resources and psychology—making Afghanistan the Soviets' equivalent of Vietnam.[87]

After Shevardnadze's visit, Shultz gained the president's approval to announce that the two superpowers had 'agreed in principle' to conclude an INF treaty and that this would probably be signed by the two leaders at a summit in Washington before Christmas. There was still significant criticism—Henry Kissinger for one complained that the deal 'undoes forty years of NATO'—but the pertinacious secretary of state had won a major diplomatic victory. There was, however, a sting in the tail. Weinberger persuaded Reagan, schizophrenic as ever about the Soviets, to take a tough line on the rest of the arms control agenda, insisting on no compromises on strategic weapons or anti-missile defences. The defense secretary never trusted Gorbachev or believed he was sincere about reform. Weinberger's hardnosed concept of diplomacy was that if the Soviets made concessions, the Americans should simply increase the pressure, extract more, and give away nothing. 'No negotiations for two years', he told the president. Although Weinberger was now increasingly isolated and on the way out—he would resign in November, ostensibly on account of his wife's health—he had effectively ring-fenced START and SDI for the rest of Reagan's presidency. In October Gorbachev tried to make his attendance at a summit conditional on American movement on strategic and space weapons but, faced with White House obduracy, he backed off. The INF deal was too important for him to risk derailment and he finally agreed to come to the US capital in December in order to sign it.[88]

Washington was a different kind of Reagan-Gorbachev summit from its predecessors. Geneva and Reykjavik had been decisive moments in the Cold War—the first by sparking mutual engagement, the second in changing the terms of the whole nuclear debate. By contrast, the Washington summit of 7–10 December witnessed few breakthroughs: the hard work had been done via painstaking diplomacy over the previous six months and the event itself was largely symbolic. Yet the symbolism was hugely important. Having dared to think the unthinkable at Reykjavik, the two leaders (now on first-name terms) had moved from thought to action in doing the unprecedented. For the first time in the Cold War the superpowers signed an agreement to reduce their nuclear arsenals, not merely setting a limit to further growth as Nixon and Brezhnev had done with SALT I. Moreover, they had agreed to eliminate a whole category of nuclear weapons that were especially feared for their quick-strike ability. Even though this amounted to only about 5 per cent of total nuclear stocks, it was a sign that the superpowers were capable of reversing their decades-long arms race. And the provisions for mutual verification, even inspections without notice, demonstrated a new level of mutual trust and openness. If anything Gorbachev, intoxicated by the spirit of *glasnost*, had proved more forthcoming on this issue than the Americans. The impression of new thinking was enhanced by his public relations offensive while in America. Images of an elegant and animated Soviet leader chatting with Steven Spielberg and Joe DiMaggio, or jumping out of his limo to press the flesh on a Washington street-corner, showed as vividly as the INF treaty that the Soviet Union was in the grip of revolutionary change.

MOSCOW: AN UNFULFILLED CLIMAX

The Soviets remained hopeful about further nuclear arms control. Gorbachev was keen to 'crown' the president's proposed visit to Moscow the following spring with 'an agreement on strategic offensive weapons'.[89] But hardline elements in the NSC, CIA, and the Pentagon had mobilized in opposition even before the Washington summit. A typical NSC paper presented Soviet concessions as intended to help Gorbachev 'consolidate his power, slow up our defense modernization and SDI programs, ease technology transfers, and split us from NATO'. NSC analyst Fritz Ermarth warned that a 'grand compromise' was afoot that could 'open the road' to 'a START deal in the spring, and a brilliant summit in Moscow'. He suggested that Frank Carlucci, Reagan's latest national security adviser, had 'better preempt'.[90] Carlucci, together with his deputy (and soon successor) Colin Powell wanted a 'hardheaded summit' that would focus on regional conflicts rather than arms control. Their aim was to slow down progress in discussing strategic and space weaponry, thereby making a Moscow 'coronation' unlikely. And they certainly did not want a repeat of Reykjavik, when the two leaders had taken the ball and run with it. NSC staffers therefore dreamed up 'a whole list of possible tricks for deflecting the momentum of conversation and buying time' in order to 'turn the tables on the Soviets and use the [Moscow summit] deadline against them'.[91]

When in Washington for the December 1987 summit, Shevardnadze sensed that decisions were now flowing upward, rather than being made at the top. Reagan was clearly hamstrung in arms control policy by the National Security Directives he had been persuaded to sign. The president confessed rather pathetically to a frustrated Gorbachev that both of them had 'problems with bureaucracy'.[92] Such obstruction was not new, of course, but at Geneva and Reykjavik Gorbachev had galvanized Reagan, who in turn generated the energy and will to surmount numerous obstacles. In the twilight of his second term, however, weary and perhaps already exhibiting the symptoms of Alzheimer's disease, Reagan lacked the ambition and stamina to cut through the red tape. And as a lame-duck president facing a legislative branch controlled by the Democrats, and with many of his own party still vehemently anti-Soviet, Reagan had much less scope to take radical action. It was not until 27 May 1988, on the eve of the Moscow summit, that the Senate voted to ratify the INF Treaty. This delay, reminiscent of the SALT II saga, handcuffed START negotiators ahead of the Moscow summit and also undermined the Kremlin's confidence in the Americans. The last straw was the refusal of the US Navy to sacrifice its sea-launched cruise missiles, which would block START until its resolution in 1991.[93]

For his part, Gorbachev was in a weaker position over START than he had been over INF. The Soviet military was jealous of nuclear 'parity' with the United States—a hard-won gain from the summitry of the early 1970s. The INF Treaty had dismantled almost five times as many Soviet missiles as American, including SRINFs against which the United States had never developed their own equivalents. So military hawks resisted additional concessions on strategic weapons, despite Gorbachev's conviction that 'without a significant reduction in military spending we will not be able to solve the problems of *perestroika*'.[94]

At the Moscow summit, which ran from 29 May to 2 June 1988, American objectives were unambitious. The White House simply aimed to 'consolidate' the gains already made, warning against 'exaggerated expectations' on the future pace of Soviet-American rapprochement or of the reform process in the Soviet Union.[95] The event was consequently bigger on pageantry than on substance. Reagan rhapsodized about liberty and enterprise to students at Moscow State University and hosted Soviet political dissidents at the US embassy. The two leaders signed ratification documents for the INF Treaty and took their 'impromptu' walk around Red Square. Gorbachev deemed Reagan's confession that the Soviet Union was no longer the 'evil empire' to be 'one of the genuine achievements' of the summit.[96]

The atmosphere was constructive and affable, with little of the ideological posturing of Geneva or Reykjavik. Overall, Moscow was more significant for Gorbachev's reform agenda than for Soviet-American relations. The summit allowed him to outflank rivals such as Yegor Ligachev on the right and Boris Yeltsin on the left, who protested that *perestroika* and *glasnost* were proceeding either too quickly or too slowly. Ahead of Reagan's arrival, Gorbachev circulated a list of domestic policy changes and then rammed them through the XIX Communist Party Conference at the end of June. These included the first elected legislature in Russia since the October Revolution. Gorbachev did not foresee that these reforms would contribute to the eventual disintegration of the Soviet Union.

The Moscow summit was therefore the 'coronation' without a crown, the unfulfilled climax of a succession of meetings that had begun in Geneva two-and-a-half years before. Its significance was largely symbolic; yet the symbolism of that moment in Red Square was profound.

*   *   *   *   *

Summitry had facilitated, indeed energized, Reagan and Gorbachev's efforts to reduce the nuclear danger and improve superpower relations through dialogue and negotiation. For brief but heady moments at the summit the two men escaped from their bureaucratic minders and dared to share their dreams. Their four meetings did not transcend the Cold War but they helped significantly to break the ice. Skilful intermediaries, notably Shultz and Shevardnadze, helped turn icebreakers into breakthroughs, most notably the INF Treaty of December 1987, which in turn served to defuse the superpower arms race. In the United States, these parleys and meetings brought flexibility and ingenuity to the policymaking process, before an internal counterattack moderated the pace of change on arms control at the strategic level. In the Soviet Union, the summits empowered Gorbachev and fostered creative political thinking, yet his innovations would eventually, albeit unintentionally, reform the empire he had inherited out of existence. And in Europe, the Reagan-Gorbachev summitry—though conducted over the heads of the Europeans—set the stage for a veritable transformation in the geopolitics of the Cold War.

NOTES

1. Michael R. Beschloss and Strobe Talbott, *At the Highest Levels: The Inside Story of the End of the Cold War* (London, 1993), 9; Memcon, President and Suzanne Massie, 11 March 1988, National Security Archive, George Washington University, Washington, DC, electronic briefing book (henceforth NSAEBB), no. 251, doc. no. 4, http://nsarchive.gwu.edu/NSAEBB/NSAEBB251/4.pdf. Mikhail Gorbachev, *Memoirs* (New York, 1996), 590.

2. General overviews include Raymond L. Garthoff, *The Great Transition: American-Soviet Relations and the End of the Cold War* (Washington, DC, 1994); Jack F. Matlock, Jr, *Reagan and Gorbachev: How the Cold War Ended* (New York, 2004); James Graham Wilson, *The Triumph of Improvisation: Gorbachev's Adaptability, Reagan's Engagement, and the End of the Cold War* (Ithaca, NY, 2014); and on summitry, David Reynolds, *Summits: Six Meetings that Shaped the Twentieth Century* (London, 2007), ch. 7.

3. Simon Miles, '"Quiet Diplomacy:" The Reagan Administration's Initial Engagement with the Soviet Union', unpublished paper presented at the annual meeting of the Society for Historians of American Foreign Relations, Lexington, Kentucky, 21 June 2014; James Mann, *The Rebellion of Ronald Reagan: A History of the End of the Cold War* (New York, 2009).

4. 'National Security Decision Directive (NSDD) 75: US relations with the USSR, 17 January 1983', in Jason Saltoun-Ebin, ed., *The Reagan Files: Inside the National Security Council* (Santa Barbara, CA, 2nd edn, 2014), 217.

5. David E. Hoffman, *The Dead Hand: The Untold Story of the Cold War Arms Race and its Dangerous Legacy* (New York, 2009), 44.

6. 'Minutes, NSC Meeting, Sanctions, 18 June 1982', in Saltoun-Ebin, *The Reagan Files*, 185.

7. 'Letter, Ronald Reagan to Liuba Vaschenko, 11 October 1984', in Kiron Skinner, Annelise Anderson, and Martin Anderson, eds, *Reagan: A Life in Letters* (New York, 2003), 380.

8. Ronald Reagan Presidential Library, Simi Valley CA (henceforth RRPL), Robert McFarlane files, Reorganized Archival Collection (henceforth RAC) Box 3, Memorandum, Shultz to Reagan: USG-Soviet relations, 3 March 1983.

9. Paul Lettow, *Ronald Reagan and his Quest to Abolish Nuclear Weapons* (New York, 2005), xi, 37–8.

10. John F. Burns, 'Gromyko rejects Reagan arms plan', *New York Times*, 3 April 1983, 10.

11. Reagan, Address to the Nation on the Soviet Attack on a Korean Civilian Airliner, 5 September 1983, The American Presidency Project (henceforth APP) website, http://www.presidency.ucsb.edu/ws/index.php?pid=41788&st=007&st1. Robert M. Gates, *From the Shadows: The Ultimate Insider's Story of Five Presidents and How They Won the Cold War* (New York, 1996), 273.

12. Ronald Reagan, *An American Life* (New York, 1990), 611.

13. Archie Brown, 'The Gorbachev Revolution and the End of the Cold War', in Melvyn P. Leffler and Odd Arne Westad, eds, *The Cambridge History of the Cold War, vol. III* (Cambridge, 2011), 244–66.

14. Letter, Reagan to Gorbachev, 11 March 1985, 1, http://www.thereaganfiles.com/19850311.pdf.

15. Asked on one occasion by an American diplomat whether he had enjoyed his breakfast, Gromyko replied 'Perhaps'. See Wilson, *The Triumph of Improvisation*, at 93.

16. Minutes, CPSU Politburo session, 11 March 1985, History and Public Policy Program Digital Archive, TsKhSD, F.89, http://digitalarchive.wilsoncenter.org/document/120771.

17. Stephen Kotkin, *Armageddon Averted: The Soviet Collapse, 1970–2000* (New York, 2008), 61; Emily Rosenberg, 'Consumer Capitalism and the End of the Cold War', in Leffler and Westad, *The Cambridge History of the Cold War, vol. 3*, 489–512.

18. RRPL, Robert McFarlane files, RAC Box 1, NSDD-153: Shultz-Gromyko meeting, 1 January 1985, 1.

19. Matlock, *Reagan and Gorbachev*, 149.

20. RRPL, Jack Matlock files, Box 45, Scope paper, Shultz to Reagan: UNGA, 7 October 1985.

21. Andrei Grachev, *Gorbachev's Gamble: Soviet Foreign Policy and the End of the Cold War* (Cambridge, 2008), 39, 53.

22. RRPL, Jack Matlock files, Box 45, Letter, unknown to Matlock: NSC meeting on Shevardnadze, undated.

23. RRPL, Jack Matlock files, Box 50, memorandum, MacFarlane to Reagan, 'How to record the summit?' 12 November 1985.

24. Letter, Gorbachev to Reagan, 24 March 1985, 3, NSAEBB no. 172, doc. 6, http://nsarchive.gwu.edu/NSAEBB/NSAEBB172/Doc6.pdf.

25. RRPL, Jack Matlock files, Box 49, Marginalia, McFarlane to Reagan: Soviet Union, 27 September 1985, Report: Soviet psychology, undated.

26. RRPL, Donald Regan files, Box 7, Memorandum, Shultz to Reagan: What to expect from Gorbachev, 14 November 1985.

27. RRPL, Jack Matlock files, Box 47, Memorandum, Matlock to McFarlane: Adelman memo, 3 July 1985; and Memorandum, Kenneth Adelman to McFarlane: US-Soviet leadership meetings (underlining in the original).

28. On Weinberger's spoiling tactics, see George P. Shultz, *Turmoil and Triumph*: *My Years as Secretary of State* (New York, 2003), 578–82, 598; Wilson, *The Triumph of Improvisation*, 95.

29. 'The summit: What it's all about—the city gets ready', *New York Times*, 18 November 1985, A6. For fuller discussion of the Geneva meeting, see Reynolds, *Summits*, 339–54.

30. Third Reagan-Gorbachev plenary meeting, 20 November 1985, NSAEBB no. 172, doc. 21, http://nsarchive.gwu.edu/NSAEBB/NSAEBB172/Doc21.pdf. See also Reynolds, *Summits,* 350–1.

31. Shultz, *Turmoil and Triumph*, 601. In a briefing paper for the president, Shultz suggested that reaching agreement for follow-up summits in Moscow and Washington might be 'the most important outcome of this summit as it could establish a process of decision-making'. RRPL, Robert E. Linhard files, Box 92178: Summit Nov. 19–21, folder 1, Shultz, Meeting with the President, 6 November 1985, 2.

32. Edmund Morris, *Dutch: A Memoir of Ronald Reagan* (New York, 1999), 568–9, 823; Gorbachev's post-summit comments are noted in the diary of Anatoly

S. Chernyaev, 24 November 1985, NSAEBB no. 172, doc. 26, http://nsarchive.gwu.
edu/NSAEBB/NSAEBB172/Doc26.pdf.

33. RRPL, Robert E. Linhard files, RAC Box 11, Letter, Reagan to Gorbachev: The
    inadmissibility of nuclear war and other principles, 31 November 1985.

34. RRPL, Jack Matlock files, Box 50, NSDD-183: Geneva meeting, 8 August 1985, 1.

35. RRPL, Jack Matlock files, Box 53, Memorandum, Michael Schneider to USIA
    Director: Forward from Geneva, 1, 5.

36. Diary entry, Chernyaev, 24 November 1985, NSAEBB no. 172, doc. 26,
    http://nsarchive.gwu.edu/NSAEBB/NSAEBB172/Doc26.pdf.

37. Hoffman, *The Dead Hand*, 235, 237.

38. Ronald Reagan, *The Reagan Diaries* (New York, 2007), 383.

39. Memorandum, Poindexter to Reagan, Gorbachev's handwritten letter, 15 February
    1986, copy at http://endofcoldwarforum.org/sites/default/files/docs/reagan/STY-
    1986-02-15.pdf.

40. RRPL, Robert E. Linhard files, RAC Box 6, Memorandum, Paul Nitze: Transition
    to defense, 4 April 1985, 2–3.

41. RRPL, Robert E. Linhard files, RAC Box 6, Email, McFarlane to Linhard: SDI,
    30 March 1985.

42. RRPL, Robert McFarlane files, RAC Box 1, Memorandum, William Clark to
    Reagan: The anti-nuclear movement, 22 April 1982, 4.

43. RRPL, Robert E. Linhard files, RAC Box 9, Memorandum, Judy Mandel to
    Stephen Sestanovich: Initiative, 27 January 1986.

44. RRPL, Robert E. Linhard files, RAC Box 12, Cable, Shultz to London: British on
    Reykjavik, 25 October 1986, 3.

45. Reagan, *The Reagan Diaries*, 388.

46. RRPL, W. Dennis Thomas files, Box 7, Memorandum, Henkel to Regan and
    Poindexter: President's views—Summit II, 2 April 1986, 1.

47. Archie Brown, *The Gorbachev Factor* (Oxford, 1996), 163; Wilson, *The Triumph of
    Improvisation*, 105–6.

48. Anatoly Chernyaev notes, 4 October 1986, NSAEBB, no. 203, doc. 5, http://
    nsarchive.gwu.edu/NSAEBB/NSAEBB203/Document05.pdf.

49. Gorbachev to Reagan, 15 September 1986, NSAEBB no. 203, doc. 1, http://
    nsarchive.gwu.edu/NSAEBB/NSAEBB203/Document01.pdf.

50. Wilson, *The Triumph of Improvisation*, 111; Shultz to Reagan, memo: Reykjavik,
    2 October 1986, NSAEBB no. 203, doc. 4, http://nsarchive.gwu.edu/NSAEBB/
    NSAEBB203/Document04.pdf (underlining in original); and NSC: Gorbachev's
    Goals and Tactics at Reykjavik, 4 October 1986, NSAEBB no. 203, doc. 6, http://
    nsarchive.gwu.edu/NSAEBB/NSAEBB203/Document06.pdf. See also RRPL, Jack
    Matlock files, Box 56, Memorandum, Matlock, Linhard and Tyrus Cobb to
    Poindexter: Points to raise with president on Reykjavik themes, undated.

51. Nicholas Thompson, *The Hawk and the Dove: Paul Nitze, George Kennan, and the
    History of the Cold War* (New York, 2009), 305.

52. US Memcon, Reagan-Gorbachev, first meeting, 11 October 1986, 6–8, NSAEBB
    no. 203, doc. 9, http://nsarchive.gwu.edu/NSAEBB/NSAEBB203/Document09.pdf.

53. 'Memoranda from Vitalii Kataev, no date', in Sidney D. Drell and George
    P. Shultz, eds, *Implications of the Reykjavik Summit on its Twentieth Anniversary*
    (Stanford, CA, 2007), 64, 77.

54. Thompson, *The Hawk and the Dove*, 303.

55. US Memcon, Reagan-Gorbachev, first meeting, 11 October 1986, 3–4, NSAEBB no. 203, doc. 9, http://nsarchive.gwu.edu/NSAEBB/NSAEBB203/Document09.pdf.

56. Matlock, *Reagan and Gorbachev*, 222–3.

57. Memcon, Akhromeyev-Nitze working group meeting, 11–12 October 1986, 52, NSAEBB no. 203, doc. 17, http://nsarchive.gwu.edu/NSAEBB/NSAEBB203/Document17.pdf.

58. Matlock, *Reagan and Gorbachev*, 225; US Memcon, Reagan-Gorbachev third meeting, 12 October 1986, 7, 16–17, NSAEBB no. 203, doc. 13, http://nsarchive.gwu.edu/NSAEBB/NSAEBB203/Document13.pdf.

59. RRPL, Al Keel files, RAC Box 2, Email, Linhard to Poindexter: Update on arms control, 24 October 1986.

60. RRPL, Al Keel files, RAC Box 3, Notes, US remark on Soviet counter, undated.

61. US Memcon, Reagan-Gorbachev fourth meeting, 12 October 1986, 13–15, NSAEBB no. 203, doc. 15, http://nsarchive.gwu.edu/NSAEBB/NSAEBB203/Document15.pdf (underlining in the original).

62. Jonathan Hunt and Paul F. Walker, 'The Legacy of Reykjavik and the Future of Nuclear Disarmament', *Bulletin of the atomic scientists* 67, no. 6 (2011), 63–72.

63. Grachev, *Gorbachev's Gamble*, 83; Notes, Chernyaev: Gorbachev's thoughts on Reykjavik, 12 October 1986, 1, NSAEBB no. 203, doc. 19, http://nsarchive.gwu.edu/NSAEBB/NSAEBB203/Document19.pdf.

64. Reagan, Address to the Nation on Reykjavik, 13 October 1986, APP website, http://www.presidency.ucsb.edu/ws/index.php?pid=36587&st=&st1. Matlock, *Reagan and Gorbachev,* 239; Grachev, *Gorbachev's Gamble*, 86.

65. Notes, Chernyaev: Gorbachev's thoughts on Reykjavik, 12 October 1986, 1, NSAEBB no. 203, doc. 19, http://nsarchive.gwu.edu/NSAEBB/NSAEBB203/Document19.pdf; Notes, Chernyaev: Politburo session, 30 October 1986, 4, NSAEBB no. 203, doc. 23, http://nsarchive.gwu.edu/NSAEBB/NSAEBB203/Document23.pdf.

66. Notes, Chernyaev: Politburo session, 30 October 1986, 4, NSAEBB no. 203, doc. 23, http://nsarchive.gwu.edu/NSAEBB/NSAEBB203/Document23.pdf.

67. The NSC had tried to amend a sentence stating that SDI was 'the key to a world without nuclear weapons' to read without 'offens[iv]e ballistic missiles' but without success. RRPL, Robert E. Linhard files, RAC Box 11, President's copy: Draft address to the nation on Iceland meeting, 13 October 1986, 3, 6, 10. Cf. Reagan, Address, Reykjavik, 13 October 1986, APP website, http://www.presidency.ucsb.edu/ws/index.php?pid=36587&st=&st1.

68. RRPL, Robert E. Linhard files, RAC Box 12, Memcon, Reagan and Thatcher, 14 October 1986, 2–3; RRPL, Robert E. Linhard files, RAC Box 11, Talking points: Reykjavik, 17 October 1986, 2.

69. RRPL, Al Keel files, RAC Box 3, Memorandum, Poindexter to Reagan: Why we can't commit to eliminating all nuclear weapons within 10 Years, 5–6 (underlining in the original).

70. Charles Moore, *Margaret Thatcher: The Authorized Biography, vol. 2* (London, 2015), 598, 609–10.

71. RRPL, Al Keel files, RAC Box 2, Memorandum, Shultz: Recommended next steps post-Reykjavik, 13 October 1986; Memorandum, Poindexter to Reagan: Where do we go from here?, undated, 1–3; RRPL, Al Keel files, RAC Box 3, Linhard,

Memorandum for the Arms Control Support Group: Instructions re defense and space, 24 October 1986, 3.

72. RRPL, Al Keel files, RAC Box 2, Memorandum, Weinberger to Reagan: Post-Reykjavik instructions for the Geneva negotiators, 19 October 1986.

73. RRPL, Al Keel files, RAC Box 2, Talking points, Shultz-Shevardnadze, 29 October 1986; Memorandum for Shultz: Your meetings with Foreign Minister Shevardnadze, undated; Draft instructions for NST delegation, Defense and space, 24 October 1986, 3; and, Email, Poindexter to Linhard: Shultz-Shevardnadze meeting, 28 October 1986.

74. Grachev, *Gorbachev's Gamble*, 94, 109; Notes, Chernyaev on 'Politburo and Central Committee conference,' 1 December 1986, 1, NSAEBB no. 203, doc. 28, http://nsarchive.gwu.edu/NSAEBB/NSAEBB203/Document28.pdf.

75. RRPL, Al Keel files, RAC Box 2, Memorandum, Weinberger to Poindexter: Comments on your post-Reykjavik follow-up, 31 October 1986; NSDD 250: Post-Reykyavik policy, 3 November 1986, NSAEEB no. 203, doc. 25, http://nsarchive.gwu.edu/NSAEBB/NSAEBB203/Document25.pdf.

76. RRPL, National Security Council: NSDD files, Executive Secretariat, Box 91297, William Cockrell to Carlucci: JCS meeting with the President, 5 January 1987.

77. Wilson, *The Triumph of Improvisation*, 126–30.

78. Alexander Yakovlev, 'Toward an analysis', 25 February 1987, 7, NSAEBB no. 238, http://nsarchive.gwu.edu/NSAEBB/NSAEBB238/russian/Final1987-02-25%20Yakovlev%20memo.pdf, and Excerpt from Politburo discussions, 26 February 1987, 2, NSAEBB no. 238, http://nsarchive.gwu.edu/NSAEBB/NSAEBB238/russian/Final1987-02-26%20Politburo.pdf.

79. Brown, *The Gorbachev Factor*, 122–6; Mikhail Gorbachev, *Perestroika: New Thinking for Our Country and the World* (New York, 1987).

80. Shultz, *Turmoil and Triumph*, 884.

81. Garthoff, *The Great Transition*, 312–13. Memcon, Gorbachev—Shultz meeting, 14 April 1987, 1–2, NSAEEB no. 238, http://nsarchive.gwu.edu/NSAEBB/NSAEBB238/russian/Final1987-04-14%20Gorbachev-Shultz.pdf.

82. Reagan, Remarks at the Brandenburg Gate, 12 June 1987, APP website, http://www.presidency.ucsb.edu/ws/index.php?pid=34390&st=&st1; Wilson, *The Triumph of Improvisation*, 129; James Mann, *The Rebellion of Ronald Reagan: A History of the End of the Cold War* (London, 2009), 194–6.

83. Garthoff, *The Great Transition*, 313–14; NSDD-278: Establishing a US negotiating position on SRINF missiles, 13 June 1987, NSAEBB no. 238, http://nsarchive.gwu.edu/NSAEBB/NSAEBB238/usdocs/Doc%203%20(Natl%20Sec%20Decision%20Directive%2006.13.87).pdf; and State Department briefing papers: NST, START, INF, etc., 11 August 1987, NSAEBB no. 238, docs 4a–4e, http://nsarchive.gwu.edu/NSAEBB/NSAEBB238/.

84. Wilson, *Triumph of Improvisation*, 134.

85. Excerpt from Politburo minutes, 9 July 1987, NSAEBB no. 238, http://nsarchive.gwu.edu/NSAEBB/NSAEBB238/russian/Final1987-07-09Politburo.pdf.

86. Grachev, *Gorbachev's Gamble*, 105–10.

87. Shultz, *Turmoil and Triumph*, 987.

88. Shultz, *Turmoil and Triumph*, 988 (Kissinger); Wilson, *The Triumph of Improvisation*, 129–30 (Weinberger).
89. Letter, Gorbachev to Reagan, 28 October 1987, 3, NSAEBB no. 238, http://nsarchive. gwu.edu/NSAEBB/NSAEBB238/russian/Final1987-10-28%20Gorbachev%20Letter %20to%20Reagan.pdf.
90. RRPL, Robert E. Linhard files, RAC Box 19, Memorandum, E. Rowny to Carlucci: Where do we go from here on arms control?, 6 November 1987; and Memorandum, Ermarth to Linhard and Sandra Kelly: Conversation with Kampelman, 3 November 1987.
91. RRPL, Robert E. Linhard files, RAC Box 19, Handwritten notes, Linhard, NSGP and summit III, undated; Memorandum, Ermarth to Linhard: Summit dynamics; and Memorandum, Rowny to Carlucci: Where do we go . . . , 2.
92. Memcon, Working luncheon with Gorbachev, 12.40pm–2.10pm, 10, 10 December 1987, NSAEBB no. 238, http://nsarchive.gwu.edu/NSAEBB/NSAEBB238/usdocs/ Doc%2019%20(Working%20Lunch%20Reagan%20Gorby%2012.10.87).pdf.
93. Matlock, *Reagan and Gorbachev*, 277–9.
94. Notes, Chernyaev: Politburo session, 25 February 1988, NSAEBB no. 251, doc. 2, 1, http://nsarchive.gwu.edu/NSAEBB/NSAEBB251/2.pdf.
95. NSDD-305: Objectives at the Moscow summit, 26 April 1988, NSAEBB no. 251, doc. 8, 1–2, http://nsarchive.gwu.edu/NSAEBB/NSAEBB251/8.pdf.
96. Gorbachev, *Memoirs*, 457.

7

Beijing and Malta, 1989

Jeffrey A. Engel and Sergey Radchenko

'A new breeze is blowing and a world refreshed by freedom seems reborn', George H.W. Bush declared in his Inaugural Address as president on 20 January 1989. 'The totalitarian era is passing, its old ideas blown away like leaves from an ancient, lifeless tree.' For a statesman this was an exciting moment, when history could be made. 'There are times', Bush continued, 'when the future seems thick as a fog; you sit and wait, hoping the mists will lift and reveal the right path. But this is a time when the future seems a door you can walk right through into a room called tomorrow.'[1]

One might have expected that in 1989 Bush would have first walked through the door marked Moscow. After the drama of the Reagan-Gorbachev summits and with Poland and Hungary already on the path of reform, much of the world was fixated on the Soviet Union and Eastern Europe. But Bush, who had met Gorbachev several times when Reagan's vice-president, was wary of the Soviet leader and his intentions. He also knew that, although Reagan's summitry had helped defuse the superpower arms race, it had not ended the Cold War. National Security Adviser Brent Scowcroft, in particular, feared that Gorbachev as a master of propaganda 'could exploit an early meeting with a new president as evidence to declare the Cold War over without providing substantive actions from a "new" Soviet Union'. In December 1988, soon after his election, Bush assured Gorbachev to his face that he had 'no intention of stalling things' but explained that he 'wanted to formulate prudent national security policies'. In fact once president, Bush and his aides decided on what they called a 'pause' in Soviet-American relations, in order to undertake a full-scale stocktaking of the Reagan era. This lasted right up to the end of May, when Bush announced that the United States would now 'move beyond containment' and encourage the spread of democracy across the whole of Eurasia 'from Budapest to Beijing' to create 'a larger home, a home where West meets East, a democratic home'. But, the cautious president warned, 'democracy's journey East is not easy . . . Barriers and barbed wire still fence in

Fig. 7.1. Bush and Deng in the Great Hall of the People, Beijing, 26 February 1989 (AP)

nations.' Gorbachev had to prove that his slogan about 'openness' was not mere rhetoric. Bush in turn made clear that 'positive steps by the Soviets would be met by steps of our own'.[2]

Yet, instead of prioritizing the Soviet Union, Bush looked initially towards China. His first foreign trip as president was to see Deng Xiaoping (see Figure 7.1).

In June, with the horrors of Tiananmen Square, however, the door marked Beijing slammed firmly in his face. And by late 1989, with Eastern Europe transformed, Bush had turned to Gorbachev. At his December summit with the Soviet leader in Malta, he declared that they stood at 'the threshold of a brand-new era of U.S.-Soviet relations' and that it was 'within our grasp to contribute, each in our own way, to overcoming the division of Europe'. In that year of surprises, 1989, this remarkable turn in American policy from Beijing to Moscow would prove of real diplomatic importance.[3]

BEIJING I: DENG AND BUSH

Like his mentor Richard Nixon, George Bush wanted to improve Sino-American relations as a potential counterweight to the Soviets and, also like Nixon, he considered himself an expert on the country.[4] 'The importance of

China is very clear to me', he told Washington insider Zbigniew Brzezinski, formerly Carter's national security adviser, in December 1988, six weeks before taking the oath of office. The Reagan administration had considered relations with Beijing, Bush said, 'almost exclusively in a bilateral relationship' but now, emerging from Reagan's shadow, he believed it would be better to bring China into a 'Transpacific Partnership' involving all the major Pacific powers, including Japan and South Korea.[5] He also hoped good relations with Beijing could offset whatever might happen with Moscow, recalling the triangular diplomacy used to such great effect by Nixon in the early 1970s. Either way he hoped to act fast. 'I'd love to return to China before Deng leaves office entirely', he told Brzezinski. 'I feel I have a special relationship there.'[6]

This was not mere hyperbole. *De facto* American ambassador to China in the mid-1970s, before full normalization of relations in 1979, Bush had always preached the value of personal friendship, whether in business or politics and he made a point during his time in Beijing of meeting as many elite Chinese figures as possible. He was not always successful—China's top leaders and Secretary of State Henry Kissinger each worked at different times to keep Sino-American channels of communication to themselves—yet nonetheless Bush managed to cultivate Deng Xiaoping, a key player in communist party politics who from 1977 led China's internal revolution away from the dogmas and violence of the previous decade's ruinous Cultural Revolution. 'He was a very short man', Bush wrote in his diary of their very first encounter, but not one to be given short-shrift. More important than this initial (and not uncommon) reaction to the diminutive Deng, Bush recorded that his Chinese counterpart 'left the door open for future visits'.[7] In the 1970s each clearly saw in the other something notable, perhaps even remarkable, and no doubt with the potential for a promising future.

Deng's very presence in Beijing by the 1970s was remarkable in its own right. At the heart of Chinese politics and diplomacy since the 1940s—purged not once but twice by Mao Zedong, most significantly in 1966 for being a 'capitalist roader'—Deng returned from internal exile in Jiangxi in 1974. He found Beijing politics no less riven by factional strife than when he had left, because the radicals (the so called 'Gang of Four' who rose to power in the Cultural Revolution) contended for influence with moderates and pragmatists while Mao suffered the debilitations of the motor-neuron disease that ultimately took his life. Deng survived, accumulated power, saw off the Gang of Four and eventually by 1979 had seized full power from his rival and Mao loyalist Hua Guofeng. Deng initiated controversial policies of 'reform and opening up' (*gaige kaifang*) that spawned rapid economic growth. The ultimate pragmatist, he allowed private ownership and limited private enterprise, famously arguing that ideological arguments mattered less than a system's productivity. 'It doesn't matter whether a cat is white or black', he explained, 'as long as it catches mice'. Viewing reform itself through a single metric, what would work best, Deng was able to accept nearly anything as long as it did not disrupt his country's hard-won peace and stability following the deprivations of the 1960s and the violent political upheaval of the ensuing decade. In the event his economic reforms would give rise to political expectations beyond anything he envisioned or could accept, with consequences that would ultimately define his legacy.

China's turn toward openness included further development of the Sino-American relationship since the Mao-Nixon summit in 1972. In January 1979 Deng visited the United States to mark the resumption of full diplomatic relations between Washington and Beijing that had been broken four decades before. 'If we look back', Deng told an aide, 'we find that all of those [countries] that were on the side of the United States have been successful [in their modernization drive], whereas all of those that were against the United States have not been successful.' History thus taught an obvious lesson: 'We shall be on the side of the United States.'[8]

During his American tour, Deng made a point of visiting Bush, the only non-governmental figure so honoured. Bush not only took time to renew formal contact but also invited Deng to an old-fashioned Texas rodeo. Their relationship continued to develop during Bush's vice-presidency (1981–9), becoming not so much a true friendship than a comfortable and frequent acquaintance—the kind in which conversations might continue over years and statements of true intimacy are frequently proclaimed because both sides know there is an artistry and theatre to diplomacy. Bush considered Deng a 'trusted' confidant, while Chinese leaders frequently praised Bush as 'an old friend'. The latter term, *lao pengyou* in Mandarin, had particular meaning, being applied only to influential foreigners with long experience of working with the Chinese. Such friends were valued in Beijing for their ability to speak plainly and for their role as interlocutors between China and the broader world. Nixon, Bush, and Kissinger earned this distinction; Presidents Carter and Reagan did not.[9]

Trust of this sort, however, frequently came at a price. Chinese officials often turned to their 'old friends' when they were in need or had an important message—or threat—to deliver. Old friends could be expected to carry even bad news faithfully and, as the noted journalist James Mann has observed, they 'can be *repeatedly* asked to deliver favours, where others are treated more pragmatically'.[10] Put plainly, the Chinese could make requests of Nixon and Bush that would never have been asked of Reagan, because they were aware that the former had invested so much of their personal reputation in maintaining strong and smooth Sino-American relations. This dynamic was well known. 'The Chinese seem to feel comfortable only in dealing with those who share a basic inclination to establish positive *guanxi* [interpersonal connection] at the human level', diplomat Richard Solomon wrote in 1999 at the end of a career that had included numerous negotiations with the Chinese. 'Yet these same friends are the ones who receive the brunt of the pressure when there are problems to be resolved for the Chinese assume—not without reason—that those who see value in the US-PRC relationship are the ones who will work to resolve the problems and thereby sustain their status as friends.'[11]

Bush relied on personal relations as the lubricant of society as well, and thus felt entirely comfortable with diplomacy conducted on this plane. 'Because I lived there [China]', he told Deng in 1979, 'I understand as well as anyone in the U.S.' the problems that Chinese leaders faced, in particular over Taiwan. He therefore hoped to serve as a conduit for better Sino-American relations writ large. 'If I can ever be helpful, I will', Bush promised at the close of the 1970s. 'Maybe someday there will be a useful role to play.'[12] The two men kept in touch, meeting whenever relations between their two nations required. Bush, for instance, was considered the logical choice in late August 1980 to undertake a much-publicized conciliation mission when then-candidate Reagan's incendiary support of the Taiwan regime threatened to undercut his diplomatic credibility. The political cartoonist Patrick Oliphant captured Bush's role as Sino-American mediator perfectly, picturing him astride a bucking bronco with Reagan's head, having just crashed into a China shop much to the consternation of its irate Chinese owners. 'Take it easy gentlemen', Bush said, 'I can explain everything'.[13]

It was a tense meeting. Behind closed doors Deng and his comrades sharply rebuked Bush for Reagan's position, criticizing even lower-ranking campaign officials for anti-Chinese rhetoric. Yet Bush's personal stock in Beijing rose, both by undertaking the mediation but also by refusing to rise to the bait of Deng's harsh words. As vice-president, Bush was tasked yet again in 1982 with journeying to China to help damp down rising tensions over Taiwan. This time the issue was American arms sales to the Nationalists. The Chinese were adamant to the point of obstinacy during the first days of Bush's trip, arguing rigidly that any American military shipments to Taiwan violated Chinese sovereignty. Progress seemed impossible, until Deng pulled Bush aside for a brief private conversation, with only their interpreters and the American ambassador present. The conversation stretched well beyond an hour, but the two men eventually emerged with the basic structure of a deal: Washington could continue its arms sales, albeit at a much lower level, while never seeking to formally separate Taiwan from the mainland (both Beijing and Taipei maintained the right to rule the other). It was not a perfect arrangement, but Bush and Deng, behind closed doors and speaking one-to-one, had found a way out of the impasse.[14] When the 1988 election heated up, there was thus a clear favourite in Beijing—George H.W. Bush. 'We had a lot of contact with him', Deng told American reporters. 'I hope he'll win the election.'[15]

Given this long association Bush's aides were hardly surprised when, in December 1988, the president-elect wondered aloud about going to Asia, and to China in particular, for his first substantive overseas trip in office. Cold War presidents typically went to Europe first. Yet Bush wanted to prioritize China because he believed in Deng as a progressive leader and also calculated that better Sino-American relations would help offset potential Soviet gains. He considered Deng's economic reforms fully embedded by 1989 after more than a decade and believed, like many American policymakers, that China had already passed a critical tipping point so that the reforms already instituted would not easily or perhaps ever be reversed. Economic change was expected to generate political change. Democratization therefore seemed to Bush not a question of whether but when—a view widely held in American policymaking circles at the time. As James Mann observed, 'Virtually all of the American analyses judged China almost exclusively by the standard of the Cultural Revolution.' By this standard, China under Deng 'looked good', and more importantly looked to be on the right path.[16]

Deng's economic reforms did indeed stir desire for a more open society as well. From the outset posters went up on the 'Democracy Wall' in Xidan Street in Beijing criticizing the government and calling for change. It was there that in December 1978 a young activist, Wei Jingsheng, had posted an essay called 'Fifth Modernization', a naïve but passionate demand for the democratization of China. The authorities tolerated the wall for some months before arresting Wei and shutting down the public forum but dissent was not extinguished. It peaked anew in December 1986 with protests at the University of Science and Technology in Hefei, where students were supported by a number of prominent intellectuals including the astrophysicist Fang Lizhi, who was then the university's vice chancellor. Party hardliners called for purges in response, prompting Deng to sacrifice his protégé and general secretary of the Chinese Communist Party (CCP), the reform-minded Hu Yaobang, who was replaced with another reformer, Zhao Ziyang. Although personally inclined towards gradual evolution in the direction of greater openness, economically and also politically, Zhao faced formidable internal opposition. This was led by Prime Minister Li Peng, who represented the conservative wing of the Chinese leadership.

By 1987 Deng Xiaoping, now well into his eighties and tiring after a decade as 'paramount leader', had officially retired from all his posts except the crucial Chairmanship of the Central Military Commission. But he still had the final say in all matters. He protected Zhao Ziyang from conservative attacks, even though clearly not sharing the general secretary's enthusiasm for political reform. Zhao was a keen economic modernizer and a vocal advocate of better relations with the United States, and losing him to the conservatives could well derail Deng's entire reform agenda. So the general secretary pressed on, with Deng's backing, but his difficulties multiplied in late 1988 and early 1989, in large part because of rash economic moves that sent prices soaring, leading to bank runs and shortages of basic goods.[17]

American intelligence analysts picked up signs of this power struggle in early 1989. Yet, equally significant for US policy towards China were the momentous changes underway in Sino-Soviet relations. Beijing and Moscow had been on a gentle upward slope towards normalization since 1982 but, even though bilateral trade had recently picked up and contacts intensified, Deng was not yet willing to bury the hatchet after decades of personal and geopolitical antagonism without first extracting something from the Soviets. His conditions were that Moscow reduce its military presence along the Sino-Soviet border and in Mongolia, withdraw from Afghanistan, and thirdly, most important perhaps, arrange for the Soviet Union's ally Vietnam to pull out of Cambodia, which it had occupied since December 1978. Progress on resolving what Beijing called the 'three obstacles' proved slow, but by late 1988 the Chinese were sufficiently satisfied with Soviet concessions to invite Gorbachev to Beijing in May 1989 for a summit with Deng. This was intended to symbolize Sino-Soviet rapprochement after a quarter-century of tension and antagonism.

Unlike Bush, Gorbachev had never met Deng Xiaoping. He had never even been to China and certainly no one considered him a *lao pengyou*. Twenty-seven years Deng's junior, Gorbachev had been in his twenties at the time of the Sino-Soviet split. Nevertheless, soon after taking the reins of power in March 1985 he, like Bush in 1989, prioritized achieving a breakthrough with China. His overtures were welcomed in Beijing, likewise his economic restructuring, but the Chinese were wary of what they regarded as the Soviet leader's excessive enthusiasm for political reform, especially after Gorbachev had unleashed the full force of democratization in 1987. Deng reportedly thought Gorbachev an 'idiot' for increasingly putting politics before economics.[18] Gorbachev, in turn, remained sceptical of the Chinese reforms in the absence of the sort of political overhaul which, he thought, a real *perestroika* required.[19] Despite these mutual reservations, relations did improve in the late 1980s, although the Chinese made very clear on several occasions that there would be no return to the past—that they would never again consent to becoming the Soviets' 'younger brother'—the patronizing term so often used by Moscow in the 1950s to Chinese irritation. Gorbachev's response was reassuring: it would now be 'difficult', he said, 'to imagine China in the role of a younger brother'.[20]

The prospect of a Deng-Gorbachev meeting in May 1989 concentrated minds in Washington. Ever since his election Bush had been seeking a diplomatic pretext for an early China visit and Beijing's invitation to Gorbachev added urgency because the president did not want to be upstaged by the wily Soviet leader. Then fate intervened. Japan's Emperor Hirohito, on the throne for over sixty years, died on 7 January 1989. Having fought the Japanese as a young naval aviator in the Pacific Theatre in 1944, Bush believed his attendance at the funeral would demonstrate not only the strength of Japanese-American relations but the power of reconciliation as well. Funeral diplomacy thus provided the perfect excuse to visit Asia more generally. He journeyed to Japan for the ceremonies in the last week of February, tacking on a quick two-day visit to China. Bush always denied that Gorbachev's forthcoming summit with Deng influenced his own calculations but many observers none-theless believed that the president's arrival in Beijing three months before Gorbachev signalled a new bout of Soviet-American one-upmanship.

Bush's trip to Beijing on 25–26 February was brief yet not without controversy. Unlike a more formal summit, he arrived without an agenda, except to reconnect with the Chinese leadership and reaffirm his commitment to the region. He was, for the most part, warmly received and the term *lao pengyou* echoed throughout his meetings. 'Every time you come', President Yang Shangkun declared, 'you discuss major issues with Chinese leaders. So you've made great contributions to the development of Sino-U.S. relations and to cooperation between our two countries. As this is your first trip to China since you've taken your present office, it is very significant. I think this shows that you, Mr. President, pay much attention to our bilateral relationship.'[21]

Some perspective on these comments is provided by a remark Bush made later to one of the authors of this chapter. 'You shouldn't take such talk seriously', Bush observed during a trip to Beijing in 2005. Hurtling through closed streets in an official limousine, Bush as an ex-president was afforded the kind of treatment typically given to current heads of state. No doubt having a son in the Oval Office helped. At every stop Chinese officials fell over each other with praise. He reciprocated in kind from the podium but was clearly unimpressed once back in the confines of his car. 'I do have a relationship there; there is warmth', he explained. 'But those kinds of welcomes, those over-the-top words, they're for show; it's what they do.' Barbara Bush was blunter: 'They say all kinds of things; especially when they want something.'[22]

What China's sweet-talking leadership wanted in 1989 was trade and invest-ment, but otherwise to be left alone, at least when it came to how the govern-ment controlled the pace and scope of change within its own borders. They drew a firm line at anything that even hinted of political meddling. 'This visit comes at a time that is very important for both our countries', Zhao said. 'The current international situation is developing and undergoing drastic changes.'[23]

Attempting to assuage American fears about a renewed Sino-Soviet alliance, Zhao promised that 'normalization of Sino-Soviet relations will not be like in the 1950s . . . Any military alliance or military relationship is out of the ques-tion.' This would be a common refrain during Bush's time in Beijing—that Gorbachev's impending visit augured nothing more than an end to an era of direct antagonism. Deng launched into a long discussion of why it must be so, citing 'accumulated problems' with 'deep historical roots' and listing Russia, alongside Japan, among the two countries that had done the greatest damage to China. It was good to have a safer border and better relations with the Soviets but, as Zhao put it to Bush, 'we must watch the deeds of Mr. Gorbachev and not just listen to his words'.[24] Premier Li Peng echoed the thought during his own formal session with the president: 'The Soviet Union has agreed to

China's conditions, or most of our conditions' required to 'restore normal state relations', he explained. 'We want relations to be normal again. A higher goal is for China and the Soviet Union to become good neighbors, but not to have an alliance relationship.' Repeating Beijing's standard mantra of exceptionalism—at once integrated into the world system yet simultaneously cordoned off from it—he added: 'proceeding from China's own security interests, we do not want an alliance with any country in the world'.[25]

That prohibition on alliances included the United States, and Chinese officials repeatedly stressed their long-standing contention that internal affairs were nobody's interest but their own. Deng and his cadre saw in the Soviet bloc's experience a case study of how governments might easily lose control over the reform process if they ceded too much to the people. 'China would not welcome the kind of labor problems that Poland is experiencing with Solidarity', Li told Bush, pointing out that the People's Republic (PRC) did not suffer from satellite countries who desired even greater reforms 'more quickly than the Soviets would like'.[26] Deng developed the point during his meeting with Bush. 'We also hope Gorbachev's reforms will gradually become fruitful', he stated, but cautioned that 'our own experience tells us that it is not easy to get fruits'. Finding common ground in their mutual scepticism towards Gorbachev, Bush agreed. 'Gorbachev is a charming man, and the Soviet Union is in a state of change', yet overall, he said, the 'byword for the United States is caution'.[27]

China's top leaders also set down clear markers on the limits of reform. There were, Zhao told Bush, some who argued that economic reform was too risky for so large a country and that 'China should go back to the old road'. But he dismissed such critics, who thought the government had transformed the nation too quickly, as 'few' and with 'no appeal'. He was more worried about 'a small number who think there are so many difficulties in reform because China is lagging behind on political reform'. They 'stand for a multi-party parliamentary system—the introduction of a Western political system'. In Zhao's view 'these people may be few, but they are vocal and active', though their 'proposition does not tally with the realities of China'. Speaking with uncharacteristic bluntness for a Chinese statesman, he explained that if their ideas were 'carried out, chaos will result, and reform will be disrupted'.[28]

Invoking the term 'chaos' meant something specific and ominous to his generation of rulers, as Bush well knew, recalling the darkest days of the Cultural Revolution. Zhao thus explicitly warned the president that the Chinese leadership would brook neither political dissent nor foreign support for radical demands. 'Some press people in the West and the U.S. feel warmly toward those in China who advocate a Western political system and have great interest in them', he continued. 'In our view, if there are Americans who support those Chinese people who are opposed to the current policies of the Chinese government, they will hurt reform as well as Sino-U.S. Friendship.'[29] Deng repeated this line. 'The overwhelming need is to maintain stability', the

Chinese leader told the president. 'Without stability, everything will be gone, even accomplishments will be ruined.' With all the things that were changing throughout the world, he concluded, 'we hope our friends abroad can understand this point'. 'We do', Bush said. 'All right, then', Deng replied in a matter-of-fact way. 'Let's have lunch.' But he had delivered his message in plain terms. His government would not condone what Gorbachev allowed within Eastern Europe, or encouraged within the Soviet Union's own borders. Any Western support for democratization within China would be regarded as a violation of sovereignty and as an attempt to foment revolt.[30]

The warning was rammed home at the end of the summit. The Americans were scheduled to host a farewell banquet, with top PRC officials in attendance. Among the prominent Chinese cultural and educational figures on the US embassy's guest list was the dissident academic Fang Lizhi. His name had been passed to the White House weeks before, yet it had rung no alarm bells. Hours before Bush landed in Beijing, however, word spread that if Fang showed up for dinner, the Chinese leaders would not. They considered attendance of a vocal critic as an insult, and thus made clear their willingness to embarrass Bush, with cameras rolling, by threatening only empty seats at a banquet given in their honour.

Bush exploded when he heard this news. 'Who the hell is Fang Lizhi?' he screamed from his suite on Air Force One as it flew from Tokyo to Beijing. (Given his frequent claim of expertise in Chinese affairs, this query was revealing because no real China Hand would have needed to ask such a question in 1989.)[31] American and Chinese officials reached an accord only at the eleventh hour whereby Fang could attend but would be seated out of sight of China's leaders. For this reason Bush remained on tenterhooks throughout his entire visit that his hosts might embarrass him—a new president—at the climax of his first foreign trip.

In the event Bush welcomed Deng and his colleagues for dinner. But Fang never made it. Detained by the authorities, he was prevented from taking his seat; American officials learned of his plight only after the dinner had finished. And so Bush left Beijing embarrassed after all, having got the message loud and clear from his Chinese counterparts—including Deng, his old friend—that China's internal affairs were none of Washington's business. How Beijing dealt with dissent, in other words, should not concern even China's *lao pengyou*.

BEIJING II: DENG AND GORBACHEV

Yet domestic affairs could not easily be insulated from international influences. As China emerged from isolation after the Cultural Revolution, its leaders found it difficult to keep shut the doors to political ideas and concepts that were fundamentally at odds with one-party rule. Such ideas seeped in from two directions: from the West and also from the rapidly reforming Soviet Union. It was the Soviet example, in particular, that worried the Chinese leaders: despite years of hostility, the two countries were bound together by invisible ideological strings because, if socialism was abandoned by the Soviet Union, it was difficult to imagine its survival in China. With Mikhail Gorbachev pressing full steam ahead with political reforms amid spiralling change throughout the Soviet bloc, his visit to Beijing carried toxic implications for China and its divided leadership.

Deng and the Politburo had little inkling of what awaited them when they set a date for Gorbachev's visit. The second half of April saw the start of widespread demonstrations, triggered by the sudden death on the 15th of the former general secretary, Hu Yaobang, long considered a champion of student causes. Students took the streets to praise Hu but also to air their many grievances about official nepotism and corruption and the lack of political reforms. The protests had deep roots, reflecting a build-up of popular frustration with massive price rises and other signs of economic malaise. Students also criticized insufficient opportunity for upward socio-economic mobility.

The CCP leadership split between proponents of crackdown or dialogue. The latter group was led by Zhao whose attitude, in the words of historian Ezra Vogel, seemed to be 'that of an understanding parent giving advice to children who were basically good'. But the hardliners, apparently with Deng's direct approval, pushed through the publication of an editorial in the official daily, *Renmin Ribao*, which blamed a 'small minority' for instigating 'turmoil'. The students were not cowed. Encouraged by all-too-visible divisions and confusion at the top, they continued to press their case, holding demonstrations in Beijing's Tiananmen Square, the nation's ceremonial and symbolic heart. By early May their demands had become increasingly radical, with many calling for outright democratization, and on the 13th some students declared a hunger strike in the Square. As the standoff escalated between the demonstrators and the party, proponents of compromise within the Chinese leadership—notably Zhao—were being marginalized, setting the course towards overt confrontation. The hardliners had drawn 'lessons' from the revolutionary consequences of reform in Eastern Europe. As observed by Yao Yilin, a key Politburo insider, if the government accepted the student movement as 'patriotic and democratic', legalizing their organization, then 'opposition parties would appear in China' and 'our country would take the same path as Poland'. This was a concession that the CCP could not and would not make.[32]

It was in this dramatic atmosphere that Mikhail Gorbachev arrived in China for the first Sino-Soviet summit in thirty years. Beijing was a sea of banners and placards. Students packed the streets leading to the city centre and Tiananmen Square overflowed with protesters. There Gorbachev was supposed to walk on the red carpet and inspect the guard of honour under the watchful gaze of international reporters. Instead these reporters were all over Tiananmen interviewing student protesters; the guard of honour could not even approach the overcrowded square and there was no way to unroll the traditional red carpet. Time and again in the run-up to the summit the Chinese leadership debated this embarrassment. As Deng put it before the visit, 'Tiananmen is the symbol of the PRC. The square has to be in order when Gorbachev comes. We have to maintain our international image. What do we look like if the square's a mess?' Official appeals to student patriotism—asking them not to let China lose face—fell on deaf ears. The one thing that the students did was to sweep the Square with their banners, expecting to welcome into their midst Gorbachev— whom many considered their prophet of democracy.[33]

They never got the chance. The welcoming ceremony was moved to the airport and the ceremonial carpet left in storage at the National People's Congress. Met by an apologetic President Yang Shangkun, Gorbachev was taken through back alleys to the Congress building for a banquet in what one Soviet participant described as a 'hall the size of a train station'. The guests were treated to various delicacies including shark fin and abalone, while a People's Liberation Army orchestra performed nostalgic Soviet songs and classical music. The pomp and ceremony served only to expose the gulf between the formal orderliness of the Sino-Soviet normalization and the upheaval right across Beijing. Student protesters, who were now holding their hunger strike just minutes away from the hall where Gorbachev and the Chinese leaders exchanged toasts, had become participants in this summit. Conscious of his mission, Gorbachev kept his distance from the turmoil playing out in the streets. He refused to heed a student petition with six thousand signatures that was delivered to the Soviet embassy, asking him to meet with them. Instead he repeatedly emphasized the USSR's refusal to interfere in China's domestic affairs. Privately, however, the Soviet leader was stunned. 'We tried to act with reserve and judiciousness', he commented soon afterwards—'although I, frankly speaking, thought that we should leave as quickly as possible' and go home.[34]

Like Bush in February, Gorbachev met with all the senior Chinese leaders. But, in contrast with the Sino-American summit, there was no intimacy to these discussions, no warm recollections of past times spent together, no small talk about playing tennis or bridge. In fact there was very little in the way of personal connections between Gorbachev and his Chinese interlocutors, even those like Yang Shangkun and Li Peng who had spent years in the USSR as students and could speak passable Russian (see Figure 7.2).

But though distant in personal terms, Gorbachev and the Chinese shared the experience of reform. 'Here we speak the same language with you', Zhao told the Soviet leader on 16 May. He then set out his vision for transforming China and developing Marxism before it outlived itself. 'We have no other way out, no other weapon but to walk the road of reforms.' Zhao appeared

Fig. 7.2. Gorbachev overshadowed in the Great Hall of the People, Beijing, 15 May 1989 (AP)

sympathetic to students even as he criticized their naiveté. Gorbachev agreed that while some of the advocates of reform in China and the USSR were 'hot heads', many were truly committed allies in overcoming the forces of inertia.

Prime Minister Li Peng represented these very forces and led the growing faction within the Party's highest echelon that advocated a harsh crackdown on the dissenters in the Square. He also had little use for Gorbachev, writing in his diary in 1987: 'Some comrades thought: we formerly had a high appraisal of Soviet reforms; in reality, Gorbachev shouts a lot and does little. Other comrades thought that Gorbachev, by his methods, created an opposition to himself, whereas the Chinese [methods] have united the great majority of officials.' After policies of *glasnost* triggered ethnic unrest within the Soviet borders, especially across the Caucasus, and political upheaval in satellites such as Poland and Hungary, Li Peng concluded that Gorbachev's reckless political reforms could well lead to the break-up of the Soviet Union. Gorbachev's visit to Beijing at such a sensitive time struck him as extremely dangerous for the CCP. He noted how the Soviet embassy had accepted the student petition (instead of turning the students away) and commented disapprovingly on the remarks by Raisa Gorbacheva at the state banquet about how, on the way in from the airport, the Gorbachevs had got out of their car and received a 'warm welcome' from the masses. When Gorbachev broached the subject of reforms, arguing that while China was ahead economically, the Soviet Union led politically, Li answered with reserve: 'Every country has its circumstances, every man walks his own road.'[35]

As with Bush's visit, the height of the summit was Gorbachev's meeting with Deng Xiaoping, which, the Chinese indicated, marked the official moment of Sino-Soviet normalization. The meeting also symbolized for many protestors the course they hoped to take. 'Gorbachev 58, Deng Xiaoping 85', read some of the banners in the streets, denoting their respective ages and highlighting the contrast between the dynamism of one and the conservatism of the other. Gorbachev came from the generation of the Soviet *shestidesyatniki*—those who had politically matured during the atmosphere of relative openness of Khrushchev's de-Stalinization. He was well-educated—a holder of a law degree from Moscow State University—and highly Westernized in ways Deng could never have been. Yet, despite these differences, Gorbachev did not look down on China and worked hard to make a good impression on Deng. He was tactful, deferential, and generally inclined to listen rather than talk, which was not always the case for the opinionated Soviet leader. He told his advisers that he would conduct the conversation as a younger person speaking to an elder, as 'this is valued in the East'.[36] For the Chinese, questions of protocol were also at the top of the agenda. They wondered, and worried, whether Gorbachev might give Deng the bear-hug communist leaders often lavished on each other, or if they would simply exchange polite handshakes. Their hope was to be presented as something other than a Soviet ally, for all the painful connotations of the past that it raised. Thus when Deng and Gorbachev met on 16 May, there was only a handshake—a small detail but one that spoke volumes about the new character of the Sino-Soviet relationship. It was respectful, it was formal, but it was by no means close.[37]

The purpose of their meeting was, in Deng's words, to 'close the past and open the future'. This was something for which Gorbachev was well prepared. After shaking hands, however, Deng unexpectedly launched into a topic that caught the Soviet leader off guard—the true nature of Marxism-Leninism. No matter how great Marx and Lenin were in their times, Deng explained, they could have hardly predicted the changes that would occur in the world. Dogmatic application of their ideology was therefore out of date, and out of the question. 'He who cannot develop Marxism-Leninism taking into consideration the new conditions is not a real Communist', he insisted. Gorbachev tried to say something profound without offending or contradicting Deng, though he himself was now less interested in defining a 'real communist' than in identifying which reform policies actually worked. Fortunately, Deng offered a way out of this potentially awkward ideological moment. Each side, he suggested, must follow its own path and develop its own brand of Marxism. No single model suited all. With this Gorbachev could heartily agree, having encouraged Eastern European regimes to pursue national paths of communist reform. Deng then launched into a long monologue, as he had done with Bush, offering a history of Sino-Soviet relations back to the nineteenth century in order to make clear the need for equality in their new relationship. Agreeing, the Soviet leader chose not to lecture Deng with his own version of history. He had come for reconciliation, not argument. 'Good', he told Deng. 'Let's put an end to this.'[38]

Despite their different backgrounds and mutual scepticism in 1989, Bush and Gorbachev followed roughly similar approaches while in Beijing. Both understood China's importance—treating the country not just as an element in a game of triangulation but also as a substantial and independent reality with which they each had to deal in its own right. Both were aware of the immense long-term significance of relations with the new China. And both were at pains to stress that they had no intention of interfering in the country's domestic affairs. Thus Gorbachev, the China novice, and Bush, the *lao pengyou*, each proved equally pragmatic when dealing with Deng's regime, perhaps realizing that they had no choice but to embrace China as it was.

TIANANMEN

This pragmatic approach was put to the test on 4 June, when an impatient Deng Xiaoping—freed from the embarrassment of Gorbachev's visit—finally ordered a brutal military crackdown in and around Tiananmen Square. Hundreds died, demonstrators and also soldiers, in combat waged through the city's streets. The events were captured by the world's media because many journalists who reported the summit had stayed to cover the demonstrations. Two images became iconic in the West: the crushing of the Goddess of Democracy—a ten-metre high, papier-maché replica of the Statue of Liberty in New York—and a lone student standing before a column of army tanks. In a single night, Tiananmen changed in the global consciousness from a place to an event—the carnage televised, its images transmitted around the world, and ultimately seared into the global canon of rebellion and repression. Yet Tiananmen elicited very different reactions in Washington and Moscow: Bush was openly horrified at the violence and felt his trust betrayed, whereas Gorbachev contained his personal feelings and worked to strengthen Sino-Soviet relations.

Washington was not surprised at the use of force. Ambassador James Lilley had been predicting a crackdown for weeks, upping his expectation of bloodshed the day before from 'likely' to 'imminent'. But Bush, despite his desire for more democracy, had gone out of his way to avoid encouraging the demonstrators, lest this inflame passions in Beijing. 'I am old enough to remember Hungary in 1956', he told reporters in Europe in late May. 'I do not want to be a catalyst for encouraging a course of action that would inevitably lead to violence and bloodshed.' Indeed, asked if there was 'any-thing concretely the West can do to help the process without interfering', Bush conceded, 'Not that I can think of '.[39]

Bush said more behind the scenes, warning Chinese officials on numerous occasions—personally and through trusted emissaries—that any resort to violence would bring serious repercussions and that American public reaction would undoubtedly force his hand. 'I have no desire whatever to be seeming to interfere in the internal affairs of the People's Republic', he wrote Deng in late May, almost repeating the Chinese leader's February lecture, 'and I want you to know that I am determined to achieve the closest possible relations between our two countries'. However, the president said he also felt compelled to 'express to you my hope that there would be no outcome with respect to the student demonstrations which would interfere with my ability to pursue the kinds of policies which would promote the goals we seek in our relationship' and that 'any solution you decide upon would avoid violence, repression, and bloodshed'. Writing, he said, as an old friend, he reminded Deng that America, and the world, was watching.[40]

But Deng, fearful for his regime's survival, took absolutely no notice. He decided to wall-off China once more—curtailing foreign media while cracking down, hard and without mercy, on those who would cause chaos in the streets. As Lilley explains, he hoped to practise the old Chinese phrase of 'closing the door so as to beat the dog'. Deng believed that the West had short memories, and ultimately needed China's trade: their ire would not last. In the blunt words attributed to him, 'you carry these things out, and the Westerners forget'.[41]

And so, despite his much vaunted special relationship with the Chinese leader, Bush had no way to halt the violence of Tiananmen Square. China was a nuclear-armed great power with a seat on the United Nations Security Council by 1989. The president could no more deploy troops in Beijing to protect the demonstrators than he could send the US Marines to Mars. At the critical hour, after PRC tanks had driven demonstrators from the square and amid reports of possibly imminent civil war throughout China, Bush was left with only one card to play—invoking his long friendship with Deng to make a personal appeal for calm.

Deng refused to accept his phone call. Chinese and American leaders had no strategic 'hot-line' in place in 1989, no dedicated means of connecting, like Moscow and Washington, in times of crisis. Indeed Chinese and American leaders had rarely, if ever, communicated by phone to that point in time. Yet these were not ordinary circumstances, and an American president typically assumes he can reach anyone in the world at a moment's notice, never imagin-ing that his call would be refused. But Deng did precisely that. Astonished, Bush's inner circle initially speculated that the Chinese leader was either too ill to pick up the phone or had been deposed. In fact, Deng's calculated refusal demonstrated the real limits of 'old friendship' with Beijing at this moment of crisis. The abortive call proved to be Bush's last fling as China's *lao pengyou*. His China policy was now bankrupt. And amid outrage among the American public about Tiananmen, Washington's relations with Beijing plunged to a low reminiscent of the 1960s, before Nixon's pathbreaking visit in 1972.

By contrast, Soviet relations with China continued to strengthen in the wake of Tiananmen. Moscow issued a limp statement of 'regret' over bloodshed and privately Gorbachev appeared 'dismayed'.[42] But he was not about to sacrifice the hard-won gains of his personal diplomacy for the sake of abstract principles. The Congress of People's Deputies—Gorbachev's new parliament established and elected in 1989—issued a carefully-worded statement appealing for 'wisdom, reason, and [a] weighted approach' in resolving the crisis.[43] Radical deputies who wanted more were given short shrift by Gorbachev. When human rights advocate Andrei Sakharov mounted the podium to demand the recall of the Soviet ambassador from China, Gorbachev—who chaired the session—simply switched off his microphone.[44] The Soviet leader later justified his approach to India's Rajiv Gandhi: 'Politicians must be careful in these matters. Especially when we are talking about a country like China. A country with more than a billion people. This is a whole civilization!'[45] In his own circle he was even more candid. When in October 1989 the Soviet Politburo received intelligence that the number of dead in the massacre might have topped three thousand, Gorbachev's reaction was: 'We must be realists. They, like us, have to hold on. Three thousand . . . So what?'[46]

Gorbachev had problems of his own, including the upheavals in the Caucasus and now the protests in the Baltic republics. He clinically separated his personal aversion to the use of force and his sympathy for the students' cause from the exigencies of power politics. Given the domestic malaise at home and uncertain gains from engagement with the West, normalization of relations with China could be presented as an impressive diplomatic achievement. Gorbachev saw China's post-Tiananmen isolation from the world as a blessing of sorts for the USSR: Beijing's need for friends offered Moscow a chance to flesh out the bare bones of the new Sino-Soviet relationship and thereby strengthen its leverage vis-à-vis the West in triangular diplomacy. Unsure that even a reformed Soviet state would ever be accepted and integrated in Europe, Gorbachev was especially interested in developing a different form of triangular cooperation—between China, India, and the USSR. Whereas the Chinese had previously given a cold shoulder to these plans, after Tiananmen Gorbachev told Gandhi that they might well change their alignment, turning away from Western nations that had condemned the regime's actions to friends in Asia whose muted criticisms suggested a deeper understanding of Beijing's particular needs. Feeling that the Americans actually wished all three of them—the Soviet Union, India, and China—something 'worse' than Tiananmen, Gorbachev told Gandhi that 'perhaps, now is the exact moment when they [the Chinese] are truly interested in ties with you and with us'.[47] By not having spoken out, Gorbachev hoped that his silence spoke volumes: he saw Tiananmen as a human tragedy but also as a useful political opportunity.

On a larger plane, Tiananmen made a significant, if often overlooked, contribution to Soviet-American relations, and to Bush's evolving approach to Eastern Europe. The crackdown of 4 June occurred on the same day as Poland held its first free parliamentary elections, in which the trade union movement Solidarity swept the board. Bush publicly (though cautiously) celebrated this democratic triumph but he feared that hardline communist regimes in Eastern Europe might yet follow the Chinese example and use force on protestors if they also felt that their existence was at stake. The instability was not simply due to internal political change but also to the opening of Hungary's border with Austria, which cut through the Iron Curtain and encouraged East Germans, in particular, to go west to the Federal Republic. Bush was now belatedly focusing on Cold War Europe. His first transatlantic trip as president had been only at the end of May, to meet with Western European allies; in July he followed up with an eye-opening visit to Poland and Hungary. The president's rhetoric was now about encouraging the march of freedom and overcoming the division of Europe.[48]

After his vivid experiences in Poland and Hungary, Bush attended the G7 summit in Paris at which he sought to focus attention on the problems of Eastern Europe. He was now coming to the conclusion that a meeting with Gorbachev should not be delayed. Strongly encouraged by French President François Mitterrand on 13 July, who emphasized that 'the important thing was that the superpowers talk and exchange views', Bush prepared a letter for the Soviet leader to explain 'how my thinking is changing'. Previously he had felt that a meeting would have to produce major agreements, especially on arms control, but now he had decided it was urgent for both of them to develop a personal relationship 'to reduce the chances that there could be misunderstandings between us'. The president proposed an informal, no-agenda meeting 'without thousands of assistants hovering over our shoulders, without the ever-present briefing papers and certainly without the press yelling at us every five minutes about who's winning'. In fact, Bush said firmly, 'it would be best to avoid the word "summit"' altogether. By early August, Gorbachev had agreed in principle, with the hope of meeting in September. But it took several weeks to sort out schedules and location.[49]

In the autumn of 1989 Bush was concerned above all about East Germany, where the gerontocratic regime of Erich Honecker was particularly resistant to reform and the Red Army was stationed in strength. Although Gorbachev's speech to the UN in December 1988—stating that 'force and the threat of force can no longer be, and should not be instruments of foreign policy'—had apparently negated the 'Brezhnev doctrine' justifying Soviet suppression of the Prague Spring, nobody could be certain how Gorbachev and the Soviet military would react if communism really began to crumble in the German

Democratic Republic (GDR). By late October, hundreds of thousands of East Germans were marching for reform. The temptation in Washington to become triumphalist was now intense but Bush admitted that the Chinese tragedy was colouring his response. 'If we mishandle change in Eastern Europe and get way out [in front] looking like an American project', he lamented in his diary, 'you would invite crackdown and negative reaction that could result in bloodshed'.[50] On 9 November, the Berlin Wall was breached and the GDR started to collapse; people power also spilled over into Czechoslovakia, Bulgaria, and Romania. On the president's personal handwritten notes from talks with global leaders and White House staff on the night the Wall came down, one word was repeated, underlined, and highlighted—'Tiananmen'.[51] Anxious to avoid provoking a similar crackdown in Berlin, Bush eschewed triumphalist rhetoric and ignored calls for him to 'dance' on the Wall.[52] With the GDR and Eastern Europe in turmoil, he was relieved that his meeting with Gorbachev was now imminent, having been firmed up for the first weekend of December in Malta.

MALTA: BUSH AND GORBACHEV

In contrast with Bush, Gorbachev had always been keen on an early meeting. The Soviet leader had requested this way back in December 1988, right after Bush's election, but the president-elect had procrastinated and by late spring Gorbachev's patience with the Americans was wearing thin. 'What were they waiting for?' he fumed. The president's change of heart in the summer was therefore encouraging and, after the fall of the Wall, Gorbachev was especially anxious to achieve superpower consensus on how to manage the pace of change in Eastern Europe.[53]

Their talks on 2–3 December took place off the coast of Malta on board a Soviet cruise liner, the *Maxim Gorky*. The sessions were rocky, literally and figuratively. A massive storm buffeted the shipboard meetings, even forcing cancellation of some sessions, though the two leaders managed to spend nearly two days in conversation together. What they achieved is hard to quantify. No great accords resulted; they resolved neither Soviet-American relations nor the future of Germany. Although Bush spoke of entering 'a brand-new era of U.S.-Soviet relations', he was not willing to publicly declare that the Cold War was over. Challenged to say as much by an American reporter a few days later, the president was evasive: 'We're fooling around with semantics here. I don't want to give you a headline. I've told you the areas where I think we have progress. Why do we resort to these codewords that send different signals to different people? I'm not going to answer it.' He rephrased the question: 'Is the Cold War the same—I mean, is it raging like before in the times of the Berlin

Blockade? Absolutely not. Things have moved dramatically. But if I signal to you that there's no Cold War, then it's "what are you doing with troops in Europe?" I mean, come on!'[54]

Given that the two alliance blocs were still facing off across a Germany in turmoil, Bush felt he was in no position to announce the end of the Cold War. But, as he was at pains to say, it was certainly not 'raging' in the way it had been in 1948–9. There was no longer a danger of war, the ideological competition was being defused and, most importantly, the tenor of personal relations between the Soviet and American leaders was now fundamentally different. 'I do want to say that the world will be a better place if perestroika succeeds', Bush told his Soviet counterpart. 'You said some U.S. elements want to see perestroika fail. I can't say there are no such elements in the U.S.—but there are no serious elements, and most Americans don't feel that way.'[55] By December, importantly, neither did the president who had come to realize that, whatever his previous misgivings about Gorbachev's sincerity, none of the revolutions of 1989 would ever have been possible without the initial impetus from the Soviet leader's reform policies. Finally persuaded that perestroika was a good thing and not merely a Machiavellian scheme to disrupt transatlantic relations and undermine America's position in Europe, Bush began the long process of learning to trust Gorbachev as well. 'I have been called cautious', he told the Soviet leader, 'but I have conducted myself in ways not to complicate your life. That's why I have not jumped up or down on the Berlin Wall.'[56]

Gorbachev began to trust as well. He appreciated Bush's refusal to inflame passions behind the suddenly defunct Iron Curtain. He also made two points of his own. First, that German unification was not something the Soviets would endorse in the near-term: 'There are two [German] states, mandated by history.' Gorbachev urged Bush to help restrain Chancellor Helmut Kohl's enthusiasm for rapid reunification, instead of letting 'history decide the outcome'. In other words, would Bush promise that the issue of Germany—arguably the most important geopolitical challenge facing the Soviet Union as 1990 loomed—would not be decided quickly or by the Germans alone? Bush replied: 'I agree and we will do nothing to recklessly try to speed up reunification.'[57]

Gorbachev's second main point was ideological. He wanted Bush to change not only his outlook but his entire rhetoric about Soviet-American competition. *Perestroika, glasnost*, indeed in many ways Gorbachev's entire political agenda boiled down to a single notion: bringing Soviet society in line with the rest of Europe and the rest of the world, thereby preparing the socialist state that decrepitly concluded the twentieth century for the rapidly approaching twenty-first. This required the West to abandon the notion that the Soviets, and by extension their Russian predecessors, were in some way divorced from Western society. For *perestroika* to succeed, his country needed to be part of Europe not only politically and economically but in mentalities as well—in other words, transcending the idea of an East-West divide. Too many Americans, in Gorbachev's view, interpreted communism's collapse as a Western triumph, or rather as the triumph of American values. 'What I dislike is when some U.S. politicians say unity of Europe should be on the basis of Western values', he told Bush directly. 'We have long been accused of exporting ideology. That is what is now being proposed by some', though of course, he told the president politely, 'not you'.[58]

Bush and his aides took Gorbachev's point. They quickly agreed to employ the terms 'democratic values' and 'universal values' rather than 'Western values'. It was a small concession, but taken together with his restraint over German reunification, a meaningful step nonetheless.[59] Anatoly Chernyaev, one of Gorbachev's closest advisers, summed up the summit a few weeks later: 'it seemed like a regular, normal affair'. Gorbachev 'acted like he and Bush were old pals—frank and simple, and openly well-intentioned'. The 'deciding factor', Chernayev added, was that 'the USSR and US are no longer enemies. This is the most important thing.'[60]

What ultimately did Malta mean? In concrete terms, not very much. It did not determine procedures for reuniting Germany, integrating Eastern and Western Europe, or helping the Soviet Union make a soft-landing in its difficult transition from socialism to capitalism and from communism to liberal democracy. Malta was, however, the first step in building the kind of trust that ultimately saw Bush and Gorbachev become like *lao pengyou*—'old friends'. Such a relationship did not guarantee diplomatic leverage, as Deng had demonstrated; it also had real limits in mitigating domestic conflict, as evidenced by Tiananmen. But *lao pengyou* could speak frankly and with mutual understanding. After Malta Bush and Gorbachev did just that— above all about Germany.

NOTES

1. George Bush, Inaugural Address, 20 January 1989, The American Presidency Project (henceforth APP) website, http://www.presidency.ucsb.edu/ws/index.php?pid=16610.

2. George Bush and Brent Scowcroft, *A World Transformed* (New York, 1998), 46; President's private meeting with Gorbachev, Governor's Island, New York, 7 December 1988, 1.05 pm–1.30pm, 5, National Security Archive, George Washington University, Washington, DC, electronic briefing book (henceforth NSAEBB), no. 261, doc no. 8, http://nsarchive.gwu.edu/NSAEBB/NSAEBB261/us08.pdf; Bush, speech in Mainz, 31 May 1989, APP website, http://www.presidency.ucsb.edu/ws/index.php?pid=17085&st=&st1=.

3. Bush-Gorbachev question-and-answer session, Malta, 3 December 1989, APP website, http://www.presidency.ucsb.edu/ws/index.php?pid=17900&st=&st1=.

4. 'Bush: 'Our Work is Not Done; Our Force is Not Spent', *The Washington Post,* 19 August 1988, A28.

5. George Bush Presidential Library, College Station, Texas, George Bush Collection (henceforth GBPL-GBC), Vice Presidential Daily Files, Alphabetical Transition Files (11/8/88–1/19/89), Transition (11/9/88–1/19/89), Bush to Brzezinski, 21 November 1988.

6. GBPL-GBC, Vice Presidential Daily Files, Alphabetical Transition Files (11/8/88–1/19/89), Transition (11/9/88–1/19/89), Bush to Brzezinski, 21 November 1988.

7. Jeffrey A. Engel, ed., *The China Diary of George H.W. Bush: The Making of a Global President* (Princeton, NJ, 2008), 46–8.

8. Quoted in Chen Jian, 'China, the Third World and the End of the Cold War', in Artemy Kalinovsky and Sergey Radchenko, eds, *The End of the Cold War and the Third World: New Perspectives on Regional Conflict* (London, 2011), 112.

9. Richard H. Solomon, *Chinese Negotiating Behavior: Pursuing Interests through 'Old Friends'* (Washington, DC, 1999), 102.

10. James Mann, *About Face, A History of America's Curious Relationship with China, from Nixon to Clinton* (New York, 2000), 135—italics added.

11. Solomon, *Chinese Negotiating Behavior,* 102.

12. James Lilley, *China Hands: Nine Decades of Adventure, Espionage, and Diplomacy in Asia* (New York, 2004), 217, 223.

13. Lilley, *China Hands,* 223.

14. Ezra F. Vogel, *Deng Xiaoping and the Transformation of China* (Cambridge, MA, 2011), 485–6. The Bush-Deng arrangement formed the basis, when formally negotiated, of a 'United States-China Joint Communique on United States Arms Sales to Taiwan' (17 August 1982).

15. Mann, *About Face,* 176. See also Mann's more polemical *The China Fantasy: How our Leaders Explain Away Chinese Repression* (New York, 2007).

16. Mann, *About Face,* 159.

17. Intelligence Research Report, State Department, 17 December 1987, State Department FOIA reading room; Intelligence Research Report, State Department, 21 October 1987, 10. Both available at https://foia.state.gov/search/results.aspx?searchText=China&beginDate=19871001&endDate=19871231&publishedBeginDate=&publishedEndDate=&caseNumber=.

18. Vogel, *Deng Xiaoping,* 423.

19. Sergey Radchenko, *Unwanted Visionaries: the Soviet Failure in Asia at the End of the Cold War* (New York, 2014), 172–80.

20. Czechoslovak Translation of the Soviet Summary of Conversations Between Mikhail Gorbachev and Li Peng in Moscow, 8 January 1986, Central State Archives (SÚA), Prague: UV KSC. See Parallel History Project, http://kms2.isn.ethz.ch/serviceengine/Files/PHP/19459/ipublicationdocument_singledocument/64ca85ed-235f-4fe0-9e33-71130bc4f517/cs/860108_cz_translation.pdf.

21. GBPL, Brent Scowcroft Files (henceforth BSF), Presidential Correspondence, Memcon, Bush's meeting with Yang Shangkun, 25 February 1989, https://bush41library.tamu.edu/files/memcons-telcons/1989-02-25–Shangkun%20[1].pdf.

22. Jeffrey Engel interview with George and Barbara Bush, 16 November 2005.

23. GBPL, BSF, Presidential Correspondence, Memcon, Bush's meeting with Zhao Ziyang, 26 February 1989, https://bush41library.tamu.edu/files/memcons-telcons/1989-02-26–Ziyang.pdf.

24. GBPL, BSF, Presidential Correspondence, Memcon, Bush's meeting Zhao Ziyang, 26 February 1989, https://bush41library.tamu.edu/files/memcons-telcons/1989-02-26–Ziyang.pdf.

25. GBPL, BSF, Presidential Correspondence, Memcon, Bush's meeting with Li Peng, 26 February 1989, https://bush41library.tamu.edu/files/memcons-telcons/1989-02-26–Peng.pdf.

26. GBPL, BSF, Presidential Correspondence, Memcon, Welcoming banquet in Beijing, China, 25 February 1989, https://bush41library.tamu.edu/files/memcons-telcons/1989-02-25–Peng.pdf.

27. GBPL, BSF, Presidential Correspondence, Memcon, Bush's meeting Deng Xiaoping, 26 February 1989, https://bush41library.tamu.edu/files/memcons-telcons/1989-02-26–Xiaoping.pdf.

28. GBPL, BSF, Presidential Correspondence, Memcon, Bush's meeting with Zhao Ziyang, 26 February 1989, https://bush41library.tamu.edu/files/memcons-telcons/1989-02-26–Ziyang.pdf.

29. GBPL, BSF, Presidential Correspondence, Memcon, Bush's meeting with Zhao Ziyang, 26 February 1989, https://bush41library.tamu.edu/files/memcons-telcons/1989-02-26–Ziyang.pdf.

30. GBPL, BSF, Presidential Correspondence, Memcon, Bush's meeting Deng Xiaoping, 26 February 1989, https://bush41library.tamu.edu/files/memcons-telcons/1989-02-26–Xiaoping.pdf.

31. Mann, *About Face*, 178. See also 'Ambassador Winston Lord', Association for Diplomatic Studies and Training, Foreign Affairs Oral History Project, 28 April 1998, http://www.adst.org/OH%20TOCs/Lord,%20Winston.pdf.

32. Vogel, *Deng Xiaoping*, 608; Chen Jian, 'Tiananmen and the Fall of the Berlin Wall: China's Path toward 1989 and Beyond', in Jeffrey A. Engel, ed., *The Fall of the Berlin Wall: The Revolutionary Legacy of 1989* (New York, 2009), 111–12.

33. Liang Zhang et al., eds, *The Tiananmen Papers* (New York, 2002), 143.

34. Mikhail Gorbachev, *Sobranie Sochinenii*, vol. 15 (Moscow, 2010), 261.

35. Zhang Ganghua and Li Peng, *Li Peng liu si ri ji zhen xiang: Fu lu Li Peng liu si ri ji yuan wen* (Hong Kong, 2010).

36. Oleg Troyanovskii, *Cherez Gody i Rasstoyaniya: Istoriya Odnoi Sem'yi (Over Years and Distances)* (Moscow, 1997), 373.

37. Excerpts from the conversation between Mikhail Gorbachev and Deng Xiaoping, 16 May 1989, http://digitalarchive.wilsoncenter.org/document/116536.

38. Ibid.

39. George Bush, The President's News Conference, 30 May, 1989, APP website, http://www.presidency.ucsb.edu/ws/index.php?pid=17077&st=Hungary&st1=1956.

40. GBPL, Scowcroft Papers on China 2 of 5 Tiananmen Square Crisis [2], White House Situation Room Files, From Washington to American Embassy Beijing, Letter from President Bush to Deng Xiaoping, 27 May 1989.

41. Lilley, *China Hands*, 309.

42. GBPL, Telcon: Kohl to Bush, 15 June 1989, https://bush41library.tamu.edu/files/memcons-telcons/1989-06-15–Kohl.pdf.

43. 'New Congress neutral on China bloodshed', *The Associated Press*, 6 June 1989.

44. Bill Keller, 'Soviet Congress ends with one last spat', *New York Times*, 10 June 1989, 1. Aleksandr Lukin, *Medved' Nablyudaet Za Drakonom* (Moscow, 2007), 280.

45. Excerpts from conversation between Mikhail Gorbachev and Rajiv Gandhi, 15 July 1989, http://digitalarchive.wilsoncenter.org/document/119291.pdf?v=6a44a2603e0ef 9559df45d0b2d1d461a.

46. Gorbachev Foundation, Moscow, Record of the Politburo meeting, 4 October 1989.

47. Gorbachev, *Sobranie Sochinenii*, 258.

48. Bush and Scowcroft, *A World Transformed* (New York, 1998), 130.

49. Bush and Scowcroft, *A World Transformed*, 126–9, 132–3; for complete text of Bush's invitation letter, see GBPL, NSC Files, Brent Scowcroft Collection, Special Separate China Notes Files, China Files, Folder: China 1989 (Sensitive) [4], Bush to Gorbachev, 21 July 1989. See also GBPL, Memcon, Bush's meeting with Mitterrand, 13 July 1989, https://bush41library.tamu.edu/files/memcons-telcons/ 1989-07-13–Mitterrand.pdf.

50. Bush and Scowcroft, *A World Transformed*, 148.

51. GBPL, Office of the President, Daily Files, Folder: Saturday, 11 November 1989.

52. Bush and Scowcroft, *A World Transformed*, 149.

53. Mikhail Gorbachev, *Memoirs* (London, 1996), 497.

54. Bush-Gorbachev question-and-answer session, Malta, 3 December 1989, APP website, http://www.presidency.ucsb.edu/ws/index.php?pid=17900&st=&st1; Bush, news conference, Brussels, 4 December 1989, APP website, http://www.presidency.ucsb. edu/ws/index.php?pid=17907&st=&st1=.

55. GBPL, NSC Files, Condoleezza Rice Files, Soviet Union/USSR Subject Files, Folder: Summit at Malta December 1989: Malta Memcons, First expanded bilateral, Maxim Gorky, 10.00–11.55am, 2 December 1989, 3, http://digitalarchive.wilsoncenter.org/ document/117430.

56. GBPL, NSC Files, Condoleezza Rice Files, Soviet Union/USSR Subject Files, Folder: Summit at Malta December 1989: Malta Memcons, First expanded bilateral, Maxim Gorky, 10.00–11.55am, 2 December 1989, 9, http://digitalarchive.wilsoncenter.org/ document/117430.

57. GBPL, NSC Files, Condoleezza Rice Files, Soviet Union/USSR Subject Files, Folder: Summit at Malta December 1989: Malta Memcons, First restricted bilateral, Maxim Gorky, 12.00–1.00pm, 2 December 1989, 5, http://digitalarchive.wilsoncenter.org/ document/117430.

58. GBPL, NSC Files, Condoleezza Rice Files, Soviet Union/USSR Subject Files, Folder: Summit at Malta December 1989: Malta Memcons, First restricted bilateral, Maxim Gorky, 12.00–1.00pm, 2 December 1989, 4, http://digitalarchive.wilsoncenter.org/ document/117430.

59. GBPL, NSC Files, Condoleezza Rice Files, Soviet Union/USSR Subject Files, Folder: Summit at Malta December 1989: Malta Memcons, Second expanded bilateral, Maxim Gorky, 4.35–6.45pm, 3 December 1989, 10, http://digitalarchive.wil soncenter.org/document/117430.

60. Anatoly S. Chernyaev diary, 2 January 1990, NSAEBB no. 298, doc. 13, http://nsarchive.gwu.edu/NSAEBB/NSAEBB298/Document%2013.pdf.

8

The Caucasus, 1990

Kristina Spohr

Another curious image from a summit. 15 July 1990. Men in suits surrounding two leaders sitting on tree trunks—one in his woolly jumper, the other in a cardigan (see Figure 8.1). Set up, of course, as media theatre but in its own way intimate and in fact one of the most significant moments in the dénouement of the Cold War. Mikhail Gorbachev and Helmut Kohl had met that morning in Moscow but then the Soviet leader flew the German chancellor down to his dacha near Arkhyz, in the remote vastness of the Caucasus mountains. He hoped that this more informal setting might enable them to resolve their crucial sticking points over German reunification.

Two days later Chancellor Kohl reflected on the significance of the Caucasus summit in a letter to French President François Mitterrand.

> I conducted my discussions with President Gorbachev on common philosophical grounds: As members of the same generation which had still consciously experienced the war and its consequences, we now faced up to the challenge to grasp the great, perhaps unique, opportunity to contribute to finally overcoming the division of Europe and to shape a peaceful, secure and free future for our continent in perpetuity.

Kohl ended the letter by listing the three main results of the summit for a unified Germany: defining its territorial scope (encompassing East and West Germany, as well as Berlin); ending the reserved rights and responsibilities of the four victor powers of 1945, thereby confirming the new Germany's full and unrestricted sovereignty; and affirming its sovereign right to choose its alliance freely according to the Helsinki Final Act of 1975.[1]

With these three achievements from the summit, Germany emerged as a key designer of the post-Cold War security architecture. Kohl had secured Gorbachev's written agreement to full NATO membership for a united Germany and to the option for NATO of deploying eastward to the Oder-Neisse line after the end of a transitional period for the withdrawal of

Fig. 8.1. On Tree Trunks in the Caucasus: Kohl and Gorbachev, 15 July 1990 (Bundesbildstelle)

Soviet troops from former East German territory. As for NATO's extension beyond eastern Germany—to this day a matter of controversy—the issue was not even addressed in Arkhyz, either by the Germans or the Soviets. What mattered was that the Caucasus deal ensured NATO's survival beyond the Cold War and cemented a new predominance on the European continent for the forty-year-old Western security institution and with it the continuation of a leading American role in Europe. Equally significant, this was happening at the same time as NATO's Cold War rival, the Warsaw Pact, was disintegrating and the Red Army, whose presence in the heart of Europe had shaped the Cold War since the demise of Hitler's Reich, was in retreat.

The mechanism and the symbolism of the summit were equally significant. The two men on the tree trunks sealing the deal on the future of Europe were the leaders of the Soviet Union and West Germany, while the president of the United States watched from some five thousand miles away. Crucial for brokering the deal was Kohl's chequebook diplomacy—using Bonn's financial muscle to leverage Soviet troops out of East Germany. It was a sign of Germany's new political confidence in global diplomacy. To be sure, during 1989–90 the administration of George H.W. Bush set down key security markers for West German diplomacy at Soviet-American meetings in Malta, Moscow, and Washington and it broadly endorsed Kohl's subsequent actions. But the Americans had not expected that the chancellor's summit diplomacy would prove so speedy, effective, and far-reaching. As the new Germany flexed its muscles, it seemed to many observers that Uncle Sam was left looking like an awkward bystander.

The Caucasus summit and the bigger story of how Germany and Europe exited the Cold War grew out of a highly dynamic triangular relationship between the United States, the Soviet Union, and the Federal Republic. In this triangularity West Germany began to act as an equal with each superpower in pursuit of its own national interests. This pattern emerged as soon as the Berlin Wall fell on 9 November 1989 and Kohl announced his ten-point programme for unification. Closer examination of the events of these formative weeks is important for understanding the summitry that followed in 1990.

AFTER THE WALL: HOW TO REIN IN THE GERMANS?

The opening of Hungary's border with Austria in May 1989 allowed East Germans the chance to leave their police state for the first time in twenty-eight years. By the early autumn thousands were leaving their *Heimat* and travelling through Czechoslovakia, Hungary, and Austria to take up their automatic right of citizenship in the Federal Republic. In late September the panic-stricken leaders of the ruling Socialist Unity Party (SED) persuaded the Czech government to close its borders, but this only increased the pressures building up within the German Democratic Republic (GDR) from the growing civil rights movement. Protestors carried placards declaring 'All the way to Hawaii without any visa' and 'Passports for everyone—marching orders for the SED'.[2]

Seeking to ease the crisis, the regime prepared new regulations for travel and permanent exit from the GDR, albeit still under official control. These were announced at 6pm on 9 November in a press conference by a media spokesman, Günter Schabowski, who knew little of the details and botched his statement. Journalists who had been bored by most of Schabowski's hour-long briefing suddenly woke up when he said things like 'allows every citizen ... exit via all GDR border crossings to the FRG ... comes into effect, according to my information, immediately, without delay'.[3] Suddenly the room emptied as the media, sensing a scoop, broadcast on the wire services and television channels stories suggesting that the Berlin Wall was now open. By midnight thousands of East Germans had flocked to the checkpoints. The border guards, scared of the crowds and unable to obtain clear instructions, simply raised the barriers. That night some 78,000 East Germans crossed into West Berlin. It was the start of a tidal wave.

So the fall of the Wall was a combination of people power, governmental paralysis, and sheer luck. Suddenly on the night of 9–10 November the German question was back on the international agenda. Gorbachev sent Kohl an urgent message warning against any statements 'designed to stimulate a denial of the existence of two German states and encourage emotional reactions' that could have 'no other goal than destabilizing the situation in the GDR'. This did not stop the chancellor from rushing to Berlin and talking about self-determination: 'We demand this right for all in Europe. We demand it for all Germans.'[4] But Washington stayed surprisingly mute. President Bush was criticized by the American media for his lack of jubilation. Secretary of State James Baker made ritual comments about 'freedom', 'democracy', and the principle of 'unification' but in practice waited on events.

A week later, this mood of caution and restraint continued to rule in the White House. Bush knew that Margaret Thatcher and François Mitterrand, leaders of the two Western European victor powers of 1945, had serious private reservations about the re-emergence of a large, unified Germany at the centre of Europe. Above all he feared a violent and bloody military crackdown by the Soviets and certainly did not want Gorbachev to believe that he was provoking disorder and that the demonstrations all over Eastern Europe had been an 'American project'.[5] The president telephoned Kohl on 17 November to warn against 'expansive rhetoric' and 'talk about reunification or a time-plan for tearing down the wall'. Bush stressed that 'unforeseeable reactions in the GDR and Soviet Union' had to be avoided. He promised to consult closely with Kohl but wanted the chancellor to avoid any precipitate action until he and Gorbachev had been able to talk at their Malta summit in early December.[6]

Kohl, however, ignored this advice and took matters into his own hands. On 28 November he presented a ten-point programme for unification in a speech to the Bundestag. After the usual genuflections towards the FRG's responsibilities to the EC, NATO, and CSCE, he set out a unilateral plan that effectively bypassed the victor powers. His blueprint to achieve unity in free self-determination focused on supporting reforms inside the GDR, creating confederative structures between the two states with the aim of an eventual federation, and anchoring these developments in the pan-European process and East-West relations.[7] One might thus argue that in contrast to the *Deutschlandpolitik* approach of the Social Democrats' *Ostpolitik* architect Egon Bahr, which had been founded on the idea of 'change through rapprochement' (*Wandel durch Annäherung*), Kohl was now pressing for rapprochement between the two Germanies through change within the GDR.

Kohl had put forward his own concrete plans for Germany, though without a timetable, knowingly taking the risk that the Allies and his neighbours might not welcome a German fait accompli. For him unification was now no longer a rhetorical aspiration but a real possibility. Crucially, in regard to security arrangements, nothing explicit was said on NATO. This upset some Western allies. So Horst Teltschik, the chancellor's close national security adviser, was 'at pains to stress that Federal German membership of NATO was not in question'.[8] Nevertheless, with his ten points, Kohl had seized leadership of the whole unification process.

Washington, even if surprised by Kohl's proposal, appeared to support it, at least on the surface.[9] The following day, 29 November, James Baker held a press conference at which he presented a set of American conditions for supporting German unification. This was clearly an effort to regain some control over the direction of events. The secretary of state laid down four principles:

1. US support for German self-determination without endorsing specific outcomes;

2. the enduring membership of a unified Germany within NATO and the European Community;

3. a peaceful and gradual movement towards unification;

4. the need for the terms of the Helsinki Final Act to be observed on the question of postwar boundaries.[10]

The second principle stood out as Baker's chief concern. If Germany were to unify, the country had to be kept inside NATO. It was clearly an implicit American assumption that the Alliance would persist and should play a key role in Europe's post-Cold War security order. A German-Soviet bargain of 'neutrality for unification'—such as Stalin had offered back in 1952—must be avoided at all costs.

The State Department had clearly lined up behind Kohl's programme, albeit with conditions. Significantly, however, the president kept quiet and little leaked out of the White House. It seems that Bush was primarily concerned with the American-Soviet relationship and the preservation of peace and stability in Europe as a whole. Nobody could be certain how the USSR would react to developments in Germany. That would become clearer, he hoped, after his meeting with Gorbachev. Although Malta had been originally intended as an informal getting-to-know-you affair (Bush had tried to avoid the word 'summit'),[11] there was now a substantive and critical issue to address. Only face-to-face, it seemed, could Bush really gauge what Gorbachev would tolerate on the German question.

MALTA: GORBACHEV'S AMBER LIGHT FOR UNIFICATION AND AMERICA'S NEW ATLANTICISM

In Malta on 2–3 December, Bush and Gorbachev touched twice on Germany. The president was at pains to distinguish between Kohl's highly emotional response to the dramatic events in East Germany and his own generally cautious approach. He emphasized, in the face of critics who blasted him for being 'timid' and refusing to 'jump up and down at the Wall', that this was 'no time for grandstanding', for a step that looked good but 'could prove reck-less'.[12] Yet he also insisted that America had special responsibilities in Europe, not least via its leadership position in NATO. Above all, Bush made clear that the United States could not be asked to 'disapprove of reunification'.[13] This was key. No triumphalism but no opposition: Bush had come out openly in support of the German people and implicitly of Kohl's ten points.

What Gorbachev said was equally momentous. He stated categorically that the Soviet Union no longer regarded the United States as 'an adversary' and considered their relationship to be 'cooperative'. He assured Bush that the USSR 'under no circumstances would start a war'. On reunification, he agreed with the president that it was best for Germany to be unified on the basis of mutually acceptable 'democratic values': self-determination, openness, and pluralism.[14] Gorbachev thus confirmed that he had torn up the Brezhnev doctrine. There would be no repeat of Soviet military interventions like Prague 1968, Hungary 1956, and Berlin 1953. On the other hand the Soviet leader underlined his opposition to rapid change: 'Mr. Kohl is in too much of a hurry on the German question. That is not good. I worry that this could be part of his pre-election game and not because of a strategic outlook . . . We should let Kohl know that his approach could damage things.' Gorbachev's position was that 'there are two states, mandated by history. So let history decide the outcome.'[15]

The general tone of the meeting was positive. Gorbachev said it was a time of 'great responsibility' and also 'great opportunity'. Afterwards, in their joint Q and A with reporters, Bush—who had previously been wary of meeting with Gorbachev—spoke out warmly in favour of 'regular contacts' to build on the 'good personal relationship' that they had established. Neither expected to totally convert the other but they had been able to talk constructively about differences 'without rancor' and 'as frankly as possible'. The president felt that 'if we hadn't sat here and talked we might not have understood how each other feels on these important questions'. So, he concluded to general laughter, 'I couldn't have asked for a better result out of this non-summit summit'.[16]

Bush took away from Malta two important impressions. First, Gorbachev had signalled at least an amber light on German unification. The Soviets did not like the prospect and wanted the president to restrain Kohl, but they would allow events to run their course. Bush felt that Baker's four principles provided an adequate framework. Second, with newfound insight into Gorbachev's position, Bush could pursue the perpetuation of NATO, as embodied in Baker's second principle. And this he did. At the NATO Council on 4 December, the day after Malta, the president told the Allies that 'it was time to provide the architecture for continued change'.[17] He then informed the press: 'The United States will remain a European power', which meant that it would 'stay engaged in the future of Europe', and he pledged that America would 'maintain significant military forces in Europe as long as our allies desire our presence as part of a common defense effort'. The president reiterated NATO's traditional support for unification, but stressed that this should occur peacefully, gradually, and 'in the context of Germany's continued commitment to NATO and an increasingly integrated European community'.[18] In making this statement, Bush had moved the United States back into the role of policy-shaper.

At Malta Bush declared that 'we stand at the threshold of a brand-new era of U.S.-Soviet relations. And it is within our grasp to contribute, each in our own way, to overcoming the division of Europe and ending the military confrontation there.'[19] But the Americans struggled to define what it meant to be on the cusp of epochal change. A fascinating insight into how they were grappling with this question at that moment can be gleaned from the typed notes and handwritten jottings (in italics) that Baker produced on 4 December:

> Overview theme: Cold War is not over yet, but moving into final stage (*structure of peace*) . . . As we move into this *post-post war era* [~~final stage of the CW~~], we must concentrate on building a new age of peace, democracy, and economic liberty: A New Atlanticism and a New Europe that reaches further East.

> General: Architecture of the New Atlanticism and New Europe should not try to develop one overarching structure. Instead, it will rely on a number of complementary institutions that will be mutually reinforcing – NATO, EC, CSCE, WEU, Council of Europe.[20]

Baker publicly sketched out some of his ideas on the 'Architecture for a New Era' in a speech in West Berlin on 12 December when he talked about transforming NATO from a 'military organisation' into a 'political alliance'. But what hit the headlines was his meeting afterwards with the East German leaders, which was interpreted as an attempt to 'shore up' the GDR government and put the brakes on Bonn's push for rapid unification.[21] This followed a quadripartite meeting the day before in the allied Kommandatura in Berlin. It seemed that the three Western allies, despite all their fine words about unification, were still happy to sit down with Moscow's representative in an old fashioned Four-Power parley, over the heads of the FRG.[22] Baker's whole trip to Berlin was therefore widely seen as a slap in the face for Kohl. It was indeed a PR disaster, and Baker later apologized to the chancellor.[23]

THE NEW ARCHITECTURE OF EUROPEAN SECURITY: 'HELSINKI II' OR A 'POLITICAL NATO'?

Baker's actions had been predicated on the assumption that East Germany was still a viable state, at least for the immediate future, and that change could be regulated and managed from above by the four Allied powers. Kohl resented this paternalistic attitude because he wanted the two Germanies to negotiate as equals with the four victor powers (2 + 4, not 4 + 0). Furthermore, a visit to Dresden on 19 December, when he was surrounded by crowds chanting *Wir sind ein Volk*, convinced him that unification was going to come much more quickly than he had previously anticipated. In the New Year the GDR government, almost insolvent, came to Kohl begging for credits but he refused to bail them out. Instead he proposed full economic and monetary union, including the generous offer of 1:1 conversion of *Ostmarks* into *Deutschmarks*. With the date for East Germany's first free elections advanced to 18 March, this gave the CDU's sister-party the *Allianz für Deutschland* a splendid political platform and it won a smashing victory, winning nearly half the vote. Clearly Kohl was now calling the shots in East as well as in West Germany. From April 1990 the arithmetic of the 2 + 4 process was effectively 1 + 4.[24]

By early 1990, in other words, German unification was only a matter of time. But how this should come about and in what form aroused intense debate in Washington and Bonn, with the two foreign ministers—Hans-Dietrich Genscher and James Baker—pitted for a while against their political bosses.

Genscher had been in charge of the Foreign Ministry in Bonn since 1974. He was also a leading figure in the Free Democratic Party—the junior partner in Kohl's Christian Democrat coalition government. On 31 January 1990 Genscher delivered a major speech in Tutzing in which he stated that, because of revolutionary changes in Eastern Europe, it would be 'necessary to give special attention to the security interests of the Soviet Union' and to avoid interfering in Warsaw Pact matters. He argued that NATO should declare unequivocally that 'whatever happens in the Warsaw Pact there will no expansion of NATO territory eastwards, that is to say, closer to the borders of the Soviet Union. This security guarantee is important for the Soviet Union and its conduct . . . Any proposals for incorporating the part of Germany at present forming the GDR in NATO's military structures would block intra-German rapprochement.' The important thing in Genscher's view was to define clearly the future role of the two alliances, NATO and the Warsaw Pact. He envisaged that these two alliances would continue but would in time 'move away from confrontation to cooperation' and then become 'elements' of a new 'cooperative security structure throughout Europe'.[25]

Genscher made his Tutzing speech without clearing his words with the chancellery. He probably did this in retaliation for Kohl's unilateral declaration of the Ten Points, but he also regarded the place of Germany in Europe's evolving security architecture as his rightful area of competence as foreign minister. Significantly, there was no reference in the speech to the future of American nuclear weapons and Western forces in Germany, although both were necessary to keep NATO's defence and deterrence capabilities intact.[26]

Genscher's approach reflected his long commitment to *Ostpolitik* and also to the Helsinki process, especially the ambition for an all-European security system under the umbrella of the CSCE. This was not far from Gorbachev's ideas for a 'common European home' and his talk at Malta about a 'Helsinki II summit' to develop 'new criteria' for this 'new phase' in international relations because he hoped to transform both the Warsaw Pact and NATO into institutions that were 'more political than military'.[27]

The German foreign minister had dropped a political bombshell. He stood in stark contrast to Kohl who had so far only cautiously engaged with the security dimensions of unification.[28] A similar rift had also emerged in Washington over the post-Cold War security order. While the National Security Council (NSC) and White House staff envisaged a united Germany in NATO, some State Department bureaucrats contemplated American and Soviet military withdrawal from Germany and possible German withdrawal from NATO's integrated military command structures (like France had done in the 1960s under President Charles de Gaulle).[29]

Baker sided broadly with his State Department staff but also agreed with some of Genscher's views. In doing so, he acted without instructions from White House. The two men met on 2 February, and then appeared in front of the world media, as they put it, 'in full agreement'. Genscher stated that there was 'no intention to extend the NATO area of defense and security toward the East'. When pressed by journalists on the details, he specified 'no halfway membership this way or that. What I said is that there is no intention of extending the NATO area to the East.'[30] Genscher had thus somewhat clarified his Tutzing formula and secured Baker's agreement. Political NATO membership should be enjoyed by all of Germany, whereas militarily the GDR would remain outside NATO. Expansion of the Alliance beyond Germany was not mentioned and did not seem a political concern at this time.[31]

The practicalities of this vision were left largely unaddressed. One key difference over procedural matters did, however, emerge. While Baker pressed for a 2 + 4 framework involving the two Germanies and the four victor powers within which to negotiate Germany's new security arrangements, Genscher continued to stress the centrality of the CSCE for this process. He even expressed the desire to see this pan-European forum institutionalized via two CSCE summits in 1990 (in Paris) and 1992 (in Helsinki).[32]

A week later, Baker was sitting in the Kremlin. In meetings with Gorbachev and Soviet foreign minister Eduard Shevardnadze, he conveyed Genscher's ideas in the guise of presenting America's own thoughts on Germany's future.[33] Choosing a slightly narrower phraseology to that of his German counterpart, Baker offered Gorbachev the guarantee that, if US forces stayed in Germany within the framework of NATO, then 'neither the jurisdiction nor the military presence of NATO would extend one inch to the east'.[34] With these striking but actually imprecise words, the secretary of state suggested that NATO's defence cover would not stretch to GDR territory. That German unification would occur was, however, taken for granted.

By the time Baker spoke with Gorbachev, Bush was at last taking the lead. He saw things somewhat differently from his secretary of state. In a letter to Kohl on 9 February, drafted not by the State Department but by his NSC staff, the president explained that the continued presence of American forces on German soil and the continuation of nuclear deterrence were both 'critical to assuring stability in this time of change and uncertainty'. And so he suggested to Kohl that a component of a united Germany's NATO membership could be what he called a 'special military status for what is now the territory of the GDR. We believe that such a commitment could be made compatible with the security of Germany, as well as of its neighbours, in the context of substantial, perhaps ultimately total, Soviet troop withdrawals from Central and Eastern Europe.' Conscious, like Baker, of the need to make NATO more palatable to Gorbachev, he argued that the Alliance should 'have a changing mission, with more emphasis on its political role'.[35]

Bush's letter showed how new language could ensure the protection and defensibility of all of unified German territory while hopefully serving as a means to overcome Soviet objections to full NATO membership for united Germany. In contrast to Baker's and Genscher's phrasings, which seemed to rule out any kind of military expansion by NATO, Bush's language potentially ruled every option in. This shift in wording represented a significant change in policy—from a more defensive to a more assertive American stance.

The White House had clearly decided that unification was to be achieved absolutely and unequivocally on Western, indeed American, terms. NATO was not only intended to survive but would serve as a vehicle to ensure the leading role of the United States in European security after the Cold War.[36] Bush saw the Atlantic Alliance as a 'force of stability' which, 'along with other multilateral institutions such as EC and the CSCE', should 'overlap to provide a common security and policy framework to complement the role of economic and political groupings'. NATO, moreover, was not only a key to the continuing US security presence. Keen to stress the increasingly political character of the Alliance—and on that point Bush, Baker, and Genscher were converging—the Americans in addition believed, to quote Baker's own notes, that 'if history is a guide, then continued US presence & influence would be constructive'.[37] Bush and Baker also agreed that the way to resolve all the external matters related to unification was not through a Helsinki II process (as Genscher and Gorbachev had proposed), nor in the form of a 'peace' settlement or treaty to wind up World War Two (a French and Soviet formula)[38] but via the much smaller 2 + 4 talks. The latter formula avoided the impression of a Four-Power diktat—anathema in Bonn.

By mid-February Baker was singing from the same hymn-sheet as Bush. The White House now considered it imperative to 'get Kohl to agree that a united Germany would be a full member of NATO and a participant in its integrated military structure, and to state that publicly'. The chancellor duly did so in a press conference after his meeting with the president at Camp David on 25 February, from which Genscher had been deliberately excluded. (This was the first time a German chancellor had been accorded the privilege of a stay at the presidential exclusive retreat in Maryland.) In private during their discussions Kohl further agreed to the continued presence of American troops and nuclear weapons on German soil.[39]

But Genscher did not give up straight away. He stuck with his long-term idea of institutionalizing the CSCE right into the spring—airing it in public again on 23 March at the WEU Assembly in Luxembourg.[40] Kohl was incensed and wrote an angry letter to his foreign minister stating firmly that he did not share Genscher's views and insisting on a unified public stance for his government.[41] This rebuke clearly had the desired effect. Thereafter Genscher stayed silent, at least in public, while West German officials began to present Kohl's Camp David position to the media as official policy, in other words broad agreement on unified Germany's NATO membership being pursued by all key actors in Washington and Bonn as an immediate goal.

The challenge now was how to sell this to the Soviets in a non-threatening way, given that Moscow was about to lose its most prized Warsaw Pact ally to the other side. The Americans and the Germans agreed on the need to 'de-demonize' the Western Alliance in the eyes of the Soviet Union. The Germans also stressed the importance of discussing their choice of NATO membership as a matter of principle, citing the Helsinki Final Act's statement about 'the right of any state to belong, or not to belong, to an alliance'.[42] The Soviets had signed up to the agreement back in 1975 and the FRG was using this to hold them to account—a tactic that worked with Gorbachev. In Malta in December 1989 he had accepted the right of the German people to 'self-determination'. In Moscow in February 1990 he conceded the right of the Germans to unify. And when he met Bush in Washington on 1 June, he consented to granting nations, in other words including unified Germany, the right to freely choose their alliance membership.[43] The Helsinki principle had therefore received a threefold confirmation from the Soviet leader.

But what really troubled Gorbachev were the practicalities. The Soviets had some 380,000 troops and military personnel in the GDR, together with 164,000 dependants. These forces comprised five armies and one air army deployed in 1,100 locations across East Germany. Put together these installations covered an area equivalent to the whole of the Saarland in West Germany. The equipment statistics were equally formidable: 4,100 tanks, 7,900 armoured vehicles, 3,500 artillery, 1,300 aircraft, and 800,000 tons of ammunition. If, as Kohl wanted, all this had to be withdrawn as a consequence of German unification, Gorbachev would have to relocate 10 per cent of the Red Army and 7.5 per cent of its equipment back home to the USSR. A logistical nightmare, with grave social implications, the move would impose massive costs on a Soviet government already teetering on the edge of bankruptcy.[44]

Aware of Gorbachev's predicament, Kohl started to dangle the prospect of West German money to ease the costs of the transition. But the chancellor's position was also sensitive. He assumed that Moscow would drive a hard financial bargain as the price for its formal consent to all of united Germany being a member of NATO—not least because, throughout June, Shevardnadze and Gorbachev kept introducing varying proposals for a unified Germany's 'dual-membership' in the Atlantic Alliance and the Warsaw Pact. Moreover, the chancellor needed Soviet agreement that Germany would achieve full sovereignty at the moment of unification despite Soviet troops remaining on German soil during what he hoped would be a short transitional period.[45]

To resolve all these matters, Kohl urgently sought a summit with the Soviet leader. In early June the chancellor arranged DM 5 billion in credits from West German banks—an offer to which Gorbachev responded 'euphorically'.[46] On the 11th the Soviet leader issued the eagerly-awaited invitation for Kohl to meet with him in the middle of July.[47] Two weeks later the chancellor came up with another sweetener. He offered a further DM 1.25 billion to cover the 'stationing costs' of Soviet troops in the second half of 1990. Conscious that the East German mark was now worthless, he also allowed Soviet troops to exchange their field bank savings into Western DMs at a favourable rate after the German economic and currency union took effect on 1 July.[48]

Just before flying to the Soviet Union, Kohl received last-minute intimation that this would be a highly personal summit, not merely an official affair in Moscow. Gorbachev invited him to visit the city of Stavropol, near where he had been born. Teltschik, the chancellor's close aide, was thrilled and considered this a striking achievement: the Soviet leader would welcome Kohl to his '*Heimat*' and so the likelihood of this state visit ending in public failure was minimal. Surely, Teltschik reasoned, the Stavropol invitation could only be read as a signal that the Russians would be friendly and forthcoming, and would not adopt very negative positions on the 2 + 4 negotiations.[49]

The chancellor's visit was in fact one prong—albeit perhaps the most important—of a Western charm offensive. The Soviet-German summit would take place immediately after NATO Secretary General Manfred Wörner had visited the Kremlin—the first time the leader of the Alliance, seen in the Kremlin as its arch antagonist, had visited the Soviet Union[50]—and just prior to a similar trip by the president of the European Commission, Jacques Delors. In other words, the chancellor's visit was not a unilateral German *démarche* but was embedded internationally. Particularly important for East-West relations was NATO's dramatic declaration at its London summit on 5 July that the Alliance was evolving from a military into a political organization. 'The Cold War belongs to history. Our Alliance is moving from confrontation to cooperation', Wörner declared. 'We look at the Soviet Union and the countries of Central and Eastern Europe as potential partners and friends.' But, he added, 'Europe is not yet immune from future risk or danger'. NATO was still essential.

'This Alliance, which has contributed so much to overcoming Europe's painful division, must play its full part alongside other Western institutions in extending the stability and security we enjoy to all European nations.'[51]

All this was helpful to the Soviet leader at an especially delicate moment of his domestic political struggle. In an effort to break the power of the Party, in March Gorbachev had arranged his election to the new post of President of the Soviet Union and was now pushing through a programme of democratization at all levels at the same time as his attempted marketization of the economy was floundering. At the 28th Party Congress in early July 1990 he faced the challenge of gaining re-election as general secretary of the Communist Party of the Soviet Union (CPSU) in the face of a substantial body of delegates now intent on his overthrow. Foreign policy was an important facet of this political battle. Conservatives in the Party and the military were furious about the proposed pullout from Germany and Eastern Europe. Gorbachev's Malta summit was denounced as a 'Munich'. General Albert Mashakov complained bitterly that 'the Soviet army is leaving the countries that our fathers liberated from fascism without a fight'. Gorbachev and Shevardnadze therefore desperately needed evidence to show that German unification would not be a threat. Meeting with Baker on 23 June, the Soviet foreign minister had repeatedly stressed the importance of the NATO summit signalling that the Alliance was changing and a 'new Europe' was being born. This, he said, was necessary for Gorbachev's whole 'political position'. Baker had taken this conversation very much to heart and it strengthened his determination to ensure that NATO issued its 'London Declaration on a Transformed North Atlantic Alliance' about evolving into a more political alliance, with smaller military forces, reduced reliance on nuclear weapons, and 'regular diplomatic liaison' with the USSR and Eastern European states.[52]

Gorbachev got through the Congress without having his wings clipped. He could now concentrate on international affairs and the upcoming summit with Kohl. Publicly in Bonn Teltschik and other government figures were at pains to play down expectations about big developments, stressing the larger purposes of the visit, including economic cooperation and the idea of a future treaty of Soviet-German friendship.[53] Nevertheless Kohl had a strong hand to play, above all the priceless asset of 'deep pockets' as Bush predicted in February—in other words his capacity for chequebook diplomacy at a time when Gorbachev's coffers were empty. It was crucial that Kohl found out just prior to departure that Gorbachev had already spent the DM 5 billion in bank loans offered in May, even though the credit had only recently been finalized.[54]

Kohl arrived in Moscow on the evening of 14 July in a Boeing 707 of the *Bundesluftwaffe*. A second plane followed with a massive entourage of press and media. During the flight there was much speculation over the question of whether this was the chancellor's most important foreign trip ever. Whatever Teltschik had told the press, expectations were sky high.

REACHING THE SUMMIT: MOSCOW, STAVROPOL, AND ARKHYZ, 15–16 JULY 1990

The first stage of the Soviet-German summit began on Sunday, 15 July at 10.00am. The venue was the Soviet Ministry of Foreign Affairs' main guesthouse—a grand neo-gothic building, formerly the mansion of a Moscow textile magnate. Gorbachev and Kohl met with only one translator for each of them, plus their foreign policy advisers Chernyaev and Teltschik.[55]

The chancellor was keen at the start to create a congenial and trustful atmosphere and to underline the enormous importance of their tête-a-tête. 'These are historically significant years', he declared. 'Such years come and go. The opportunities have to be used. If one does not act, they will pass by.' Citing Bismarck's famous phrase, he told Gorbachev, 'you have to grab the mantle of history'. Kohl was trying to convey his sense of the unique responsibility that the two of them had to shape the future. He understood this as 'a special opportunity' of 'our generation'—a generation that had been 'too young in the Second World War to become personally guilty, but which, on the other hand, had been old enough to experience those years consciously'. Now, he said, it was their duty to use the opportunities before them to reshape the world.[56]

Gorbachev picked up on Kohl's train of thought, and expressed his desire for them to seize the 'great opportunities that had opened up'. While he wanted to take 'the notion of one world as the starting point,' Gorbachev left no-one in doubt how significant Russian-German relations were to him. In fact he saw their cultivation as being on a par with the ongoing 'normalization of relations with the United States'. Kohl, Germany, and this summit had thus all been elevated, at least in the Kremlin leader's mind, to the same level as superpower relations.[57]

Having created a rapport, it was time to move on to practicalities. Kohl's first move was to make an offer of a fundamental nature: a 'comprehensive treaty' with the USSR within a year. Explaining how to progress in this direction, into 'a new era of relations', he reminded Gorbachev that the first all-German election would be held on 2 December. The subtext was clear. This dramatic West German offer of a new treaty depended on the chancellor personally—and specifically on his re-election, this time as the leader of a unified Germany. So the Soviet-German summit had better be a success.[58]

More immediately, Kohl expected to conclude bilateral agreements in three areas: 1) a definitive plan for Soviet troop withdrawal (to underline German sovereignty), 2) Soviet acceptance of unified Germany's NATO membership, and 3) a decision on the upper limit of the armed forces of a united Germany.[59] He furthermore emphasized that at the end of the 2 + 4 talks full sovereignty had to be granted at the same moment as German unification.[60]

The chancellor also mentioned economic cooperation with and financial assistance for the Soviet Union. He underlined that these were issues that had to be handled by the West as a whole; and so he had lobbied hard on behalf of Gorbachev over the past weeks at the conferences of the European Council in Dublin and the G7 in Houston. Even though these summits had failed to put money on the table, Kohl reminded Gorbachev that in purely bilateral German-Soviet aid packages he personally had kept his word. And there had been no need for written agreements or lengthy bureaucratic negotiations. He ticked off what he had done for Gorbachev. Food relief in February 1990. The DM 5 billion credit in May. The generous deal to allow Soviet troops in East Germany to convert their *Ostmark* savings into DM. And finally the honouring of the bankrupt GDR's commitments toward the Soviet Union, including its export agreements (worth some DM 20 billion) and also DM 1.25 billion to help pay for Soviet forces in East Germany.[61]

The chancellor had made his moves cleverly and carefully, first creating a good atmosphere and then spelling out what he had done for Gorbachev. The Soviet leader was not, however, immediately won over. He responded that what Kohl was doing was clearly of 'great importance for Germany' but warned that it also created 'great psychological and political problems for the Soviet Union'. Trust was therefore essential. He noted that some of the Soviet top brass, as well as journalists, were shouting that he was 'selling the fruits of great victory in World War II for German Marks'. Finally getting down to specifics himself, Gorbachev insisted that the new Germany should be formed within the borders of FRG, GDR, and Berlin and that it should never acquire or develop atomic, biological, and chemical (ABC) weapons. He also stated that 'the military structures of NATO could not be extended to GDR territory' and that a 'transitional settlement had to be arranged for the presence of Soviet troops'.[62]

At no point so far had Gorbachev explicitly stated his consent to unified Germany's NATO membership. Instead, by using Baker's February phrases on the non-extension of NATO jurisdiction, he had in passing hinted at his answer to this key security question. But what might have sounded like the long-desired Soviet concession on the NATO question remained initially opaque. Did Gorbachev now take for granted all-German political membership of NATO? The Soviet leader merely kept repeating the language that 'NATO military structures would not be extended to the GDR' and that Soviet troops would remain in East Germany for a transitional period.

So Kohl tried to pin him down, step by step. The chancellor's first concern was full sovereignty upon unification (even if the Red Army remained for an interim period) and the termination of Four-Power rights; when he raised this, Gorbachev answered in the affirmative. Then the chancellor moved on to seek clarification on the NATO issue. Gorbachev fudged his replies: 'De jure was clear'. Germany would be a member of NATO. 'De facto, however ... the present territory of the GDR would not belong to the NATO as long as Soviet troops were stationed there'. As rendered in the Soviet minutes, his position was that 'despite de jure membership of Germany in NATO, its eastern part would remain in the sphere of influence of the Warsaw Pact'.[63]

Although frustrated by Gorbachev's meanderings, Kohl did not unpick this point further at this juncture. Instead he and Gorbachev agreed that a bilateral treaty would be prepared concerning the Soviet transitional troop presence in East Germany for three to four years, as a bilateral agreement between their two states rather than on the old basis of Allied occupation rights. Kohl twice reminded Gorbachev pointedly that the longer the Soviet troops remained in East Germany, now without a purpose, the greater the problems would be for both Gorbachev and the Soviet army. He suggested retraining courses and housing programmes for Red Army members returning to the Soviet Union—and, using his lever of chequebook diplomacy, added these would be paid for by the Germans.[64]

These military questions, together with the fraught issues of NATO membership and German financial aid, were matters to which the two leaders would return the next day in the Caucasus. But during their first one-on-one in Moscow both men had laid their cards on the table. Meeting briefly in plenary session with their delegations between 11.35 and 12.10, Kohl again struck a positive note, thanking Gorbachev for the friendly welcome and for what he referred to as 'extraordinarily good and constructive talks'. He said that they now knew that Germany would be reunified at the end of this year but, in contrast with 1870, German unity in 1990 was coming about through agreement with her neighbours. And to consolidate this message of peace, cooperation, and reconciliation, Kohl stressed that he wanted to see a comprehensive treaty concluded between unified Germany and the Soviet Union within a year.[65] At the press conference later that day Kohl and Gorbachev radiated confidence and comradeship. 'Smiling and bantering like old friends', in the words of the *New York Times*, they said that they 'expected major progress in their talks on lifting the last obstacles of German unity'. All this was a far cry from Kohl's notorious *Newsweek* interview of 1986 when he apparently compared Gorbachev's skill in public relations with Goebbels-style propaganda, which had soured relations between them for a couple of years.[66]

In public neither leader gave any specific indication of what progress they were making but, to the media, they 'hinted repeatedly that agreement on German membership in NATO and on the size of a future German army were possible'.[67] And then the summit caravan moved south from Moscow. After lunch the two leaders (and a slimmed down entourage of advisers and journalists) flew off to Stavropol in the North Caucasus. Here, in a symbolic act of German-Soviet reconciliation, Kohl and Gorbachev laid wreaths at a gigantic basalt war memorial in honour of the Red Army's fallen heroes, etched with the reliefs of three soldier faces, in a city that less than half a century earlier had been under the jackboot of Nazi occupation.

Kohl's invitation to Stavropol—near where Gorbachev had been born and where he had started his political career—was an unusually personal gesture. No other Western leader had ever been hosted there by Gorbachev. In doing so, the Soviet president underscored the importance ascribed by the Kremlin to this summit with the man likely to become the first chancellor of a united Germany. Stavropol, Gorbachev told journalists, lay at an altitude of 2,300 feet. Pointing to the Caucasus Mountains in the distance, he said: 'We want to develop our relations further upward . . . It will take time to reach the height of Mt. Elbrus, but in our prospects we want to go even beyond that.'[68]

That evening Kohl, Gorbachev, and their delegations were whisked off by helicopter to Gorbachev's mountain dacha, a former hunting lodge near the resort village of Arkhyz, where their talks would continue next day. As soon as they arrived, they changed into informal clothes and walked—Kohl in his cardigan and Gorbachev in his woolly jumper—down to the edge of a rushing mountain stream. For the world press this proved a perfect photo opportunity. It was also a remarkable first: an iconic moment of rare spontaneity for a summit, especially one in the Soviet Union where all such events had previously been meticulously staged and highly formal. The two sides then had a congenial and relaxed dinner in the fresh mountain air. But while everyone else went to bed at 10.00, Kohl caught Gorbachev and had another go on the question of Germany's NATO membership. Kohl asked for no restrictions. Gorbachev looked at him in silence. On the crucial issue of the summit, they were still struggling for words.[69]

The next morning, 16 July, the Soviet leader remained evasive. He linked the establishment of Germany's full sovereignty to some big principles, including 'the non-extension of NATO's military structures to the territory of the present GDR'. He was brusquely reiterating what he had said the previous day. Genscher then countered that 'the concluding document had to pronounce that Germany had the right to join the alliance of its choice'. By using the word 'right' the foreign minister was holding Gorbachev to the Helsinki principle of self-determination to which he had already subscribed, most recently in Washington six weeks earlier. Obviously, Genscher added, 'Germany would choose NATO'. Put on the spot, Gorbachev consented to this but said he preferred to see as little as possible in writing about an explicit German commitment to NATO. After they debated the matter for some minutes, Kohl summed up the discussion: their deal was that, as a fully sovereign state, united Germany 'had the right to be a member of an alliance and that this membership meant NATO' but the Alliance did not have to be explicitly mentioned in the concluding summit document. Gorbachev agreed.[70]

After an interlude over the separate treaty about the presence of the Soviet troops in the GDR, Gorbachev then reverted to the question of NATO—going on to the offensive once again and testing Kohl and Genscher's resilience. He baldly demanded 'the assurance that NATO structures will not be extended to

GDR territory as long as Soviet troops are stationed there'. And as he ground on about the issue, he seemed to undercut his earlier concession about Germany's NATO membership, flatly re-asserting that he wanted 'the new sovereign Germany to declare that it understood the Soviet concerns and that no extension of NATO to the territory of the GDR would occur'. Shevardnadze jumped in on what he called this 'very serious question', adding his own twist: 'One should not permit NATO structures to be extended to the GDR and nuclear weapons to be deployed there after the withdrawal of Soviet troops.'[71]

For almost four hours, they went to and fro on these all-important word-games. Sometimes Gorbachev gave ground to the Germans, only then to backtrack, reiterate old positions, and dig in his heels. Negotiating with such an interlocutor was really wearing and required great attention and skill on the part of Kohl and Genscher. They had to hold their nerve and keep their focus. But this they did. The tactic that crystallized under pressure was that, at each juncture, Kohl kept summarizing the consensual points in a matter-of-fact way (one, two, three) while leaving the more controversial points and disputed formulations to the side, only to return to them having achieved progress in other areas. Genscher tended to enter the discussions, often to great effect, by formulating statements of principle that the Soviets would find impossible to evade. With this negotiating tactic, working as team, the German tandem managed painstakingly to accumulate a consensus.[72]

The outcome of this protracted duel at the summit was as follows: when Germany became fully sovereign upon unification, all of the new country would come under NATO's umbrella. For the transitional phase while Soviet troops were still present in the GDR, only units of the *Bundeswehr* that were not integrated into NATO could be stationed there. After the Red Army had left, German troops under NATO command could also be transferred there but not any foreign troops or nuclear weapons. The chancellor conceded to Gorbachev that, since sovereignty would only come about in the concluding document of the 2 + 4 talks, the bilateral treaty concerning the presence of the Soviet troops on the territory of the present GDR would have to wait. They concurred on a Soviet withdrawal period of three to four years (with Kohl again promising financial aid for housing and retraining for these troops back in the USSR—which would eventually amount to another DM 17 billion).[73] During that time the *Bundeswehr* would also be reduced to a maximum of 370,000 troops.

It is noteworthy that Kohl and Genscher never explicitly discussed the issue of NATO enlargement into Eastern Europe with Gorbachev and Shevard-nadze. Their assumption seemed to be that they were simply debating the enlargement of the territory of an existing member of the Alliance. But as a result of this process, the Warsaw Pact would lose a member and be forced to concede territory and position. In time this asymmetry would prove the thin end of a very significant geo-strategic wedge in Russia's relations with the West.

Immediately after returning to Bonn, Kohl held an upbeat press conference about the historic agreement on German unification and continued membership of NATO. The chancellor was 'smilingly self-confident and securely self-deprecatory', in the words of one journalist. He promised that a united Germany would recover its place at the heart of Europe peacefully, without again becoming a threat to its neighbours. He announced that the USSR would pull all its troops out of the GDR no later than the end of 1994—in other words, exactly fifty years after they entered Germany in the final months of World War Two. The Caucasus talks were no Rapallo, he insisted—no repeat of the notorious German-Russian compact of 1922. Instead, Kohl emphasized that a transformed Germany, firmly committed to European integration and European ideals of democracy, had negotiated on behalf of its allies with the Soviet Union for an ideal all of them had supported over the last forty years.[74]

Although not sinister, the Caucasus was certainly a Rapallo-like surprise. The Big Four allies were astonished that the chancellor managed to extract from Gorbachev key concessions to resolve the conundrums that had bedevilled East-West relations for months. As Douglas Hurd, Britain's foreign secretary, admitted after the 2 + 4 ministerial meeting on 17 July, the agreement had 'brought about a sea-change in the negotiations' and put the Six 'firmly in the end game'. Now that the Soviet Union had 'accepted the essential Western points on pol[itical]-mil[itary] issues', he noted, there was 'a realistic prospect of wrapping the whole process up' at the next 2 + 4 ministerial in Moscow on 12 September.[75]

The Americans, too, had to acknowledge that Kohl's summit agreement was a game-changer. Bush welcomed it as being 'in the best interests of all the countries of Europe, including the Soviet Union'. He also made a point of saying that the United States had 'been in the forefront of suggesting the best way for stabilization and peace would be a united Germany, a unified Germany as a full-fledged member of NATO'. But privately administration insiders conceded that 'it would have been much nicer if the deal Gorbachev and Kohl seem to have struck could have been announced when all the major powers were represented'. Not only were Bush and Baker not at the summit; the secretary of state was completely taken by surprise. For weeks, he and his staff had been telling the press that they expected no break in the German impasse until the autumn. Representative Lee Hamilton of Indiana, a prominent Democratic spokesman on foreign affairs, stuck the knife into the Republican administration: 'This makes clearer than ever that the Germans are leading Western policy toward the Soviet Union.' He added coyly: 'I am not saying that it is George Bush's fault, and I am not saying that we have become a non-power' but Hamilton's implication was clear.[76]

Nothing could hide that fact that the 2 + 4 talks had been rendered almost irrelevant because—as one West European ambassador observed—'not even a fig leaf was left' to conceal the fact that West Germany had essentially negotiated its own terms. The transformation in Germany's international position was seen by American commentators as quite phenomenal. 'Kohl used to come here as a supplicant', one Republican senator remarked on Capitol Hill, 'but now he comes into a room up here and senior people defer to him. He is polite and good-humored of course, but he dominates conversations'. The German chancellor had clearly left his mark: with the outcome of the Caucasus summit he had made history (see Figure 8.2).[77]

*   *   *   *   *

In 1989–90 Bush and Baker had set the broader European security parameters for German unification, based on a 'new Atlanticism', in the sequence of superpower meetings in Malta, Moscow, and Washington. The Germans— following initial differences of approach on the part of Kohl and Genscher— willingly followed suit after the chancellor met the president at Camp David in February 1990. With general American backing, the Germans were emboldened to go it alone and themselves sealed the 'Germany-in-NATO' deal, with all that it entailed, at the Caucasus summit. On the basis of America's provision of the security framework, Kohl had the scope to negotiate with Gorbachev. And at the summit he proved that he had the skill to successfully conduct personal politics, as well as bargaining masterfully with his 'deep pockets'.[78]

Bonn was clearly acting in line with Washington; there were no doubts about Kohl's true loyalty to the Atlantic Alliance and the United States. But the Caucasus summit also showed that Germany was now assertively pursuing its own national interest, at its own pace and by cultivating its own personal diplomacy. Kohl's friendly and mutually trusting interaction with Gorbachev in turn laid the foundation for much improved bilateral German-Soviet relations that would persist long after Gorbachev's departure and the disappearance of the Soviet Union. The Caucasus was therefore a far cry from the constipated summitry at Erfurt and Kassel in 1970–1 through which the leaders of the two Germanies, each closely tied to its superpower patron, took the first tentative steps towards transcending their country's division. By 1990 the GDR was a failed state, on the verge of being subsumed into the Federal Republic, and the West German chancellor was being welcomed as an equal at the personal retreats of the American and Soviet presidents. The successful Caucasus meeting demonstrated Germany's international emancipation on the world stage.

What, then, were the implications of the Caucasus for the post-Cold War order? In his rudimentary but fascinating jottings during the winter of 1989–90, James Baker had talked of a 'post post-war' security architecture (in other words finally moving on from 1945) in which 'old' but 'newly transformed' Western institutions (especially NATO and the EC) as well as the CSCE should complement each other. In this context it is important to note that Kohl made no deals with Gorbachev regarding NATO's territory and

Fig. 8.2. 'The Bonn/Moscow Alliance: The War is Over' (*Der Spiegel*, 23 July 1990)

scope beyond the narrow confines of resolving the question of German unification. In 1990 the future place of NATO in an undivided Europe was left entirely open. But there was now no question that the United States would remain a European power after the end of the Cold War. By contrast, Russia's future position was highly equivocal.

NOTES

1. For the letter, see Helmut Kohl, *Ich wollte Deutschlands Einheit* (Berlin, 1996), 442–3.
2. Quotations in Mary Elise Sarotte, *1989: The Struggle to Create Post-Cold War Europe* (Princeton, NJ, 2009), 35.
3. Extract from Schabowski press conference, 9 November 1989, in *Cold War International History Project Bulletin*, no. 12–13, doc. 7, 157–8, https://www.wilsoncenter.org/sites/default/files/CWIHP_Bulletin_12-13.pdf.
4. Philip Zelikow and Condoleezza Rice, *Germany Unified and Europe Transformed: A Study in Statecraft* (Cambridge, MA, 1997), 103.
5. George Bush, *All the Best, George Bush: My Life in Letters and Other Writings* (New York, 2013), 446, 451; George Bush and Brent Scowcroft, *A World Transformed* (New York, 1998), 148–9.
6. Hanns Jürgen Küsters und Daniel Hofmann, eds, *Dokumente zur Deutschlandpolitik: Deutsche Einheit—Sonderedition aus den Akten des Bundeskanzleramts 1989/90* (Munich, 1998) (henceforth *DESE*), doc. 93, 539.
7. Helmut Kohl's Ten-Point Plan for German Unity (28 November 1989), http://germanhistorydocs.ghi-dc.org/sub_document.cfm?document_id=223.
8. Keith Hamilton and Patrick Salmon, eds, *Documents on British Policy Overseas, Series III, vol. 7, German Unification 1989/90* (Abingdon, 2009) (henceforth *DBPO III/7*), doc. 59, 140.
9. Marc Fisher, 'Kohl Proposes Broad Program for Reunification of Germany', *Washington Post*, 29 November 1989, 1.
10. See *DBPO III/7*, doc. 76, 173, fn 2; and Karl Kaiser, *Deutschlands Vereinigung: Die internationalen Aspekte—mit den wichtigen Dokumenten* (Bergisch Gladbach, 1991), doc. 14, 169.
11. Bush, *A World Transformed*, 132.
12. GBPL, First Restricted Bilateral Session with Chairman Gorbachev of Soviet Union, 12.00–1.00pm, 2 December 1989, 5, https://www.wilsoncenter.org/sites/default/files/Malta%20_Summit–Copies_from_HW_Bush_Archives.pdf.
13. GBPL, Second Expanded Bilateral Session, 4.35–6.45pm, 3 December 1989, 6, https://www.wilsoncenter.org/sites/default/files/Malta%20_Summit–Copies_from_HW_Bush_Archives.pdf.
14. GBPL, Second Expanded Bilateral Session, 4.35–6.45pm, 3 December 1989, 2, 9–10, https://www.wilsoncenter.org/sites/default/files/Malta%20_Summit–Copies_from_HW_Bush_Archives.pdf.
15. GBPL, First Restricted Bilateral Session with Chairman Gorbachev of Soviet Union, 12.00–1.00pm, 2 December 1989, 4–5, https://www.wilsoncenter.org/sites/default/files/Malta%20_Summit–Copies_from_HW_Bush_Archives.pdf.
16. Remarks at Q&A session, 3 December 1989, 1.20pm on board 'Gorky', The American Presidency Project (henceforth APP) website, http://www.presidency.ucsb.edu/ws/index.php?pid=17900&st=&st1.
17. Quoted in Sarotte, *1989*, 79.
18. Bush, News Conference in Brussels, 4 December 1989, APP website, http://www.presidency.ucsb.edu/ws/index.php?pid=17907&st=&st1. See also Alan Riding,

'Bush Says Soviets Merit West's Help to Foster Reform', *New York Times*, 5 December 1989, A1, A17.

19. Remarks at Q&A session, 3 December 1989, 1.20 pm on board 'Gorky', APP website, http://www.presidency.ucsb.edu/ws/index.php?pid=17900&st=&st1.

20. James A. Baker Papers, Mudd Library, Princeton, NJ (henceforth BP), Box 108, Folder 12, JAB notes from 12/4/89 following POTUS-Gorbachev mtg @Malta, Brussels, Belg. (WEU was the Western European Union.) Underlinings are in the original typescript; italicized phrases and deletions are handwritten additions by Baker.

21. Quotes from Thomas L. Friedman, 'Baker in Berlin, Outlines Plan To Make NATO a Political Group', *New York Times*, 13 December 1989, A1, A18. See also Speech by Secretary of State James Baker to the Berlin Press Club (Extracts), 13 December 2015, printed in Lawrence Freedman, ed., *Europe Transformed: Documents on the End of the Cold War* (London, 1990), 397–8.

22. Werner Weidenfeld et al., *Geschichte der deutschen Einheit, vol. 4—Außenpolitik für die deutsche Einheit: Die Entscheidungsjahre 1989/90* (Stuttgart, 1998), 179–87. See also Craig R. Whitney, '4 Powers to Meet on German Issues—Bonn-East Berlin Ties Prompt First Such Talks Since "72"', *New York Times*, 11 December 1989, A1, A7.

23. BP, Box 104, Folder 1, 1989 Oct.–December, 12/17/1989, Letter Baker to Kohl.

24. *DESE*, doc. 158, 754–5. See also Serge Schmemann, 'Vote Is Moved Up By East Germans; Coalition Widened: Ballot Is Set For March—All Parties Agree on the Early Election, Showing Anxiety About Public's Mood', *New York Times*, 29 January 1990, 1. See also Gerhard Ritter, *Hans-Dietrich Genscher, das Auswärtige Amt, und die deutsche Vereinigung* (Munich, 2013), 59–69.

25. Quoted from the Tutzing speech as printed in Freedman, ed., *Europe Transformed*, 440–1. See also Kaiser, *Deutschlands Vereinigung*, doc. 23, 191. On Central-Eastern European troop withdrawal demands, see *DBPO III/7*, doc. 129, 263.

26. Richard Kiessler and Frank Elbe, *Ein runder Tisch mit scharfen Ecken: Der diplomatische Weg zur deutschen Einheit* (Baden-Baden, 1993), 79–80.

27. GBPL, Second Expanded Bilateral Session, 4.35–6.45pm, 3 December 1989, 7, https://www.wilsoncenter.org/sites/default/files/Malta%20_Summit–Copies_from_HW_Bush_Archives.pdf.

28. *DESE*, doc. 153, 741; Horst Teltschik, *329 Tage: Innenansichten der Einigung* (Berlin, 1991), 123. See also *DBPO III/7*, docs 105 and 109, 223–4 and 231.

29. See Frank Costigliola, 'An "Arm Around the Shoulder": The United States, NATO and German Reunification, 1989–90', *Contemporary European History* 3, no. 1 (March 1994), 95; cf. Mick Cox and Steven Hurst, '"His Finest Hour?" George Bush and the Diplomacy of German Unification', *Diplomacy & Statecraft* 13, no. 4 (2002), 136.

30. Quote from Zelikow and Rice, *Germany Unified and Europe Transformed*, 176.

31. See *DESE*, doc. 159, 756; BP, Box 108, Folder 14, JAB notes from 2/2/90 press briefing following 21/2 mtg w/FRG FM Genscher, WDC—Handwritten note. For further detail, see Kristina Spohr, 'Precluded or Precedent-Setting? The "NATO Enlargement Question" in the Triangular Bonn-Washington-Moscow Diplomacy of 1990–1991', *Journal of Cold War Studies* 14, no. 4 (2012), 18–32.

32. *DESE*, doc. 159, 756–7. See also Teltschik, *329 Tage*, 128–9.

33. *DBPO III/7*, doc. 124, 255; Aleksandr Galkin und Anatolij Tschernjajew, eds, *Michail Gorbatschow und die deutsche Frage: Sowjetische Dokumente 1986–1991* (München, 2011) (henceforth *MGDF:SD*), doc. 71, 312.

34. *MGDF:SD*, doc. 71, 312. This is the official German translation of the Soviet minutes of the Gorbachev-Baker meeting (for which no American transcript has so far been found): '... daß die Vereinigten Staaten ihre Anwesenheit in Deutschland im Rahmen der NATO aufrecht erhalten—die Jurisdiktion oder militärische Präsenz der NATO in östlicher Richtung um keinen einzigen Zoll ausgedehnt wird.'

35. *DESE*, doc. 170, 784–5.

36. See Bush, *All the Best*, 460–1. See also Costigliola, 'An "Arm Around the Shoulder"', 101–2. According to Costigliola, citing US House of Representatives, Committee of Armed Services meetings in February, March, and April 1990, the Bush administration also believed that a 'robust US military role through NATO, particularly with nuclear weapons, helped counter any German temptations to develop a full panopoly of modern armaments'.

37. BP, Box 108, Folder 14, 1990 Feb, JAB notes 2/20/90 MTG w/GB, Czechoslovak pres @WH; and JAB notes from 2/6/90 MTG. w/Czech. Pres. Havel, Hradcany Castle, Prague, Czechoslovakia.

38. BP, Box 108, Folder 16, 1990 April, JAB Notes from 4/4/90 mtg w/FRG FM Genscher @Dept of State.

39. As explained by an NSC staffer to the British. *DBPO III/7*, doc. 154, 307–8. Joint News Conference following Discussions with Chancellor Helmut Kohl, 25 February 1990, APP website, http://www.presidency.ucsb.edu/ws/index.php?pid=18188&st=&st1. See also *DESE*, doc. 192, 860–73; Sarotte, *1989*, 126–7.

40. For the speech, see Hans-Dietrich Genscher, *Unterwegs zur Einheit: Reden und Dokumente aus bewegter Zeit* (Berlin, 1991), 258–68, esp. 265–6. See also Hoover Institution Archives, Zelikow-Rice Papers 1989–1995, Box 1, Letter, Zelikow to Genscher, 24 January 1995, 5.

41. Teltschik, *329 Tage,* 182–3.

42. *DESE*, doc. 278, 1130. Cf. the US record of the meeting which is distinctly shorter on these points, GBPL, Memorandum of Conversation, Kohl and Bush, 17 May 1990, 11.40–12.55pm, 4, https://bush41library.tamu.edu/files/memcons-telcons/1990-05-17-Kohl%20[2].pdf.

43. Summing up their meeting on 3 June, Bush stated: 'I believe, as do Chancellor Kohl and members of the alliance, that the united Germany should be a full member of NATO. President Gorbachev, frankly, does not hold that view. But we are in full agreement that the matter of alliance membership is, in accordance with the Helsinki Final Act, a matter for the Germans to decide.' Bush, News Conference with Gorbachev, 3 June 1990, APP website, http://www.presidency.ucsb.edu/ws/index.php?pid=18549&st=&st1.

44. For troop data, see Celeste A. Wallander, *Mortal Friends, Best Enemies: German-Russian Cooperation after the Cold War* (Ithaca, NY, 1999), 71.

45. Helmut Kohl, *Vom Mauerfall zur Wiedervereinigung: Meine Erinnerungen* (Munich, 2009), 297–326. See also 'Reaktion auf Gorbatschows Deutschland-Rede—Westen lehnt Vorschlag ab—Kohl: Doppelte Bündniszugehörigkeit nicht realistisch', *Süddeutsche Zeitung*, 13 June 1990.

46. Sarotte, *1989*, 160.

47. Teltschik, *329 Tage*, 265.

48. Mallaby to FO (relating conversation with Teltschik), 12 July 1990, *DBPO III/7*, doc. 215, 429–30.

49. Teltschik, *329 Tage*, 310.

50. Serge Schmemann, 'Gorbachev meets with NATO's chief', *New York Times*, 15 July 1990.

51. Manfred Wörner, opening statement to NATO summit meeting, London, 5 July 1990, http://www.nato.int/cps/en/natohq/opinions_23718.htm?selectedLocale=en.

52. Andrei Grachev, *Gorbachev's Gamble: Soviet Foreign Policy and the End of the Cold War* (Cambridge, 2008), 185, 189–90; BP, Box 109, Folder 2, 1990 June, copy of 6/23/90, send to POTUS re: mtg w/USSR FM Shev. For the London Declaration, see http://www.nato.int/docu/comm/49-95/c900706a.htm.

53. Teltschik, *329 Tage*, 313; *DBPO III/7*, doc. 215, fn 2, 429–30.

54. *DESE*, doc. 192, 869; Kohl, *Meine Erinnerungen*, 294–6, 328; Teltschik, *329 Tage*, 318–19.

55. *DESE*, doc. 350, 1340; Hans Klein, *Es begann im Kaukasus* (Berlin, 1991), 64.

56. *DESE*, doc. 350, 1340.

57. *DESE*, doc. 350, 1340–1.

58. *DESE*, doc. 350, 1341–3.

59. *DESE*, doc. 350, 1343; see also Klein, *Es begann im Kaukasus*, 35. NB: Whereas Kohl was willing to reduce the *Bundeswehr* from some 500,000 to 370,000 men (while the East German army was to be abolished), the Soviets had been pressing for an even bigger reduction down to 240,000. Angela Stent, *Russia and Germany Reborn: Unification, The Soviet Collapse, and the New Europe* (Princeton, NJ, 1999), 134–5.

60. Kohl, *Meine Erinnerungen*, 334.

61. *DESE*, doc. 350, 1343; cf. Teltschik's comments reported in *DBPO III/7*, doc. 215, 429. Cf. Stefan Bierling, *Wirtschaftshilfe für Moskau: Motive und Strategien der Bundesrepublik Deutschland und der USA 1990–1996* (Paderborn, 1998), 333.

62. *DESE*, doc. 350, 1344–7.

63. Compare *DESE*, doc. 350, 1346–7, with *MGDF:SD*, doc. 102, 464.

64. *DESE*, doc. 350

65. *DESE*, doc. 352.

66. Serge Schmemann, 'Kohl Sees Soviets Amid Upbeat Mood—He and Gorbachev Predicting Gains on German Unity', *New York Times*, 16 July 1990, 1; William Tuohy, 'Misquoted About Gorbachev, Kohl Says: Chancellor Denies Comparing Soviet Leader to Nazis' Goebbels', *Los Angeles Times*, 3 November 1986, http://articles.latimes.com/1986-11-03/news/mn-14904_1_kohl-spokesman. Despite denials by Kohl's office, *Newsweek* stood by its version of what Kohl had said: 'He is a modern Communist leader who knows something about public relations. Goebbels, one of those responsible for the crimes of the Hitler era, was an expert in public relations, too.'

67. Schmemann, 'Kohl Sees Soviets Amid Upbeat Mood', 1.

68. Schmemann, 'Kohl Sees Soviets Amid Upbeat Mood', A6. See also Kohl, *Meine Erinnerungen*, 336–8.

69. Kohl, *Meine Erinnerungen,* 339.

70. See *DESE*, doc. 353, 1355–7. For the Soviet transcript of this 16 July meeting see *MGDF:SD*, doc. 104, 470–88.

71. *DESE*, doc. 353, 1357–8.

72. *DESE*, doc. 353, 1358–60.

73. Bierling, *Wirtschaftshilfe für Moskau*, 333; Vladislav Zubok, 'With His Back Against the Wall: Gorbachev, Soviet Demise, and German Unification', *Cold War History* 14, no. 4 (November 2014), 641–3.

74. Craig R. Whitney, 'Kohl Outlines a Vision: A Neighborly Vision', *New York Times*, 18 July 1990.

75. *DBPO III/7*, doc. 219, 435–6.

76. R.W. Apple, 'Bush Hails Soviet Decision', *New York Times*, 17 July 1990, A1; Andrew Rosenthal, 'Bush Declares He Does Not Feel Left Out by Gorbachev and Kohl', *New York Times*, 18 July 1990, A1, A7. On American surprise, see also Zelikow and Rice, *Germany Unified and Europe Transformed*, 342–3.

77. Apple, 'Bush Hails Soviet Decision', A1.

78. The total costs of German financial aid to the Soviet Union and its successor states was about DM 100 billion in the period 1989–94. Bierling, *Wirtschaftshilfe für Moskau*, 332–3.

IV

Conclusions

9

Summits, Statecraft, and the Dissolution of Bipolarity in Europe, 1970–90

Kristina Spohr and David Reynolds

This book has explored two major issues—the evolution of the Cold War and the practice of international summitry. More specifically, it has investigated the interaction between them: how systemic developments influenced the behaviour of leaders and how leaders in turn tried to shape the processes of change. Fearful that cold war might spark hot war, and even nuclear annihilation, from the 1970s statesmen resorted to summit diplomacy in the hope of finding a *modus vivendi* and perhaps even a peaceful exit from the whole era of confrontation. This concluding chapter first draws out the overall arguments of the book and then offers some observations on how summitry and statecraft exerted a distinctive influence in helping to transcend the bipolar order in Europe.

FROM CONFRONTATION TOWARDS DÉTENTE, 1945–69

As an ideological confrontation the Cold War dates back to 1917, to the collision of the new Soviet ideology of Marxism-Leninism with the values of Wilsonian capitalist democracy. Unveiled as the old European order was collapsing at the end of World War One, both these ideologies were evangelical in nature and global in scope. But their expansive implications were not fully realized until the end of a second, even more destructive, world war which mobilized Soviet and American power as the key forces in the defeat of Imperial Japan and Nazi Germany. Here we find the origins of the Cold War order.

In 1945 the atomic bomb proved America's trump card in the Pacific War but Washington's monopoly of this new weapon of mass destruction was intolerable to Stalin, triggering a superpower arms race that became a leading motif of East-West conflict. Such was the dynamism of postwar technological innovation that this spiralling competition produced ever larger nuclear arsenals and a dangerous diversity of weaponry. By the 1970s each superpower possessed sufficient intercontinental missiles to destroy each other and the Soviets were now on a par with the Americans. So the arms race shifted to a theatre level, where Soviet advances in intermediate-range weapons raised the spectre of a nuclear war in Europe that would leave the continent totally destroyed.

America and Russia entered the heart of Europe in 1945 in order to crush Nazism. They were, however, fundamentally at odds about what should replace the Third Reich—a Sovietized state of the sort imposed on most of Eastern Europe after 1945 or a country based on the American-led Western model? Given the economic and military potential of Germany, neither could afford to let the other get its own way. They therefore ended up dividing the country into two rump states—the Federal Republic of Germany and the German Democratic Republic—each a superpower client. Yet even a divided Germany was not a source of stability because American policy towards the Federal Republic entailed building up its strength and prosperity, promoting its rearmament, and welcoming it into NATO. This rehabilitation of German power in 1945–55 alarmed Soviet leaders haunted by memories of Hitler's surprise attack in 1941: for them security meant an East European buffer zone, Western ratification of the borders won at great cost by the Red Army in 1945, and the perpetuation of German partition to minimize any future threat. So, having initially repressed their zone of Germany, in the 1950s the Soviets built up the East German state as their European frontline. For the United States, likewise, its German client became central to the country's whole position in Europe. West Germany had emerged as a major economic power and German territory was vital for forward-based systems in any future war between West and East. In a larger sense, Washington viewed Western Europe as the global heartland and was determined to shape its future direction in America's interest. The historically unprecedented commitment made by the United States in 1949 to North Atlantic security became the bedrock of US foreign and defence policy.

And so the European Cold War was a complex palimpsest of international problems. The underlying ideological antagonism between the superpowers was rooted in 1917, but the geopolitical conflict stemmed largely from World War Two. America and Russia were drawn into Europe to defeat Nazi Germany; they stayed in part to control postwar Germany. Around the two Germanies they constructed two antithetical European blocs. And their rivalry was raised to a lethal level by the spiralling nuclear arms race.

The division of Germany and Europe was, however, never intended to be permanent. West Germany's Basic Law committed the state to ultimate reunification and, equally important, reunification on liberal democratic terms. This challenged the existence of not only East Germany but also of the larger East European order. America and the other NATO allies were committed to German unity in principle but did little to advance it in practice, as became clear when the Berlin Wall was erected in 1961. In fact, the Americans quietly welcomed the sealing off of East Berlin as a way to reduce East-West tensions: as Kennedy quipped, 'a wall is a hell of a lot better than a war'.[1] West Germany therefore had to come to terms with the likelihood of partition for the foreseeable future and this fundamental fact of diplomacy was the catalyst for a major shift in policy when the Social Democrats became the governing party in Bonn from 1969. Unlike the Christian Democrats, who had shaped the first two decades of the Federal Republic around a policy of binding Germany to the West through new alliances with America and France, the Social Democratic Party (SPD)—led by Willy Brandt, a former mayor of West Berlin—looked east and sought to build a relationship with the East German state. Brandt wanted to make the Cold War liveable for the German people as a whole—to develop a *modus vivendi* with a regime that, he hoped, would disappear in the long run but, in the short term, had to be accepted as a fact of life. Here were the German roots of détente.

Although Europe formed the cockpit of the Cold War, this was also a global struggle and détente had a global dimension. In 1949—the year the two Germanies were created, together with NATO—China's long civil war had reached its climax. Mao Zedong's victory over the Nationalists tipped the world's most populous country into the communist camp and it soon came to war with the United States over Korea. Initially Mao's China was dependent on the Soviet Union but by the 1960s the Sino-Soviet alliance had fallen apart and in 1969 the two countries seemed on the brink of war themselves. And, while Nikita Khrushchev sought to develop Russia's consumer society, Mao tried to rejuvenate Chinese communism by launching the Cultural Revolution and proclaiming the People's Republic as the true champion of Marxism-Leninism against Moscow's 'bourgeois revisionism'. By the 1970s the Sino-Soviet split had turned an apparently simple East-West confrontation into a triangular powerplay with America, Russia, and China each trying to manipulate the other two for its own ends. By this time, too, America was in a weaker position compared with its postwar heyday. The long and divisive Vietnam War stirred up public debate about strategic over-commitment and eventually undermined the economy with high inflation and a massive trade and payments deficit. America's crisis mirrored a larger Western economic malaise. In 1971 the Bretton Woods financial system collapsed into a chaos of fluctuating exchange rates and the 1973 oil price explosion shook the hitherto stable foundation of Western postwar growth based on cheap energy. This crisis of capitalism provoked self-doubt in the West's capacity to sustain the Cold War contest.

Geopolitical and economic shifts were thus preconditions for détente at the global level in the early 1970s. But, as in Germany, leaders were essential: men with a vision, a grasp of where the world was going, and also the political mandate to act. Brandt's global counterpart was Nixon, who talked of a 'pentapolar' world, with several centres of power that had to be balanced and managed. As a right-wing Republican and former commie-basher, he was also in a far stronger position to engage with the two Red giants, Moscow and Beijing, than the Democrats, saddled with failure in the Vietnam War. None of this is to deny that the Soviet bloc was interested in reducing tension but the diplomatic initiative for détente came essentially from the West—and it did so in the form of summitry.

THE COLD WAR AND THE SUMMITS
OF THE 1970s AND 1980s

Churchill had called as early as 1950 for a 'parley at the summit' to defuse international tensions, but summit meetings proved marginal in the darkest days of the Cold War. After Potsdam in 1945 Stalin did not meet again with Western leaders and their encounters with his successor, Khrushchev, proved unproductive; Paris in 1960 and Vienna in 1961 actually damaged East-West relations. The nuclear test ban treaty of 1963 owed little to summitry: it was instead a direct response to the Cuban crisis of 1962 which had brought the superpowers to the brink of nuclear war. As it became clear that the Cold War was here to stay, the question of how to manage co-existence at the strategic and ideological levels became salient in the 1970s. With the two Germanies and the America-Russia-China triangle now facts of international life, statesmen needed to communicate across the ideological divide. Hence the importance of the three pieces of summitry examined in the first part of this book—the pair of meetings between the leaders of West and East Germany in Erfurt and Kassel in 1970 and Nixon's visits in 1972 to Beijing and then Moscow.

One striking feature of these early 1970s encounters is the sense of drama, of venturing out into the unknown and coming face-to-face with the adversary. These, one might say, were journeys of reconnaissance, which is why Henry Kissinger's staff named the briefing book for his first trip to China 'Polo I'—alluding to the Venetian traveller Marco Polo who opened up China in the Middle Ages. Making the same point more pungently, Willy Brandt said that his talks with Willi Stoph were about 'getting a smell of each other'.[2] Location also mattered. Unlike some earlier Cold War meetings, such as Geneva in 1955 and Vienna in 1961, the summits of the early 1970s did not take place in neutral cities. Visiting Erfurt in 1970, Brandt was the first West German leader to step onto the soil of the German Democratic Republic (GDR). Similarly, before 1972 no American president had ever ventured to the heart of the two great communist empires. In short, Brandt and Nixon were going to the Other. What's more they were seen doing so. These meetings were major media events, captured in press photos and television film and beamed around the planet. Some four hundred journalists from all over the world covered the Erfurt meeting, forty-six of them accompanying Brandt on his special train from Bonn. Likewise, Nixon's summits in Beijing and Moscow were carefully scheduled and choreographed for prime-time television in the United States.

But these summits were not merely performative acts: substance also mattered because leaders met in order to talk. Initially they were often talking *at* each other. Erfurt was characterized by long monologues, in which both leaders set out familiar, highly polarized positions in dogmatic language—'duel rather than dialogue' to quote Benedikt Schoenborn. In Beijing, too, the American and Chinese leaders stuck to basic positions on key issues such as Taiwan. But what mattered was the novelty of talking, of bridging what Prime Minister Zhou Enlai called 'the vastest ocean in the world—twenty-five years of no communication'.[3] Whatever their limitations and constraints, these initial meetings served as icebreakers—to borrow the language of Brandt and his close adviser Egon Bahr, the first small steps in a longer journey towards more meaningful engagement. The crux at Erfurt was to secure a second meeting, and to hold it on West German soil. During this follow-up encounter in Kassel the framework was laid for more detailed negotiations that would produce the *Grundlagenvertrag* of 1972. In other words, talking *at* became talking *with*. On the superpower level this same transition occurred before the summits because of Henry Kissinger's privileged position as the president's right-hand man and special messenger. His visits to Beijing thrashed out the agenda for Nixon's own visit; similarly his backchannel to the Kremlin via Ambassador Anatoly Dobrynin laid the groundwork for the president to go to Moscow. And that Nixon-Brezhnev summit in May 1972 combined symbolism with substance: not only were the leaders of the two rival superpowers seen to be talking *to* each other, they also agreed and signed major accords on arms limitation (SALT I), technology, and culture.

The range of agreements concluded in Moscow reminds us of a further point. Summitry between leaders had the potential to create a larger 'social space' for more extensive and intensive dialogue. Nixon's 1972 visit was intended as the first in a series of annual summits, bringing each leader to the other on a regular basis (Washington/San Clemente 1973, Moscow/Yalta 1974). These alternated between America and Russia, combining official meetings in the capital with informal get-togethers at the leaders' country retreats. This promising pattern was, however, broken after only two years by the Watergate debacle. At a lower level summitry encouraged networking among officials, as in the two Germanies after Kassel, and this diversification of contacts extended onto the public plane. For Brandt and Bahr the essential point of engaging with the GDR was to thaw the Cold War at a human level—allowing ordinary citizens more chance to communicate through family visits, postal services, sports teams, and the like. As Bahr put it, 'the man in the street must see some change'.[4] A similar humanization of relations began to occur between the United States and the Soviet Union. Agreements signed in Moscow in 1972 permitted exchanges between intellectuals, scholars, musicians, and other performers. Détente, it seemed, was starting to de-other the Other—at all levels.

Although historical phases postulated by scholars are always somewhat artificial, it is reasonable to say that whereas the summits discussed in the first part of the book were dramatic breakthroughs that helped to thaw the Cold War, by the mid-1970s we can discern a new phase—one of consolidation. This involved institutionalizing the changes brought about by détente, reflecting on their implications (good and bad), and identifying possible ways to move on. The aim was to make the Cold War more liveable. Yet by the end of the decade this optimistic mood had dissipated amid new superpower tensions and the growing sense of crisis in the West. Living with the Cold War became more a matter of muddling through, as examined in part two.

The positive sense of liveability (amelioration) was most apparent in the Helsinki Final Act—signed at a unique summit/international conference that consummated a long process of negotiation known as the Conference on Security and Cooperation in Europe (CSCE) among thirty-five states. These included America and Russia, but most of the signatories were Europeans from both sides of the Cold War as well as neutrals. The complex Helsinki agreement involved two key elements. The first was a territorial understanding recognizing the European borders established in 1945. This affirmed the Soviet sphere of influence in Eastern Europe and helped to address the Kremlin's underlying security angst. The second element was 'respect for human rights and fundamental freedoms' and the promotion of human contacts (such as travel and marriage), the exchange of information, and cultural and educational cooperation. This reflected the larger Western desire to humanize the Cold War and served to enlarge and institutionalize the Moscow 1972 concept of a shared social space across the Cold War divide. Taken as a whole this summit was intended to draw a line under World War Two, ease East-West tension, and begin the normalization of Cold War relations through additional CSCE meetings. The latter, however, made little progress.

The momentum of détente was also not sustained at the superpower level. The flurry of annual Soviet-American summits from 1972 onward ran out of steam after Nixon's fall, with only two more formal summit meetings over the rest of the decade—Vladivostok in November 1974 and Vienna in July 1979. Meanwhile superpower relations worsened over their widening geo-ideological competition in Asia, Africa, and Latin America. The optimistic mood of Sino-American rapprochement in 1972 also evaporated: establishment of formal diplomatic relations did not occur until 1979. And, despite a West German-Soviet summit in 1978 to conclude a twenty-five year trade treaty, German-German relations stalled after the meetings of 1970–2 because the GDR was now intent on consolidating itself as a distinct nation, not just a separate state.

The decline of East-West summitry amid the waning of détente also reflected changes at the top. The summits of the early 1970s had depended on strong Western leaders, especially Nixon and Brandt—both of whom had strategic visions about policy as well as a tight grip on power. But in 1974 Nixon was toppled by Watergate and Brandt by the Guillaume spy affair—two events of major international consequence that stemmed from apparently maverick domestic incidents, except that each scandal reflected the leader's dangerously personalized governing style. Nixon's successor, Gerald Ford, did not have the same political clout and the man who replaced him, Jimmy Carter, lacked credibility abroad and support at home. On the Soviet side, too, political leadership was ebbing. In the early 1970s Brezhnev had used summitry to strengthen his domestic position. The 1972 summit with Nixon elevated him to a position of supremacy within the Soviet state, sidelining Alexei Kosygin and Nikolai Podgorny who had initially shared power with him after the ousting of Khrushchev. And Brezhnev rushed to conclude the Helsinki accords so as to have another diplomatic accomplishment to proclaim at the 1976 Party Congress. But his declining health, compounded by the fact that he did not finally die until 1982, left the Kremlin increasingly in political limbo and the West without a viable interlocutor.

Summitry did not disappear entirely, however. In the second half of the 1970s it was driven by the Western Europeans in reaction to the friction and drift at the superpower level. This aroused a profound sense of insecurity, especially in the minds of Valéry Giscard d'Estaing and Helmut Schmidt, the leaders of France and the Federal Republic, who directed the Western response. Part of their concern was economic—Western Europe was far more vulnerable to the oil shock than energy-rich America and also more seriously ravaged by stagflation—but they also feared that the lack of a new financial order to replace Bretton Woods would be exploited politically by Moscow. Acting on their shared concerns, Giscard and Schmidt convened the Rambouillet economic summit in November 1975, precursor of the annual meetings of key Western leaders that became known as the G7.

The Western sense of insecurity was military as well as economic. The five-year interim SALT I agreement had been signed in 1972, but it took the rest of the decade to decide on the next stage. And SALT II, finally signed in 1979 at Vienna, seemed deeply unsatisfactory to America's allies in Western Europe. The treaty focused on superpower strategic arsenals and ignored the recent Soviet deployment of intermediate-range nuclear forces (INF), especially

SS-20s, which threatened Europe but not the United States and to which the West had no direct equivalent. As with the G7, it was an inner circle of Western leaders (from America, Britain, France, and West Germany) who grappled with this security question in January 1979 at Guadeloupe.

This was a distinctive summit: secret and highly informal, intended primarily as an exchange of views between allies. In consequence, the talking immediately got down to substance and the dialogue, often very frank, helped to tease out individual national perspectives so that the Western 'Big Four' could come up with a common policy to deal with the adversary. The intensity of these exchanges served, however, to exacerbate Schmidt's sense of insecurity about the American position on arms control and led directly to his dual-track policy of arms reduction negotiations combined with new deployments of American INFs—with a clear emphasis on exploring the former track before implementing the latter. This became NATO policy by the end of 1979 and might well not have happened without Guadeloupe and Schmidt.

NATO ministers announced the dual-track decision on 12 December 1979. Two weeks later on 27 December Soviet troops intervened in Afghanistan and Carter then responded with a boycott of the Moscow Olympics. These events— each seen by the other side as offensive and threatening—abruptly ended diplomatic dialogue between the superpowers and precipitated what was variously called 'the New Cold War' or 'the Second Cold War'. The East-West crisis deepened in 1981 when the Polish government, under Soviet pressure, imposed martial law in an effort to suppress the free trade union movement, Solidarity, in direct violation of the Helsinki Final Act. The nadir of this renewed Cold War came in 1983 when Carter's successor, Ronald Reagan, denounced the Soviet Union as an 'empire of evil' and pushed through the implementation of the dual-track INF deployment in Europe. Such was the paranoia in Moscow that, in the autumn, the Kremlin perceived NATO's 'Able Archer' exercise as the prelude to an American attack on the Soviet Union and prompted it to consider a pre-emptive nuclear strike. The sense of mutual alienation seemed total: 'for the first time in nearly fifteen years', observed American journalist Strobe Talbott, 'the Americans and the Soviets were no longer negotiating in *any* forum'.[5]

Nevertheless communication did continue across the Cold War divide in Europe. The Federal Republic, in particular, was keen to keep open channels to the East because of the German question. Schmidt urged Brezhnev to resume dialogue with the White House and also sought to sustain the economic nexus created in the wake of détente, especially the pipeline to bring Siberian natural gas three thousand miles to Western Europe. In a similar way, his Christian Democrat successor Helmut Kohl facilitated the so-called *Milliardenkredite* to the GDR in 1983 and 1984—trying to exploit the East German debt crisis in order to reduce border tensions and gain humanitarian concessions. These continued European-level contacts reflected attempts to live with Cold War, in the rudimentary sense of muddling through and trying to cope. There had been serious ups and downs in East-West relations before (for instance, from the high of the 'spirit of Geneva' in 1955 to the depths of the Cuban Missile Crisis in 1962). But, in contrast to the early Cold War, there now existed in the early 1980s a mesh of ties at various levels which the Western Europeans, especially in Bonn, were desperate to protect and maintain.

By 1984 the West had got through the immediate crisis of the new Cold War but prospects of a renewed thaw seemed bleak. The best to be hoped for, it seemed in Western capitals, was a re-launch, at some point, of superpower arms control negotiations from a position of strength. But when the talking did resume, quite surprisingly it resulted in a totally new relationship with the Soviet Union. Why this occurred is perhaps the most important conundrum in recent international history and it deserves closer attention here.

Structural factors within the Soviet bloc were, of course, extremely important. The command economy proved increasingly unproductive and uncompetitive, requiring massive artificial subsidies to keep it going. The revenue from Soviet oil exports and the provision of détente-era credits from the West had helped in the short term but oil prices collapsed in the mid-1980s while the credits built up a huge debt burden across Eastern Europe. A return to economic autarky was, however, not an option because the Soviet bloc needed continued access to the West in order to keep up technologically, especially in the dawning computer age, and also to placate ordinary people with more sophisticated consumer goods. The socio-economic malaise was exacerbated by imperial overstretch. With roughly a quarter of GDP being channelled into the armed forces and the military-industrial complex, manpower and resources were not available for the rejuvenation of the civilian economy. But breaking the mould of Soviet defence and foreign policy was enormously difficult because of the military's stranglehold over political life.

Such systemic conservatism could only be transformed by innovative leadership. This, however, was sorely lacking right across the Soviet empire. Brezhnev's long but now sclerotic hold on power since 1964 was matched, even exceeded elsewhere. For instance, the tenure of János Kádár dated back to the Soviet crackdown in Hungary in 1956. As long as such ageing men stayed in charge, the entrenched position of key interest groups in the party, bureaucracy, and the military remained intact and with this a fundamental aversion to any radical change. The situation descended into farce in the USSR after Brezhnev died in November 1982, followed in short order by Yuri Andropov in February 1984, and Konstantin Chernenko in March 1985. Only then did the Soviet elite reluctantly jump a generation from men born before World War One, to choose Mikhail Gorbachev, born in 1931. Crucially, Gorbachev was not haunted by 1941 and, as part of the university-educated middle class of the Khrushchev years, he had been able to see alternatives to the Soviet system thanks to visits around Western Europe during the détente era of the 1970s.

Upon his accession to power, Gorbachev moved cautiously, talking mainly about galvanizing the existing economic system: his first slogan was *uskorenie* (acceleration). But the sluggishness of reform forced him into more radical measures—*perestroika* (restructuring) and *glasnost* (openness, or frankness)— and then to accept that socio-economic change required political reform as well, by giving people a greater stake in the system through controlled democratization and devolution of power to the individual republics. Each of these steps entailed protracted battles with the conservatives, especially the military-industrial complex. In order to reduce the burden of defence spending on the economy, Gorbachev became increasingly interested in arms control with the West. This pushed him into summitry.

In the ensuing transformation of superpower relations, Gorbachev was the crucial change-agent but he could not have acted alone. Reagan, despite his notorious Cold Warrior image, had been seeking an American-Soviet summit even in the Brezhnev era and he responded warmly to this young and dynamic new Kremlin leader. During their first meeting in November 1985 in Geneva Gorbachev noted that it was 'almost seven years since the last summit'—a period, he said, during which communication had largely taken place 'via the press'. But after only an hour's conversation with the American president, he said, he found himself deeply impressed by Reagan's 'idea about dialogue': they were 'talking *to* each other rather than *about* each other'. Over the next few years their relationship had many ups and downs but this human bond remained fundamental. As Reagan remarked in his memoirs, 'there was a chemistry between Gorbachev and me that produced something very close to a friendship'.[6]

No agreements were signed in Geneva but Reagan and Gorbachev had clearly struck a chord. At their second meeting in Reykjavik in October 1986, this trust emboldened them into a passionate dialogue about a nuclear-free world. Even though pulling back from the brink of such a revolutionary step, much to the relief of their aides, the two men had clearly developed radically new conceptions of security. On his side, Reagan repudiated the traditional American doctrine of deterring war though Mutual Assured Destruction as literally mad: his Star Wars project (SDI) was intended to abolish nuclear weapons for the benefit of the world. Gorbachev, likewise, moved beyond security as a zero-sum game, benefiting one side only at the expense of the other, to talk about 'sufficient security' rather than superiority.

In December 1987, at their third meeting in Washington, the two men finally realized some of their hopes by signing the INF treaty, which represented an unprecedented breakthrough after four decades of the Cold War. Whereas the SALT talks in the 1970s were simply about arms limitation, the INF treaty actually eliminated a whole category of nuclear weapons. This was possible in large measure because, unlike the erratic summitry of the 1970s, the sequence of meetings in quick succession from 1985 had built up personal trust between the leaders and generated real momentum to reach a common goal.

A novel feature of these 1980s superpower summits was simultaneous rather than consecutive translation. Each politician could now listen via earphones to professional interpreters instead of waiting for the other man's comments to be translated before embarking on his own speech. This greatly reduced the length of meetings and, more important still, directly linked words to tone and body language in something close to a real-time conversation. One senior Russian aide reckoned that simultaneous interpreting set the conduct of Soviet-American relations 'on a completely new road'.[7]

For all these reasons—mutual trust, shared ideas, and new technology—the Reagan-Gorbachev meetings were more productive than the similar burst of Soviet-American summitry in 1972–4. This had merely relaxed tension (détente), whereas Gorbachev and Reagan had used creative summitry to establish real cooperation (entente). Although fully expecting that competition between their two systems would continue, they were making the Cold War liveable in a far more basic sense than in the 1970s. Not only had they defused the nuclear confrontation and the fear of annihilation that had been endemic since 1945, their summitry also transcended the ideological divide by helping to 'de-other' the Other. Again this process started with Geneva, with its cosy images of the two leaders joking around the fireplace, and culminated in their fourth summit in Moscow in May 1988 when Reagan repudiated his 'evil empire' speech in 1983 as something from 'another time, another era'.[8]

Thanks to these arms control summits, which enabled him to reduce the grip of the Soviet military-industrial complex, Gorbachev was able to focus more intently on domestic reform and his expanding agenda of *perestroika* and *glasnost*. At first he managed to keep control of events but in 1989 the new course he had initiated took on a life of its own in Eastern Europe, where his reform programme was picked up by new and younger leaders. In Hungary and Poland the result was a multi-party democracy, and soon political revolution was spreading across the bloc through East Germany, Czechoslovakia, Bulgaria, and Romania by the end of the year. This was in no way what Gorbachev had intended but he did not intervene. Stating in July that 'what the Poles and Hungarians decide is their affair' and that 'we will respect their decision whatever it is', he repudiated the 'Brezhnev doctrine' which had justified past Soviet interventions.[9] He was proclaiming a new set of 'universal' values and thus put his international credibility on the line. Moreover, through the summits and the INF treaty, he had locked himself into a novel relationship with the West, which would be jeopardized if he used force to hold the bloc together. Here we see a classic example of the interaction between domestic and foreign policy.

The revolutions of 1989 by themselves did not change the map of Europe. The Soviet Union also still maintained a sphere of influence in Eastern Europe through Comecon, the Warsaw Pact and, above all, the presence of the Red Army. The weak link was, however, the German Democratic Republic. When the Berlin Wall was breached in November 1989, the exodus of East Germans to the West undermined the GDR state and raised the spectre of chaos and instability at the heart of Europe. November 1989 opened up fundamental questions about the German state, nation, and territory. It also threatened to unpick the European peace settlement of 1945 that had been woven around the partition of a truncated Germany. To resolve these issues peacefully summitry proved essential—but that was no easy task.

First of all, their resolution posed a major challenge for American diplomacy and leadership. The crisis of 1989 occurred at a moment of transition between two presidencies. Reagan's successor, George H.W. Bush was initially suspicious of Gorbachev and he prioritized relations with China. But the violent crackdown in Tiananmen Square by Deng's regime in June 1989—just as Poland and Hungary had begun their transitions to democracy—forced him into a fundamental rethink of geopolitical priorities. The Chinese repression ended immediate hopes of improved relations with Beijing, but Eastern Europe was now in flux and Bush wanted to ensure that change happened without violent conflict, especially given the Soviet military presence. This meant that he had to engage with Gorbachev, and their informal meeting in Malta on 2–3 December 1989 (dubbed by Bush the 'non-summit summit') was rather like the Reagan-Gorbachev icebreaker in Geneva in 1985—fostering confidence and understanding between previously wary leaders. The two men haggled about ideology: was the Soviet Union now embracing 'Western values' or did Russia and America simply espouse common 'democratic values'? But they agreed that these values included openness, pluralism, and self-determination. This triad of Helsinki principles provided the essential criteria with which they tackled the issue of German unification: that, they affirmed, would be the crux of their 'New Relationship' in Europe after 1989.

The second challenge for summitry was forging a consensus between Washington and Bonn. After the fall of the Berlin Wall Chancellor Kohl unilaterally seized the initiative with his ten-point plan setting out a path towards eventual 'state unity'. At this stage he was running well ahead of Washington and it took time and effort for Bush to catch up. Gorbachev's commitment at Malta on the principle of peaceful self-determination provided reassurance for the president that there would be no war over German unification. At the same time Bush made clear publicly that the United States intended to remain a military power in Europe. With the GDR rapidly imploding into the Federal Republic, the Americans successfully ensured that the process of unification would be handled by the two Germanies but in conjunction with the great-power quartet of 1945. When Gorbachev met Bush again at the summit in Washington in late May 1990, the Soviet leader conceded the right of a united Germany to choose its alliance, which of course in practice meant NATO. Bush had managed to create a framework for German unification that did not jeopardize American interests.

This agreement allowed Kohl and Gorbachev to deal directly on the specifics. Their July 1990 meeting was the climactic German-Soviet summit of the Cold War, taking place in the Kremlin and then at Gorbachev's mountain retreat in the Caucasus. The latter venue was especially important because it permitted a degree of informality not possible in Moscow: the two men were seen on global television in a cardigan and a woolly jumper sitting on tree stumps. They also laid wreaths at a war memorial dedicated to the Soviet dead of World War Two—an important symbolic act of reconciliation by leaders too young to have participated in the conflict and ready to draw a line under past antagonisms. Kohl and Gorbachev were now setting their sights on the future, on a new world order. To them history seemed thrillingly palpable: in Kohl's words this was 'now a historic moment in world politics' when one could feel the pressure of events forcing decisions.[10] At the Caucasus summit Gorbachev explicitly accepted a unified Germany's full membership of NATO, while Kohl provided sufficient financial sweeteners to secure timely withdrawal of the Red Army from German soil. This bargain paved the way for the four occupying powers to surrender their victor rights and for the re-establishment of a united and fully sovereign Germany on 3 October 1990, forty-five years after the defeat of the Third Reich. The German question had finally been resolved, by consent not force, with summitry playing a significant part in that dénouement.

The way German unification was settled had implications for the continent at large because the division of Germany had taken shape within the wider framework of a continent split into two rival military alliances. In fact, the phased withdrawal of the Red Army from Germany accelerated the general collapse of the Warsaw Pact. In contrast, NATO not only survived but came to encompass former East German territory. Other Western structures from the early Cold War also persisted, including the Federal Republic and the European Community. With the Soviet Union squeezed out of Europe and the American presence reaffirmed, the West was seen to have 'won' the Cold War. This seemed even more evident during 1991 as the remorseless logic of Gorbachev's devolution of power to the republics played itself out and the USSR fell apart, taking with it both him and the Communist Party of the Soviet Union. On Christmas Day 1991, three-quarters of a century after the Bolshevik Revolution, the Red Flag was lowered for the last time from the top of the Kremlin. The strongest successor state, Russia, which had formed the core of the USSR, now found itself on the margins of Europe, not at its heart.

Did the sudden disintegration of the Soviet Union in 1991 mean the end of the Cold War in a more fundamental sense, because the state that had set out in 1917 to export communist revolution was now on the scrap heap of history? That was the assumption in the heady days after the Soviet collapse, especially among triumphalists in the United States who anticipated the dawning of a unipolar era in world history in which America was the 'sole superpower' and the source of universal values. Clearly some of the hallmarks of the Cold War had disappeared during the Gorbachev era—first the spiralling nuclear arms race, then the stark ideological confrontation, next the partition of Germany and Europe, and finally the Soviet Union itself. The new Russia grappled with democratization and, like China, with the challenges of capitalism and integration in the global economy.

Yet other features of the Cold War had not been transcended. Germany was now united but it remained a neutered power, renouncing a military and diplomatic role that was commensurate with its current economic strength or paralleled its aggressive self-assertion in the period 1870–1945. *Westbindung* and self-restraint remained axiomatic: the consensual policy of integration agreed by West Germany and its allies from 1949 continued after 1990 through the persistence of NATO and the deepening of the EU. In 1870 German unification was forcibly imposed on its neighbours; in 1990 re-unification was the result of peaceful negotiation within institutional structures adapted from the Cold War era.

This point also reminds us that, even after the Iron Curtain had been lifted, the Europeans were not masters of their own destiny, as they had been—for good and ill—throughout the nineteenth century and in many ways right up to 1945. The defeat of Nazi Germany had been accomplished not by the Europeans but by two new superpowers, entirely or partly from outside Europe, who became the power brokers of Cold War Europe. After 1991 only one of them, the United States, remained a force in the heart of Europe—again by European consent as much as American will. In this way, too, the Cold War architecture had not been entirely dismantled.

The other superpower imploded despite the efforts of Western leaders in their summitry of 1989–90 to support Gorbachev's process of reform. In the process Moscow lost its Eastern European satellites and then its peripheral republics. Subsequently the West made various efforts to draw Russia into its new European security order: the North Atlantic Cooperation Council (1991); the 'Partnership for Peace' programme (1994); the 'NATO-Russia Founding Act' (1997) which created the Permanent Joint Council, replaced in 2002 by the NATO-Russia Council. All proved ineffectual. In this situation of continuing geo-strategic uncertainty, the Central and East European countries clamoured for rapid inclusion into the institutions of the West to escape from the historic embrace of the Russian bear.

By 2004 both NATO and the EU had expanded to the borders of Russia. This, however, created a backlash in Moscow. Playing on a widespread feeling of humiliation and alienation, Vladimir Putin, Russia's hardline nationalist leader from 2000, strove to recreate a buffer zone in Eastern Europe and also trumpeted an ideology of difference from the West—the old theme of the Other. Putin's rhetoric was rooted in the traditional Janus-like posture of Russia as a vast Eurasian empire extending from the Baltic to the Pacific that looked both east and west; in its own way not fully European. Far from conforming to shared values within an institutionally regulated Europe, Putin's Russia acted like a loose cannon, undermining the stability and predictability that the summiteers of 1989–90 had so desired.

The three issues of Germany, America, and Russia therefore remind us that there was no totally 'new' world order after 1991. So did the peaceful dénouement of the Cold War merely paper over deeper cracks? Did summitry encourage consensus by fudging fundamental areas of disagreement? Did peace, in short, come at a price? Yes, of course, it did. Because solving one problem usually requires ignoring others, or at least giving them lower priority. We must therefore acknowledge that, in spite of all the positive achievements of summitry between 1970 and 1990, Europe's Cold War order had not been completely transcended. Older balance-of-power problems continued to exist, stemming from the Cold War and long before.

But none of this should obscure the larger historical point. The map of Europe and the dynamics of international politics changed fundamentally over the two decades since those first steps towards to détente by Brandt and Stoph, Nixon and Brezhnev. By the end of 1991 the nuclear arms race had been defused and the German question resolved, while the collapse of the Soviet Union terminated the bipolar clash of ideologies that had underpinned the Cold War. Here was a complete transformation of the international order and, unlike other comparable ruptures such as 1815, 1870, 1918, and 1945, it had been accomplished without a European or world war and indeed with relatively little domestic violence.

CREATIVE SUMMITRY AND THE MANAGEMENT OF THE COLD WAR ENDGAME

What role, then, did summitry play within this remarkably peaceful transformation of the international order? How far were statesmen simply responding to huge systemic shifts? To what extent did these leaders actually shape the processes of change? This book has identified three moments of particularly creative synergy during the 1970s and 1980s when leadership at the summit made a difference to the course of history.

In the first instance, 1970–3, summit meetings were important in starting to get to know the Other, after a period of intense hostility when the world came close to nuclear war. This was done not just behind closed doors but in the full glare of the international media, helping thereby to influence public attitudes on both sides of the Iron Curtain. Substantive agreements also resulted, driven through from the top by national leaders, particularly the German treaties and the superpower arms control agreements signed in Moscow. The agency of key leaders clearly mattered: Nixon had a geopolitical vision of how the global balance was changing and also the anti-communist credentials to go to Beijing and Moscow without being damned as an appeaser. On the German side, the *Ostpolitik* initiatives of 1970–2 would have been inconceivable for Christian Democrat chancellors like Adenauer and Kiesinger, who lacked Brandt's passionate engagement with the problems of Berlin and national division. Nixon and Brandt each worked in dynamic partnership with a close aide (Kissinger and Bahr) who combined bold strategic thinking with an aptitude for quiet backchannel diplomacy.

The Reagan-Gorbachev round of summits constitutes our second example of how human agency in response to systemic pressures served as a catalyst for historical change. These men were the two great heretics among Cold War leaders, who not only did not believe in nuclear deterrence but also were willing to act on their convictions. And they sparked each other's radicalism through the frequency and intensity of their encounters—annually over four years between 1985 and 1988. Reagan and Gorbachev challenged a fundamental premise of the Cold War, namely that security depended on the threat of nuclear annihilation. Their deepening dialogue and growing trust enabled them not merely to think the unthinkable but speak the unspeakable. In the end they went on to do what had previously been unimaginable, by signing a treaty in 1987 to abolish a whole category of nuclear weapons. This revolutionary moment was not simply the consequence of systemic forces—the Western defence build-up and Star Wars or Gorbachev's need to break the hold of the Soviet military-industrial complex. It also reflected a fundamental convergence of values made possible by parleys at the summit. Reagan made this point explicit at their meeting in Moscow in 1988 by consigning his 'evil empire' rhetoric to a past era. And, as with our first example from the 1970s, effective partnerships with and between key advisers were essential—Reagan and Shultz, Gorbachev and Shevardnadze. But unlike the Nixon-Brandt era, these partnerships were not with personal aides, outside formal diplomatic channels, but with foreign ministers and their bureaucracies. This helped ensure that moments of summit chemistry were formalized in lasting agreements.

Although playing no direct role in the revolutions of 1989, summitry was very important in the subsequent East-West dialogue over the vital question of German unification within the orbit of NATO. Herein lies the third key episode of summit synergy that we have identified in this book. In these discussions over Germany, Kohl was Gorbachev's main interlocutor, supported by Bush. As with our other two examples, mutual trust, shared visions, and constructive partnerships were vital, together with the ability to sense a decisive moment. But Kohl, Gorbachev, and Bush all saw themselves as heralds of a new era and as creators of something truly novel—a united Germany in an undivided Europe—in the process trying to integrate a reformed Soviet Union into the global economy within what Bush called a 'New World Order'. Apart from NATO's overtures, another sign of this was the international operation to drive Saddam Hussein out of Kuwait in the Gulf War of 1991, entailing unprecedented Soviet-American cooperation in the United Nations that would have been inconceivable during the Cold War. The alienation of post-Soviet Russia by the late 1990s should not blind us to the intentions and spirit of the statesmen of 1990–1.

What were the features of such historically creative summitry? First, the facilitation of personal trust at the very top. Summit meetings are high-risk ventures, leaving leaders exposed and potentially humiliated if things go wrong—as happened, for instance, between Kennedy and Khrushchev in 1961 in Vienna. But where the gamble pays off and the meeting succeeds, it can be a catalyst for change. Political leaders, by definition, have the potential to shape policy decisively within their own countries, cutting through the bureaucratic red tape that often ties up routine diplomacy. Catalytic partnerships, such as the one between Reagan and Gorbachev, can also reorient the agenda of international politics and create a more predictable environment for diplomacy. The effectiveness of such personal connections is enhanced by good working relationships with and between their aides and ministers. Such men convert bright ideas into practical policies, for instance Shultz and Shevardnadze who provided essential reinforcement for the Reagan-Gorbachev duo. Some of these aides also act as 'sherpas', secretly preparing the way to the summit. Examples include Kissinger for Nixon, Bahr for Brandt, and Teltschik for Kohl.

Although summit meetings take place behind closed doors, summitry often has a public, performative side. Symbolic moments, enacted for and disseminated by the global media, can have huge impact in changing perceptions, even in helping to 'de-other' previously antagonistic regimes and cultures. Some of these iconic images have been mentioned in this book. One thinks of Nixon's handshake with Zhou Enlai, Reagan strolling with Gorbachev around Red Square, and Kohl and Gorbachev in leisure-wear amid the mountains the mountains of the Caucasus. These pictures signalled a moment of transformation in international relations far more eloquently than any number of official communiqués.

Yet summits are sometimes deliberately low profile and informal. Helmut Schmidt was an inveterate advocate of meetings away from the limelight, without an agenda or pressure for formal agreements. His prime concern was a frank exchange of ideas in order to advance mutual understanding. 'Dressing down' was sometimes seen as useful to build up a relaxed atmosphere: the Western Big Four in their shirtsleeves in the beach hut at Guadeloupe, for instance. Terminology also mattered. The word 'summit' was anathema to Schmidt because it evoked pageantry, pomp, and publicity. Similar feelings led George H.W. Bush to call his Malta meeting with Gorbachev a 'non-summit summit'.

Historically creative summitry also requires give and take. As we have seen, real or perceived weakness often prompts the initial contacts: Nixon needed to talk in the early 1970s, Gorbachev in the mid-1980s. But even when the instigator of a summit feels strong, as Reagan did when making overtures to Brezhnev, the weakness of the Other can be especially dangerous in the nuclear age, provoking rash gambles such as Khrushchev placing missiles in Cuba in 1962. Summitry in the face of a potential third world war was therefore not simply a zero-sum game in which one side deliberately sought to make the other side lose. Instead it demanded compromises out of which mutually beneficial stability could grow. The summits analysed in this book show just this: in order to ensure peace and gain predictability in the conduct of international affairs, leaders met, talked, and even learned from each other. This is not to deny that each side wanted to gain advantages in a continuing Cold War but the first and foremost aim was the avoidance of armed conflict, which so easily could escalate to nuclear holocaust. This was classically seen in the Reagan-Gorbachev summits and in the meetings that resolved the German question while trying to respect Gorbachev's own needs and declining domestic position. The aspiration of summitry in the late 1980s was to conjure up a new international order out of a revolutionary moment without provoking chaos and anarchy.

To be truly transformative, summitry requires a combination of pragmatic politics and grand vision—crisis management to expedite conflict resolution. At this level of creativity, statecraft at the summit is the art of the possible in pursuit of the improbable. In human terms, going to the summit requires a huge physical and intellectual effort—preparing, travelling, performing, and then selling. And timing is of course critical: you need to be in a position to talk; so does your interlocutor; and finding the moment is even more delicate when more than two leaders are involved. All this requires judgement—but also more than a modicum of luck.

The most skilful statesmen are always alert to the tides of history, sensing when the current runs against them but also knowing when to surf the waves. Bismarck, a German protestant, talked of trying to 'see God striding through world history' and then catching 'the hem of his garment so that we are carried on with it as long as we must go'. Lenin, a historical materialist, did not invoke God but he used a similar image, insisting that statesmen had to accept the confusion and complexity of a revolutionary process and dare to take their chances, rather than assuming that historical change happened in 'the peaceful, calm, smooth and precise manner of a German express train pulling into a station' on to which they could climb in a leisurely fashion.[11] Similarly, Nixon and Brandt discerned very clearly the situational constraints within which they operated but were also intent on shaping historical outcomes. And the men who presided over the climax of the Cold War explicitly saw themselves as making history rather than simply being made by it. As Reagan said to

Gorbachev at Geneva, 'To hell with the past, we'll do it our way'. In his 1990 meeting with Gorbachev, Chancellor Kohl recalled Bismarck's injunction that 'you had to grab the mantle of history' and declared that these were 'historically significant years', when one should not waste the chance to take 'decisions that could have long-lasting, positive effects'.[12] Kohl captured that double sense of fateful moment and unique opportunity that entrances statesmen of vision, skill, and nerve—the men who dare to parley at the summit.

NOTES

1. Quoted in Michael R. Beschloss, *The Crisis Years: Kennedy and Khrushchev, 1960–1963* (New York, 1991), 278.
2. Vermerk Brandt über das Gespräch mit Stoph, 19 March 1970, *Berliner Ausgabe* VI, 281.
3. Richard Nixon, *The Memoirs of Richard Nixon* (London, 1978), 560.
4. Memorandum of conversation by Egon Bahr, 26 October 1969, *Dokumente zur Deutschlandpolitik, VI. Reihe, Band 1: 21. Oktober 1969 bis 31. Dezember 1970* (Munich, 2002), doc. 1, 3–4.
5. Strobe Talbott, *Deadly Gambits: The Reagan Administration and the Stalemate in Arms Control* (New York, 1984), 4. Italics added.
6. First Reagan-Gorbachev plenary meeting, 19 November 1985, 2, http://www.thereaganfiles.com/geneva-summit-transcripts.pdf; Edmund Morris, *Dutch: A Memoir of Ronald Reagan* (New York, 1999), 823; Ronald Reagan, *An American Life* (New York, 1990), 707.
7. Sergei Tarasenko, quoted in William Wohlforth, ed., *Witnesses to the End of the Cold War* (Baltimore, 1996), 19.
8. Michael R. Beschloss and Strobe Talbott, *At the Highest Levels: The Inside Story of the End of the Cold War* (London, 1993), 9.
9. R.J. Crampton, *Eastern Europe in the Twentieth Century* (London, 1994), 408.
10. Hanns Jürgen Küsters und Daniel Hofmann, eds, *Dokumente zur Deutschlandpolitik: Deutsche Einheit—Sonderedition aus den Akten des Bundeskanzleramts 1989/90* (Munich, 1998) (henceforth *DESE*), doc. 352, 1354.
11. Vladimir Lenin, 'Can the Bolsheviki hold state power?' *Prosveshcheniye* no. 1–2, 14 Oct. 1917, https://www.marxists.org/archive/lenin/works/1917/oct/01.htm.
12. Reagan-Gorbachev dinner, 20 November 1985, 7, http://www.thereaganfiles.com/geneva-summit-transcripts.pdf; *DESE*, doc. 350, 1340, 1354.

Bibliography of Secondary Sources

Books

Adomeit, Hannes, *Imperial Overstretch: Germany in Soviet Policy from Stalin to Gorbachev* (Baden-Baden, 1998)

Aijazuddin, Fakir S., *From a Head, Through a Head, To a Head: The Secret Channel Between the US and China Through Pakistan* (Oxford, 2000)

Aleksandrov-Agentov, A. M., *Ot Kollontai do Gorbacheva* (Moscow, 1994)

Baring, Arnulf, *Machtwechsel: Die Ära Brandt-Scheel* (Stuttgart, 1982)

Bell, Daniel, *The End of Ideology: The Exhaustion of Political Ideas in the Fifties* (Glencoe, IL, 1960)

Bennett, G., and K. A. Hamilton, eds, *Documents on British Policy Overseas: The Conference on Security and Co-operation in Europe, 1972–1975*, series III, vol. 2 (London, 1997)

Berg, Hermann von, *Vorbeugende Unterwerfung: Politik im realen Sozialismus* (Munich, 1988)

Berridge, G. R., *Diplomacy and Theory* (Basingstoke, 2nd edn, 2002)

Beschloss, Michael R., *The Crisis Years: Kennedy and Khrushchev, 1960–1963* (New York, 1991)

Beschloss, Michael R., and Strobe Talbott, *At the Highest Levels: The Inside Story of the End of the Cold War* (London, 1993)

Bierling, Stefan, *Wirtschaftshilfe für Moskau: Motive und Strategien der Bundesrepublik Deutschland und der USA 1990–1996* (Paderborn, 1998)

Bischof, Günter, Stefan Karner, and Barbara Stelzl-Marx, eds, *The Vienna Summit and its Importance in International History* (New York, 2014)

Bock, Siegfried, Ingrid Muth, and Hermann Schwiesau, eds, *DDR-Außenpolitik im Rückspiegel: Diplomaten im Gespräch* (Münster, 2004)

Bozo, Frédéric, et al., eds, *Visions of the End of the Cold War in Europe, 1945–1990* (New York, 2012)

Brands, Hal, *From Berlin to Baghdad* (Lexington, KY, 2008)

Brands, Henry W., *Reagan: The Life* (New York, 2015)

Brandt, Willy, *Begegnungen und Einsichten: Die Jahre 1960–1975* (Hamburg, 1976)

Brandt, Willy, *Erinnerungen* (Berlin, 1989)

Brezhnev, Leonid, *Peace, Détente, and Soviet-American Relations: A Collection of Public Statements* (New York, 1979)

Brinkley, Douglas, and Luke A. Nichter, eds, *The Nixon Tapes: 1971–1972* (Boston, 2014)

Brown, Archie, *The Gorbachev Factor* (Oxford, 1996)

Brzezinski, Zbigniew, *Power and Principle: Memoirs of the National Security Adviser, 1977–1981* (London, 1983)

Bush, George, *All the Best, George Bush: My Life in Letters and Other Writings* (New York, 2013)

Bush, George, and Brent Scowcroft, *A World Transformed* (New York, 1998)

Callaghan, James, *Time and Chance* (London, 1987)

Campbell, David, *Writing Security: United States Foreign Policy and the Politics of Identity* (Manchester, 1992)

Carter, Jimmy, *Keeping Faith: Memoirs of a President* (New York, 1982)

Carter, Jimmy, *White House Diary* (New York, 2010)

Chernyaev, Anatoly S., *My Six Years with Gorbachev* (University Park, PA, 2000)

Cohen, Raymond, *Negotiating across Cultures: International Communication in an Independent World* (Washington, DC, 2nd rev. edn, 1999)

Crampton, R.J., *Eastern Europe in the Twentieth Century* (London, 1994)

Dallek, Robert, *Nixon and Kissinger: Partners in Power* (New York, 2007)

Del Pero, Mario, *The Eccentric Realist: Henry Kissinger and the Shaping of American Foreign Policy* (Ithaca, NY, 2009)

Dijkink, Gertran, *National Identity and Geopolitical Visions: Maps of Pride and Pain* (London, 1996)

Dobrynin, Anatoly, *In Confidence: Moscow's Ambassador to America's Six Cold War Presidents (1962–1986)* (New York, 1995)

Drell, Sidney D., and George P. Shultz, eds, *Implications of the Reykjavik Summit on its Twentieth Anniversary* (Stanford, CA, 2007)

Dunn, David H., ed., *Diplomacy at the Highest Level: The Evolution of International Summitry* (London, 1996)

Engel, Jeffrey A., ed., *The China Diary of George H.W. Bush: The Making of a Global President* (Princeton, NJ, 2008)

Engel, Jeffrey A., ed., *The Fall of the Berlin Wall: The Revolutionary Legacy of 1989* (New York, 2009)

Fiebig-von Hase, Ragnhild, and Ursula Lehmkuhl, eds, *Enemy Images in American History* (Oxford, 1997)

Fischer, Beth A., *The Reagan Reversal: Foreign Policy and the End of the Cold War* (Columbia, MO, 1997)

Fischer, Thomas, *Neutral Power in the CSCE: The N+N States and the Making of the Helsinki Accords 1975* (Baden-Baden, 2009)

Freedman, Lawrence, ed., *Europe Transformed: Documents on the End of the Cold War* (London, 1990)

Galkin, Aleksandr, and Anatolij Tschernjajew, eds, *Michail Gorbatschow und die deutsche Frage: Sowjetische Dokumente 1986–1991* (München, 2011)

Gao, Wenqian, *Wannian Zhou Enlai* (Zhou Enlai's Later Years) (Hong Kong, 2003)

Gardner Feldman, Lily, *Germany's Foreign Policy of Reconciliation: From Enmity to Amity* (Lanham, MD, 2012)

Garthoff, Raymond L., *Détente and Confrontation: American-Soviet Relations from Nixon to Reagan* (Washington, DC, 1985)

Garthoff, Raymond L., *The Great Transition: American-Soviet Relations and the End of the Cold War* (Washington, DC, 1994)

Garton Ash, Timothy, *In Europe's Name: Germany and the Divided Continent* (New York, 1993)

Gates, Robert M., *From the Shadows: The Ultimate Insider's Story of Five Presidents and How They Won the Cold War* (New York, 1996)

Genscher, Hans-Dietrich, *Erinnerungen* (Berlin, 1991)

Genscher, Hans-Dietrich, *Unterwegs zur Einheit: Reden und Dokumente aus bewegter Zeit* (Berlin, 1991)

Geyer, David C., and Douglas E. Selvage, eds, *Soviet-American Relations: The Détente Years, 1969–1972* (Washington, DC, 2007)

Giscard d'Estaing, Valéry, *Le pouvoir et la vie: vol. 2—L'affrontement* (Paris, 1991)

Glad, Betty, *An Outsider in the White House: Jimmy Carter, his Advisors, and the Making of American Foreign Policy* (Ithaca, NY, 2009)

Gleijeses, Piero, *Visions of Freedom: Havana, Washington, Pretoria, and the Struggle for Southern Africa, 1976–1991* (Chapel Hill, NC, 2013)

Gong, Li, *Kuayue honggou: 1969–1979 nian Zhong Mei guanxi de yanbian (Across the Chasm: The Evolution of China–U.S. Relations, 1969–1979)* (Zhengzhou, 1992)

Gorbachev, Mikhail, *Perestroika: New Thinking for Our Country and the World* (New York, 1987)

Gorbachev, Mikhail, *Reykjavik: Results and Lessons* (Madison, CT, 1987)

Gorbachev, Mikhail, *Memoirs* (New York, 1996)

Gorbachev, Mikhail, *Sobranie Sochinenii, vol. 15* (Moscow, 2010)

Grachev, Andrei, *Gorbachev's Gamble: Soviet Foreign Policy and the End of the Cold War* (Cambridge, 2008)

Grebing, Helga, et al., eds, *Willy Brandt: Berliner Ausgabe, vol. 6* (Berlin, 2005)

Guo, Simin, and Tian Yu, eds, *Wo yanzhong de Mao Zedong (As I Saw Mao Zedong)* (Shijiazhuang, 1990)

Hamilton, Keith, and Patrick Salmon, eds, *Documents on British Policy Overseas, Series III, vol. 7: German Unification 1989/90* (Abingdon, 2009)

Hanhimäki, Jussi, *The Flawed Architect: Henry Kissinger and American Foreign Policy* (New York, 2004)

Hanhimäki, Jussi M., and Odd Arne Westad, eds, *The Cold War: A History in Documents and Eyewitness Accounts* (Oxford, 2003)

Hanhimäki, Jussi M., et al., eds, *The Routledge Handbook of Transatlantic Security* (London, 2010)

Harder, Hans-Joachim, ed., *Von Truman bis Harmel: Die Bundesrepublik Deutschland im Spannungsfeld von NATO und europäischer Integration* (Munich, 2000)

Hartmann, Robert T., *Palace Politics: An Inside Account of the Ford Years* (New York, 1980)

Haslam, Jonathan, and Karina Urbach, eds, *Secret Intelligence in the European States System, 1918–1989* (Stanford, CA, 2013)

Hilger, Andreas, ed., *Diplomatie für die deutsche Einheit: Dokumente des Auswärtigen Amts zu den deutsch-sowjetischen Beziehungen 1989/90* [Schriftenreihe der Vierteljahrshefte für Zeitgeschichte] (Munich, 2011)

Hoffman, David E., *The Dead Hand: The Untold Story of the Cold War Arms Race and Its Dangerous Legacy* (New York, 2009)

Holdridge, John, *Crossing the Divide: An Insider's Account of the Normalization of U.S.–China Relations* (Lanham, MD, 1997)

Hutchings, Robert L., *American Diplomacy and the End of the Cold War: An Insider's Account of US Policy in Europe, 1989–1992* (Washington, DC, 1997)

James, Harold, *International Monetary Cooperation since Bretton Woods* (Oxford, 1996)

Jarausch, Konrad H., and Martin Sabrow, eds, *Weg in den Untergang: Der innere Zerfall der DDR* (Göttingen, 1999)

Ji, Chaozhu, *The Man on Mao's Right: From Harvard Yard to Tiananmen Square—My Life Inside China's Foreign Ministry* (New York, 2008)

Jian, Chen, *Mao's China and the Cold War* (Chapel Hill, NC, 2001)

Jin, Chongji, et al., eds, *Zhou Enlai zhuan, 1949–1976 (A Biography of Zhou Enlai, 1949–1976)* (Beijing, 1998)

Johnson, Robert D., *Congress and the Cold War* (New York, 2006)

Jordan, Hamilton, *Crisis: The Last Year of the Carter Presidency* (London, 1982)

Kaiser, Karl, *Deutschlands Vereinigung: Die internationalen Aspekte—mit den wichtigen Dokumenten* (Bergisch Gladbach, 1991)

Kaiser, Monika, *Machtwechsel von Ulbricht zu Honecker: Funktionsmechanismen der SED-Diktatur in Konfliktsituationen 1962 bis 1972* (Berlin, 1997)

Kalinovsky, Artemy, and Sergey Radchenko, eds, *The End of the Cold War and the Third World: New Perspectives on Regional Conflict* (London, 2011)

Keworkow, Wjatscheslaw, *Der geheime Kanal: Moskau, der KGB und die Bonner Ostpolitik* (Berlin, 1995)

Keys, Barbara, *Reclaiming American Virtue: The Human Rights Revolution of the 1970s* (Cambridge, MA, 2014)

Khan, Sultan M., *Memories and Reflections of a Pakistani Diplomat* (London, 1997)

Kiessler, Richard, and Frank Elbe, *Ein runder Tisch mit scharfen Ecken: Der diplomatische Weg zur deutschen Einheit* (Baden-Baden, 1993)

Kissinger, Henry, *White House Years* (Boston, 1979)

Kissinger, Henry, *Years of Upheaval* (Boston, 1982)

Kissinger, Henry, *Years of Renewal* (New York, 1999)

Kissinger, Henry, *On China* (New York, 2011)

Klein, Hans, *Es begann im Kaukasus* (Berlin, 1991)

Kohl, Helmut, *Ich wollte Deutschlands Einheit* (Berlin, 1996)

Kohl, Helmut, *Vom Mauerfall zur Wiedervereinigung: Meine Erinnerungen* (Munich, 2009)

Kornienko, Georgii, *Kholodnaia voina: svidetel'stvo ee uchastnika (The Cold War: An Account from a Participant)* (Moscow, 2001)

Kotkin, Stephen, *Armageddon Averted: The Soviet Collapse, 1970–2000* (New York, 2008)

Kotkin, Stephen, with Jan T. Gross, *Uncivil Society: 1989 and the Implosion of the Communist Establishment* (New York, 2009)

Küsters, Hanns Jürgen, and Daniel Hofmann, eds, *Dokumente zur Deutschlandpolitik: Deutsche Einheit—Sonderedition aus den Akten des Bundeskanzleramts 1989/90* (Munich, 1998)

Laber, Jeri, *The Courage of Strangers: Coming of Age With the Human Rights Movement* (New York, 2005)

Lederach, John P., *Building Peace: Sustainable Reconciliation in Divided Societies* (Washington, DC, 2010)

Leffler, Melvyn P., and Odd Arne Westad, eds, *The Cambridge History of the Cold War, 3 vols* (Cambridge, 2011)

Lettow, Paul, *Ronald Reagan and his Quest to Abolish Nuclear Weapons* (New York, 2005)

Lévesque, Jacques, *The Enigma of 1989: The USSR and the Liberation of Eastern Europe* (Berkeley, CA, 1997)

Li, Ping, et al., eds, *Zhou Enlai nianpu, 1949–1976 (Chronology of Zhou Enlai, 1949–1976)* (Beijing, 1997)

Li, Zhisui, *The Private Life of Chairman Mao* (New York, 1994)

Lilley, James, *China Hands: Nine Decades of Adventure, Espionage, and Diplomacy in Asia* (New York, 2004)

Lüthi, Lorenz M., *The Sino-Soviet Split: Cold War in the Communist World* (Princeton, NJ, 2008)

Maier, Charles S., *Dissolution: The Crisis of Communism and the End of East Germany* (Princeton, NJ, 1997)

Mann, James, *About Face: A History of America's Curious Relationship with China, from Nixon to Clinton* (New York, 2000)

Mann, James, *The China Fantasy: How Our Leaders Explain Away Chinese Repression* (New York, 2007)

Mann, James, *The Rebellion of Ronald Reagan: A History of the End of the Cold War* (New York, 2009)

Mastny, Vojtech, and Malcolm Byrne, eds, *A Cardboard Castle? An Inside History of the Warsaw Pact, 1955–1991* (Budapest, 2005)

Matlock, Jack F. Jr, *Reagan and Gorbachev: How the Cold War Ended* (New York, 2004).

Menil, George de, and Anthony M. Solomon, *Economic Summitry* (New York, 1983)

Michel, Judith, *Willy Brandts Amerikabild und –politik 1933–1992* (Göttingen, 2010)

Möller, Horst et al., eds, *Akten zur Auswärtigen Politik der Bundesrepublik Deutschland, vols 1975–1979* (Munich, 2006–10)

Moore, Charles, *Margaret Thatcher: The Authorized Biography, vol. 2* (London, 2015)

Morris, Edmund, *Dutch: A Memoir of Ronald Reagan* (New York, 1999)

Mourlon-Druol, Emmanuel, and Federico Romero, eds, *International Summitry and Global Governance: The Rise of the G7 and the European Council, 1974–1991* (London, 2014)

Münkel, Daniela, *Kampagnen, Spione, geheime Kanäle: Die Stasi und Willy Brandt* (Berlin, 2013)

Nakath, Detlef, *Deutsch-deutsche Grundlagen: Zur Geschichte der politischen und wirtschaftlichen Beziehungen zwischen der DDR und der Bundesrepublik in den Jahren von 1969 bis 1982* (Schkeuditz, 2002)

Neier, Aryeh, *The International Human Rights Movement: A History* (Princeton, NJ, 2012)

Nelson, Mike, and Barbara Perry, eds, *41: Inside the Presidency of George H.W. Bush* (Ithaca, NY, 2014)

Newsom, David, *The Soviet Brigade in Cuba: A Study in Political Diplomacy* (Bloomington, IN, 1987)

Nianyi, Wang, *Da dongluan de niandai (In the Years of Great Upheaval)* (Zhengzhou, 1988)

Niedhart, Gottfried, *Entspannung in Europa: Die Bundesrepublik Deutschland und der Warschauer Pakt 1966 bis 1975* (Munich, 2014)

Nixon, Richard, *RN: The Memoirs of Richard Nixon* (New York, 1978)

Nixon, Richard, *Leaders* (New York, 1982)

Nove, Alec, *An Economic History of the USSR, 1917–1991* (New York, 3rd edn, 1992)

Oberdorfer, Don, *The Turn: From the Cold War to a New Era* (New York, 1991)

Ouimet, Matthew J., *The Rise and Fall of the Brezhnev Doctrine in Soviet Foreign Policy* (Chapel Hill, NC, 2003)

Pang, Xianzhi, and Jin Chongji, eds, *Mao Zedong zhuan, 1949–1976 (A Biography of Mao Zedong, 1949–1976)* (Beijing, 2003)

Pei, Jianzhang, chief ed., *Xin Zhongguo waijiao fengyun (Winds and Clouds in New China's Diplomacy)* (Beijing, 1994)

Pfeil, Ulrich, ed., *Die DDR und der Westen: Transnationale Beziehungen 1949–1989* (Berlin, 2001)

Pipes, Richard, *Vixi: Memoirs of a Non-believer* (New Haven, NJ, 2003)

Pleshakov, Constantine, *There Is No Freedom without Bread: 1989 and the Civil War that Brought Down Communism* (New York, 2009)

Plokhy, Serhii, *The Last Empire: The Final Days of the Soviet Union* (New York, 2014)

Potthoff, Heinrich, *Im Schatten der Mauer: Deutschlandpolitik 1961 bis 1990* (Berlin, 1999)

Preston, Andrew, and Fredrik Logevall, eds, *Nixon in the World: American Foreign Relations, 1969–1977* (New York, 2008)

Putnam, Robert D., and Nicholas Bayne, *Hanging Together: Cooperation and Conflict in the Seven-Power Summits* (London, 2nd edn, 1987)

Qian, Jiang, *Pingpang waijiao shimo (Ping-Pong Diplomacy: The Beginning and the End)* (Beijing, 1987)

Qian, Jiang, *Xiaoqiu zhuandong daqiu: Pingpang waijiao muhou (Little Ball Moves Big Ball: Behind Ping-Pong Diplomacy)* (Beijing, 1997)

Radchenko, Sergey, *Unwanted Visionaries: The Soviet Failure in Asia at the End of the Cold War* (New York, 2014)

Raßloff, Steffen, ed., *'Willy Brandt ans Fenster!' Das Erfurter Gipfeltreffen 1970 und die Geschichte des 'Erfurter Hofes'* (Jena, 2007)

Reagan, Ronald, *An American Life* (New York, 1990)

Reagan, Ronald, *The Reagan Diaries* (New York, 2007)

Reynolds, David, *One World Divisible: A Global History since 1945* (New York, 2000)

Reynolds, David, *Summits: Six Meetings that Shaped the Twentieth Century* (London, 2007)

Rhodes James, Robert, ed., *Winston S. Churchill: His Complete Speeches, 8 vols* (New York, 1974)

Roberts, Priscilla, ed., *Behind the Bamboo Curtain: China, Vietnam, and the World Beyond Asia* (Washington, DC, 2006)

Rose, Jonathan, *The Literary Churchill: Author, Reader, Actor* (New Haven, 2014)

Saltoun-Ebin, Jason, ed., *The Reagan Files: Inside the National Security Council* (Santa Barbara, CA, 2nd edn, 2014)

Sargent, Daniel J., *A Superpower Transformed: The Remaking of American Foreign Relations in the 1970s* (New York, 2014)

Sarotte, Mary Elise, *Dealing with the Devil: East Germany, Détente, and Ostpolitik, 1969–1973* (Chapel Hill, NC, 2001)

Sarotte, Mary Elise, *1989: The Struggle to Create Post-Cold War Europe* (Princeton, NJ, 2009)

Sarotte, Mary Elise, *The Collapse: The Accidental Openin g of the Berlin Wall* (New York, 2014)

Schmidt, Karl-Heinz, *Dialog über Deutschland: Studien zur Deutschlandpolitik von KPdSU und SED (1960–1979)* (Baden-Baden, 1998)

Schönfelder, Jan, and Rainer Erices, *Willy Brandt in Erfurt: Das erste deutsch-deutsche Gipfeltreffen 1970* (Berlin, 2010)

Schwarz, Hans-Peter, et al., eds, *Akten zur Auswärtigen Politik der Bundesrepublik Deutschland, vols 1968–69* (Munich, 1999–2000)

Seidel, Karl, *Berlin-Bonner Balance: 20 Jahre deutsch-deutsche Beziehungen— Erinnerungen und Erkenntnisse eines Beteiligten* (Berlin, 2002)

Service, Robert, *The End of the Cold War: 1985–1991* (London, 2015)

Shen, Zhihua, *Mao, Stalin and the Korean War: Trilateral Communist Relations in the 1950s*, trans. Neil Silver (London, 2012)

Shultz, George P., *Turmoil and Triumph: My Years as Secretary of State* (New York, 1993)

Skinner, Kiron, Annelise Anderson, and Martin Anderson, eds, *Reagan: A Life in Letters* (New York, 2003)

Smith, Gerard, *Doubletalk: The Story of SALT* (Lanham, MD, 1985)

Snyder, Sarah B., *Human Rights Activism and the End of the Cold War: A Transnational History of the Helsinki Network* (New York, 2011)

Solomon, Richard H., *Chinese Negotiating Behavior: Pursuing Interests through 'Old Friends'* (Washington, DC, 1999)

Spero, Joan E., and Jeffrey A. Hart, *The Politics of International Economic Relations* (London, 5th edn, 1997)

Spohr, Kristina, *The Global Chancellor: Helmut Schmidt and the Reshaping of the International Order* (Oxford, 2016)

Steck, Stefan, *Neue Ostpolitik: Wahrnehmung und Deutung in der DDR und den USA, 1961–1974—Zur Symbolik eines politischen Begriffs* (Hamburg, 2012)

Stent, Angela, *Russia and Germany Reborn: Unification, the Soviet Collapse, and the New Europe* (Princeton, NJ, 1999)

Stueck, William, *The Korean War: An International History* (Princeton, NJ, 1997)

Sukhdorev, Viktor M., *Iazyk moi—drug moi: Ot Khrushcheva do Gorbacheva* (Moscow, 2008)

Suri, Jeremi, *Power and Protest: Global Revolution and the Rise of Détente* (Cambridge, MA, 2003)

Suri, Jeremi, *Henry Kissinger and the American Century* (Cambridge, MA, 2007)

Talbott, Strobe, *Deadly Gambits: The Reagan Administration and the Stalemate in Arms Control* (New York, 1985)

Teltschik, Horst, *329 Tage: Innenansichten der Einigung* (Berlin, 1991)

Thomas, Daniel, *The Helsinki Effect: International Norms, Human Rights, and the Demise of Communism* (Princeton, NJ, 2001)

Thompson, Nicholas, *The Hawk and the Dove: Paul Nitze, George Kennan, and the History of the Cold War* (New York, 2009)

Tian, Zengpei, and Wang Taiping, eds, *Lao waijiaoguan huiyi Zhou Enlai (Senior Diplomats' Remembrance of Zhou Enlai)* (Beijing, 1998)

Troyanovskii, Oleg, *Cherez Gody i Rasstoyaniya: Istoriya Odnoi Sem'yi (Over Years and Distances)* (Moscow, 1997)

Tucker, Nancy, ed., *China Confidential: American Diplomats and Sino-American Relations, 1945–1996* (New York, 2001)

Tudda, Chris, *A Cold War Turning Point: Nixon and Mao, 1969–1972* (Baton Rouge, LA, 2012)

Tudda, Chris, *Cold War Summits: A History, from Potsdam to Malta* (London, 2015)

Vaïsse, Justin, *Neoconservatism: The Biography of a Movement* (Cambridge, MA, 2010)

Vance, Cyrus, *Hard Choices: Critical Years in America's Foreign Policy* (New York, 1983)

Villaume, Poul, and Odd Arne Westad, eds, *Perforating the Iron Curtain: European Détente, Transatlantic Relations, and the Cold War, 1965–1985* (Copenhagen, 2010)

Vogel, Ezra F., *Deng Xiaoping and the Transformation of China* (Cambridge, MA, 2011)

Wallander, Celeste A., *Mortal Friends, Best Enemies: German-Russian Cooperation after the Cold War* (Ithaca, NY, 1999)

Wang, Bingnan, *Zhongmei Huitan Jiunian Huigu (Nine Years of Sino-American Talks in Retrospect)* (Beijing, 1985)

Wang, Nianyi, *Da dongluan de niandai (In the Years of Great Upheaval)* (Zhengzhou, 1988)

Webb, Michael C., *The Political Economy of Policy Coordination: International Adjustment since 1945* (Ithaca, NY, 1995)

Weidenfeld, Werner, et al., *Geschichte der deutschen Einheit, vol. 4—Außenpolitik für die deutsche Einheit: Die Entscheidungsjahre 1989/90* (Stuttgart, 1998)

Westad, Odd Arne, *The Global Cold War: Third World Interventions and the Making of Our Times* (Cambridge, 2005)

Wilson, James G., *The Triumph of Improvisation: Gorbachev's Adaptability, Reagan's Engagement, and the End of the Cold War* (Ithaca, NY, 2014)

Wohlforth, William, ed., *Witnesses to the End of the Cold War* (Baltimore, MD, 1996)

Wolf, Markus, *Spionagechef im geheimen Krieg: Erinnerungen* (Munich, 1997)

Xia, Yafeng, *Negotiating with the Enemy: U.S.-China Talks during the Cold War, 1949–1972* (Bloomington, IN, 2006)

Xu, Dashen, ed., *Zhonghua renmin gongheguo shilu (A Factual Record of the People's Republic of China)* (Changchun, 1994)

Xu, Jingli, *Jiemi Zhongguo Waijiao Dangan (Declassifying Chinese Diplomatic Files)* (Beijing, 2005)

Xue, Mouhong, ed., *Dangdai Zhongguo waijiao (Contemporary Chinese Diplomacy)* (Beijing, 1988)

Yang, Mingwei, and Chen Yangyong, *Zhou Enlai waijiao fengyun (Diplomatic Winds and Clouds of Zhou Enlai)* (Beijing, 1995)

Zaloga, Steven J., *The Kremlin's Nuclear Sword: The Rise and Fall of Russia's Strategic Nuclear Forces, 1945–2000* (London, 2002)

Zelikow, Philip, and Condoleezza Rice, *Germany Unified and Europe Transformed: A Study in Statecraft* (Cambridge, MA, 1997)

Zhang, Ganghua, and Li Peng, *Li Peng liu si ri ji zhen xiang: Fu lu Li Peng liu si ri ji yuan wen* (Hong Kong, 2010)

Zhang, Liang, et al., eds, *The Tiananmen Papers* (New York, 2002)

Zhang, Ying, *Sui Zhang Wenjin chushi Meiguo: Dashi furen jishi (Serving in the United States with Zhang Wenjin: Account of An Ambassador's Wife)* (Beijing, 1996)

Zhonggong zhongyang wenxian yanjiushi (Chinese Communist Party Central Committee Document Research Office), ed., *Mao Zedong nianpu, 1949–1976 (Chronology of Mao Zedong, 1949–1976)* (Beijing, 2013)

Zubok, Vladislav M., *A Failed Empire: The Soviet Union in the Cold War from Stalin to Gorbachev* (Chapel Hill, NC, 2007)

Zwahr, Hartmut, *Die erfrorenen Flügel der Schwalbe: DDR und 'Prager Frühling': Tagebuch einer Krise 1968–1970* (Bonn, 2007)

Articles and Chapters

Alexandroff, Alan S., and Donald Brean, 'Global Summitry: Its Meaning and Scope', *Global Summitry* 1, no. 1 (2015), 1–26

Bange, Oliver, 'The GDR in the Era of Détente: Conflicting Perceptions and Strategies', in Poul Villaume and Odd Arne Westad, eds, *Perforating the Iron Curtain: European Détente, Transatlantic Relations, and the Cold War, 1965–1985* (Copenhagen, 2010), 57–78

Bange, Oliver, 'The Stasi Confronts Western Strategies for Transformation 1966–1975', in Jonathan Haslam and Karina Urbach, eds, *Secret Intelligence in the European States System, 1918–1989* (Stanford, CA, 2013), 170–208

Bock, Siegfried, and Karl Seidel, 'Die Außenbeziehungen der DDR in der Periode der Konsolidierung (1955–1972/73)', in Siegfried Bock, Ingrid Muth, and Hermann Schwiesau, eds, *DDR-Außenpolitik im Rückspiegel: Diplomaten im Gespräch* (Münster, 2004), 53–68

Bozo, Frédéric, 'Détente versus Alliance: France, the United States and the Politics of the Harmel Report (1964–1968)', *Contemporary European History* 7, no. 3 (1998), 343–60

Brown, Archie, 'The Gorbachev Revolution and the End of the Cold War', in Melvyn P. Leffler and Odd Arne Westad, eds, *The Cambridge History of the Cold War, vol. III: Endings* (Cambridge, 2010), 244–66

Chen, Jian, 'Tiananmen and the Fall of the Berlin Wall: China's Path toward 1989 and Beyond', in Jeffrey A. Engel, ed., *The Fall of the Berlin Wall: The Revolutionary Legacy of 1989* (New York, 2009), 96–131

Chen, Jian, 'China, the Third World and the End of the Cold War', in Artemy Kalinovsky and Sergey Radchenko, eds, *The End of the Cold War and the Third World: New Perspectives on Regional Conflict* (London, 2011), 101–21

Colley, Linda, 'Britishness and Otherness: An Argument', *Journal of British Studies* 31, no. 4 (1992), 309–29

Costigliola, Frank, 'An "Arm Around the Shoulder": The United States, NATO and German Reunification, 1989–90', *Contemporary European History* 3, no. 1 (March 1994), 87–110

Cox, Michael, and Steven Hurst, '"His Finest Hour?" George Bush and the Diplomacy of German Unification', *Diplomacy & Statecraft* 13, no. 4 (2002), 123–50

Danhui, Li, 'Zhou Enlai in the Sino-American Rapprochement', *Lengzhan guojishi yanjiu (Cold War International History Studies)*, no. 6 (Summer 2008)

Di, He, 'The Most Respected Enemy: Mao Zedong's Perception of the United States', *China Quarterly* 137 (March 1994), 144–58

Duffy, Gloria, 'Crisis Mangling and the Cuban Brigade', *International Security* 8, no. 1 (Summer 1983), 67–87

Engel, Jeffrey A., 'When George Bush Believed the Cold War Ended and Why That Mattered', in Mike Nelson and Barbara Perry, eds, *41: Inside the Presidency of George H.W. Bush* (Ithaca, NY, 2014), 100–21

Fischer, Thomas, '"A Mustard Seed Grew into a Bushy Tree": The Finnish CSCE Initiative of 5 May 1969', *Cold War History* 9, no. 2 (2009), 177–201

Giauque, J.G., 'Bilateral Summit Diplomacy in Western European and Transatlantic Relations, 1956–63', *European History Quarterly* 31, no. 3 (2001), 427–45

Harmer, Tanya, 'Brazil's Cold War in the Southern Cone: 1970–1975', *Cold War History* 12, no. 4 (November 2012), 659–81

Hershberg, James G., and Chen Jian, 'Informing the Enemy: Sino-American "Signaling" and the Vietnam War, 1965', in Priscilla Roberts, ed., *Behind the Bamboo Curtain: China, Vietnam, and the World Beyond Asia* (Washington, DC, 2006)

Howarth, Marianne, 'Die Westpolitik der DDR zwischen internationaler Aufwertung und ideologischer Offensive (1966–1989)', in Ulrich Pfeil, ed., *Die DDR und der Westen: Transnationale Beziehungen 1949–1989* (Berlin, 2001), 81–98

Hunt, Jonathan, and Paul F. Walker, 'The Legacy of Reykjavik and the Future of Nuclear Disarmament', *Bulletin of the Atomic Scientists* 67, no. 6 (2011), 63–72

Kochavi, Noam, 'Insights Abandoned, Flexibility Lost: Kissinger, Soviet Jewish Emigration, and the Demise of Détente', *Diplomatic History* 29, no. 3 (June 2005), 503–30

Kramer, Mark, 'The Demise of the Soviet Bloc', *The Journal of Modern History* 83, no. 4 (December 2011), 788–854

Kuisong, Yang, 'The Sino-Soviet Border Clash of 1969: From Zhenbao Island to Sino-American Rapprochement', *Cold War History* 1, no. 1 (August 2000), 21–52

Mark, Chi-Kwan, 'Hostage Diplomacy: Britain, China, and the Politics of Negotiation, 1967–1969', *Diplomacy & Statecraft* 20, no. 3 (2009), 473–93

Marquardt, James J., 'Transparency and Security Competition: Open Skies and America's Cold War Statecraft, 1948–1960', *Journal of Cold War Studies* 9, no. 1 (Winter 2007), 55–87

Melissen, Jan, 'Pre-Summit Diplomacy: Britain, the United States and the Nassau Conference, December 1962', *Diplomacy & Statecraft* 7, no. 3 (1996), 652–87

Mundzeck, Lisa, 'Der "Geist von Erfurt": Das Gipfeltreffen am 19. März 1970 in der deutschen Presse', in Steffen Raßloff, ed., *'Willy Brandt ans Fenster!': Das Erfurter Gipfeltreffen 1970 und die Geschichte des 'Erfurter Hofes'* (Jena, 2007), 82–100

Nakath, Detlef, 'Das Dreieck Bonn – Ost-Berlin – Moskau: Zur sowjetischen Einfluß-nahme auf die Gestaltung der deutsch-deutschen Beziehungen (1969–1982)', in Ulrich Pfeil, ed., *Die DDR und der Westen: Transnationale Beziehungen 1949–1989* (Berlin, 2001), 99–115

Niedhart, Gottfried, '"The Transformation of the Other Side": Willy Brandt's Ostpolitik and the Liberal Peace Concepts', in Frédéric Bozo, Marie-Pierre Rey, Bernd Rother, and N. Piers Ludlow, eds, *Visions of the End of the Cold War in Europe, 1945–1990* (New York, 2012), 149–62

Phillips, Steven, 'Nixon's China Initiative, 1969–1972,' in United States Department of State, ed., *Documenting Diplomacy in the 21st Century* (Washington, DC, 2001), 130–46

Preston, Andrew, and Fredrik Logevall, 'Introduction: The Adventurous Journey of Nixon in the World', in Andrew Preston and Fredrik Logevall, eds, *Nixon in the World: American Foreign Relations, 1969–1977* (New York, 2008), 3–24

Raßloff, Steffen, and Thomas Rothbart, 'Das erste deutsch-deutsche Gipfeltreffen 1970 in Erfurt', in Steffen Raßloff, ed., *'Willy Brandt ans Fenster!' Das Erfurter Gipfeltreffen 1970 und die Geschichte des 'Erfurter Hofes'* (Jena, 2007), 48–81

Reynolds, David, 'Summitry as Intercultural Communication', *International Affairs* 85, no. 1 (2009), 115–27

Reynolds, David, 'Science, Technology, and the Cold War', in Melvyn P. Leffler and Odd Arne Westad, eds, *The Cambridge History of the Cold War, vol. III: Endings* (New York, 2011), 378–99

Roberts, Adam, 'An "Incredibly Swift Transition": Reflections on the End of the Cold War', in Melvyn P. Leffler and Odd Arne Westad, eds, *The Cambridge History of the Cold War, vol III: Endings* (Cambridge, 2010), 513–34

Romero, Federico, 'Cold War Historiography at the Crossroads', *Cold War History* 14, no. 4 (2014), 685–703

Rosenberg, Emily, 'Consumer Capitalism and the End of the Cold War', in Melvyn P. Leffler and Odd Arne Westad, eds, *The Cambridge History of the Cold War, vol. III: Endings* (New York, 2011), 489–512

Rotter, Andrew J., 'Saidism without Said: Orientalism and U.S. Diplomatic History', *American Historical Review* 105, no. 4 (2000), 1205–17

Sarotte, Mary E., 'A Small Town in (East) Germany: The Erfurt Meeting of 1970 and the Dynamics of Cold War Détente', *Diplomatic History* 25, no. 1 (Winter 2001), 85–104

Savranskaya, Svetlana, and Taubman, William, 'Soviet Foreign Policy, 1962–1975', in Melvyn P. Leffler and Odd Arne Westad, eds, *The Cambridge History of the Cold War, vol. II: Crises and Détente* (Cambridge, 2010), 134–57

Schmidt, Helmut, 'The 1977 Alastair Buchan Memorial Lecture', *Survival* 20, no. 1 (Jan.–Feb. 1978), 2–10

Schoenborn, Benedikt, 'NATO Forever? Willy Brandt's Heretical Thoughts on an Alternative Future', in Jussi M. Hanhimäki et al., eds, *The Routledge Handbook of Transatlantic Security* (London, 2010), 74–88

Shiyan, Wei, 'Inside Stories of Kissinger's Secret Visit to China', in Jianzhang Pei, ed., *Xin Zhongguo waijiao fengyun (Winds and Clouds in New China's Diplomacy), vol. 2* (Beijing, 1991)

Shiyan, Wei, 'Kissinger's Second Visit to China', in Jianzhang Pei, *Xin Zhongguo waijiao fengyun (Winds and Clouds in New China's Diplomacy), vol. 3* (Beijing, 1994)

Soutou, Georges-Henri, 'La décision française de quitter le commandement intégré de l'OTAN (1966)', in Hans-Joachim Harder, ed., *Von Truman bis Harmel: Die Bundesrepublik Deutschland in Spannungsfeld von NATO und europäischer Integration* (Munich, 2000), 185–208

Spohr, Kristina, 'Precluded or Precedent-Setting? The "NATO Enlargement Question" in the Triangular Bonn-Washington-Moscow Diplomacy of 1990–1991', *Journal of Cold War Studies* 14, no. 4 (Fall 2012), 4–54

Spohr, Kristina, 'Helmut Schmidt and the Shaping of Western Security in the late 1970s: The Guadeloupe Summit of 1979', *International History Review* 37, no. 1 (2015), 167–92

Stelkens, Jochen, 'Machtwechsel in Ost-Berlin: Der Sturz Walter Ulbrichts 1971', *Vierteljahrshefte für Zeitgeschichte* 45, no. 4 (1997), 503–33

Suckut, Siegfried, 'Probleme mit dem "großen Bruder": Der DDR-Staatssicherheitsdienst und die Deutschlandpolitik der KPdSU 1969/70', *Vierteljahrshefte für Zeitgeschichte* 58, no. 3 (2010), 403–39

Suri, Jeremi, 'Explaining the End of the Cold War: A New Historical Consensus', *Journal of Cold War Studies* 4, no. 4 (2002), 60–92

Wenger, Andreas, 'Crisis and Opportunity: NATO's Transformation and the Multi-lateralization of Détente, 1966–1968', *Journal of Cold War Studies* 6, no. 1 (2004), 22–74

Westad, Odd Arne, 'Moscow and the Angolan Crisis, 1974–1976: A New Pattern of Intervention', *Cold War International History Project Bulletin*, no. 8–9 (1996–7), 21–32

Xia, Yafeng, 'China's Elite Politics and Sino-American Rapprochement, January 1969–February 1972', *Journal of Cold War Studies* 8, no. 4 (Fall 2006), 3–28

Zavisca, Jane, 'Explaining and Interpreting the End of Soviet Rule, *Kritika* 12, no. 4 (2011), 925–40

Zhang, Ying, 'Random Recollection of Premier Zhou's Later Years', in Zengpei Tian and Wang Taiping, eds, *Lao waijiaoguan huiyi Zhou Enlai (Senior Diplomats' Remembrance of Zhou Enlai)* (Beijing, 1998), 374–83

Zubok, Vladislav, 'With His Back Against the Wall: Gorbachev, Soviet Demise, and German Unification', *Cold War History* 14, no. 4 (2014), 619–45

Index

Printed and bound by CPI Group (UK) Ltd, Croydon, CR0 4YY